Luminos is the Open Access monograph publishing program from UC Press. Luminos provides a framework for preserving and reinvigorating monograph publishing for the future and increases the reach and visibility of important scholarly work. Titles published in the UC Press Luminos model are published with the same high standards for selection, peer review, production, and marketing as those in our traditional program. www.luminosoa.org

The publisher and the University of California Press Foundation gratefully acknowledge the generous support of the Ahmanson Foundation Endowment Fund in Humanities.

Between Household and State

Between Household and State

The Mughal Frontier and the Politics of Circulation in Peninsular India

Subah Dayal

UNIVERSITY OF CALIFORNIA PRESS

University of California Press
Oakland, California

© 2024 by Subah Dayal

This work is licensed under a Creative Commons [CC BY-NC-ND] license.
To view a copy of the license, visit http://creativecommons.org/licenses.

Suggested citation: Dayal, S. *Between Household and State: The Mughal Frontier and the Politics of Circulation in Peninsular India*. Oakland: University of California Press, 2024. DOI: https://doi.org/10.1525/luminos.216

Library of Congress Cataloging-in-Publication Data

Names: Dayal, Subah, author.
Title: Between household and state : the Mughal frontier and the politics of circulation in peninsular India / Subah Dayal.
Description: Oakland, California : University of California Press, [2024] | Includes bibliographical references and index.
Identifiers: LCCN 2024014802 (print) | LCCN 2024014803 (ebook) | ISBN 9780520402362 (paperback) | ISBN 9780520402379 (ebook)
Subjects: LCSH: Households—India—Deccan. | Borderlands—India—Deccan. | Politics and culture—Mughal Empire—History. | Mughal Empire—Politics and government. | Deccan (India)—Politics and government—17th century.
Classification: LCC DS461 .D314 2024 (print) | LCC DS461 (ebook) | DDC 954.02/5—dc23/eng/20240802

LC record available at https://lccn.loc.gov/2024014802
LC ebook record available at https://lccn.loc.gov/2024014803

32 31 30 29 28 27 26 25 24
10 9 8 7 6 5 4 3 2 1

In memory of the oldest teachers, and my mother

M. Z. A. Shakeb (1933–2021)
Rahmat Ali Khan (1942–2022)
Devika Dayal (1953–2020)

CONTENTS

List of Illustrations ix
Note on Transliteration xi

1. The Household in Connected Histories 1
2. The Military Barrack: Identifying Households, Becoming Mughal 32
3. From Court to Port: Governing the Household 61
4. The Adorned Palace: Narrating Ceremony and Relatedness 87
5. At Home in the Regional Court: Critiquing Empire 114
6. From Battlefield to Weaving Village: Disciplining the Coast 144
7. Postscript: Forgetting Households, Making Dynasties 180

Notes 199
Acknowledgments 247
Bibliography 251
Index 275

ILLUSTRATIONS

MAPS

1. Mughal India and the Indian Ocean world   2
2. Physical terrain of peninsular India   2
3. Deccan sultanates in the Hyderabad-Karnatak   11
4. Mughal sites in the northern Deccan   35
5. Indo-Africans, Iranians, and Marathas on the Konkan and Kanara coasts   74
6. Indo-Africans, Marathas, and Indo-Afghans on the southern Coromandel coast   148

FIGURES

1. Muster or descriptive roll of Malik Ahmad   33
2. The household of Mustafa Khan Lari of Bijapur   64
3. Nusrati, *tarjī'-band* for Muhammad 'Adil Shah and Khadija Sultana's wedding   88
4. Hakim Atishi, *'Ādilnāma* (The book of 'Ādil)   115

NOTE ON TRANSLITERATION

All long vowels and the letters *ayn* and *hamza* are indicated in Persian and Urdu words. Non-English words such as *ghar* used frequently across book are not italicized after the first mention. With the exception of direct transliterations, diacritics have been eliminated in proper names (excluding *ayn* and *hamza*). Quotations from VOC archival documents retain the spelling of seventeenth-century Dutch.

1

The Household in Connected Histories

Our taxi could go no further, so we walked up the ascending path to the hill fort's entrance. Twenty kilometers north of our destination, Burhanpur, a small city in central India situated between the valleys of the Tapti and Narmada Rivers on the western end of the Satpura Hills, the winding mud road we were traveling vanished abruptly into the side of a steep hill. At a height of 260 meters, Asirgarh (fort) is the doorway to the Indian peninsula, where Hindustan ends and the Deccan begins. Before entering its enormous black gates, we turned around to take in the view—a single frame where the repetitive image of thorny *kīkar* trees on the flat, beige plains of northern India gives way to a contrast of lush green against the black soil of a plateau or tableland. Looking south from Asirgarh, one place ends and another one begins.

In 1601, when Emperor Akbar finally captured this fort, thousands of soldiers in the army of the Mughal Empire—the largest political power of precolonial India—marched across the contrasting landscapes of Hindustan and the Deccan.[1] But legend has it that Asirgarh had never been taken by force; nor did it belong to any particular ruler for long. Singular, yet akin to many sites across the Indian subcontinent, Asirgarh ensconced the sediments of multiple pasts. At the fort's center is the mosque built by the Faruqi dynasty of Khandesh (ca. 1382–1601), with Persian inscriptions recording the additions built by each Mughal emperor alongside vestiges of the Holkar family of Indore, who lost it to the English East India Company in 1819. Inside what remains of the colonial cantonment lie the graves of dead British officers.

For me, the journey to Asirgarh marked the beginning of multiple haphazard itineraries over many years to make sense of what happened in the decades *after* the Mughals marched south into peninsular India. Walking across this vast

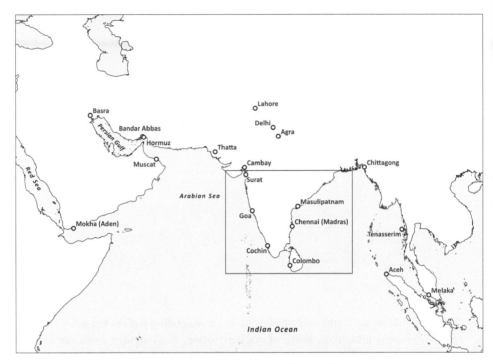

MAP 1. Mughal India and the Indian Ocean world. Drawn by Kanika Kalra.

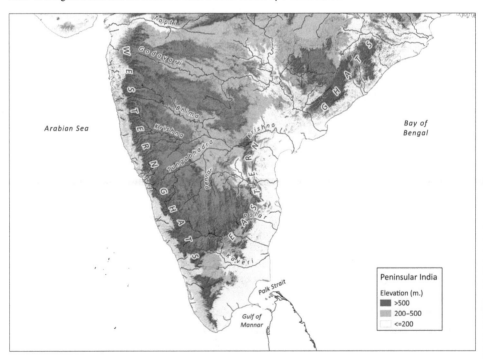

MAP 2. Physical terrain of peninsular India. Drawn by Kanika Kalra.

landmass, tracing the relationships between the many contrasting landscapes that stretch across modern-day states from Maharashtra to Tamil Nadu, led to many places where borders of all kinds—social, cultural, linguistic, and political—were both pronounced and amorphous. For example, the tiny village of Gabbur in Raichur, a district in Karnataka where the streets buzz with the sound of Kannada, Marathi, Telugu, and Urdu, defying the linguistic boundaries of the modern-day nation-state of India. Or Gandikota, a village where the rise and fall of political dynasties, so neatly marked in official Persian chronicles, made it impossible to differentiate a fort from the landscape of red rocks in the gorge of the Pennar River in southeastern Andhra Pradesh. At the opposite end of the peninsula in the lands below the Narmada River—the geographic feature often used to mark the borders of northern and southern India—stood another famed fort, Senji, less than a hundred kilometers east from the bustling port-city of Pondicherry in present-day Tamil Nadu (southeastern India).[2] Here, too, one place ended and another began. The Deccan plateau's boulders gave way to the Karnatak lowlands, the coastal plains where cotton was grown, spun, woven, and then shipped across the Indian Ocean to be sold in markets from the Persian Gulf to Thailand. Asirgarh and Senji were the two hill forts that bookended the northern and southern limits of the Mughal frontier in peninsular India.

From the central plateau to riverine deltas and, finally, to the coasts of peninsular India, my itineraries across diverse ecologies went beyond stops at monumental ruins. At times, I followed the journeys of smaller kinds of discarded material evidence, the myriad objects that historians use to reconstruct the past. Such detritus, discarded reams of paper with a few lines on them sometimes stored in the niches of fort walls now housed in modern archives, describe the weathered faces of ordinary soldiers, name their fathers and forefathers, and note the places they called *ghar* or home—the cities and locales from which they hailed or the lineages they had served for generations. Or in long forgotten poetic verses that praised their bravery in battles fought across places called Hindustan, the Deccan, and the Karnatak.

The mobility of people, goods, and ideas across the physical and geographic features that mark the boundaries of northern and southern India has been a persistent feature of the subcontinent's past and present. Yet, these two parts are often imagined very differently in both popular and scholarly understandings. The relative sociocultural homogeneity of the so-called Hindi belt of the north is often contrasted with the striking heterogeneities of language, food, clothing, and regional political parties of the south. And yet, history told from the vantage of political centers such as Delhi, located in the northern plains, has shaped how the "far south" of the subcontinent is imagined and subsumed into definitions of India. In other words, delineations of the subcontinent before it was divided up by modern nation-states often begin from a northern perspective, oblivious to the peninsula's bewildering layers of languages, castes, sects, and social practices. On the other hand, a narrative of local exceptionalism is commonly evoked to mark southern alterity from the normative north.[3] As much as these popular stereotypical divides between *north* and *south* speak to the crises of modern-day national identities, they are rooted in a deep history of overlapping sovereignties and contestation between the regions that forged the Mughal frontier, long predating the invention of "India" by European colonialism.[4] This book travels as an itinerary across the expanse of peninsular India to figure out how definitions of these spaces transformed when their institutions, personnel, and resources circulated, fusing into each other over the course of the seventeenth century.

. . .

By the year 1600, much of the globe fell under empires. These large, expansive political formations, each often under a single dynastic line that ruled over diverse subjects, managed to hold together many different linguistic, ethnic, and social groups. Empires built complex state institutions, such as the military, bureaucracy, and court, and fostered new circuits of cultural and artistic patronage.[5] Early modern empires were not stationary. They were not fixed in any one capital city or heartland but rather moved relentlessly—from Istanbul to Damascus and Cairo, from Madrid to Mexico City, from Delhi to Burhanpur. In doing so, they generated new frontiers across distant spaces.[6] When acquiring more territories, they were not single-handedly overrunning shrubby, blank frontiers and quickly replacing them with all things imperial. On the contrary, empires confronted challenges from preexisting political formations; they negotiated with regional powerbrokers, incorporated new social groups, and improvised mechanisms for holding down tenuous conquests.

As many historians have demonstrated, expanding precolonial states, from the Islamic world to late imperial China, were much invested in keeping track of their subjects and resources, even if the mechanisms for doing so were not nearly as comprehensive as those of colonial or modern states.[7] Irrespective of the nature and scope of this mechanisms, the collective scholarship of recent decades has challenged the dichotomy between the premodern vs. modern states that lay at the heart of James Scott's classic work, *Seeing Like a State*.[8] Mughal South Asia was no exception to this pattern. Here, too, imperial agents had to count, list, and inventory how many soldiers, horses, guns, and grain were in stock, thus devising mechanisms for organizing, categorizing, and mobilizing subject populations and an enormous breadth of resources. In doing so, early modern empires on the move fundamentally transformed how their subjects, also on the move, identified themselves, defined where they belonged, and declared certain spaces home. Precolonial states were therefore not necessarily "the enemy of people who move around."[9] If anything, they were invested in developing techniques to incorporate mobility into state institutions to create partially "legible state spaces" within their frontiers.[10] On the Mughal frontier in peninsular India, senses of belonging to a home or *ghar* were reconfigured just as the imperial state determined how to tie myriad mobile castes and communities into its major institutions like the army and the bureaucracy.

Between Household and State focuses on regimes of circulation and how they shaped the politics of belonging through an archivally grounded analysis of many different kinds of Asian and European literary and documentary sources. This book is the first to make sense of a fraction of an enormous documentary deposit produced by the moving Mughal frontier, reading that deposit in tandem with a range of other materials generated in the spaces between the courts and coasts of peninsular India. The book's itinerary between forts, military barracks, regional capital cities, provincial market towns, villages, and small port cities emphasizes how everything from goods and skilled labor to bureaucratic practices and kinship relations moved back and forth between different places across premodern South Asia prior to European colonization. I argue, that such patterns of circulation produced practices of social identity anchored in the household,[11] a key site for interlocking social, political, economic, and cultural exchanges and, above all, for shaping the institutions of empire—the predominant political formation in much of the early modern world.[12]

The patterns of circulation mapped out in this book contrast with two images of movement and migration in premodern India. The first conjures this part of the world as a timeless, fixed entity where nothing—neither people, nor goods, nor ideas—ever moved. A second image is of unidirectional movement from one place to another that accounts only for external movements to and from the Indian subcontinent, understood in terms like *influence, invasion,* or *migration*. In contrast to both immovability and unidirectional influence, circulation as a pattern of exchange entails moving between the same places, regions, and cities again and again, such that, over time sites develop overlaps, similarities, and codependencies. Whether the back and forth between multiple ecological and political zones of specialized laboring groups and skilled artisans, or of literary texts and social elites between courtly centers, it is now accepted that circulation was the dominant form of mobility in South Asian society well before colonialism.[13] In each of this book's chapters, I focus on how a particular form of movement worked in a specific social site, and I reconstruct how mobile social classes encountered and participated in state institutions, particularly the army, the bureaucracy, and the court. Thus, for instance, elite literati evaluated the growth of these state structures, circulating ethical critiques of power and politics in multiple languages. Participation in regimes of circulation required social elites to sometimes transcend cultural, sectarian, and ethnic boundaries and, at other times, to harden and harness social hierarchies to entrench their networks in hinterland and coastal economies.

Lying at the intersection of household studies and connected histories, this book develops two interrelated methodological issues. First, a focus on the household enables us to examine different scales and clusters of social relations in the human past.[14] It helps us move down vertically, if you will, to the relations of elite power with other social groups. An artificial divide between the "court" and "state," on the one hand, and between cultural history and literary studies, as well as between social and economic history, on the other hand, has reified the study of elite power in premodern South Asia. The household is a key site that collapses such divides by unveiling how a range of anonymous subjects shaped political and economic processes that have largely been understood as the reserve of premodern elites. Moving between the court and the coast, this book therefore extends the analytical gaze to rank-and-file soldiers, weavers, artisans, farmers, and slaves whose participation (voluntary or forced) in familial networks was vital to mobilizing resources for imperial power.

Second, the household also bridges two distinct transregional lines of inquiry that have decentered Eurocentric models of modernity by reconstructing connections across Asia, Africa, and the Middle East in the centuries prior to colonialism. There are two different routes, one via land and the other via sea, that are reimagined via this connective tissue in recent scholarship. On the one hand, at the center of this discussion have been the Islamic empires of the Middle East and South Asia—the Ottomans, Safavids, and Mughals—which endured for variable durations between the twelfth and the nineteenth centuries from the Balkans to Bengal. One way to study the connections between these empires has been through cultural institutions and the shared sociolinguistic worlds of Arabic and Persian, lingua francas of the Islamic world that operated alongside other cosmopolitan languages and multiple regional vernaculars. In recent years, comparative perspectives on the "Persianate" have examined the shared ecumene of social elites who circulated across Iran, Central Asia, and the Indian subcontinent, dismantling colonial and nationalist biases that artificially separated the histories of these kindred geographies.[15]

The other route to reconstruct connections in a world before Europe begins along the seas. Alongside elite Perso-Arabic literary and courtly circulation that connected imperial capitals, a parallel development in the period from 1500 to 1800 was the transformation of the global economy when the Indian Ocean and the Atlantic became linked for the first time in world history.[16] An earlier generation of historians reconstructed the flow of commodities such as textiles, spices, and silver by drawing on the archives of the Portuguese Estado da Índia and the world's first transnational corporations—namely, the Dutch, English, Danish, and French East India Companies.[17] The exclusive reliance on European-language archives meant that this historiography at times ended up reaffirming the teleology of "European expansion in Asia," without any engagement with materials in non-European languages. Indeed, even the most recent iterations of this scholarship continue to rely almost exclusively on European-language sources.[18] Partly, this asymmetry has to do with the paucity, accessibility, and nature of sources in non-European languages as opposed to the well-organized and preserved records of the entities that came to colonize large parts of the world.

Between Household and State intervenes between these two distinct historiographical strands that rarely speak to each other by placing the household as the link between maritime histories of peninsular India with studies of imperial and regional courts further inland. Methodologically, it contends that we take seriously, and even prioritize making sense of the cultural and moral sensibilities of precolonial actors, visible in documentary and literary genres in non-European languages first, instead of always turning to the easily accessible archives of trading companies, European travel accounts, works by missionaries, and Jesuits, either as a default or as an alibi for tracing the rise of colonialism. Within regional scholarship, this book departs from static dynastic narrations of the Mughal past centered on the city of Delhi in north India to track an empire on the move, marching across war fronts in central and southern India, the only region of the subcontinent that was never fully incorporated into the imperial realm. By linking Persianate literary and cultural worlds with the Indian Ocean littoral, from military forts and regional courts to the weaving villages of the Coromandel Coast, the book follows itinerant households—comprised of Iranians, Marathas, Africans, and Afghans—whose conflicts over matters of identity, politics, and economic power created regimes of circulation that modified senses of belonging in the Mughal world.

EMPIRE AND HOME AT THE MARGINS

The concept of *ghar* or home lies at the heart of this book. Literally meaning house, dwelling, mansion, habitation, abode, or home, ghar is a present-day vernacular term used to refer to the physical space of an actual building or structure.[19] Perhaps its most recognizable and evocative usage comes from Rabindranath Tagore's iconic novel *Ghare Baire* (*The Home and the World*, 1916) in which the split between the home and the world outside it stood for the Indian subcontinent's place in global modernity.[20] While ghar immediately conveys a sense of returning to a space of comfort, permanence and ease, it was, in times past, and remains to this day, a place of intense contention, uncertainty, and anxiety, as the most important physical and conceptual site of intrafamilial conflict. Every neighborhood, village, town, and city in modern South Asia is riven with stories about decades-long fights over a single ancestral ghar, home, bungalow or *kothī*, or family properties over which a deceased patriarch's progeny battle each other, very frequently turning to the courts, at times against or alongside a widowed maternal head.[21] Among innumerable vernacular proverbs that evoke this term, the most prevalent refer explicitly to the sense of belonging associated with the idea of ghar.[22] Take, for instance, *ghar kā bhedī lankā dhāye* (an insider reveals the house's secrets and sinks it) or *dhobī kā gadhā, nā ghar kā nā ghāt kā*, which literally means "the washerman's donkey has no home, neither at the house [ghar] nor the washing steps [ghāt]." The latter proverb's idiomatic English translation, "a rolling stone gathers no moss," inadequately captures its contemptuous tone, which conveys a sense of judgment upon those who lack a sense of belonging or loyalty to any one side.

Ghar also mediates the most mundane hierarchies of power between state and citizen. When the modern government clerk asks an average citizen queuing up to apply for a ration card, to fill out some paperwork, or to have their ID checked, the first question will be *"bāp kā nām?"*—what is your father's name? This is often followed by *"ghar kahān hai?"*—where is your home? While the first marks descent from a male ancestor, the second question may refer to a distant district, city, place of birth, ancestral land, or village. The crabby bureaucrat assumes from merely looking at a citizen that they likely do not belong to a metropolitan city or region. Implicit in the second question is that the citizen is "out of place" in a particular context and that everyone in the queue has come from somewhere else. The declaration of your ghar in these everyday encounters with the state captures how the experience of unbelonging for most people in the Indian subcontinent was, and still is, rooted in circulating *within* and across its dizzyingly heterogenous regions, rather than outside it. Belonging to another place, conversely, means not belonging somewhere else. The hierarchical bureaucratic interrogation of ghar captures the glaring inequalities that have driven people to move from one region of the subcontinent to another for centuries.[23]

The fixity of ghar with a specific place within the modern-nation state differs considerably from the meanings of this term in the pre-national works considered in this book. Rather than being fixed in place, ghar in the early modern period referred to a shared sense of belonging grounded in the circulation of households from multiple ethnic, linguistic, and social backgrounds. Ghar was a continuum of relations not limited to just sociological (kin) relations nor entirely bound to one space or territory. Ghar was a fraught site of relationships within and beyond the household unit, as well as a mediator of layered political sovereignties across regions. Belonging within the vertical hierarchy of a ghar worked in tandem with the ties forged horizontally between elite households.

Ghar, derived from the Sanskrit word *griha*, was an enduring concept in premodern South Asian texts and societies. Through late Vedic texts such as the *Grhyasutras* (ca. 800 to 500 BCE) that laid out norms for the performance of domestic rituals, Jaya Tyagi has shown that the notion of griha referred to a house's physical structure, relationships between members of the household, and their social linkages to larger communities outside it.[24] The display of rituals such as marriage, birth, and death within one griha signaled participation in wider communities, or transactions with new lineages and with other more extended *kulas* (lineages). Here, griha is not necessarily place-bound, so much as a conceptual space of social ties that produce the householder and his multiple linkages.

The two senses of ghar as a home, house, dwelling, abode, and habitation *and* as a single cell, receptacle, groove, channel, or drawer convey that it is a singular entity that functions as part of a larger unit or whole.[25] Where do we find the concept of ghar in later centuries, particularly in Islamic South Asia? The equivalent Persian word *khāna* has a range of meanings, including house or dwelling, on the one hand, and compartment or partition, on the other. It is the latter meaning of khāna that is used today in common Hindustani parlance, along with the term for family and household, *khāndān*.[26] In political histories of northern India, one way of making sense of this term has been to examine how the Mughal dynastic line and the royal household created mechanisms for incorporating high-ranking nobility into imperial service as loyal *khāna-zād* (house-born) servants.[27]

Moving beyond the northern Indian plains, the Mughals also transformed senses of belonging to a ghar elsewhere, linking it with place-bound concepts such as *watan* (abode, homeland, residence, dwelling or country) and *mulk* (domains). In peninsular India, where monarchical sovereignty was weak, generational service under an itinerant lordly household remained the fundamental form of political organization; the declaration of one's house indicated an occupation tied to years of service under a patriarchal head. Belonging to a ghar was a privilege. The Mughal state tapped into the circulation of different social groups as a resource for governing across regions, working with invocations of ghar to organize, identify, and count its new subjects and resources.[28]

In seventeenth-century sources, we may deduce three meanings of ghar. First, the idea of ghar was tied to the subcontinent's most important social category—*jāti* or *qaum* (translated as caste or sub-caste[s])—that is, endogamous social groups that determined how people married, ate, lived, worked, interacted, and distanced themselves from each other. Rather than understanding it as a timeless, fixed, and stationary category, scholars have shown how jāti evolved and intersected with ghar to form the basis of social mobility and circulation in particular contexts and time periods.[29] Ghar was the fundamental socioeconomic resource or unit that members augmented and preserved by consolidating occupational status or control over a range of property rights over generations.

Second, ghar may also be understood then as the smallest unit upon which more transregional, bigger concepts such as *watan* and *mulk* could depend. Like these transregional Arabic terms, ghar also did not refer to a bounded geographic territory.[30] Like the term *watan*, which signaled multiple referents of place and lineage, vernacular terms that transmitted senses of belonging were also fundamentally tied to occupation, taxation, and institutions of resource management common across the Islamic world.[31] Thus, in the subcontinent, households with *watan jāgīr* (hereditary patrimonies) had stronger ties to specific places, villages, and towns where they had a home or ghar for centuries and held onto particular bureaucratic offices for multiple generations, thus mediating the state's reach and control over distant resources. This meaning of ghar is most visible in administrative documents.

A third meaning can be found in literary representations where ghar can refer to a bounded political category and encompasses more than one household. For example, the Deccan is referred to as a ghar in literary works, as a broad region to be protected by the multiple lineages that had served in it for generations. It was from this conceptual terrain that the most sustainable political threat to Mughal imperial supremacy—the Marathas, the paradigmatic political formation at the intersection of household and state—emerged in the eighteenth century.[32] This book is a synchronic portrait of the preceding decades, usually dismissed as a messy interregnum bracing for the rise and fall of proper, fully formed dynastic kingdoms, when the multiple entanglements of ghar began mediating state power.

Grounded in a tradition of social history, the household moves us toward a less romantic, nostalgic vision of premodern political formations and elite power, whose connections with nonelite communities, be they soldiers, weavers, poets, artisans, or peasants, are often presumed but rarely explained. So much of Mughal history is Delhi-centered and focused on the greatness of individual glamorous emperors while the historiography of the Deccan sultanates of the south focuses only on the court. What imperial and regional politics meant to the lives of those beyond the court remains far less articulated. The household offers a site to measure the reception of an empire, where alliances, feuds, and material exchange created new forms of affinity, belonging, *and* social exclusion.

This book rejects primordial identity as the singular and most important lens through which we write about power and politics in premodern South Asia. At the same time, the cross-societal entanglements of household power push against the idea that the world before colonialism was some sort of kumbaya. We may move away from viewing precolonial state and society through opposite lenses as either largely syncretic and pluralistic with all social groups living in perfect harmony *or* as inherently and essentially discrete, sectarian communities always at odds with each other. That is, one of the main goals of this book is to examine political relationships between precolonial "Hindu" and "Muslim" familial lineages in a single, mutually constituted analytical frame. Instead of either assuming timeless premodern affinities or focusing on a single ethnicity, linguistic, or religious group, the household recalibrated state power irrespective of identity. In other words, measuring the degree of "indigeneity" or "foreignness" in Iranians, Turks, Afghans, Rajputs, and Marathas to retell "a history of hatred" is the least interesting question to ask about social elites and power in premodern South Asia.[33] By examining how these ascriptive social identifications formed in the first place through established institutions at work on the margins of empire, we see how the precolonial state incorporated patterns of mobility and circulation, thus linking lineages of service to definitions of caste and community. Instead of fixating on ethnic factionalism as a timeless phenomenon, historians of the Deccan, in particular, may want to learn from studies of the gendered household in other parts of the subcontinent that have long uncoupled premodern identity from static meanings of place, sect, and language.[34] Extending the analytic of ghar unlocks how nested connections constituted through regimes of circulation forged a multivalent politics of place across peninsular India.

Before considering this book's historiographical and methodological stakes in further detail, I first map the political and social landscape of Mughal South Asia at the turn of the seventeenth century in the following section. I begin by

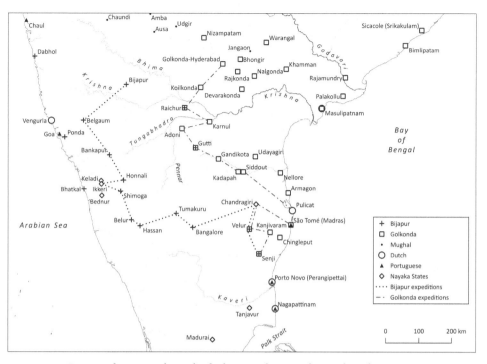

MAP 3. Deccan sultanates in the Hyderabad-Karnatak. Drawn by Kanika Kalra.

contrasting the top-down rhetoric of absolute opposition between the imperial north and regional Sultanates of the south with a bottom-up approach of how contending households anchored themselves in these states and produced overlapping and layered sovereignties across these regions. Through this discussion, my goal is to mark how ghar and its aforementioned multivalent meanings—as a socioeconomic unit, as a volatile site of intrafamilial conflict, and as a political category of belonging—were constituted by regimes of circulation integral to the everyday work of imperial institutions.

THE MUGHAL EMPIRE, DECCAN SULTANATES, AND THE INDIAN OCEAN IN THE SEVENTEENTH CENTURY

Nearly seventy years after the Central Asian prince Babur (d. 1530) established the Timurid dynastic line, founding the Mughal Empire in northern India, the renowned historian and courtier Abu'l-Fazl (d. 1602), writing in 1596, looked toward the subcontinent's southern half. He castigated the Muslim rulers of the south as "ingrates" who rose up in rebellion much too often while, at the same time, he observed that this "vast territory is like another Hindustan" (ān mulk-i wasī' ke hindūstān-i dīgar ast).[35] Abu'l Fazl articulated the coconstitution of these inseparable parts, which was also echoed in the work of the Bijapuri historian, Muhammad Qasim Firishta (d. 1620) in his early seventeenth-century chronicle, *Gulshan-i Ibrāhīmī* (Garden of Ibrahim), when he looked northward in the opposite direction and he too embedded the Deccan within Hindustan.[36] In a time of continuous military conflicts and political competition, marking the alterity of the north from the south, and vice versa, would become common across Mughal and Deccan court chronicles throughout the sixteenth and early seventeenth centuries, thereby establishing a trope that obscured the shared mechanisms of rule and overlapping arrangements of power that developed between these two regions.

This opposition framed the rivalry between the expansionist Sunni Muslim Turko-Mongol Timurids of northern India and the five smaller Turkoman regional Deccan sultanates, with both Shiʿi and Sunni kings ruling for variable lengths of time across the period comprising the ʿAdil shahs of Bijapur (ca. 1490–1686), the Qutb shahs of Golkonda-Hyderabad (ca. 1496–1687), the Nizam shahs of Ahmadnagar (ca. 1490–1636), the Barid shahs of Bidar (ca. 1538–1619), and the ʿImad shahs of Berar (ca. 1529–1574), all of which emerged from the peninsula's first Muslim dynasty, the Bahmanis (ca. 1347–1527).[37] The periodic Shiʿi inclinations of the ruling monarchs of these southern sultanates and the influx of émigré Central Asian elites resulted in strategic alliances with Safavid Iran to deter the Mughals, creating a web of triangular political and diplomatic relations.[38]

Despite being under Mughal suzerainty in the seventeenth century and after the effective defeat of Ahmadnagar in 1626, two of the regional sultanates, Bijapur and Golkonda, endured into the late seventeenth century. It wasn't until 1636 that the Deccan sultanates officially ceded territories to the Mughals by signing a deed of submission or *inqiyādnāma*, whereby they recognized the overlordship of the Mughal emperor.[39] The decades after this event have long been dismissed as ones of decline and decay, yet they also present a series of contradictions.[40] For example, in the subsequent fifty years after accepting Mughal supremacy, the regional Islamic sultanates would also reach their largest territorial extent when they extended beyond the central plateau and into the Karnatak, the Kaveri River delta, and the coastal lowlands along the Indian Ocean littoral. Here as well, the Mughal-Deccan warfront encountered the political successors of the Vijayanagara Empire (ca. 1336–1565), the *nayaka* states of Madurai, Tanjavur, and Senji in the Tamil zone and Ikkeri and Mysore in the Kannada-speaking regions of peninsular India.[41]

Throughout the seventeenth century, the Mughals fought a war of attrition and there were constant disagreements among members of the royal household about the ethics of subduing coreligionist Muslim rulers of the south and about the difficulty of extracting revenue in that region's much more unwieldy and variable ecology.[42] Attempts to incorporate the peninsula invigorated a familiar and very old pattern of politics wherein social elites from different sociological and cultural backgrounds affirmed their independence, undercutting imperial and regional monarchs by accumulating resources along the coasts, away from court capitals.[43] In many different parts of peninsular India, where monarchical forms of sovereignty had long been weak,[44] the introduction of imperial institutions simultaneously facilitated a drive toward regional centralization under elite households from a variety of caste, regional, and linguistic backgrounds. This pattern of an elasticity between monarchical sovereignty and elite social groups continued in the Deccan sultanates, well-illustrated for the preceding Vijayanagara Empire, and also conditioned Mughal imperial presence in peninsular India.[45]

These two parts of the subcontinent shared some broad features, such as the common religion of the ruling dynasts, Islam, and a cosmopolitan language, Persian, but they had different degrees of social diversity. Persian was the shared language of literary production and governance under the Mughals in the northern Indian plains and it intersected with other rich literary traditions of Sanskrit, Braj, and Awadhi in court.[46] In contrast, in peninsular India, three linguistic layers had developed by the seventeenth century. These consisted of Persian at the very top, the language of elite courtly literature and bureaucracy. It was followed by a second layer of Dakkani, a regional vernacular form of Hindawi or early Urdu, written in Perso-Arabic script and used across the southern sultanates. Dakkani's historical antecedents went back to the Delhi sultanate's (ca. 1206–1526) expansion toward the southern Indian peninsula in the fourteenth century.[47] Persian and Dakkani coexisted alongside the peninsula's rich literary traditions in regional vernaculars such as Marathi, Telugu, Kannada, Tamil, and Malayalam.[48] A range of sectarian and religious communities made up the subjects of Indo-Islamic states, ranging from followers of various Sufi orders to Vaishnava, Jain, and Sikh communities across northern India to various Shaiva, Vaishnava, Jain, and Buddhist sects in peninsular India.[49]

Looking outward, peninsular India's political geography was inexorably tied to the seas, whereby political centers located in the drylands of the central plateau or tableland had long sought control over "shatter zones" or "secondary centers" along major riverine conjunctures as well as those tied to more fertile areas of rainfall along the Eastern and Western Ghats of the peninsula that connected to port cities along the littoral.[50] Looking westward to the Arabian Sea, in the first half of the seventeenth century, elite households from the Bijapur sultanate enmeshed themselves in economic networks along the Konkan and Kanara coast (across the modern-day states of Maharashtra, Goa, and Karnataka). Looking eastward from the sultanate of Golkonda, this expansion was at first in the northern Coromandel (north of the Krishna River, from Masulipatnam to Bheemunipatnam in modern-day Andhra Pradesh).[51] In the second half of the century, the Mughal-Deccan frontier converged toward the southern Coromandel (south of the Krishna River toward the Kaveri River delta, stretching across southern Andhra and northern

Tamil Nadu), which was the center of weaving and textile trade across the Bay of Bengal.

Shortly before the Mughals established themselves in the northern plains in the third decade of the sixteenth century, another set of actors had arrived in South Asia via the Indian Ocean—namely, the Europeans, starting with the Portuguese who conquered Goa on the Konkan coast, seizing it from the sultanate of Bijapur in 1510.[52] For centuries, many different communities had sought access to the peninsula's key commodities—black pepper and cotton textiles—tying all political formations in this diverse region to the maritime routes of the western and eastern Indian Ocean. This maritime orientation was unlike that of northern India, where the Mughals first expanded in the Indo-Gangetic plains and only later turned their attention toward the seas. The Mughals acquired the prosperous port city of Surat after conquering Gujarat in the late sixteenth century in the west and Bengal in the east in the early seventeenth century. Over the course of the next few decades, these frontier zones between the Portuguese Empire in Asia and the Mughals, along with their various satellite states, produced an uneasy relationship between "unwanted neighbors," as elucidated in the work of Jorge Flores.[53] The Portuguese were eventually eclipsed by the world's first transnational companies that brought a peculiar and new form of sovereignty into the Indian Ocean, the company-state.[54] The English Company, founded on a charter issued by Elizabeth I (r. 1558–1603) in 1600, first attempted to enter the subcontinent via Gujarat. The Dutch formed the VOC (Verenigde Oostindische Compagnie) or the United East India Company in 1602, which made its way first to the eastern Indian Ocean via the Coromandel coast and only much later tapped into the western Indian Ocean around 1621.[55] This book's chapters begin right at this moment in the seventeenth century's first half, when the Mughal army, after defeating the Ahmadnagar sultanate, first occupied the northern Deccan in the 1620s. The remaining two sultanates accepted imperial overlordship and began expanding toward the Indian Ocean littoral, and the Portuguese, the Dutch, and the English negotiated their operations along the Konkan, Kanara, and Coromandel coasts with the powerful itinerant households affiliated with the regional sultanates of the south and Vijayanagara's successor states.[56]

The cast of characters here stay within the seventeenth century, a period that holds a contradictory position in both historiography and popular imagination. While some view it as mere extension of the age of absolute monarchs in the sixteenth century, at the other end, late Mughal historians often skip hurriedly over it to explain the momentous changes of the better-studied eighteenth century. Neither an addendum to or a continuation of a preceding golden age in the sixteenth century nor the precursor or cause of decline in the subsequent one, the seventeenth century's overlapping and contested sovereignties are now being made sense of on their own terms across different parts of the early modern world.[57] Scholars addressing the vantage point of different provinces in seventeenth-century India have thus emphasized the need to make sense of how regional politics shaped imperial state-making.[58]

OVERLAPPING SOVEREIGNTIES AND CONTENDING HOUSEHOLDS

By contrasting the top-down rhetoric of an absolute opposition between the imperial north and the Sultanate south with a bottom-up portrait of household participation in the day-to-day workings of early modern states, this section provides the reader with a prelude to the messy social worlds of different households reconstructed across the book's chapters by bringing together both literary and nonliterary sources generated by "court" and "state," a dichotomy I address in the introduction's last section.

Disputes over the definition of political boundaries and military resources could not disentangle the codependent and overlapping sovereignties of the Timurid Mughals of Hindustan with the Turkoman dynasties of the ʿAdil shahs of Bijapur and the Qutb shahs of Golkonda in the south. Alongside a begrudging admiration of the Mughals, southern chroniclers often referred to their northern competitors as emperors descended from Timur (*bādshāh-i tīmūrī nizhād*), or scaled them down derogatively as the emperor of Delhi (*bādshāh-i-dihlī*) or the king of Lahore (*shāh-i-lahūr*), or referred to them simply through the ethnic marker of "mughal" or Mongol, which the Mughals themselves never used.[59] Similarly, the domains of Hindustan (*vilāyat-i-mughal / mughal hindustān*) were depicted as a distinct and delimited space that lay north of the River Narmada, to which Mughal soldiers often withdrew after confrontations with regional armies.[60] Political turncoats and military renegades traversed different layers of border and threshold (*sarhad-i-mamālik*), seeking protection under a rival political regime.[61] But the problem of military retention and desertion was acute in a region where elite households in the neighboring sultanates were also expanding recruitment just as Mughal troops began to encamp across forts in the erstwhile regions of the Ahmadnagar sultanate (ca. 1490–1636), north of the River Krishna.[62] In the very heyday of imperial expansion in the seventeenth century, peninsular India became the epicenter of the empire, with the political-military campaigns in the southern centers becoming sites of improvisation where heightened centralization was constantly mediated by nonimperial state forms.

When the empire began expanding its limits beyond the Indo-Gangetic heartland, new groups were drawn into becoming "Mughal," bringing imperial practices into dialogue with regional circulation regimes and senses of ghar or belonging tied to a lineage of service. There was a fundamental difference in the way the royal dynastic line related to elite social groups in the imperial north versus in the southern sultanates. In peninsular India, military-aristocratic orders and hereditary officials maintained troops at their own expense to mobilize in times of war.[63]

The vast majority of fighters under these household chiefs were mercenaries with variable levels of control and ownership over their own weapons, horses, and food.[64] Unlike Mughal Hindustan, the Deccan sultanates did not have an elaborate *mansab* ranking system nor an ideological structure that tied distinct elite lineages to kingly power.[65] In the period of Mughal suzerainty, we see the fusion of these two imperial and regional state forms, which was also heightened when patriarchal heads of household faced shortages of resources, disputes within their families, and new incentives for joining up with different masters or entering the imperial ranks.

What did this tension in the seventeenth century between layered sovereignties and the improvising of empire look like from the bottom up? Which households enabled and extended the premodern state's reach? Often concerned with explaining the endpoints of events or the final outcomes, historians have outlined the rise and fall of the sultanates, Mughal expansion in the Deccan, and the ascendance of the Marathas and Indo-Africans to verify the seventeenth century's political turbulence in terms of absolute concepts of alliance-making.[66] My purpose here in zeroing in on a sample of the documentary evidence is twofold: (1) to trace out different social actors' definitions of ghar and how they marked its uncertain terrain of belonging; and (2) to identify which regimes of circulation impinged on the day-to-day transactions between household(s) and state.

Documentary evidence in Persian provides vignettes of two types—high-caste, hereditary village-level officials and nonhereditary, military-aristocratic lineages—circulating back and forth between regional capitals, forts, and provincial towns, deploying a common set of strategies to harness state power. In a detailed study of one *watandār* (holders of hereditary patrimonies) Maratha household, the Jedhes, A. R. Kulkarni has shown that these lineages were likely to fight each other in the battlefield, remaining loyal in service to a particular master rather than falling neatly into ethnic camps, rarely uniting to protect the *watan* as a whole.[67] Furthermore, to one-up and compete against one's own kin required drawing on "the family feud as a political resource,"[68] whereby members had to link their ghar with networks of other lineages, regardless of whether they were one of their own kind or not.

From urging cultivators to till the lands and requesting the right to tax inland market towns to resolving irate complaints about relatives and disciplining forest communities to clear strategic forts, these day-to-day tasks anchored different lineages of service to state power. When the Mughal war front first moved into peninsular India, evocations of ghar or khāna tied Maratha, Indo-African, Turko-Persians, and Afghans into a web of relations with imperial and regional states. This was not a neat, mutually exclusive hierarchy of administrative labors divided between hereditary Hindu upper-castes and Muslim émigré elites;[69] on the contrary, the evocations of ghar as a socioeconomic unit and a political category embodied the internal fragility of these ethnic and sectarian categories.

We may extend these arguments to trace one example of a household feud from the 1640s to the 1660s in order to show how its members partook in the Mughal frontier's overlapping sovereignties. In this instance of a ghar in turmoil, Kedarji Khopade, son of Narsoji, a *desai* (hereditary chieftain) of the areas around Rohida fort (present-day Maharashtra state), deplored the *harām-zādagī* (wickedness, villainy, rascality, illegitimacy) of his cousin Khandoji Khopade, son of Dharmoji. Both Kedarji and Khandoji were identified as *wārisdār* (heirs) who coshared official duties and responsibilities for governing areas around the village of Utroli. The Khopades were one of many elite Maratha *watandārs* of the Maval, a region of twelve valleys on the eastern side of the Sahyadri Mountains, in Bhor, south of the modern city of Pune, whose support had long been critical for reigning kings and emerging political contenders.[70] Starting in the 1640s, Kedarji's primary points of contact were the nonhereditary officials appointed to the transferable position of *havaldār* (literally, custodian or person in charge or governor of a port city, appointed directly by the sultan) who, in turn, reported on the activities of the hereditary officeholders to the king.[71] Sultan Muhammad ʿAdil Shah (r. 1627–56) of Bijapur noted that subjecting a devoted and loyal servant like Kedarji, a *halālkhor* (faithful, loyal), to such tyranny was unjustified (*īn chunīn ziyādatī shudan munāsib nadārad*). Thus, on November 4, 1650, one havaldār, Sankaraji Banaji, was urged to punish the wicked cousin Khandoji and help the loyal Kedarji right away.[72] Still, five years later, the family dispute remained unresolved when cultivators and peasants from the area journeyed to the court with complaints about the injustices of Khandoji. At this point, the king threatened to transfer Kedarji's *deshmukhī* (chieftaincy) to someone else if he failed to rein in his kin, holding him responsible for the actions of Khandoji.[73]

While most of the correspondence offers a viewpoint from the perspective of the court, we also hear from the beleaguered head of household, Kedarji, whose words were likely spoken to a scribe in Marathi and interpolated in an undated lengthy Persian ʿ*arzdāsht* or written petition. Kedarji began by laying out the financial strains on his khāna or ghar, going to great lengths to explain that he was "the eldest of nine brothers and had a large house(hold) (*az īn nuh kas birādarān īn kamīne birādar-i buzurg wa khāna-yi buzurg dārad*), for which he had to spend the entire amount of the cess (*nān-kār*) on the household's expenses, including those of his defiant cousin.[74] He added that his annual income was barely enough to keep up with the maintenance and development of the villages and towns, deliver revenues to crown officials, and give a share to each of his brothers. While his ghar was under these material constraints, Khandoji Khopade, with the backing of two Indo-African havaldārs and the ascendent Maratha Bhonsles, was misusing various sources of revenue generated through *inʿām* (rent-free lands) granted to the Khopade family. Recently, Khandoji had looted a village, destroying and stealing property, killing three cultivators, and injuring about ten to twelve people. With exasperation and fear, Kedarji noted that his ten to twenty mounted horsemen did not stand a chance against his relative's master, Shivaji Bhonsle (d. 1680), with his four-thousand strong cavalry. So, for the time being, Kedarji, along with his sons, decided to escape with life and limb intact. Closing with formulaic phrases that appealed to the sultan as the giver of justice (*dād*), he ended his letter with wishes for the state's continued longevity.[75]

Khandoji was not one to keep quiet and so he sent two of his men to the court to speak with the sultan. In turn, Kedarji warned the king that those people were telling all lies (*ān tamām khilāf wa durogh ast*) and that he should not believe their false speech (*zabānī ghair wāqi'a*). He urged that Khandoji be ordered to present himself to the court, in front of the king and the entire *qabā'il* (household), to settle these matters once and for all. On March 9, 1660, a *farmān* renewed Kedarji's appointment as *desai*, including a list of all the villages and forts under his purview, the market towns where he could collect necessary taxes, and his right to extract forced labor from villagers (*rābti-yi begārī*), though this likely did not stop his cousin from wreaking havoc on the cultivators and residents around Rohida.[76] This renewed commitment was contingent specifically on Kedarji stepping up to support the Indo-African military commander Siddi Jauhar Salabat Khan, who had recently agreed to lay siege at the Panhala fort in the western Deccan, against the Bhonsles, in exchange for an appointment in Karnul in the Karnatak, in the southern war front beyond the central plateau.[77] Households with stronger ties to place could reign in their defiant kinfolk if they offered soldiers for the campaigns of itinerant military households circulating between two ecological zones at the northern and southern ends of the Mughal frontier. From the perspective of these minute negotiations, then, the Mughals, Marathas, and Indo-Africans all begin to appear as contingent categories, not necessarily motivated by a principle of absolute alliance-making but by much more prosaic concerns of beating out one's extended kin over the rights to control a ghar.

What do we make of this microportrait of one household's evocations of this concept in a moment of crisis? For Kedarji, the house(hold) was an entity with constant material and economic needs, with one too many mouths to feed. Hardly a static site of natural and durable bonds, the one thing constant in it was vehement disagreement over how to use its resources and the circulation of its members to mobilize resources. A ghar's internal dynamics necessitated forging crisscrossing relationships with other familial formations with different occupational functions in the state. The possibility of villagers, cultivators, and laborers fleeing from agricultural lands or traveling to the regional capital to relay their grievances required the patriarchal head to ensure social order, which was being disrupted by his own kin. The circulation and mobility of subject populations was both a resource and a threat that bound the interests of different ghar together. Although entrenched in a specific region, the ghar of watandārs like the Khopades was interlinked with larger networks of other groups such as the Indo-Africans, who were mobilizing resources dispersed across two connected ecological zones, the Deccan and the

Karnatak. At the lowest levels of governance, patrimonial power did not exist as an ideal type with a straightforward link between the sultan-head of household-subjects.[78] The agency of patriarchal heads was often circumscribed, limited, and contingent on a range of circumstances. The internal politics of a ghar compelled household chiefs to constantly seek alliances across religious, caste, or kin divides, at times to force compromise on their subjects or to sustain their grip on offices over generations, a pattern that chapters 3 and 6 of this book will illustrate.

Finally, Kedarji's small trials also speak to the third meaning of ghar or khāna explored in this book—namely, as a political category with far more elasticity than how we conceptualize social identities in the postcolonial present. The web of relations within which Kedarji's household was embedded is reaffirmed by literary representations of seventeenth-century politics. Whether Indo-Africans, Marathas, or Central Asian émigrés, the different social groups we see performing the daily tasks of the state in documentary genres also constituted the changing moral and ethical meanings of ghar under the penumbra of empire.

In popular discussions today, the seventeenth century is often held up as a point of origin, of sorts, to which modern-day anxieties about religion, language, and regional identities can be traced. To name just one example of the polarizing narratives associated with this century, we need look no further than the famed rivalry between the Mughal emperor Aurangzeb (d. 1707) and the Maratha warrior Shivaji, used today to naturalize categories such as "Hindu" and "Muslim." And yet, in the eyes of the poet Nusrati (d. 1674?)—one of the most prominent observers of this period and a character who appears across this book's chapters—the problem with these two figures was grounded, above all, in a deep history of familiarity rather than in fundamental, essential, and irreconcilable differences. To this political poet, ghar was a moral rubric through which he gauged the actions of all households—whether émigré Turko-Persians, Afghans, Indo-Africans, or Marathas—admonishing them equally for sinking the name and fame of their houses (*dubāyā āpas nām-o-nāmūs-o-ghar*). Lamenting the decline of monarchical power in the seventeenth-century Deccan, Nusrati would observe that the home had caught fire from two sides (*dikhiyā do taraf te lagī ghar ko āg*).[79] The intrafamilial feud of Khopades was thus nested within a larger sense of ghar as a political category to which multiple cosharers belonged all the while contesting, disputing, and disagreeing with each other. Subsequent chapters of this book will consider a continuum of literary and nonliterary evidence to reconstruct the messy entanglements of the household form and how its regimes of circulation harnessed wider cross-sections of society within the premodern state.

But before starting our journey across peninsular India, let's turn to the book's methodological and historiographical stakes. In the following section, I evaluate the twin historiographies of the northern and southern halves of the subcontinent, where the category of the state is often posited against that of the court, an artificial binary that collapses when studying the household form through a connected histories approach. This dichotomy also shapes the pervasive theme of elite factionalism that unites the twin historiographies, which I also unpack in the next section by drawing on comparative critiques that urge studying the constitution of social elites through *practices* of social identity across the premodern world (rather than as a pregiven, absolute, and primordial value assigned to communities).

BEYOND COURT AND STATE IN MUGHAL SOUTH ASIA

Although some scholars may try to feign reinvention, first monographs are, in some ways, an homage to or a reflection of our training, bringing into collision lessons learned from a long list of teachers. This book is no exception. It began because I started searching for the place of households in connected histories.[80]

The household, the basic building block of a society, is commonly defined as a stationary unit with a fixed number of occupants, grounded in place. Is it possible to examine this everyday sociological category through the practice of connected histories—that is, by reading sources in multiple languages from vastly different linguistic, geographic, and philosophical worlds, often used to reconstruct histories of global diplomacy, mobility, and transregional interactions? The foundational unit of the household constituted larger jāti formations, the subcontinent's most salient form of social hierarchy.[81] It is worthwhile, then, to ask this question: What is the place of household and caste mobility in recent scholarly paradigms that emphasize transnational, interregional connections as the Persianate, Persian cosmopolis, or Eurasian interactions in the era before the nation-state? A short answer could be, there is none!

But, as the subsequent chapters will show, the story of how elite households participated in and transformed the imperial frontier reveals the connected histories of circulation across much smaller, more proximate geographies.[82] It offers a picture of mobility across much shorter distances and itineraries, or what Kären Wigen has called "pattern interactions" or "cross-cultural isomorphisms," in this instance of caste and household moving between multiple ecological zones.[83] Households in circulation within the peninsula, whether from Khandesh to the Kanara and Konkan coasts or from Telangana to the southern Coromandel, shift our attention away from much larger-scale horizontal movements between two similar sites to vertical encounters across different hierarchies of power. Studies of diplomacy have shown exchanges between major courts and capitals, between Delhi, Isfahan, and Istanbul. Or, covering movement across even larger distances, from the viewpoint of the European factory on the coast, historians of "European expansion in Asia" reconstruct the familiar story of European agents from Lisbon, Amsterdam, and London, as well as their encounters in the Indian Ocean.[84]

The earliest explorations in connected histories (before it became a thing) had, indeed, shown the utility of working across the archives of courts and states, illuminating smaller geographies of circulation, attuned to formations of caste and household at the edges of imperial states or in their "shatter zones."[85] And yet, the household has not been the subject of connected histories in the way that dynasty continues to capture the imagination of global historians. The terms *dynasty* and *family* remain two ends of an uneasy tension in our modern imagination of both present and past political forms, constituting various definitions of the entity called the state.[86] A line of rule based on descent within a family, a group of people with a common ancestor, is seen as an entity with arbitrary rules, nepotistic, informal, lacking structure, and held together by affective ties. In contrast, for the historical past, the dynastic form and establishment of rule under a single (usually) male ruler is seen as a fully-realized political model from which all others are a deviation (stateless, tribe, chiefdom, and various other terms imply the opposite of monarchy). According to this model, the four levels of ruler, dynasty, court, and realm have defined the basic features of kingly authority throughout human history.[87] In this top-down perspective, then, the king figure is synonymous with the state, a model that has long been unsettled by scholars pointing to different institutional arrangements and innovation possible within patrimonial power.[88]

This study of the intersections of household and state power and how they shaped regimes of circulation in the Mughal frontier resonates with work done by other scholars on the family and the improvisation of empires. Historians of many different parts of the world have shown that early modern empires amassed resources through a wide web of networks across distant regions, particularly through relations with the most basic unit of social organization, the family or household, which remains less examined, partly owing to a naturalism assumed inherent in this category.[89] One study has detailed the strategies that military households deployed to meet their obligations to the Ming state (ca. 1368–1644), building a bottom-up perspective on how imperial power worked at an everyday level.[90] In a similar vein, earlier studies on the Ottoman Empire's Arab provinces illuminated the administrative strategies of military households in integrating the imperial order into regional politics. More recently, combining (central) Ottoman Turkish and (provincial) Arabic materials shows how provincial literatis' networks of kin and friends created sensibilities that helped forge a cohesive imperial identity.[91] Further afield, the family remains a key site for examining how core moral concepts like honor enabled urban households to maintain local ties while serving the monarchy in sixteenth-century Granada. The role of the family and the specific practices of patrimonial power in merchant capitalism, too, have been illuminated across early modern Europe.[92]

Historians of comparative Islamic empires, particularly when evaluating post-Mongol Eurasia, have also contested this linear progression from prestate/kinship to kingly power in a few different ways, particularly when studying elite warbands and their mechanisms for incorporating new groups.[93] By examining Persianate historical writing for its discursive practices, Ali Anooshahr has shown how Turko-Mongol groups invented origins and traditions necessary for establishing dynastic power, unraveling a continuous tension in how aristocratic lineages forged the early Mughal state.[94] In the eastern Islamic world, recent work on Safavid urban history points to the household or family as the most productive site for writing the social history of time periods identified as so-called golden ages when getting past the king figure is difficult, partly owing to the kinds of sources we have available. Rejecting simplistic, linear change-over-time chronological narratives and idealized definitions of norms of comportment (*adab*), Kathryn Babayan understands the seventeenth-century household anthology as the key site where imperial discourse and proscriptions were received, critiqued, and contested, putting the household and the state into dialogue with each other.[95]

Echoing historians of comparative Islamic empires, scholars working across different periods and regions of South Asia have posed compelling questions from a range of unconventional sources to analyze the household as a site for social history. Place-based histories of greater Rajasthan (in northwestern India), in particular, have been at the forefront of understandings of caste, clan, and definitions of community. Tanuja Kothiyal and Divya Cherian thus urge building histories of the state from below, going beyond the dynastic line and supra-households such as that of the Mughals, while also emphasizing the need to study premodern social power in terms of its inherent inequalities and hierarchies.[96]

Studying the period of the Mughals, and Islam's expansion in South Asia more broadly, so often synonymous with a neat line of dynastic rulers, often entails displacing the study of the household to its outer edges. Thus, in a rich and generative recent volume on the household in the subcontinent across time, the household within Indo-Islamic political formations remains absent.[97] The family is either examined through archaeological evidence or through normative texts that governed gender relations in the ancient and early medieval periods *before* Islam (roughly before 1200 CE.) or *after* the Mughals in the eighteenth century during the early colonial period when regional lineages forged independent successor states and we typically begin accounting for the household's role in state power.[98] By examining the household role's in the intervening seventeenth century, this book attempts to answer the call that "an adequate understanding of South Asian society requires us not only to bring the state back in; it must bring non-Hindus back in, too," even though it is no longer fashionable to prioritize the state as an object of analysis.[99]

Scholarship has come a long way since Sir Jadunath Sarkar's diagnosis of the Deccan, the central plateau of peninsular India, as the "Spanish ulcer of the Mughal empire." And there have been considerable advances beyond examining Mughal emperor Aurangzeb's (r. 1658–1707) personhood and grudges against the south, or locating the cause of imperial decline in the incorporation of southern nobility, or validating Mughal success at collecting revenue in the newly conquered provinces.[100] One way to work beyond the south as a foil for the north, a trope shared in all the aforementioned works, is to investigate the long history of borrowing and cohabitation that brought the institutions of northern and southern Indian states to mirror each other.

A renewed interest in social history has taken Mughal scholarship usefully beyond the court to the streets of Delhi and the provinces of northern India to examine elite power through popular sovereignty as represented in literary sources, on the one hand, and through a microhistory of law as visible in the documents of a family of landlords in Malwa, on the other.[101] Collapsing the binary between courts and states by examining both literary and documentary evidence, reconstructions of the public sphere and political culture in Mughal north India set aside the search for change-over-time narratives.[102] Going outside the capital city of Delhi, we see that variations between the ideals depicted in chronicles and actual uses of social categories have also been carefully observed in work on the changing profiles of *zamīndār* (rural potentates) within regions in the imperial heartland, showing the utility of comparing regional documentation against ideal taxonomies drawn from court chronicles.[103] All these works on north India call for a history of reception going beyond idealized representations of imperial discourse, power, and values in ruler-centric court literature.

The historiography of the Deccan sultanates has also, in recent years, witnessed an efflorescence across many disciplines, ranging from the study of court culture and literature to political history. Multiple museum exhibitions and recent monographs have addressed the place of Deccan sultanates in the Islamic world, turning to the question of their diplomatic ties and cultural exchanges with the three gunpowder empires—the Timurid Mughals of India, the Safavids in Iran, and the Ottomans in the Middle East and North Africa.[104] One interdisciplinary project has combined monumental architecture and landscape archaeology with textual evidence to reveal the continuities of southern India's political systems at the intersections of Arabic and Sanskrit literary worlds in the sixteenth century. By incorporating material culture, Richard Eaton and Phillip Wagoner underscored shared patterns of elite power and the role of secondary cities or "shatter zones" in defining sovereignty in the Deccan, a conclusion also reached in the aforementioned early collaboration of Narayana Rao, David Shulman, and Sanjay Subrahmanyam earlier in the Nayaka world.[105] In addition, Richard Eaton has also written a synthetic pan-Indian political history, building on the argument about the salience of a shared cultural cosmopolis.[106]

Drawing on this idea of a cosmopolis, the Persian language has become the primary agent in recent political and intellectual histories of the Deccan. For example, by exploring Persian texts beyond ruler-centric chronicles that take the court as the primary site of sociability, Emma Flatt has illuminated ethical modes of living and courtly disposition based on the cultivation of esoteric, scribal, and martial skills in the period before 1600, prior to Mughal hegemony.[107] Likewise, Roy Fischel's recent political history draws on Persian chronicles to examine origin narratives and kingly ideologies in the period prior to imperial incorporation, affirming the tropes of opposition between a local identity in the face of imperial conquest.[108] In contrast to the rich tradition of accounting for state-society relations in early Mughal scholarship, as well as Abhishek Kaicker, Nandini Chatterjee, and Farhat Hasan's recent calls to return to social history in Mughal north India and forego the search for golden ages, the court remains the more privileged site of studying the Deccan sultanates.[109]

In part, the focus on court-centric literature stems from the tendency to assume a lack of accessible documentary evidence in and about the southern sultanates. And yet, it is exactly in this contradictory period of Mughal suzerainty and purported decline that the Sultanates produced the largest deposits of Persian documentary genres (which offered us a window into the trials of the internal strife in the Khopade household), emulating imperial bureaucratic practices in the very writing of their materials at the moment when elite households were driving processes of regional centralization.[110] How regional Islamic sultanates actually worked on a mundane, day-to-day level, or how their bureaucracies, armies, and administrations changed in the wake of a growing imperial occupation remains unresolved. We must turn west to the historians of the Maratha Deccan in the eighteenth century to understand everyday systems of governance that exercised social power in peninsular India and helped shape categories such as caste and household.[111]

Recent calls to move away from studying "states" and "state-formation" to "courts" and "courtly societies," particularly for Persianate Islam and culture, do so at times without accounting for the sub-continent's basic form of social organization—jāti—a variable that defies boundaries of the socioeconomic versus those of religion, culture, and language. To live well in a part of the world as unequal as the Indian subcontinent, social elites have always had to go out and fight wars, besiege cities, monopolize roads and rivers, stock rice and grain, increase cultivation, and control natural and human resources. In doing so, multireligious and multilingual elites encountered a range of other noncourtly social groups in agrarian and coastal economies. To be sure, in the era before nationalism, members of elite households transcended differences of language, region, kinship, and sect, but they did so without disturbing hierarchies of caste and status across different regions. In this book, the cantankerous itineraries from the capital city of Bijapur to the port of Devanampattinam (identified as Teganapatnam in VOC documents) collapse such binaries to reveal the coconstitutive and interdependent spheres of state and court, at the intersections of which premodern power worked. To bridge the divides between the court and the state, this book's chapters are also an experiment with method and discipline, connecting social history with literary studies and historical sociology.

Finally, using the analytic of ghar bridges the divide between court and state, which has generated a corollary fixation on the ethnic composition of pre-modern social elites, shared across the twin historiographies of the north and south. The roots of who was a foreigner and who was not in peninsular India ultimately lie in colonial ethnography, which assumed a fixed, static definition of pre-modern India, as I have argued elsewhere.[112] Historians categorized Mughal and Deccan subimperial elites (and their subjects) in terms of their distance or proximity to a pre-conceived notion of "Indianness." These definitions of belonging derived almost exclusively from Persian chronicles, which follow interelite high politics with the ruler at its center, with little or no mention of social groups beyond the court.[113] Frozen chronicle representations, however, do not reveal much about the valence of labels used for precolonial social groups or whether or not these groups earnestly believed in their purported identities; nor do they reveal how those further down the social ladder may have understood such categories. This book follows from the earliest generation of historians who studied a formidable range of archival sources beyond the official chronicle to show how ethnic identities of elites were hierarchically understood and in what manner they played prescribed functions in the imperial state.[114] It builds on this tradition, however, by attending to the constantly shifting meanings of ghar and its role in creating new definitions of becoming "Mughal," rather than with a fixed definition of this capacious entity that continues to cast a long shadow on practices of social identity present, even today, in this part of the world.

SOURCES AND ORGANIZATION

This study relies on a range of sources in Persian, in the panregional idiom of Dakkani, and in Dutch, along with a smaller number of sources in English and Portuguese. At various points in this introduction, I have echoed a critique of the Persian court chronicle, the paradigm of the Persianate, and Indo-Persian historiography more broadly, as the single most utilized body of sources used to write about the Mughal past and shape historical memory in the subcontinent for centuries thereafter.[115] These official chronicles had a strong, linear chronological frame, and notions of universal time were usually compiled in political centers and authored by immigrant first- or second-generation Persian clerical elites. Their audiences were a small circuit of users, listeners, and readers of Persian. In contrast to the chronicle form, the much larger body of Persian documentary sources generated by the Mughal occupation of peninsular India are the least examined sources from the seventeenth century, and I put them in dialogue with a range of other materials. These documents are a window into the everyday interactions of the Mughal bureaucracy with people beyond the court, the social space of Persographia as Nile Green has called it, where Persian functioned alongside many different writing systems and oral spheres across the subcontinent.[116]

The focus here on synchronic convergences within the seventeenth century rather than a neat, evolutionary change-over-time narrative stems from the desire to generate an interdisciplinary conversation on a thick yet disparate spread of literary and nonliterary multilingual materials produced in this period.[117] Specialists of non-Western premodern societies have long confronted bodies of evidence that defy modern disciplinary boundaries and force us to rely on multiple methods for reconstructing worlds before Europe.[118] How and why should the literary specialist of a regional vernacular read heroic verse about a historic battle alongside a bureaucratic document that tells us about the salaries of the soldiers who fought those battles, likely only studied by the social historian? By doing a simultaneous reading of such polyvocal sources, this book affirms the radical equality of literary and nonliterary ways of being, emphasizing the need to inhabit both in order to reconstruct the precolonial past. It shows that the "worldmaking"[119] of literary sources was anchored in political and economic alliances and tensions in ways for which neither literary scholars nor economic historians readily account. The book moves between imperial and regional capital cities and multiple ecological zones—from the arid, drylands of the central plateau to both the southwestern and southeastern coasts of peninsular India—in order to show how microhistories of a region can have deep connections with debates in global history.[120]

Much recent work on the north and south of India has shown that Persian texts were one among many linguistic traditions that circulated within and beyond courts, emphasizing the utility of supplementing this transregional language with textual materials in other languages.[121] Contributing to this conversation, I turn to *masnavī* (narrative poems in rhymed couplet form) written in Dakkani on martial-heroic themes that comment on the politics of the Mughal frontier and the transformations of ghar or senses of belonging in the seventeenth century. The longer narrative form of the masnavī allowed poets to develop parallel scenes, divergent contrasts, and the dramatization of many different events and figures, making it more conducive and accessible than other stricter and shorter Perso-Arabic forms such as *ghazal* (love lyric).[122] As the oldest living scholar of these two poetic forms in Dakkani Urdu, Mohammad Ali Asar, has shown, masnavī was the preferred form among literati across the Deccan sultanates, although ghazal also grew here from the fourteenth to seventeenth centuries. By contrast, in northern India, after the eighteenth century, ghazal remains the better studied and canonized poetic form of classical Urdu studies.[123]

Many regional histories on the periods from 1500 to 1800 have recently made the case for making sense of similar premodern martial works in a range of literary and oral traditions that help collapse the easy association of premodern languages with fixed notions of identity.[124] Dakkani or proto-Urdu[125] occupies a curious position in studies of regional languages in early modern South Asia. From its very inception in the fourteenth century, circulation across the north and south was integral to the evolution of this tongue, which continued in the eighteenth century when southern poet innovators working in this panregional idiom moved northward.[126] Rather than fixing it into cliches about local identity, sources in this language offer fertile ground for further collapsing the exaggerated divide between the north and south.

Scholars point to Dakkani's role in Sufi households that adopted it in order to spread Islam in southern India. Others have looked at its distinct adaptations of Perso-Arabic forms such as the *ghazal*.[127] Like Urdu of all varieties, Dakkani is based on a dialectal base situated between Panjabi and Khari Boli Hindi.[128] By the seventeenth century, Islamic sultanates of the south were broadly, spatially identified with different linguistic territories with regions of Kannada-speaking ʿAdil shahs of Bijapur, Marathi-speaking Nizam shahs of Ahmadnagar, and Telugu-speaking Qutb shahs of Golkonda. Dakkani occupied a panregional position, presiding over and across all these sultanates of peninsular India, below Persian but above regional vernaculars. Despite scholars having undertaken painstaking, decades-long work in regional universities on the literary history of this language before the eighteenth century, many questions remain regarding its role in shaping modern Urdu, which is often only associated with northern India.[129] For the purposes of the social historian and this book, I engage with a modest slice of these literary materials from the seventeenth century, particularly when political poets evoked the idea of ghar in this language to capture the fusing of the north and south alongside senses of belonging under Mughal rule.

From port cities, villages, and bazaars along the littoral, this book reconstructs provincial household economic activities through the Dutch East India Company's archives (VOC), a body of sources often used to recount the story of diplomacy, courtly interactions, and European-Asian encounters. *Between Household and State* instead uses this European archive to reconstruct the story of inter-Asian exchanges, revealing the complex mechanisms through which indigenous elites transcended differences in language, sect, and caste to preserve existing social inequities and to maintain hierarchies in the Indian Ocean economy. In contrast to published European travel accounts and the more well-known records of the English East India Company, partly because this entity would eventually come to rule as a colonial power over the subcontinent, the Dutch materials from the period before 1700 are underutilized and less examined. Finally, in addition to juxtaposing Dutch documents against textual traditions in regional Indian vernaculars, *Between Household and State* examines how indigenous documents were translated in this European archive to reconstruct the voices and stories of inter-Asian interactions.

Each chapter of this book focuses on a single sociospatial context, reconstructing particular regimes of circulation and mobility, which were central to configuring the meanings of ghar at the intersections of household and state power. I examine particular sites in each chapter as windows onto the temporal and spatial conjuncture of circulating relations and processes. Regimes of circulation and relations of belonging worked differently at different levels of scale, a fact that enables zooming in and out of specific clusters of social relations in each chapter. Rather than being a linear itinerary from point A to B, this book moves back and forth across the expanse of peninsular India, across different sets of scales between court and coast. Each social site illuminates the household's role in shaping the meanings of home or ghar, an everyday concept of belonging that was recalibrated through routine encounters in precolonial India's largest empire.

In chapter 2, the book opens at the military barrack, where we examine the first form of circulation—the movement of armed men and animals who interacted with different kinds of bureaucratic workers, scribes, clerks, and state inspectors. The act of identifying the itinerant soldier, verifying his ghar or home(s), was the building block of the process of becoming Mughal. From an interconnected network of military barracks in the south-central provinces (present-day Madhya Pradesh and Maharashtra), I foreground the materiality of early modern states, reconstructing the day-to-day interactions of military circulation that tied the common soldier in service (naukarī) under various households to the state. Turning to the labels that classified people according to various identification of ghar, along with labels for lineage, language, occupation, and region, the chapter unsettles the meanings of ethnic terms such as Irani, Turani, Turk, Rajput, Maratha, Afghan, Deccani, and Habshi.

This chapter shows that, in a manner that was akin to other early modern empires, Mughal institutions emboldened and schematized social hierarchies to enhance the state's coercive capacities. This chapter's bottom-up exploration of the bureaucratic encounters that produced new notions of social identity contributes to the book's larger contention that precolonial identifications were neither fuzzy nor fluid.[130] Moving armies and their personnel brought the institutional mechanisms of northern and southern India closer to each other. As a greater variety of social groups, some more legible than others, came under the purview of imperial procedure, scribes generated a spectrum of labels to make distinctions between them. In a layered war front, greater centralization required improvisation on and incorporation of pre-existing regimes of circulation to form pansubcontinental institutions of military recruitment that could incorporate subjects constantly on the move. From this foundational discussion of the first regime of circulation in military barracks, where bureaucratic encounters shaped the meanings of ghar, we move to other social sites, including the court, regional capitals, market towns, and port cities.

In chapter 3, we travel with one of the most prominent elite households that first negotiated with the imperial overlords encamped in the northern Deccan. Through Persian administrative documents, vernacular narrative poems, and VOC archives, the chapter examines a southern Iranian Shi'i émigré's confrontations with a Shaivite Kannada-speaking warrior chief while simultaneously facing opposition from his own son-in-law and other extended kin embroiled in different nodes in the agrarian hinterland around the Konkan and Kanara coasts in southwestern India (present-day Maharashtra and Karnataka). Here, I examine intrafamilial conflicts and the circulation of relatives dispersed across small market towns and entrepôts. To compete with their own kin, elite political players strategically used Europeans on the coast—namely, the Portuguese Estado da Índia and the VOC—to consolidate their control over the agrarian hinterland. At the same time, increasing pressure from the Mughals in the north brought into focus the fundamental role of hereditary village-level occupational groups, such as accountants and headmen. This chapter demonstrates how ties of service between different types of precolonial households unsettles our present-day understandings of ethnic and religious difference, often conceived along the neat binary between Hindu versus Muslim. The intrafamilial feud between a father-in-law and son-in-law or between rival siblings from a lineage of village accountants over resources were strikingly alike and analogous across different sectarian and ethno-linguistic groups.

In chapters 4 and 5, we turn to the circulation of culture—its producers, representations, and politics—in the social site of regional court capitals (Bijapur and Hyderabad-Golkonda in the present-day states of Karnataka and Telangana). These chapters consider the cross-pollination of political commentaries in two languages, Persian and Dakkani, and how multilingual literary representations therein conveyed changing senses of belonging to a ghar under imperial occupation. Chapter 4 explores the theme of cultural circulation, using multilingual literary representations for the analysis of bonds that crossed lines of gender and status. Starting at the site of the adorned palace, it reconstructs the marriage of an itinerant regional queen and the movement of her literary entourage across regional capitals. Poets, free and enslaved, produced images of celebration and bonds of relatedness that political historians usually skip over as irrelevant to politics. I argue that ghar lay at the center of literary representations that memorialized different modalities of kinship in court politics, whereby poets and participants evoked the home as an idealized space that could be built based on marriage, slave patronage, or fosterage. In Persian chronicles such as the *Muhammadnāma* (The book of Muhammad, ca. 1646), *Hadīqat al-Salātīn* (Garden of sultans, ca. 1646) to vernacular narrative poems such as *Mezbānināma* (The book of hospitality, ca. 1633), regional literati conceptualized ghar as both a site of volatility and contention that disrupted monarchical power and, concomitantly, as a space of celebration, consumption, and hospitality where new aristocratic lineages anchored themselves into royal authority. This chapter argues that the patronage bonds between those depicted and those who produced poetic representations saw ghar as a site where divisions of gender, status, and class were crossed to articulate a politics of belonging in the shadow of empire.

Comparing changes over the course of the seventeenth century, chapter 5 turns to the transformed senses of belonging to a ghar as observed by poets in the regional capital city who observed the evolution of imperial rule. I juxtapose the work of a émigré Iranian poet writing in Persian and a regional Deccani poet writing in Dakkani Urdu, both of whom composed narrative poems in the regional court of Bijapur (present-day Karnataka), where they formulated similar critiques of empire. It reconstructs how the Mughals were perceived by two different kinds of Muslim poets who, under the patronage of provincial households, observed their imperial neighbors with a mix of awe, mistrust, and suspicion. This chapter traces what changed about household power and the critique of empire from the first to the second half of seventeenth century by examining two martial poems, Hakim Atishi's ʿĀdilnāma (The book of ʿĀdil, ca. 1628) and Nusrati's ʿAlināma (The book of ʿAli, ca. 1665). These invectives elucidate the fragility of imperial and regional kings and sectarian identities in precolonial South Asia. Here, through multilingual literary representations, I show how poets took political positions on household patronage, collapsing solidarities of religion and a simplistic imperial versus regional binary. Both poets' criticisms of the Mughals were less about asserting an exceptional regional or Deccani identity and more about reflecting on the limits of monarchical power and age-old threats to it from familial formations.

In chapter 6, the book's final itinerary lands at the Mughal frontier's southernmost limits on the Coromandel coast (southern Andhra Pradesh and present-day Tamil Nadu) in southeastern India, where members of provincial households sought new alliances that cut across sectarian, linguistic, and caste lines to discipline the littoral economy. It considers representations of ghar as a political category in the seventeenth century's final decades, when multiple household lineages—Indo-Africans, Miyana Afghans, and the Maratha Bhonsles—competed for political power, with the latter eventually posing the most sustained and viable threat to Mughal supremacy. Moving away from the well-rehearsed story of sultanate decline and "elite factionalism," the chapter once again shifts our attention to the competitive socioeconomic arenas inhabited by multiple households in coastal areas where regional kings were of little relevance. Its first part returns to ghar and its shifting meanings as a political category in the poet Nusrati's final work, Tārīkh-i Sikandari (The history of Sikandar, ca. 1674), which represents the rivalry between two prominent households, the Miyana Afghans and the Maratha Bhonsles.

In the second half of the seventeenth century, we find these intimate enemies, emerging from the same political ghar in the Deccan, extending their networks into the social and economic life of the eastern Indian Ocean littoral. The interelite competition that we see in chronicles and poems did not take place in a vacuum within the world of courts alone. Marathas, Miyanas, and Indo-Africans were engaging with economic networks of merchants, artisans, weavers, and European trading companies. Intrafamilial conflict and interelite household competition was enmeshed in larger processes of proto-industrialization, the growth of markets across the world, creating transactions and encounters between new social groups.[131] Elite households drew these preexisting networks and resources across two interdependent ecological zones, the Deccan and the Karnatak, strengthening their autonomy from monarchical power. This chapter interrogates the underlying mechanisms of interelite alliances within the coastal economy, which simultaneously depended on disciplining weaving communities and sustaining existing hierarchies of status and caste in a coastal ecology. Restoring the social order took precedence over absolute principles for upholding notions of identity and community.

The conclusion considers the afterlives and memory of seventeenth-century tensions between the household and the state in the early nineteenth century. It examines Munshi Muhammad ʿAzimuddin's *Tārīkh-i Dilīr-jangī* (The history of Dilir Jang, ca. 1839), an eclectic Persian-Urdu-English "family history" that was produced for the recently exiled Miyana Afghan Nawabs of Savanur (in the Haveri district of present-day Karnataka). Many such hybrid texts were produced in the early nineteenth century when such little kingdoms, descendants of martial households that had carved out their autonomy from Mughal and Deccan sultans in centuries past, were now increasingly beholden to the authority of the British East India Company. The chapter examines how the author of this polysemic text constructed a genealogical past, reproducing documents to and from company officials to assert the competing claims of his exiled patron, Nawab Dilir Khan Dilir Jang Bahadur, and his intransigent nephews, nieces, and sisters-in-law, all of whom were staking a claim to Savanur's now much-reduced fortunes. Engaging with the distinct modes of memorializing familial versus dynastic pasts, the conclusion grapples with the question of why, at distinct moments of colonial modernity, family was obscured and dynasty underscored, thus, radically transforming how we remember the landscape of familial and kingly sovereignty in South Asia today.

2

The Military Barrack
Identifying Households, Becoming Mughal

Elephants, horses, matchlock guns, forts, and cannons are the objects that come to mind when we imagine early modern warfare. An illegible piece of paper, the size of the palm of our hand, measuring around eight by four and a half inches, is not something we think of as moving alongside enormous armies conquering lands from Damascus to Delhi. And yet, thousands of such fragments, called *'arz-o-chehreh* (descriptive or muster rolls) survive in archives across the Indian subcontinent.[1] A distant ancestor of the modern-day soldier's dog tag, the scattered detritus of the muster roll offers images of men arriving at military forts queuing up to have their names recorded. But this single sheet of paper did much more than that—it recorded detailed information about both horse and soldier. A scribe described man and horse's physical appearance, and then interrogated the soldier about his name, his city or region of origin, the language he spoke, who his father was, and which occupational group he belonged to—all social identifications people used to define themselves and others in premodern times. Spartan pieces of paper that bore witness to an active war reveal the many moving parts of the Mughal army's vast infrastructure in northernmost limits of peninsular India, where the imperial-regional war front began. Thousands of such intimate event-marked portraits capture the theater of early modern warfare.

Our journey across peninsular India begins here with a focus on the sociospatial site of the military barrack, one node in the Mughal frontier's vast infrastructure. From here, I reconstruct the bureaucratic encounter that generated the first meaning of ghar, the naming of home(s), for the purpose of social identification. Birthplaces, lineages, villages, cities, and forefathers were named, categorized, and defined through a dialogue between an imperial scribe and an ordinary soldier, bringing new social groups into the processes of becoming Mughal. Low-level

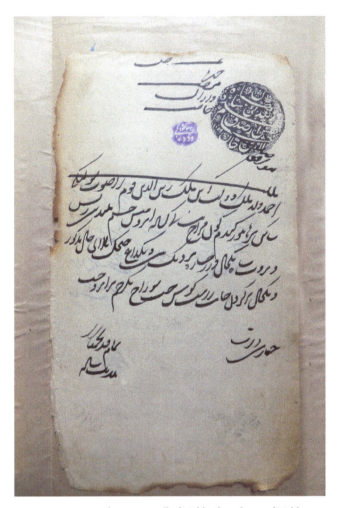

FIGURE 1. Muster or descriptive roll of Malik Ahmad, son of Malik Daulat, son of Malik Zainuddin, Rajput Solanki of Burhanpur. Mughal Record Room, Telangana State Archives, Acc. 35–699, Hyderabad, India.

administrative documents in Persian generated at the war front in peninsular India reveal how the Mughal state sought to harness the mobility and circulation of different social groups moving between political borders.[2] This chapter shows which gradations of categories the state saw when anchoring multiple households into its day-to-day functions.

The early modern state is viewed here from a bottom-up perspective and, crucially, as a material and mobile entity not fixed to a single center but forged at the crossroads of an imperial-regional battlefront in interaction with its nonelite subjects. What does this object called the muster roll tell us about how soldiers, scribes, spies, inspectors, and paymasters from different social groups, affiliated by service to elite households, participated in state institutions? Historians often turn to what is written "in" a document to extract and produce narrative history—the usual stuff of when and where a battle happened, who won, who lost, and so forth. However, materiality, on the other hand, what a piece of historical evidence looks like, what kind of ink and paper it is fashioned from, how the contents are laid out, what formulae or codes signify different kinds of information, and the way it was produced also embody social formations and can tell us about how people and institutions interacted.[3]

In three parts, this chapter examines how materiality and mobility connected lineages of service under household chiefs to the state. Deposits of muster rolls can be found across different parts of South Asia. At first glance, this humble document type appears to offer little to the historian searching for a good, linear story. But these kinds of materials and the everyday function they fulfilled reveal the relationship between service and the ascription of social identities in premodern India. I begin by describing the physical appearance and social life of muster rolls, what they looked like, how they were collected, and how they operated in the world. Second, I turn to the social classifications we find on the muster roll, or its content, tracing out patterns of how mobile people understood themselves and others through a great variety of social identifications. In the third part, I illuminate the Mughal Deccan's social and political conditions in the seventeenth century through a descriptive and demographic analysis of a cache of muster rolls. I put the region into a broader conversation about how early modern regimes bureaucratized and mobilized military resources across the world. To this end, I make three interrelated arguments. First, a pointillistic description of materiality and process unveils the humanity behind these documents, not just as objects for the historian's consumption (and her desire to produce narrative) but as an embodied object that had a well-defined purpose, function, and journey in its own time. One of the more interesting things about materiality and documents, in particular, is that they persist and, therefore, can be taken up in different times and places and by people who put them to use for unintended functions. The movement, borrowing, and transmission of muster-writing practices across Mughal Hindustan and the Deccan illustrates how materiality transcended the spatial and temporal limits of political forms, fusing the infrastructure and institutions of two regions.

The movement of a material practice reflects, then, the circulation of soldiers and scribes, the social categories they used to identify themselves, and the Mughal Empire itself. Comparing hundreds of social identifications on muster rolls addresses a much larger question at the heart of global history—the hunt for an absolute thing called premodern identity—a search that is by no means unique to South Asian pasts.[4] The documentary sediments left by early modern conquest illustrate how the movement of massive militaries into new territories created the need for clarifying notions of loyalty, identity, and community.[5] Muster rolls show that in the wake of imperial expansion, soldiers and scribes used ever-finer

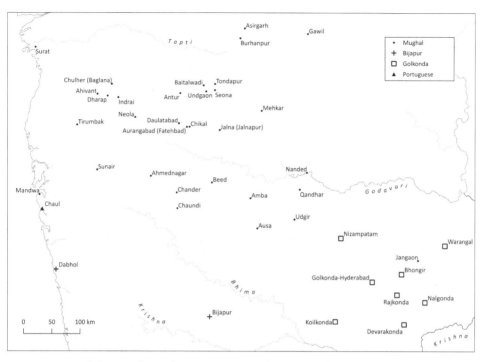

MAP 4. Mughal sites in the northern Deccan. Drawn by Kanika Kalra.

categories of self-identification that are difficult to understand with modern-day notions of ethnicity, tribe, and clan.[6] Twentieth-century historians had used colonial terms like "warlike tribes" and "martial races" to categorize people who participated in premodern armies.[7] However, social identifications, both of today and of centuries past, cannot be seen as self-contained, static, or timeless. Rather, through regular interactions between state and subject, social labels take on multidimensional and shifting meanings.

And finally, learning about how the muster roll worked tells us about how the Mughal Empire worked in peninsular India. Definitions of the term *Mughal* changed over time as the empire moved beyond Hindustan (northern India) and into other parts of the subcontinent. Documentary genres produced on a battlefront, like muster rolls, reveal the history of caste in circulation and the mobility of imperial institutions forged in interaction with preexisting regional social and political forms. Through the office of branding and mustering, I unveil the comprehensive institutional mechanisms of Mughal governance and its improvised, everyday workings.[8] With regional warrior households spearheading territorial expansion, the Deccan sultanates began to emulate Mughal centralizing institutions, particularly the branding of horses and mustering. Relatedly, the Mughal army incorporated provincial elites whose contingents were more socially homogenous into the cavalry sharing the same background as their chief. By tracing changes in pansubcontinental military recruitment networks, I contend that the Mughal army's enduring presence in this warfront actually made political-military campaigns in the southern centers much closer to the heart of the empire. Rather than having been a deviation from or an exception to imperial norms that made the empire decline in the eighteenth century, during the heyday of imperial expansion in the seventeenth century, peninsular India was the site of heightened centralization endlessly conditioned by interactions with nonimperial state forms.

As stated in the introduction, even today, the most conspicuous meaning of ghar emerges from the everyday encounters between bureaucrats and ordinary citizens. The Mughal scribe-soldier documentary dialogue investigated here traces the genealogy of this modern-day interaction. This fleeting, yet routine, dialogue captures how different social groups' senses of belonging changed as they moved between one ecological and cultural zone of the subcontinent to another. Even today, this bureaucratic interrogation of one's father's name and the place identified as home is followed by a further inquiry about the surname, —a crucial signifier through which people make sense of and slot each other into varying social categories across the subcontinent. These three inquiries may be followed up by clarifications of birth place, residence, caste, language, and so forth. At the heart of this encounter lies the naming of one's home(s) or ghar to a state agent, capturing experiences of internal migration, displacement, and circulation in the present and the past. The social context and processes that produced the Mughal descriptive roll remind us of its purpose as a premodern identity card of sorts, not one held by the bearer but one preserved at different sites of registration, where it was held for future uses by different offices that dispensed the state's revenues in the form of a salary.[9] Given the documentary record from the Mughal Deccan, it would be ahistorical to think that this kind of encounter—where a state agency interrogates subjects to derive mutually understood, but not always stable, social identifications—was unique only to the last two hundred years of South Asian history. And yet, this assumption has been prevalent in decades of scholarship.[10] Through a fragmentary documentary trail I explore here the lineages of this type of encounter between state and subject and suggests ways forward for writing the history of caste in circulation across precolonial Mughal South Asia.

FROM IDEAL TO PRACTICE: WRITING THE MUGHAL MUSTER

The Mughal army occupies an almost mythical status in the historian's imagination of premodern India.[11] In its prime, contemporary observers were also enthralled by its sight. In the late 1620s, the Persian émigré poet Hakim Atishi (whom we will meet in chapter 5), who settled in Bijapur, recounted the imperial army marching toward the city of Gulbarga in the northern Deccan so vast and limitless that all the world's muster writers could not account for its sum (*sipāhī ke lashkar nawīsān-i dahr / ze jama' hisābesh naburdand bahr*).[12] Atishi observed an everyday task, the accounting of thousands of Mughal soldiers performed by inconspicuous muster masters or *lashkar nawīs*, also known as *chehrah nawīs* or *chehrah āqāsī*—military scribes who counted, described, and cataloged pairs of men and horses. The muster master, along with other staff, produced many kinds of documents to keep track of human and animal resources on the Mughal Deccan warfront which, by the early to mid-seventeenth century, included four *sūba* or provinces—Khandesh, Berar, Aurangabad, Telangana and lay north of the River Krishna (see Map 4).

Detailing the identities of thousands of man-beast pairs with both individual and dual characteristics stands in stark contrast to the Mughal army's legendary ineffability, captured in Atishi's observation above. Innumerable muster rolls scattered across the subcontinent unintentionally give face to the nameless troops and cavalry units that traversed vast distances across the subcontinent. Muster rolls survive in such large numbers partly because they functioned as valuable stand-ins for pay slips transferable to the soldier or his lord as cash salary at stipulated intervals. To do so, state agents produced a standardized, portable inanimate object, creating a correspondence between moving humans and animals and profiles on paper.

So how did people, in an era long before thumbprints, photographs, and QR codes, recreate the likenesses of individuals on paper and why? Akin to modern objects like the driver's license that lists the color of a person's eyes, hair, and birthmarks, along with their photo, address, and signature, the muster roll recorded an ordinary soldier's physiognomy, together with his social background, through a sequence of formulaic phrases. Producing a person's exactness on paper may seem impossible in the age before print and photography, but preindustrial states devoted innumerable human and material resources to producing documents that did so with great care.

From the muster to portraiture, we now know that the Mughals were obsessed with knowing who people were.[13] Scribes were not simply describing a soldier's and horse's outer forms but gauging whether they were fit for service, at times noting whether personnel were worthy of promotion based on their moral and physical characteristics. Mughal musters are reflective of wider physiognomic practices and enumeration in the early modern world, but the practice of describing man and horse together on a single page also sets them apart from contemporaries. From the Atlantic to the Mediterranean, several studies have investigated the meanings of physical descriptions—from sailors to slave sale registers and manumission documents. For example, recording *hilya* or a description of the face was part of a long pre- and early Islamic textual tradition of '*ilm al-firāsa* or the art of reading physiognomy, which sought to connect outer characteristics with the inner qualities and moral attributes of a slave.[14]

Imperial scribes judged skin tone, scars, nose and eyebrow shapes, eye color, length of facial hair, and moustaches to be able to slot people into categories. Muster rolls enabled early modern regimes to confirm that a soldier and his horse actually existed, so that revenues could be disbursed to household chiefs who paid for soldiers' salaries and the maintenance of horses. These unique pieces of paper bound two individual creatures, man and horse, whose identities were both separate and united, into a mutually dependent relationship. Like modern identity documents that follow prescribed procedures, the muster roll was written with precision and its appearance reflected this; moreover, it adhered to formula or standardized conventions. In what follows, I describe the muster roll's materiality (texture, layout, ideal format, and formulaic language) and its documentary ecology and lifecycle, before turning to the difficulties, gaps, and everyday obstacles encountered in actually producing it.

In a sample of 2,438 musters from the 1630s to the 1660s, roughly 8 percent or 203 musters are of *khāssa mansabdār* (rank-holding household chiefs paid directly from the imperial treasury), all of whom were from the lowest ranks of Mughal nobility (below the rank of three hundred *zāt*/one hundred *sawār*), while the remaining 2,235 are musters of *tābinān* or retainers/troopers affiliated with a single *mansabdār* (rank holder).[15] A *mansabdār's* dual numerical rank included *zāt*, which indicated his position and salary in the imperial hierarchy, and *sawār*, which showed the number of horsemen the official was required to maintain in service. Provincial documents from the earliest period of Mughal presence in southern India shed light on the military's lowest echelons, who were far removed from the world of the ruling elites with ranks above one thousand, which previous studies have focused on.[16]

Mughal Deccan administrative documents measure around eight by four and a half inches and were written in the notoriously difficult to read *shikastah* (literally meaning broken) calligraphic style on unsized paper made from cloth detritus. Even after four hundred years of use, reuse, and damage, the appearance of these sheets is very white, consistent, and of high quality, suggesting the paper used for administrative documents was not cheap to manufacture and access to it was limited to specific offices and officeholders. Unsized paper, used for writing musters and related documents, is burnished and its fibers absorb ink to penetrate deeper than the paper's surface, which then prevents forgery and alteration. Sized paper used for manuscripts, on the other hand, allows for rewriting and corrections.[17] We find no marks of corrections, crossing out, rubbed ink in Mughal musters from the seventeenth century.

The unforgeability of administrative paper was, however, no guarantee against the production of fake documents. Because they served as proxy pay slips, a descriptive roll could be forged for the sake of collecting salaries for men and horses who did not exist! Hinting at the dissonance between the actual, physical, and abstract paper presence of Mughal soldiers, one mid-eighteenth-century observer, perhaps from disbelief, noted imperial forces in Delhi as being *mawjūdī, nah kāghazī* or "actually present, not merely on paper."[18] While changes on a written muster were almost impossible to make, the evil of false musters is something that even the colonial historian William Irvine lamented, citing it in the etiology of imperial decline in the eighteenth century.[19] But, as we shall see in the subsequent discussion, improvisation was characteristic of the office of mustering and branding at the very outset of imperial expansion in southern India in the early seventeenth century, as scribes and inspection staff dealt with the problem of absentee soldiers who failed to report for mustering.

The use of space, format, layout, and the different hands detectable on a page reveal the descriptive roll's multiple functions and stages of reuse. Given the modest size of low-level provincial documents, space on paper was a precious resource. These materials were quite unlike Mughal decrees (*farmān*), written on long and grand rotuli, with wasteful broad line spacing, exquisite calligraphy, meant for the purpose of being read aloud at court, what in the Fatimid context Marina Rustow has called "instruments of performance."[20] Unlike higher classes of documents meant for public viewing, the muster circulated within the restrictive and everyday paper ecology of a provincial military bureaucracy. Lines of text were closely spaced and designated to be written on particular sections of a sheet's front and back. Provincial scribes had neither the white space nor the energy to impress listeners in court, so they wrote with economy and brevity, squeezing in as few words as possible to capture the soldier's body and being. They were more concerned with generating descriptive rolls with accuracy and efficiency than with producing narrative or explaining cause and effect information, which historians can more easily extract from other classes of documents and literary materials.

All Mughal administrative documents consist of several blocks of writing on the back and front of the sheet, each with different types of information. Let us cast our eye to the top of the document first. At the center top, a header of three to four stacked lines identifies the genre or type of document (*'arz-o-chehrah/fihrist-i mullāzimān*), the office holders or level of staff the document was concerned with (*khāssa mansabdār/tābinān*), and the site where it was produced (Burhanpur/Malwa/Daulatabad). The title and main descriptive section are oriented horizontally on the front side. The extension of single letters in words enabled scribes to space each line and organize their writing. All the text in each writing block follows a nested baseline, with words stacked on top of each other toward the end to save space and fit in as much as possible. Turning to the back side, we find that not all text blocks are oriented horizontally, with later endorsements (*zimn*) and commentary (*sharh*) on the back written diagonally with an upward orientation. Endorsements named individuals who provided surety for the person whose descriptive roll was being recorded and the commentary explained what actions had been taken. The breed and condition of the soldier's horse was noted on the document's obverse along with a mark (*dāgh*), which was also branded onto the horse's hindquarters.[21]

Administrative paper was stored and used on multiple occasions. Signs of reuse on the page indicate at least two stages of use—the first when the paper was issued, sealed, and authorized for a particular office; in that case, a circular *nasta'līq* seal was placed in the top right corner. Right below the seal or next to it, we see the generic phrase *muwāfiq-i asl ast* meaning true copy, written in a hand different from the main body text of the document. The difference between the original (*asl*) and duplicate (*naql*) copy manifests itself as archival notation on the muster's page as well. The document's reverse indicates the second time the paper was used to verify soldier and horse. After two to three months, the copy would be verified against the mark on the horse's hindquarters with the day, month, and year using the formulaic phrase *muqābalah namūd* written on the back, left edge of the document.

As with men and horses, the quality of writing and description on musters corresponded to hierarchies in the imperial army. Not all were written with care and precision, there being variable levels of detail on different rolls for each type of military staff and service. Three classes of *chehrah* include around 203 musters of imperial rank holders paid directly from the treasury (*khāssa mansabdār*), with their numerical (*zāt*) and cavalry (*sawār*) rank sometimes recorded. These higher-status *khāssa* musters were written in better quality, darker ink and in a more legible hand than the over two thousand lower musters of horsemen (*tābinān*), written in weaker ink with a much quicker hand. In a third set of musters, we find a broad variety of military personnel (*ahshām*) with specialized occupations, followers, and infantry. These specialized military personnel include mounted matchlockmen or musketeers (*barqandāzān*),[22] infantry (*piādeh*), cavalry (*sawār*), musketeers (*bandūqchī*), and menial servants who were village musicians (*shāgird pesha bajantarī*), archers (*daig andāzān*), and other laborers, who had musters written with a quicker hand, containing the fewest physiognomic details.

We may now turn to the established norms for creating a correspondence between the soldier's face and horse's body with what was on paper. What rules did the muster master follow while creating a description? The template and formulae for writing *chehrah* can be found in contemporary administrative manuals. In his *Siyāqnāma*, Delhi-based Khatri litterateur Nand Ram Mukhlis (ca. 1697–1750) laid out instructions for describing the countenance not just of soldiers and horses but a whole range of objects from elephants, camels, and bulls to different kinds of weapons, daggers, swords, guns, armor, and articles of clothing.[23] The manual's section, which is titled "*dar bayān-i nigāresh chehrahāye bāyad dānist*," noted what to pay attention to when recording these short portraits. Mukhlis starts with a sample description of a certain individual—"Muhammad Beg, son of Hasan 'Ali Beg, son of Razaq Beg, from the *qaum* of *mughal turkmān* [Mughal Turkmen], a resident of Mashhad, of wheatish complexion, broad forehead, open eyebrows, sheep-eyed, long-nosed, with a black beard and moustache"—and then outlines each facial feature's possible ways of description.[24]

The manual lists parts of the face with the set of words appropriate for their description: complexion (*dar bayān-i rang*), forehead (*dar bayān-i pishānī*), eyebrows (*abrū*), eyes (*chashm*), nose (*bīnī*), cheeks (*'āriz wa rukhsār*), temples and locks of hair (*shaqīqeh wa zulf*), ears (*gūsh*), lips and chin (*lab wa zankhandān*), beard and moustache (*rīsh-o-burūt*), and height expressed in terms of the soldier's age (*qad*). The location of birthmarks (*masseh*), moles (*khāl*), wound scars and whether they were from a gun, sword, or spear (*zakhm-i shamshīr/tufang/barchī*), branding marks (*dāgh*) and smallpox scars (*dāgh-i chichak*) on any part of the face had to be recorded. A limited range of adjectives and phrases could be used to record each part. Eyes, for instance, could fall into the following six categories— deer-eyed (*āhū chashm*), sheep-eyed (*mīsh chashm*), blue-eyed (*azraq*), cat-eyed (*gurbeh chashm*), cataract (*gul chashm*), and blind (*kūr*). Eyebrows could be either joint (*pivastah*), slightly joint (*qadrī pivastah*), or unjoint (*uftadah abrū*), while complexion could be wheatish (*gandum rang*), greenish in color (*sabzfām*), white (*safīd pūst*), or reddish (*sorkh pūst*).

As with soldiers, the terminology for recording horses was specific— with combinations of colors and patterns: dark red (*nīleh surang nīleh*), streaked with grey lines or brindle (*turaq turaq lākvardī*), reddish or chestnut (*surang surmayī surang*), red and black mixed or bay (*ablaq mishkī ablaqī surang*), or greenish brown stripes or grullo (*turaq kishmishī turaq*). Specific terms for unique patterns on the animal's forehead signified particular kinds of horses:

> If the forehead is black and has stripes of red with some white [*turaq-i surang wa andak safīd*], record it as *nīl*. And, if the forehead is white and all four hands and legs are also white [stockings up the leg], write down *pechakliyān*.[25]

Prescriptions in a manual bring us to the process and ideal steps for creating the muster. The scribe, reflecting on the soldier and horse standing in front of him, might have seen man and animal with a mixture of these characteristics and made modifications to prescribed descriptions. While the muster's first part required asking the soldier specific questions about his father's name, regions, and place(s) of residence, its latter part, with the physical description, probably did not entail any dialogue or interrogation, with the scribe merely looking and selecting phrases to create the soldier's physical description on paper. The language of description— Persian—especially in its formulaic documentary form, was probably not familiar to most soldiers. Part of this encounter may have unfolded in Dakkani or Hindawi, panregional idioms that soldiers may have been somewhat familiar with, in addition to other languages they spoke, such as Marathi, Telugu, and Kannada.

In its ideal form, the office of branding and mustering observed a few sequential steps which had been streamlined in 1573 during the reign of Mughal emperor Akbar (r. 1556–1605). This shift in military recruitment is frequently recounted in administrative manuals and chronicles.[26] By the time the Mughal army moved toward the northern Deccan in the 1630s, these procedures were standardized with a clear division between those who were documented and those who produced the document. Regular soldier mustering and branding of horses established the basis on which Mughal military commanders drew a salary in the form of revenue assignments or cash. Soldiers were supposed to produce their horse along with their weapons, which they owned or could borrow from their military commander.[27] Depending on an officer's location, whether at court or in a province, anywhere from a fourth to a third of his horsemen were supposed to show up for mustering in order for the officer to draw salary. Failure or delays in doing so could result in the loss of up to a fourth (*chauthāī*) of his pay. The officer would have to return a portion of his pay according to the number of days he had delayed in branding, even in cases where a horse died between the date of verification and the date of branding.[28]

Scribes and inspectors had well-defined functions. A separate department under a provincial paymaster (*bakshī*), along with a superintendent (*dārogha*), was responsible for the verification of brands (*dāgh-o-tashīhah*). The *bakshī* was not stationed in a single place but circulated with army units to different sites to supervise the branding of horses, while frequent orders were issued to the clerk (*mutasaddī*) for branding and verification of select individuals.[29] In branding certificates, we see frequent mentions of the names of the superintendent (*dārogha*), assessor (*amīn*),[30] and an officer who authenticated accounts and documents (*mushrif*).[31] The *dārogha* would decide if the horse was healthy and permit the brand to be applied, sign the muster with a date and the phrase "one man and horse(s) were verified" (*yak nafar wa rās ba tashīhah rasīd*). A certificate with the seals of the *dārogha, amīn*, and the *mushrif* was issued to the military commander whose men had been inspected. Most musters from the Deccan are copies from the office of the provincial paymaster, who would have retained duplicates for the second inspection, which was supposed to take place after a gap of two or three months. In some instances, the seal corresponds with the name of lower-level officers, such as that of the *mushrif*, whose names are also mentioned on the page.[32]

The muster functioned within a wider documentary ecology; its functions were enhanced by a number of auxiliary documentary forms. A second layer of materials supplemented the muster roll and the horse's branding certificate (*dāgh nāma-yi aspān*) by attesting and transmitting summaries to other offices and reporting on different households that served in distinct military occupations. The provincial centers in Daulatabad and Burhanpur received some summaries, such as the report of branding and verification (*roznamcha-yi dāgh-o-tashīhah*). Death certificates for horses (*saqtī nāma-yi aspān*) were issued to the persons who had been assigned to ride them.[33] An auxiliary class of materials, unique to provincial administration, includes several kinds of summary indices (*fihrist*) that confirmed appointments and salary increments. These single sheets of paper show multiple dates of use that recorded changes in service and salary for generations from one or more households that had been in service, suggesting they were modified for future recordings.

Archival notation suggests these *fihrist* or personnel lists were likely part of larger bound registers as they are marked with a folio number in upper-left-hand corners, indicating they were filed as part of larger sets or series of documents.[34] Unlike in the Ottoman context, full registers have not survived intact from Mughal India.[35] But endorsements on the back of the lists suggest different sites within the province through which the registers would have moved, while also including comments by high-level imperial agents on salary or rank increases granted.[36] While lists of imperial servants (*fihrist-i mullāzimān*) employed in various occupations at checkpoints and forts show changes in salary, rank, and grants, a supplementary diary of branding and verification (*fihrist-i roznamcha-i dāgh wa tashīhah*) attested the day-to-day activities of the office of mustering. One such *fihrist*, for instance, recorded the service changes of two households—one of Muhammad Arab, Kamaluddin Turbati, a macebearer (*gurzburdār*), and the other of Muhammad Sharif and the other sons of Khwaja Nad ʿAli Sabzwari, who formerly served as *wāqiʿa nawīs* (intelligencers or news writers) under Prince Aurangzeb. Endorsements (*zimn*) and commentary (*sharh*) on the back noted the *sūbadār* or provincial governor Shah Nawaz Khan's evaluation of the son, Muhammad Sharif, as a young, industrious man, endorsing that his rank should be increased to one hundred *zāt* and fifteen *sawār*.[37] These summary indices supplemented the physical descriptions of military staff recorded on muster rolls. Therefore, a vast array of auxiliary documentary genres—from reports, branding certificates, summaries, and lists—were generated to affirm the work of mustering and branding. Copies were moved within provincial offices and stored for multiple uses.

Meticulous details on the muster belie the difficulties that arose in its production. Comparing the ideal imperially mandated processes of mustering against actual practices suggests that scribes and soldiers interrupted, modified, and adjusted their work to regional exigencies, thereby modifying imperial institutional mechanisms. We see central imperial institutions persisting despite changes in environment and social context, with regional constraints requiring the improvisation and adaptation of standardized practices. Military scribal staff modified norms to keep up with the task of tracking soldiers, weapons, and animals on a precarious battle front. In such circumstances, problems of staff shortages and soldier desertion also prevented formal procedures from being fully implemented.

In practice, the prescribed norms of mustering and branding had to contend with constraints on the ground and everyday modifications of imperial orders. One memorandum (*yāddāsht-i-chehrah*), from January 19, 1638, emphasized the validity of musters produced for a certain Muhammad Rafiʿ, son of Muhammad Shafiʿ in Ellichpur, in contradiction to an imperial *farmān*. The imperial order had stipulated that all troops should have their horses branded at Daulatabad (which lay more than three hundred kilometers southwest of Ellichpur); the original descriptive rolls and branding certificates (*chehrah nawīsī wa dāgh namūdah asl*) with the seal of the *sūbadār* were to be sent to the imperial court. It also added that a *mansabdār* should preserve the duplicate muster for himself (*naql rā pīsh-i khud nigāh dārad*).[38] The muster leaves (*awrāq-i chehrah*) brought by Muhammad Rafi', despite being produced at the wrong place, were to be considered valid. The muster roll was written and copied for multiple sites of preservation with at least one set of copies entering the personal archive of the lord whose men and horses were being inspected and identified.[39] Fixing mustering at one site was a problem because scribal staff were not always available. Imperial orders were therefore adjusted to these everyday challenges as long as the eventual outcome of mustering and verification was reached. The gap between the development (ideal) and implementation (practice) was real and accretive. Even so, the adjustments made on the ground to deal with practical difficulties did not undo the office's main purpose, which was to track and control the movement of human and animal resources.

Memoranda commenting on branding and mustering reveal fraught relationships between different officeholders responsible for branding and inspection, contending over what fell under each scribe's and inspection official's purview. The skilled staff who could produce the muster with its prescribed formulae and codes were stretched thin on a battle front. In an undated memorandum, a *chehrah nawīs* voiced a complaint against his superiors:

> When this humble servant writes the muster, the *amīn* compares and checks [*muqābalah namūdah*] which horse is *turkī*, *yābū*, and *tāzī*. After that, the *dārogha* compares it and sends it for branding. If by any chance, there happened to be differences, the *dārogha* and *amīn* discuss it and let the *chehrah nawīs* know. So, my request is that an order be issued to the *dārogha* and *amīn* [to work with me] and that if there are differences at the time of verification, they too should be held answerable, as per their responsibility. Although this humble servant writes the muster, these two individuals should be comparing as well as taking greater care and caution for the correct entries of the verification.[40]

From the muster master's perspective, he was responsible only for writing the description, not for verifying whether it was accurate. The *dārogha* and *amīn* were responsible for inspecting and checking the correspondence between paper and men and horses. The scribe recognized the limits of his ability to describe a person accurately on paper. Given such disagreements between military personnel, it should come as no surprise, then, that instead of the stipulated six months, one year to one and a half years, the gap between the original and the second date of branding in actual muster rolls is much longer. They show intervals of three to five, and sometimes as great as seven years.[41] Across different sites where the imperial army was spread out, mobility posed a reoccurring problem and limited the ability of still-evolving institutional mechanisms to inspect resources at regular intervals. Moreover, successfully fixing a location for branding horses and ensuring that the *dārogha* and *amīn* actually turned up also proved to be an obstacle to mustering in line with formal procedure.[42]

The exasperation evident in the above scribe's complaint sometimes translated to the common practice of deserting posts. When a *chehrah nawīs* fled, the work of branding and mustering was assigned to *topchī* or the commissaries of ordnance who, along with the *dārogha*, were put to the task. But, with the *topchī* also absent, *mewrah* or runners who carried messages between different forts and occasionally served as soldiers, were told to attend to branding.[43] From the *topchī* to the superintendent to the messenger, no other staff but the muster master actually knew how to formulate a descriptive roll. Highly specialized scribes were the only ones who could differentiate personnel in a moving army, enabling the incorporation of new social groups into what it meant to be Mughal. However, the scarcity of scribal labor meant that implementing imperial aims in a war front was often checkered with logistical challenges. Even high-level imperial actors witnessed these daily challenges. They acknowledged the Deccan sultanates' continued resilience more than fifteen years after their formal subjugation, attempting to implement several different measures to increase the region's revenues.[44] Mustering and branding lay at the core of maintaining conquest and territorial expansion. Hence, its inadequate implementation, the dearth of soldiers turning up for branding, and scribes fleeing their posts alarmed Mughal officials.[45] Ideal Mughal infrastructures, described in stationary chronicles and manuals, when viewed from the ground up through mobile documentary cultures, show that while centralization was required, even desired, actually realizing it was another matter.

The frequent image of absent soldiers and absent scribes raises questions about the human interactions that underlay the muster roll—when soldier and scribe did meet, what kind of questions were asked? How far did the soldier's self-identification match the scribe's description? Perhaps just as comic relief from the tedium of describing mundane imperial procedures, the seventeenth-century Venetian traveler Nicolò Manuzzi recounted one such encounter between a *kāyasth* (Hindu scribal caste) clerk and a soldier:

> In Shāhjahān's time a soldier went to draw his pay, and the official, who was a *kāyasth*, could not attend to him at once, as he was busy. The angry soldier threatened him, saying he should have to smash his teeth with his sword. The official said nothing, and paid him; then, jesting, said that with his pen he could do more than he with his sword. The sharp-witted scribe, to get his revenge for the menace, wrote in the book where was entered the soldier's descriptive-roll that he had lost two of his front teeth. For it is the practice in the Mogul country to write the names and personal marks of those who are employed. Some months elapsed, and the soldier appeared again for his pay. The clerk opened the book and found by the description that he was not the man entitled to that pay, for he had two front teeth more than were recorded in the register of descriptive rolls. The soldier was put to confusion; his protests and

arguments were unavailing; and seeing no other course if he would not lose his pay and his place, he was obliged to have two front teeth extracted to agree with the record, and in that way got his pay.[46]

Whatever the veracity of this account may be, the written word lay at the center of interaction between scribe and soldier. While most conversations between scribe and soldier probably included a standard, routine set of queries and were perhaps less cantankerous than the one above, the act of description was fraught with challenges. How were the soldier's answers heard and then modified, adapted, and translated on to paper? The scribe quickly pared down the soldier's answers into the information required in the muster's minimal format, without losing the details and specificity of what he had just been told. Physical descriptions of man and horse constituted just one portion of the muster. The scribe would not simply have had to look at the soldier; he would also have had to ask specific questions about how many generations a family had served in the imperial army, about the regions and place(s) of the soldier's origin, residence, and occupations, and about the ethnonym with which the soldier identified himself. The next section of this turns to this portion of the interrogation between state agent and subject that generated an array of social identifications on the muster roll. This everyday catechism between scribe and soldier was the fundamental building block that came long before singular notions of clan and community defined what it meant to be a Mughal.

INSCRIBING THE MUGHAL SOLDIER: NAMING, ETHNICITY, AND IDENTIFICATION

It is well known that a diversity of ethnic, linguistic, regional, and occupational groups constituted Mughal South Asia's social fabric. On administrative documents, scribes used the Arabic term *qaum* with a range of meanings—for example, *people, family,* and *kindred*—to define caste.[47] Under the broader umbrella of the term *Mughal*, scholars distill roughly seven to eight categories of "subnational or ethnic," "caste and community" or "racial group": Irani, Turani, Indian Muslim, Rajput, Afghan, Deccani, and non-Muslims or Miscellaneous. These aggregate categories, however, do not appear exactly as such on the musters. What we find on the document are many variations, reversals, and cross-cutting combinations of these ideal classifications. In political histories, we hear of such groups as opposing elite court factions battling for power in capital cities like Delhi, Hyderabad, and Bijapur.[48] But, what did these social identifications mean to ordinary subjects and how did they hear and utilize the terms, if at all? A single phrase on the muster roll, usually written after the soldier's name, such as *qaum-i rājpūt chauhān* or *jamā'at-i maratha bhonsle* (referring to a people or group, modified by various identifiers of place, lineage, region, city, clan, and language), helps answer this question by reconstructing what signifiers of ethnic terms may have meant to mobile premodern actors.

Modern-day notions of ethnicity are inapplicable to understanding resonant yet vastly different pre-modern understandings of this concept. In precolonial societies, "ethnicity" signified a broad set of categories, including lineage, agnatic derivation from a common male ancestor, kinship, language, religion, denomination, occupation, city, region, or family organization. On dynamic, porous battle fronts across the early modern world, neatly defined territorial, spatial units and seamless, vertical lines of descent did not determine how people, who were constantly on the move, identified themselves. Premodern states pathologized, recognized, and differentiated descent through multiple identifiers of place, residence, occupation, region, and language. Postnomadic empires incorporated warbands by tying itinerant mounted horseman to rulers through administrative and institutional mechanisms rather than hereditary lines of descent.[49] Historians of Timurid-Mughal dynastic lines have shown the utility of a range of horizontal social practices that tied different social groups to the imperial project. From the common practice of intrafamilial adoption, when wives of kings and high-ranking elites took the children of other kin into their household, to the custom of taking fosters (*koka*) for strengthening a ruler's ties to Sufi lineages—all these practices illustrate how, in a patriarchal but extremely mobile society, different practices created new social identities.[50]

We want to extend these questions explored at the level of the royal household to consider practices in the state's everyday institutions that interfaced with other parts of society. Routine bureaucratic tasks of registration and verification produced definitions of who was who and how each person should be identified, categorized, and verified. Like other early modern imperial polities, Mughal institutions emboldened and schematized social hierarchies to enhance the state's coercive capacities. Precolonial identifications had meaning. It was not as if any individual could shapeshift and become whosoever he or she pleased. In other words, precolonial identifications were neither "fuzzy" nor "fluid."[51] Historians have demonstrated that social classifications corresponded to fixed hierarchies in Mughal society.[52] Some social groups were more valued than others (as were some groups of horses compared to other breeds), and the imperial government regulated the proportion of men belonging to his own group that a household chief could recruit.[53] For instance, an individual hailing from a certain city in Iran, who had settled in northern India and had joined the Mughal court, was unlikely to recruit soldiers who also hailed from the same place and region. Mughal *mansabdārs* had a variety of soldiers under them who often did not share a common social background with their lord or chief. Further, the ethnic identities of subimperial elites were hierarchically understood and they played prescribed functions in the imperial state.

So, what happened to ethnicity when armies of household chiefs and their soldiers crossed long distances? More conceptual categories were needed to clarify and keep track of who was who. When the Mughal Empire marched south, everyday interactions of scribes and soldiers sorted out who got to be an outsider and who got to be an insider. A dizzying assortment of soldiers and scribes used ever-finer social categories to define themselves, regardless of the ideal and aggregate types laid out in Persian chronicles.[54]

Broadly speaking, there were two types of soldiers in the Mughal army: "northern," which included a variety of groups hailing from different parts of Islamicate Eurasia based in northern India; and "southern," which included those recruited near or around the battle front within south-central India. The Mughal military recruitment was akin to a *khānazād* system within the army organization in which entire households or generations of families were often employed under a common male ancestor.[55] While contingents of northern horsemen generally did not have a shared background, regionally recruited southern cavalry enlisted in homogenous units, a recruitment pattern already prevalent in the Deccan sultanates. In other words, political loyalties were generally unbound by ethnicity; it was possible to serve under a lord or household chief with whom a soldier did not share a common social, cultural, or linguistic background. Scribes and soldiers heard, used, and modified broad, more essentialized labels, such as Rajput (along with clan modifiers such as Chauhan, Solanki, etc.) and Deccani, to cut across religious, regional, and ethnic lines. At the same time, groups like the Afghans, which served in both imperial and regional sultanates' armies, transcended political boundaries. They enlisted in more homogenous units composed mainly of Afghans but they also served in heterogeneous contingents under non-Afghan chiefs.

How did scribes define the term *Mughal* and all the social groups that fell under this political unit when the very limits of this idea were expanding? Were imperial taxonomies simply replicated by provincial scribes or did the imperial army's movement and circulation set off processes of realignment and widen the range of identification categories? The way we think about these diverse identifications in Mughal India is very different from the way in which we think about different social groups in modern South Asian nation-states today. The essentialized notions of ethnicity, lineage, territory, and religion that underlie today's classification systems are often inapplicable to the plurality of identifications we find on precolonial documents. In what follows, I analyze broad patterns of how such categories appear on muster rolls to reveal the multivalent and capacious meanings of social groupings.

We may begin with the broadest term associated with the geographic south—the heavily-debated "Deccani," the meanings of which evolved over time, depending on whom one asked or whom was being opposed in which historical context.[56] The label *Deccani* did not always correspond to city, language, clan, agnatic descent, or ethnicity. It was, at best, a regional and political category into which a whole range of groups—Afghans, Habshis, Marathas, and a variety of Muslims based in southern India—could belong because they had served in the Deccan sultanates or had resided in the region that was not a part of Mughal Hindustan.⁵⁷ One royal order, dated June 26, 1668, stipulated that one fourth deduction be made on the salaries of all Deccanis who had served in Bijapur or Golkonda and later joined imperial service (*jamā 'at-i dakhanīyān ke az bijāpūr wa haidarābād bā irādeh bandagī-yi khalāyaq panāh mī āyand*).⁵⁸ The only exception to this deduction was any person who had recently arrived from Iran who, instead of joining the sultanates, had come directly into imperial service. The term *Deccani* had little to do with religion or fixed notions of space, as it could include local- and foreign-born elite, whether Hindu or a Muslim, and could refer to someone with Central Asian, African, or Maratha descent.

There are seven variations, then, through which this broad term for southerner appears on Mughal musters—*dakkanī* (of the Deccan region), *rājput-i-dakkanī* (referring mostly to Marathas but sometimes also to Habshis or Abyssinians), *pandit zunnārdār dakkanī* (a Brahman or wearer of the sacred thread from the Deccan), *rājpūt chauhān dakkanī* (claiming descent from Chauhan lineage, referring to Maratha soldiers), *shaykhzada dakkanī* (a Sunni Muslim from the Deccan), *pandit dakkanī* (a Brahman from the Deccan), *rajpūt bhonsla dakkanī* (a Maratha of the Bhonsle lineage, from the Deccan). Among the retainers, of the 5,000/5,000 rank *mansabdār* Maloji Bhonsle were Kayyaji, the son of Ranguji, and Temaji, the son of Kanhaiyaji, both identified as *rājpūt chauhān dakkanī*.⁵⁹ We may presume, citing a Chauhan warrior lineage, that both these men were Marathas.⁶⁰ Based on these variations, we can conclude that the identifications for southern or regionally recruited cavalry exhibit one or more of four characteristics—region, occupation, lineage, and jāti.

Indo-Africans also used the capacious term *dakkanī* to identify themselves. While the term *maratha* occurs only three times in the over two thousand musters from 1641 to 1656, many other groups embraced the term *rājpūt dakkani*, even non-Marathas, like Habshis or Abyssinians/Ethiopians, who had resided in southern India for centuries.⁶¹ For instance, among the Abyssinian commander Habash Khan's horsemen, *rājpūt-i-dakkanī* was used to describe Mansur and Daulat, his sons, while other soldiers in his unit were identified with the more specific phenotypical label of *habshī*, an Arabic term used to identify Indo-Africans of Abyssinian or Ethiopian descent.⁶²

Retainers under southern *mansabdārs* shared their chief's social background, a regional recruitment norm prevalent in the Deccan sultanates. From the twelve musters for troops under *mansabdār* Narsoji Dhangar, for instance, ten soldiers identified as *dhangars* (cattle herders and shepherds from western India),⁶³ and two remaining ones as Marathas (*rājpūt dakkanī*), but both groups were broadly from the same region in the western Deccan.⁶⁴ Roughly 60 percent of the 154 musters of troops, under the 5,000/5,000 rank Maratha *mansabdār*, Maloji Bhonsle, hailed from the Deccan (identified with the following variations: *rājpūt dakkanī, rājpūt chauhān dakkanī, pandit zunnārdār dakkanī, rājpūt bhonsla dakkanī*).⁶⁵ The imperial army embraced preexisting patterns of military recruitment in the Deccan by recruiting contingents organized around region, occupation, and lineage.

Single occupations or forms of military labor were sometimes the basis for homogenous contingents in both imperial and regional armies. For instance, in the muster rolls from 1641 to 1654, certain types of specialized military work were assigned to one particular social group. Musketeers (*bandūqchī*) and mounted matchlockmen (*barqandāzān*) stationed in the Deccan were overwhelmingly identified as *rājpūt*. These distinct groups of military laborers had specific salary disbursements. For example, under the *rājpūt chauhān mansabdār* Ghansham (who held a rank of one thousand), out of a total of 121 mounted musketeers (*barqandāzān-i hindūstān*), only seven were not Rajputs from Baksar (present-day Bihar in eastern India). All of Ghansham's men were granted a monthly salary (*māhiyānā*) of four and three quarters rupees on the day their horses were branded.[66] Similarly, single hereditary occupational groups also constituted the Deccan sultanates' much smaller *khāssa* armies. Identified under the broad label of menial occupations (*shāgird pesha*), these included horse keeper or equerry (*sā'is*), water carrier (*pakhālī*), horse breeder (*kabādī*), torch bearer (*mash'alchī*), with fixed specific salary rates.[67] Therefore, specialized military occupations were the basis for more homogeneity among certain groups that often hailed from one region and shared a background.

Northern and southern recruiting systems fused together particularly through the use of the most common term for warrior groups—*rājpūt*—which defied the logic of religion and region. While historians have often defined Rajputs as Hindus, the actual identifications on muster rolls contradict the association of this dilatable social identity with religion.[68] The term *rājpūt* appears in several different forms, most frequently occurring as *rājpūt chauhān* (members of the Chauhan order with alleged descent from branches of the Chahmana lineage).[69] It modifies less frequently occurring clan names like *kachwaha, solānkī, jadon, khokar, badgujar, bundela*, and even some curious combinations, such as *rājpūt-i kurd* (?) and *rājpūt-i zunnārdār* (a Rajput wearing the sacred thread, possibly a Brahmin Rajput?).[70] Half of the fifty-two musters with the identification *rājpūt chauhān* do not have Indic names, so we have no reason to assume that they were all non-Muslims.

Premodern names were not an essential indicator of religious identity. We find a great diversity of Indic and Islamic ethnonyms and exonyms on musters with the identification *rājpūt*. For instance, Dawood, son of Kalu, and Chand Muhammad, son of Noor Muhammad, served under the *mansabdār* Kar Talab Khan, and both men identified themselves as *rājpūt chauhān* when their horses were branded on March 14, 1648.[71] Similar instances of Rajput Muslims can be found listed under other lineages like Kachwaha and Solanki.[72] Although the identifications on the vast majority of the sample musters are not glossed with collective, abstract nouns like *qaum* or *jamāʿat*, occasionally these terms were used to clarify groups such as Solanki Rajputs, who could be Hindus or Muslims.[73]

Moving onto the remaining northern soldiers, we see that far more intricate pluralities may be observed in the case of Iranis, Turanis, and Afghans. Unlike southern soldiers, these labels show finer variations of region, city, area of residence, agnatic descent, ancestry, language, and occupation. Under the broad category of Iranis and Turanis, which may also be understood as Tajiks (urban, settled elites) versus Turkic (nomadic military) groups,[74] we find city names and regions (Sistani, Khurasani, Badakshi, Ghaznawi, Tabrizi, Andijani, Mawaraunnahri, Mashhadi, Isfahani, Turbati, Tashkandi, etc.), as well as various nongenealogical ancestries (Turkomen, Baharlu, Jalayir, Mughal Sadat, Mughal Barlas, Qalmaq, Jalayir, Arghun, and so forth). Examples of ancestries modified by place or language include Jalayir of Andijan and Chagatay Jalayir. Place name *nisbat* denominations were sometimes modified by ethnicity (Arab Bukhari) or sect (Sadat Bukhari), signifying a Central Asian Arab and a *sayyid* from Bukhara (in present day-Uzbekistan), respectively.[75] Such specifications of space, city, ancestry, and language identifications were entirely absent from southern troops.

The ethnic marker "Mughal" or Mongol also appears on musters as a category that bridges Iranis and Turanis.[76] Scribes and soldiers used the term Mughal along with modifiers of lineage, sect, city or region—Mughal-i-sur, Mughal Tuni, Mughal Mazandarani, Mughal Sadat, Mughal Sadat Husayni, Mughal Isfahani, Mughal Badakhshi, Mughal Musawi, Mughal Nahavandi. In a later context of the eighteenth century, Simon Digby also observed Central Asian presence in the Deccan through the saintly biography, *Malfuzāt-i Naqshbandiyya*, which produced in the Mughal provincial capital of Aurangabad.[77] He also noted the blurring of nomadic and sedentary ethnic divisions in the Deccan and the rather loose application of the label *Mughal* to both Iranis or Tajiks and Turanis or those of Turkic stock. Indeed, the *Malfuzāt* represents the culmination of a much longer Mughal military presence in the Deccan, already evident in the musters from the early seventeenth century, where ethnographic markers were well defined but evolved homologously during conquest. Thus, in the context of a moving imperial army, a certain second-generation Turani, Turktaz Khan Bahadur, could "adopt Maratha customs" while serving in the imperial army.[78] In some cases, Digby also discerned that certain *chehrah āqāsī* were exclusively appointed to record Turani soldiers' rolls. To muster masters who had recently arrived from Mughal Hindustan in the 1630s and 1640s, specificities among northern soldiers may have, therefore, been more legible than the internal variations among southern troops.

Such variations are visible among Afghans, the only group that exhibits both northern and southern recruitment patterns.[79] That is to say, muster rolls show many Afghans serving in heterogenous contingents, not sharing the same background as their *mansabdār*, but also simultaneously enlisted alongside masses of other Afghan soldiers in more homogeneous contingents under both Afghan and non-Afghan chiefs. For instance, all but two from the twelve surviving musters of 1,000/800 rank *mansabdār* Usman Khan Rohilla were labeled either Afghan or Afghan Khalil.[80] Contingents with a majority of Afghan soldiers also served under non-Afghan chiefs, such as 4,000/4,000 rank *mansabdār* Rashid Khan Ansari and his son, a *mansabdār* of 1,500/1,000 rank, Asadullah, who had more than 50 and 80 percent Afghan soldiers respectively.[81] Ethnic-based military recruitment was, therefore, more prevalent among Afghans than Iranis and Turanis. Pre-existing Afghan settlements in northern India, established on the basis of different descent groups and lineages (coming primarily from what is today southeastern and southwestern Afghanistan), may have shaped Afghan soldier recruitment in the imperial army when it began moving towards peninsular India.[82]

Scribes labeled Afghans with great precision. The word *Afghan* appears on musters by itself or modified by several other markers that signified agnatic descent (*tā'ifa* and *qabīla*),[83] group (*gurūh*), and factions (*firqa*), as well as names of cities and regions within Mughal Hindustan and Central Asia. The first category of Afghan musters in our sample contains Pakhtun descent groups composed of many different lineages (*-zai* or sons of the purported apical ancestor Qays);[84] the second show affiliations to geographic regions and cities within and beyond Mughal Hindustan; and a third indicate cross-cutting with other overarching categories such as Turani and Irani, representing a very long process of Afghan ethnogenesis. Tajiks and Turks had long been absorbed into the aforementioned lineages, which do not signify static, fixed origins, but ones that were transformed further with the continuous movement of Afghans into the Indian subcontinent.

The second category of Afghan labels, citing cities and regions within and beyond Mughal India, demonstrate a process of gradual differentiation. Examples of labels with geographic modifiers include Afghan-i Turbati (in present-day Balochistan), Afghan-i Tabrizi (from Tabriz in northwestern Iran), Afghan-i Qandhari (from Qandahar in present-day southern Afghanistan). These locales, both near and far from the Afghan homeland, suggest that some geographic labels may refer to Tajiks or settled urban elites, a sizable minority that inhabited the Sulayman Mountains, alongside the aforementioned pastoral-nomadic lineages.[85] From geographic regions within Mughal north India, we find Afghan-i Kashi (from Benaras or Varanasi in northern India), Afghan-i Mewati (from Mewat, a region south of Delhi that spans the present-day states of Haryana and Rajasthan), and Afghan Rohilla (from the Rohilkhand region in present-day Uttar Pradesh in northern India). The third and last set of labels show cross-cutting and overlap with other overarching categories during a period when confessional and ethnic identities were in flux. These include Afghan-i Turki, referring to someone who could be from both a Sarwani/Yusufzai/Kakar and Barlas/Qipchaki ancestry.[86] Similarly, the label Afghan-i Bakhtiyari refers to people who cut across the nomadic versus sedentary dichotomy (i.e., people who held multiple occupations, such as herders, merchants, and farmers) and variably identified themselves as Tajik, Pakhtun, or *sayyid*, depending on the context.[87] The wide variety of Afghan labels, associated with lineages, geographies, and multivalent ancestries, attest to the slow processes of ethnogenesis, an outcome of large population movements and circulation across transregional distances.

While the descriptive roll offers direct clues about soldiers' identifications, unearthing the social groups to which scribal staff belonged is nearly impossible from the documents themselves. Overall, very little can be said about who muster masters were or what their level of literacy was with the language of administration—Persian.[88] While musters offer intricate physiognomic and social portraits of the Mughal soldier, they offer no trace or definitive sign of the Mughal scribes who generated this documentary genre. Since we do not find any signatures or any attestations with scribes' names, the muster master's social identity is far more difficult to deduce from clues on the page. I have yet to come across names of provincial *chehrah nawīs* that might illuminate which social groups held this office in the Mughal military. While citing names of higher-level scribal clerks, such as *wāqi'a nawīs* (intelligencer), and inspection staff, such as the *dārogha, amīn*, and *mushrif*, was fairly common across different classes of Mughal documents, the muster master remained anonymous.[89]

One possible reason for the lack of specificity in regionally recruited soldier identifications in comparison to northern soldiers may have had to do with the scribes who wrote the muster. In the formative period when military offices were being established in the 1630s and 1640s, northern scribes, such as Kayasthas and other literate groups, may have accompanied the imperial army to the battle front.[90] To them, the specificities of northern soldiers may have been far more legible than the internal differences between less familiar groups from the Deccan. Especially since regionally recruited horseman served in more homogeneous contingents, scribes rarely seem to have interrogated particularities of cities, regions, and clans. The full integration of Maratha Brahmins as a scribal class into Mughal military administration may explain why late seventeenth-century musters show greater detail and specification of place and region than the early and mid-seventeenth-century materials analyzed here.[91] Prior to this period, more specific labels (names of regions, cities, denomination, agnatic descent, etc.) described northern soldiers while capacious labels (Deccani) defined regionally-recruited personnel. In the sample of over two thousand muster rolls from the 1630s to the 1660s examined in this chapter, the interplay between scribes' (administrative/literate) and soldiers' (lay/illiterate) understandings and uses of widely accepted identifications demonstrate the distance of new social groups from and their gradual incorporation into imperial institutions.

To sum up, what does the analysis of the aggregate and the minutiae on the muster tell us about precolonial understandings of social identifications? The way people saw themselves and others changed as they moved across new landscapes.

The need for ever-finer categories contradicts the ideal types we associate with being Mughal, embodied in the idea that precolonial India was a fully formed, static, and pregiven entity. We know the story of a Mughal Hindustan in the postcolonial nation-state's self-image, with a strong center that held in balance a variety of subjects.[92] But the minute identifications on musters reveal multiple ways of being Mughal, with subnational or ethnic groups, crossing sectarian, lineage, and regional divides. The idea that social identifications have inherent absolute values and are self-contained borrows from nineteenth- and twentieth-century understandings of ethnicity and race that tie social groups to fixed notions of territory and kinship.[93] Linking identifications to territory, descent, language, and sect prevents us from appreciating the inherent mobility of social taxonomies in precolonial times, wherein the movement of large armies changed the way everyday actors used, invented, and understood social categories. Just as contingents of regional soldiers joined the Mughal camp, changing the usages of bureaucratic social taxonomies, regional polities also embraced imperial institutional mechanisms. The outcomes of early modern conquest were not merely ones of absolute opposition, erasure, or a single battle transforming a blank frontier into an imperial outpost overnight. Rather, a gradual process unfolded, which meant that materiality moved across political borders, setting off processes of borrowing and cohabitation between empire and region.

IMPERIAL AND REGIONAL INTERSECTIONS

Eclectic categories for social identifications do not tell the tale of porous pre-modern identities nor of a monolithic Mughal state that came from northern India, taking over everything in the south that stood in its way. Zooming out diachronically, when compared to scholarship on other periods of South Asian history (ancient and medieval), Mughal historians are not unique in pointing out the deviance and exceptionalism of southern India. As Janaki Nair has argued, the category of "south India" has operated as an eternal exception to attest to the normativity of northern India across many different historical periods, a persistent convention in the subcontinent's historiography. [94] Despite overlapping mechanisms of rule, a Mughal centricity pervades both regional and imperial historiographies and much of the story we know, especially of the seventeenth century, is one of Mughal ascendency and Deccan sultanates' decline.[95]

By investigating what muster rolls look like and what is actually in them, we learn that the social identities distilled by modern historians were often broken down by premodern state and subject or were absent altogether. Muster rolls show the emerging proximity and integration of Mughal-Deccan state forms. Instead of casting the Deccan as an anomalous region where Mughal ambitions came to die, the muster master's daily paperwork can be viewed as a process of institutionalization, whereby centralizing power structures adjusted to regional circumstances and patterns of recruitment. Moving armies and their personnel brought the institutional mechanisms of northern and southern India closer to each other. On a layered war front, greater centralization required improvisation and incorporation of existing regional patterns of war-making for pansubcontinental soldier recruitment.

Looking at regional records closely, we find that mustering of men and horses was one practice the Deccan courts began to implement in the seventeenth century, possibly in emulation of the Mughals, but certainly owing to the intensification of military campaigns under regional households in the Hyderabad-Karnatak. Under imperial suzerainty, semi-autonomous regional elites increasingly challenged sovereign power, which necessitated the standardization of military recruitment. At the same time, as we saw through the examination of social identifications, the Mughal army absorbed regionally recruited contingents in which troops shared the same background as their chief, a feature of military organization in Deccan courts.

A reevaluation of Mughal presence in southern India requires that we place empire alongside coexisting regional political forms—that is, the independent, non-Timurid Deccan sultanates whose administrative-military structures came to intersect with Mughal norms.[96] Studies of soldiering in regional sultanates' armies are much more sparse than works on military recruitment in Mughal Hindustan, although scholars have drawn out the ideal, normative articulations of centralized military revenue collection systems in the Deccan sultanates.[97] In the sultanate of Bijapur, two administrative distinctions shaped soldier recruitment. Officials appointed to centrally administered districts called *mu'āmalā* or *qal'ah* were supervised by a havaldār appointed by the sultan, while others were assigned to cultivable lands (*muqāsā*) in districts called *tappa* or *pargana*. There were several kinds of *pargana* administration, with smaller portions of land under the purview of hereditary subordinate territorial chiefs (*deshmukh/desai*), usually Maratha Brahmins, Lingayats, and other literate groups. Both aristocratic-military orders and hereditary officials maintained troops at their own expense, mobilizing them in times of war.[98] The vast majority of fighters under these chiefs were mercenaries with variable levels of control and ownership over their own weapons, horses, and equipment.[99] Unlike Mughal Hindustan, the Deccan sultanates did not have an elaborate *mansab* ranking system or an ideological structure that tied distinct aristocratic lineages to kingly power.[100]

From the time of the Bahmanis (ca. 1347–1527) on, a stratification of power remained the norm in southern Indian sultanates well into the seventeenth century, with a very small portion of the army (*khāssa khayl*) maintained directly by the king. Aristocratic military and hereditary chiefs thus recruited and maintained much of the armed forces.[101] For instance, on the eve of war with the Nizam shahs of Ahmadnagar in the late 1620s, the appointment of selected Golkonda commanders was determined through their social composition, occupation of soldiers, and the kind of revenue assignment that an appointee had been given by the sultan:

> ʿAli Khan Beg Afshar, who was one of the servants of *kevān pāsbān* [Sultan ʿAbdullah Qutb Shah], was given *tankhwāh* [share of the revenue] of 10,000 *hun* [gold coin], had a hundred young valiant Turks [*sad jawān bahādur-i turk*] in his contingent. Maryam Beg Zulfiqar, who was also a high-ranking servant of this court, got a *jāgīr* of 10,000 *hun*, had under him a hundred mounted gunners [*sawār tufangchī*]. Muhammad Sayyid Badakhshi was a brave young man in service of the court. Two of these aforementioned men were given *tankhwāh*. Sayyid Babu and Malik Makhdum Dakkani and few other brave men from the Deccan [*ahl-i-dakkan*] were also appointed as *sardārs* of *muqāsā* or cultivable lands and given *tankhwāh*.[102]

Chiefs of distinct lineages, who were tied to regional sultans through revenue assignments, controlled troops with a shared background or specialization in the same type of military labor. In the late 1620s, one Maratha *sardār*, Vithoji Kantiya, who had lent support to the Golkonda sultan against the Nizam shahs of Ahmadnagar and the forces of Bijapuri minister Murari Pandit, reached the city of Hyderabad. Soon after arriving with his wife, sons, nephew, and close relatives (*zan-i vithojī wa pisar wa birādar zādeh wa qarābitān*), along with an army of two to three thousand Maratha soldiers (*afwāj-i marāthā*), Vithoji fell ill and passed away. Praising his troops' loyalty and devotion (*ʿubūdīyat wa fidwīyat*), Sultan ʿAbdullah Qutb Shah (r. 1626–72) then appointed Vithoji's sons and nephew to a *jāgīr*.[103] This pattern of incorporating household chiefs, their extended kin, and troops was common across the sultanates and it intensified in the seventeenth century as more and more territories came within the penumbra of a layered Mughal imperial conquest led by regional families. With the sultanates accepting imperial suzerainty, military expeditions intensified—as did the contentions between regional sultans and the most powerful military chiefs, who often asserted their autonomy, mobilizing their armed contingents to fortify independent strongholds. At a palpable distance from regional sovereigns, with greater control over manpower and independent military resources, both imperial and regional regimes depended on aristocratic-military households to facilitate territorial expansion.

Consider the case of Bijapur, where this tension between kingly and aristocratic centralization came to a head in Sultan Muhammad ʿAdil Shah's reign (r. 1627–56), specifically through the implementation of horse branding.[104] Unlike in Mughal Hindustan, in the Deccan sultanates there was no equivalent to the muster master's office, as the authority to brand horses and muster soldiers was still delegated to each aristocratic-military household chief. An excerpt from a *dastūruʾl-ʿamal* or administrative manual, perhaps the only surviving one we have from the Deccan sultanates, stipulated the instructions for branding horses.[105] When first appointed to a *jāgīr* or *muqasa*, each household chief had to count the number of horses and men under him, placing his individual branding mark on the horse (*ʿalāmāt-i dāgh-i khud*). On the other hand, the horses of ministers (*wazīr*) would have the royal branding mark (*dāgh-i sarkārī bādshahī*). When household heads appeared at court, they would report on their army's count and the condition of their troops in distant provinces. A chief or commander of counting (*zābiteh shumār*) would compare any previous counts and investigate any discrepancies. The manual prescribed that some minor carelessness could be overlooked but any grievous error should be reprimanded (*agar taghāfil kardanī ast taghāfil kunand agar tahdīd kardanī ast tahdīd numāyand*). If the horse had already been branded and confirmed to return to service for another household chief, the master of brands would refresh this brand with his own brand (*agar aspī dāgh zadeh shudeh sābit-i dīgar be chākrī rujū ' shavad sāheb-i dāgh dāgh-i khud bar ān dāgh tāzeh kunad*).[106] While directives to regularize branding may have come from regional sultans, semi-autonomous provincial elites held on to their own brands, controlling the authority to regulate men and horses. Contemporary evidence from the seventeenth century attests to this tiered hierarchy between sultans and household chiefs, with the latter responsible for branding while reporting on the armies' conditions to the king.[107] Faced with the growing assertion of aristocratic-military and hereditary territorial elite households, the Deccan sultans therefore attempted to centralize military administration and incorporate Mughal recruitment procedures.[108] Despite this attempt to standardize military recruitment, the authority to brand remained under the control of regional household chiefs.

To sum up, in regional sultanates, the number of troops directly controlled by the sultan was much smaller than the number of soldiers under lesser grandees or heads of military households. With the increase in military expeditions, attempts were made to reorganize armies through centralizing mechanisms such as branding. Military commanders and hereditary territorial chiefs recruited their own men, maintaining weapons and horses with relative autonomy from sovereigns. As discussed here, this pattern of regional recruitment—sharing the chief's social background—transformed the Mughal army's profile when it began to recruit contingents within peninsular India. In regional sultanates, the onus of branding and mustering still fell on the aristocratic-military and hereditary chiefs rather than in a bureaucratic office with multiple scribes and inspectors, as was the case in Mughal military encampments that lay across the River Krishna.

MATERIALITY AND MILITARIES IN GLOBAL PERSPECTIVE

The story of the muster does not end at the River Krishna in south-central India. The Mughal muster's materiality and mobility resonate well beyond the subcontinent. Everyday archival practices translated the innate human need for creating conceptual categories into portable objects that lay at the core of military bureaucracies across the world. To hear their echoes, consider for a moment the following two musters from opposite ends of the globe, Potosí (in present-day Bolivia) and Burhanpur (in central India):

> Pedro Juan Dávila native of the Villa of Madrid, tall of body, brown face, graying, with a gap between the teeth, of the age of twenty-two years, son of Pedro Dávila. Enlisted this same day, and is named as corporal of the Guzmáns & the Captain's squadron, he has his own harquebus and they gave him sixty pesos for two payments. [December 23, 1624][109]

> Malik Ahmad, son of Malik Daulat, son of Malik Zainuddin, of the *qaum* of Rajput Solanki. resident of Burhanpur, wheatish complexion, broad forehead, open eyebrows, sheep-eyed, long nose, beard and moustache black, one mole on the cheek close to the nose, with one small pox mark on top of the abovementioned mole, one mole on the neck on the right side, piercing in the left ear, scar on the left eyebrow, *zāt* of twenty-four or *chahār bīstī*, approximate age/stature of thirty-three years.

> Striped horse, some white hair on the forehead, on the left lobe dry scars, on the hindquarter few less visible scars, with a white line on either side, Turki horse.
> Dated on 9 Zu al-Qa'dah.
> Of the 19th Regnal Year [December 17, 1645]
> It was checked and declared that the horse has become infirm.[110]

It is of course the case that Malik Ahmad, a Rajput Solanki, resident of Burhanpur in central India, and Pedro Juan Dávila, originally from Madrid in Spain and residing at that time in Potosí in South America, never met in real time. Yet the descriptive template to translate these men onto paper, one in Persian and the other in Spanish, is strikingly alike. The soldiers are identified in terms of place, height, complexion, distinct facial features like moles and scars, their ages, and agnatic descent. While Malik Ahmad's description is paired with that of his horse, Pedro Juan Dávila was a harquebusier or foot soldier with a matchlock. Both were perhaps soldiers of fortune who offered their military labor to armies settling into new lands. Malik Ahmad moved between the frontier city of Burhanpur to military forts dispersed across south-central India that had recently come under Mughals, while Dávila crossed the Atlantic to reach the famous Andean silver-mining city of Potosí, then under Spanish rule.[111]

The lives of Malik Ahmad and Pedro Juan Dávila were indeed connected, but not because they intersected in time and space. Rather, both lived in inland cities where imperial infrastructures were being implemented—Potosí and Burhanpur—centers of the Atlantic and the Indian Ocean, places that connected the global flow of goods and people. Gujarati textiles made their way overland via Burhanpur to port cities on the western coast of India, where they were exchanged for silver coins from Potosí. The growing presence of two early modern empires shaped the social fabric and political institutions of booming commercial cities where different worlds and kinds of people collided. In Potosí, an ethnic clash between Basques and other groups starting in 1622 led to martial law in 1623–24, when 230 foot soldiers were rounded up and their musters produced.[112] In

Burhanpur, on the other hand, lords paid directly from the imperial treasury failed to send their soldiers for mustering and branding; among them, Malik Ahmad appears to have been a low-ranking chief with very few retainers of his own, moving from a modest numerical rank of twenty-four to eighty *zāt* in the Mughal army.[113]

In both these worlds, people, animals, and things had to be tracked and accounted for to make sure no one fled and nothing was wasted. While the language for recording Dávila and Ahmad's physiognomy resonates, their musters survive today in different archival modes. Unlike the palm-sized single sheet of Mughal documents, the Potosí musters were recorded in larger registers, part of a miscellany of expenses and costs listed in composite records that accounted for the use of crown money. Arguably, from sailors to slaves and convicts, versions of descriptive rolls may be found in the archive of any early modern empire, performing the work of tracking, counting, listing, and describing imperial resources.[114] Large, bureaucratic, centralized empires across the early modern world created mechanisms for reading and categorizing humans into what we today understand as caste and/or ethnicity. This object captures the dynamic continuum from mercenary to the professional soldier that scholars have long argued cannot be viewed as a teleological transition or as a path to modernization.[115] For the global historian, the prodigious scatter of Mughal musters embodies the unevenness, overlap, and improvisation shared across military recruitment systems in different contexts throughout the early modern world.

Event-marked portraits bring marginal military personnel into the imaginary of the historian who, on first glance, may find little story to tell from such materials. And yet, this portrait of the everyday work performed in the Mughal war front's military sites, has shown otherwise. Shaping the state from the bottom up, the quiet everyday interactions between rulers and ruled created change over time and space. Since their discovery in the early twentieth century, Mughal archives from southern India have been simultaneously ubiquitous and invisible in writing the Mughal past. Despite frequent citation of over "150,000 documents from the Deccan," these materials have remained relatively inconspicuous in studies of Mughal India.[116] In part, this concurrent acknowledgement and elision emerges from the dissonance between what the historian expects to demonstrate from these materials and what the document actually places before us. Part of the difficulty is that these materials do not lend themselves easily to narrating the way that court chronicles or other more elaborate forms of writing such as stylized prose or *inshā'* or the records from *qāzī* courts allow. Despite these challenges, previous generations of historians and archivists laid the groundwork for examining Mughal documentary genres, particularly for verifying chronicle-derived narrative histories, which have remained the dominant way of writing the Mughal past. By mostly bracketing Persian chronicles, this chapter has reexamined one documentary genre on its own terms and within the context of its production in the Mughal-Deccan battlefront.

The muster roll bore witness to cultures of circulation and mobility, where ordinary subjects participated in empire's two core institutions—the military and the bureaucracy. This artifact unsettles the idea that the "pre-modern state was, in many crucial respects, partially blind; it knew precious little about its subjects, their wealth, their landholdings and yields, their location, their very identity."[117] On the contrary; the Mughals were obsessed with knowing who people were, but not necessarily for the purpose of discovering the authenticity or the absolute value of a thing called identity. The muster represents a literate state's attempts to develop mechanisms of identification for keeping track of the itinerant soldier and his most prized asset, the horse, along with a whole host of other resources. At the heart of this identification lay the soldier's declaration of ghar or home, articulated through multiple signifiers of lineages of service, place, language, occupation, and region. The scribe had a part to play in schematizing the northern versus the southern soldier, marking different degrees of heterogeneity within these categories. Imperial institutions shaped senses of where one's home was and what the experience of circulating on a war front layered with multiple political formations meant. From these fundamental material and bureaucratic processes of circulation through which homes were named and identified, we journey, in the next chapter, to the regional capital city of Bijapur and the Kanara and Konkan coasts. Here, we consider the politics of ghar within one itinerant household that negotiated the limits of an imperial-regional warfront, while articulating shifting senses of belonging through polyvocal critiques of what it meant to make and unravel the home in the Mughal world.

3

From Court to Port
Governing the Household

Traveling by car or train across peninsular India, the portion of the subcontinent surrounded by water on all but one side, reveals many different ecological zones. If we board a train in the Deccan railways system, for instance, from the city of Bijapur, the dry, rugged central plateau gives way to the lush, green eastern slopes of the Sahyadri Mountains or the Western Ghats, which run along the Konkan and Kanara coasts, overlooking the Arabian Sea. Moving in the southeastern direction, we would reach the coastal Coromandel Plains, looking out at the Bay of Bengal. Today, as in centuries past, these varied geographic landscapes were given definitions based on where the traveler began the journey, whether they viewed this vast landform from Hindustan, the Deccan, or the Karnatak.

We move south from the encampments of the Mughal army to the regional capital of Bijapur. From here, we follow one elite Indic Muslim household's circulation to and from the port cities and hinterlands of the Konkan and Kanara coasts of southwestern India. The household at its center has fascinated generations of historians, as more materials have come to light in recent years in Portuguese and Dutch that illuminate its chief's long political career in the sultanate of Bijapur from the 1620s to 1640s, when the regional sultanates nominally accepted imperial overlordship after decades of conflicts and negotiations. The household of Mustafa Khan or Muhammad Amin, a second-generation Iranian, traces its roots to the city of Lar in southern Iran. He served as prime minister, becoming instrumental in bringing the young Muhammad ʿAdil Shah to the throne. After a succession struggle, he emerged as the chief negotiator, brokering peace with the Mughals in 1636. One of his daughters married Sultan Muhammad ʿAdil Shah of Bijapur in 1633; the wedding was an event celebrated in court chronicles.[1] Although political historians discuss Mustafa Khan's political and diplomatic negotiations in

European sources, a sizable body of literary and documentary materials about him and his household in Persian and Dakkani have not been integrated into the well-rehearsed story of yet another "foreigner" or Iranian émigré with a fickle commitment to defending the Deccan against the Mughals.[2] The prevailing scholarly concern has been to gauge exactly how foreign premodern Muslims of various ethnic, linguistic, and regional origins in South Asia really were, finding an absolute measure of their distance from something called the local environment.[3]

The reason for this lacuna, particularly in the periods long before early colonialism and English East India Company rule in the eighteenth century, is the prevailing scholarly paradigm used for writing about India before Europe, particularly in the period under the Mughals—the study of the intersections of the Indic and Islamicate/Persianate cultural worlds.[4] This model has usefully undone the colonial idea of homogenous Muslim conquests over hapless Hindu principalities, enabling the study of syncretic, composite cultures and significantly broadening the range of texts used for writing cultural history.[5] Recently, however, the model has also been reevaluated and critiqued for overemphasizing the separateness of the Hindu and Muslim worlds and for, at times, leaving out the study of status and caste within and across these social groups. While cultural histories of southern India have made the case for influence between separate Sultanate (i.e., Islamicate/Persianate) and post-Vijayanagara *nayaka* (i.e., Indic) polities evident in borrowing courtly tastes, cultural dispositions, and norms of comportment, I argue that we should also look at the circulation, borrowing, and mirroring of social practices—for example, those associated with multilingualism and the parallel roles of Hindu and Muslim office holders in the regional bureaucracy.[6]

By bridging the cultural and political worlds of a figure like Mustafa Khan, social practices, whether those connected with listening to the rhymes and rhythms of a new literary idiom or those having to do with fighting over the control of a bureaucratic office, enabled families, only a generation or two old, to make a ghar in peninsular India. The operations of Mustafa Khan and his relatives at the intersections of household and multiple monarchical powers reveal two sides to the politics of belonging in peninsular India: the polyvocal literary expression of political ambitions and the consolidation of occupational roles in bureaucratic offices. By participating in the ecology of multilingualism and working the regional administration, this household built a sense of home in a space with many internal sociocultural frontiers.

In the first part of this chapter, I consider vernacular works, where Mustafa Khan is depicted as a user of and listener to multiple languages and I thereby show him as transcending the social-linguistic frontiers of the Deccan (Persianate/Islamicate) and the Karnatak (Indic). I examine the *Fathnāma-yi Ikkeri*, a martial work written in masnavī or rhymed couplet form, which depicted a battle between this Muslim warrior chief of the Deccan and the Shaiva Keladi chief, Sivappa Nayak (d. 1660), of Ikkeri and Bednur in the Karnatak, and show how this work emphasized the cultural differences between these rivals and then collapsed them altogether to signal the Indic Muslim patron's cognition of and command over an intimate enemy. Rather than using the Persian chronicles to mark the cultural separateness of émigré households, I urge us to examine understudied representations of such households in other vernaculars that present alternative practices of creating ghar in peninsular India.

Elite power was not sustained by depicting political aspirations in literary representations alone. In the second part of this chapter, then, I turn to documentary evidence in South Asian and European languages to illustrate the second prong of an émigré household's politics of belonging. Focusing on moments of conflict against kingly authority, I show how centrally appointed bureaucrats, who were members of Mustafa Khan's household, attempted to transform their offices into hereditary appointments, all while mediating relationships with the Portuguese and the Dutch. The second part of my argument here locates elite Muslim formation and place-making practices within the debate about subcaste or jāti, South Asia's most salient sociological category, broadly defined as an endogamous social group with lineage and kinship ties. As identified in the book's introduction, histories of caste have yet to fully consider the place of Islam and the role of Muslim familial mobility in the production of jāti and state-formation.[7] Through the household of Mustafa Khan, I show how relatives tried to use their administrative posts as venal offices, which would be associated with certain rights and privileges, thereby establishing a pattern that has been evocatively demonstrated for different Hindu scribal castes across the subcontinent.[8]

Moving beyond heroic depictions of a household chief, I then show how different kinfolk strengthened mechanisms for inheriting and competing for bureaucratic offices, devising new ways of navigating the competitive terrain of politics in peninsular India. By unraveling silences in the literary archive, I analyze competing voices in translated letters from European archives, along with Persian documents that reveal how relatives occupying different bureaucratic offices collided with monarchical authority, seeking to perpetuate their hold over important nodes of trade on the Kanara and Konkan coasts. These centrally appointed positions—such as that of the *havaldār* (literally meaning custodian or person in charge or governor of a port city, appointed directly by the sultan), which was usually held by Muslim elites—were much more stringently regulated by the monarch, were transferred frequently from one revenue assignment to another, and did not afford the rights and privileges that came with hereditary offices, usually held by upper-caste Hindus at the village level. The conflicts between Mustafa Khan's relatives provide an example of the mirroring of a social practice and jāti formation across sectarian lines. In the period of Mughal suzerainty in the Deccan and increased imperial pressure, a wider range of social groups sought to entrench their occupational roles through family mobility across land and sea. In turn, the internal conflicts within this émigré, Muslim, and military-bureaucratic

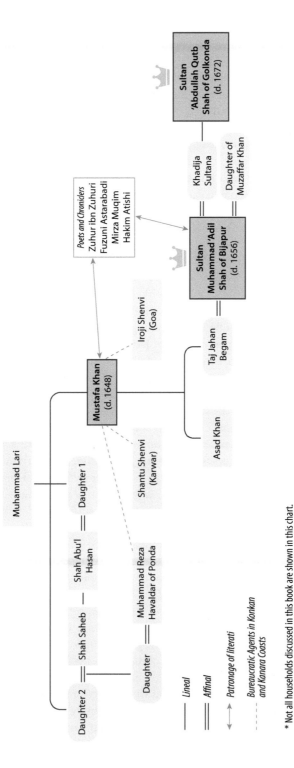

FIGURE 2. The household of Mustafa Khan Lari (d. 1648) of Bijapur. Drawn by Matilde Grimaldi.

household determined the outcomes of the Luso-Dutch conflict on Konkan and Kanara coasts, following a pattern that resonates with earlier studies of the Indian Ocean world.[9]

In what follows, I first present a brief biography and overview of Mustafa Khan and his household, highlighting prominent relatives visible across different archives. After laying out who was in this household and where they journeyed, I then home in on the portrait of Mustafa Khan's political ambitions in the *Fathnāma-yi Ikkeri*, which memorialized his battle with the *nayakas of* Ikkeri and Bednur in the Karnatak. The chapter's final section turns to conflicts among relatives of this family. By comparing correspondence in Persian, Portuguese, and Dutch about these feuds, I show how relatives in key bureaucratic offices mobilized resources to challenge kingly authority and exploited competition between Portuguese Goa and the Dutch East India Company on the coasts of southwestern India.

THE HOUSEHOLD OF MUSTAFA KHAN

Mustafa Khan emerged as a key negotiator when the Deccan sultans accepted Mughal suzerainty in 1636. In the war campaigns that ensued thereafter, first toward the southwestern Kanara and Konkan coasts, his extended kin established strongholds in Belgaum and Bankapur, far from the Mughal headquarters in Burhanpur, Daulatabad, and the regional capital cities of Bijapur and Hyderabad (see map 1). Mustafa Khan was known as "Khan Baba" in Persianate texts; he was called the "Iranian Olivares" by the Portuguese in Goa; and the Dutch observers stationed in the factory at Vengurla called him the "stadthouder van Decan" (state-steward of the Deccan). The role of Mustafa Khan in mediating relations with the Mughals has been substantially evaluated through European-language sources.[10]

A powerbroker in Bijapuri politics and in Mughal-Portuguese relations in the southwestern Deccan, Mustafa Khan played a role as kingmaker in the succession crisis of 1627. His extensive contacts in Goa, as well as his network of Shenvi Brahmin agents dispersed along the Konkan and Kanara coasts, are examined by Jorge Flores who notes the following: "his relationship with [Sultan] Muhammad ʿAdil Shah was characterized by frequent ups and downs as the *valido* fell and rose several times." In contrast with what we may expect of an émigré Iranian, Mustafa Khan was also categorically mistrusted by the Mughal emperor Shah Jahan for never fully aligning with the empire.[11] In 1635 and 1643, European observers reported how the Bijapur sultan placed Mustafa Khan under house arrest twice at his bases in Belgaum and Bankapur, where he would spend much of the latter part of his career in the 1640s.

Reports from the VOC factory at Vengurla that supplement Portuguese observations of Bijapuri politics relay contradictory information about the family of Mustafa Khan and the fraught place of Sultan Muhammad ʿAdil Shah in it, since both men made ambiguous promises to the VOC about ousting the Portuguese from the Konkan coast. VOC observers weighed the potential of a Bijapuri attack against the Mughals, for which the sultan wanted to mobilize resources via the factory at Vengurla and redirect them to the Karnatak war front. Pieter Paets, the chief merchant at Vengurla, reported rumors circulating about the Bijapur sultan's intention to raise war against the Great Mughal by calling forth the maximum forces from the Karnatak. The Dutch merchant expressed the concern that if the Mughals entered the equation, all the promises that Bijapur had made to the VOC about retaking the Konkan would not be kept.[12]

Another close interlocuter of Mustafa Khan was one Pieter Andries, a *chirurgijn* or doctor, frequently sent to attend to him and brought information from the prime minister's household dispersed between Belgaum and Bankapur.[13] Mustafa Khan assured the doctor that he (instead of the sultan) could fulfill the promise to the VOC and send his son, Asad Khan, to take over Goa, with the assistance of thirty to forty thousand men.[14] Much of the correspondence from the factory at Vengurla referring to different members of Mustafa Khan's household does not so much answer the question of what happened as it dwells on the possibility of the Mughals marching farther south and the question of whether or not the elite households of the sultanates would offer assistance to Europeans on the coasts if an imperial attack were to happen.

Marriages within and across different households strengthened Mustafa Khan's position as prime minister of Bijapur. These were not straightforward political alliances, but they likely produced a terrain of familial politics with a constant threat of disunion, a reality that is not explicitly stated in our archives. Mustafa Khan's other important kin included two brothers-in-law, Shah Abu'l Hasan and Shah Saheb, and a man named Muhammad Reza, who was also Shah Saheb's son-in-law and the havaldār of the important city of Ponda, which lay north of Portuguese Goa.[15] Mustafa Khan was therefore Muhammad Reza's *māmā* or maternal uncle-in-law, an affinal tie that carried with it the burden of many obligations, both explicit and implicit. At the same time, as stated earlier, through the marriage of his daughter, Mustafa Khan was also the father-in-law of Sultan Muhammad 'Adil Shah. Although the elite Muslim daughters and sisters who made these relationships possible are invisible in the archives (except for faint glimpses of festive Persianate texts commemorating conjugal ties discussed in the next chapter), we may surmise that the bonds forged through these marriages were fragile.

In the absence of a consanguine agnatic male ancestor—the maternal uncle— a figure long reviled and represented in South Asian literary traditions (best illustrated in the cunning characters of Shakuni *māmā* and the tyrannical Kans *māmā* from the epic *Mahabharata*),[16] occupied the fraught role involved in stepping in as the patriarch and making major decisions, such as marrying off his sister's daughters into other households, which often meant exercising control over extended kin and controlling and allocating the household's resources. One key figure was Muhammad Reza, who had married the daughter of Mustafa Khan's sister. He held the office of the havaldār or governor of Ponda, a bureaucratic position responsible for collecting customs on imported war supplies, controlling the movement of everyday goods into the capital city, and allocating resources to the Karnatak war front. The governor of Ponda was in a position to demand more not only from his powerful maternal uncle-in-law, Mustafa Khan, but also from his cobrother-in-law, the king Muhammad ʿAdil Shah, to secure his office's autonomy. The unsaid affective hierarchies governing these familial ties and the elite women who were integral to them, although they are silent in the archive, shaped a volatile political terrain. As this chapter's final section will show, Mustafa Khan was, in some ways, struggling to exercise authority over his multiple feuding *dāmād* (sons-in-law), a son-in-law through his daughter (the king, Muhammad ʿAdil Shah), and a nephew-in-law married to his sister's daughter (the port city bureaucrat, Muhammad Reza).

Finally, the trajectory of Mustafa Khan's career cannot be adequately understood without evaluating how his household participated in peninsular India's ecology of multilingualism. The household chief's movement beyond the regional capital city of Bijapur into the southwestern Karnatak in the 1640s coincided with an expansion of his cultural patronage. Mustafa Khan presided over a multiethnic and multilingual literary circuit, which produced texts not just in Persian but also in the panregional literary idiom, Dakkani. Mustafa Khan's literary circuit included Iranian émigré poets and court chroniclers who wrote in Persian, as well as lesser-known poets who eulogized him in the heroic mode in the more widely recognized Dakkani. To make sense of how this émigré household participated in multilingualism, in the next section we turn to the words one of these poets, Mirza Muqim, who traveled south beyond the court and capital city, accompanying his itinerant patron's armies for a campaign at the fort of Ikkeri in 1644.

A PATRON OF MANY TONGUES

The rich scholarly conversation about how literary expression in multiple languages shaped the politics of belonging in premodern South Asia resonates with our case study, illuminating why it matters to study a figure like Mustafa Khan in languages beyond Persian.[17] Before turning to the text at hand, Mirza Muqim's *Fathnāma-yi Ikkeri*, this debate's broad arguments are worth reiterating here.

Literary portraits of Self versus Other in South Asia's regional vernaculars have shown the complex and layered meanings of representations about political violence and conflict, particularly when they are coded through the tropes and languages of religious, ethnic, and linguistic difference.[18] In a different context, Ramya Sreenivasan argued that multilingual patronage across genres addressed a range of audiences, expressing degrees of vassalage between the court of the Mughal emperor Akbar and Raja Man Singh of Amber.[19] Similarly, in the context of discussing fifteenth-century Gujarat, Aparna Kapadia has shown how polyphonic heroic verse, combining cosmopolitan Sanskrit with panregional Dimgal, composed for a small Rajput chieftain, Ranmal of Idar, in the hinterlands of western India, spoke to the universal ideals of Indic kingship, on the one hand, and the regional context of competing warrior lineages, on the other. The images in *Fathnāma-yi Ikkeri's* of an aspiring warrior patron, Khan Baba, with a household dispersed between coast and country, very much echo the tropes of martial prowess elucidated for the *Ranmallachanda*. The poet Mirza Muqim constructed images of gore and blood on the battlefield, used political insults and ethnography to apprehend a familiar rival, and finally resolved a military conflict by moving between lowly Dakkani and high Persian to address his patron's multiple aspirations. As Kapadia notes, the portraits in such uncanonized texts do not necessarily affirm an inclusive nature of the terms of political engagement. A closer and more meticulous appraisal of the cultural and cosmic traits of one's rivals often entailed an assertion of sectarian and religious difference.[20]

In peninsular India, as discussed in this book's introduction, historians often link the problem of multilingualism to the question of ethnicity and something called local identity. Some studies emphasize the idea that Muslims of Iranian stock in southern India only associated with Persian while the literary idiom of Dakkani was used only by Muslims born in peninsular India.[21] These conclusions partly stem from the tendency to rely on Persian court chronicles in a space where the sociological base of this language was admittedly very small—but one of many spoken and written tongues with multiple textual traditions.[22] Moving beyond Persian, still others have made the case for disassociating language with ethnicity and religion altogether—for instance, by exploring Telugu poets who eulogized Persian-speaking patrons.[23]

In such a multilingual environment, the choice to depict Khan Baba in the panregional literary idiom of Dakkani was by no means an anomaly or an extraordinary endeavor. Contemporaries who followed and described Khan Baba's troubling second house arrest by Sultan Muhammad 'Adil Shah in 1643 were all part of a wider circuit of literati taking sides for and against this household chief and his often-sidelined son-in-law, the king. Mirza Muqim's composition, *Fathnāma-yi Ikkeri*, complements the narrative projected by Khan Baba's Persian chronicler friends, such as Zuhur ibn Zuhuri and Fuzuni Astarabadi, who saw the episode of his arrest as an example of erroneous judgment by the sultan and an instance of a trying time that tested their patron's endurance.[24] It should come as no surprise, then, that this patron chose two tongues to capture his political ambitions, not just in Persian but in Dakkani, that the latter of which competed for the same patronage circuits as Persian.[25]

Let us turn now to the broad features of the work at hand, *Fathnāma-yi Ikkeri*. In terms of its overall structure, this narrative poem is divided into seven sections, each with a heading in Persian followed by a narration in Dakkani. Its plot follows the stages of war-making and conquest—from the first news of trouble on the frontier to the preparations and planning for battle, a description of war-making, and, finally, diplomacy and the moment of negotiating peace with the enemy.

The scenes include various dramatizations of a historical event. For instance, the poet versifies multiple conversations of a pensive sultan holding court with his advisors, pivoting to the moment when he turns to his prime minister and father-in-law Mustafa Khan's wise counsel about how to resolve Sivappa Nayak's revolt. Then come the names and titles of officials and heads of other prominent households who accompany the hero on his campaign. Mustafa Khan's household and his army then make a treacherous journey beyond the court in the Deccan into the unfamiliar wilderness and formidable forts of the Karnatak; this is followed by descriptions of the ethnicities of his troops who were of varied lineages, hailed from different lands, and spoke many languages. Emulating the tone of reportage also common in chronicles, Mirza Muqim dramatizes the exchange of letters and ambassadors between the hero, Mustafa Khan, and his enemy, Sivappa Nayak, who begs for mercy and forgiveness and in the poem's closing scene, submitting at the end of the siege of Ikkeri. As a result, the sultan expresses his deep gratitude to Mustafa Khan by presenting him with honors.

More than in contemporary Persian chronicles, in this poem the figure of the sultan serves as a foil to its hero, Mustafa Khan. The king appears only briefly in the beginning and the end, in both scenes to praise, promote, and express gratitude toward the hero. The purpose of such heroic depictions was not merely propaganda on the patron's behalf or some tool to legitimize him.[26] Mirza Muqim portrays Mustafa Khan in this text foremost as a user—listener and speaker—of kindred competitive tongues, Persian and Dakkani. And yet, this portrait is less about citing the patron's stake in the vernacular. Instead, the shifting use of each language within the poem signals the narrative arch of political incorporation and a politics of linguistic code-switching at the crossroads of two geographic subregions, the Deccan and the Karnatak. Going beyond conventional binaries of court chronicles, Mirza Muqim sketches a Mustafa Khan in the opening act of military conflict, hurling obscene Dakkani insults at the enemy. And moments later, in the closing act of negotiating peace, the same prime minister delivers a speech entirely in Persian, gesturing toward his rival's political incorporation.

Mirza Muqim opens the Ikkeri episode with Sultan Muhammad 'Adil Shah pensive and worried about the fort's fall. The sultan calls on Khan Baba, who assures him that he will take care of Ikkeri as the sultan praises his skills in battle. After some deliberation and consultation with court astrologers, he decides on a day for the siege. The army begins the journey on 22 Shawwal, 1053/Wednesday, January 3, 1644, camping at Bankapur for a few days until the day of battle on 10 Zu al-Qa'dah, 1053/January 10, 1644.[27] Muqim constructs a scene of Mustafa Khan's army marching into the city of Bankapur, followed by a long list of other prominent household chiefs who accompanied him. This list includes broad categories of ethnicities used to categorize soldiers (much like the descriptive rolls examined in chapter 2), such as Habshis, Afghans, Mughals, Chaghatays, Qizilbash, Marathas and Turks. Along with their names, the poet extols their virtues on the battlefield. A common convention used across many Persianate texts, ethnographic observations of armies present the hero—in this case, Mustafa Khan—as surrounded by an extended network of kinfolk, who were not necessarily tied by blood nor religion but by ties of service. The poet writes of those who accompanied Mustafa Khan on the Ikkeri expedition in these words:

> *chaliyā siddī rehān solāpur kā,*
> *silah band marjān bednūr kā.*
>
> along went Siddi Rehan of Solapur,
> fastening his weapons, he set off for Bednur.
>
> *ketī aur gāntī marāthī vazīr,*
> *jinan nanūn likhne na āwe dabīr.*
>
> they there were Kate, Ghorpade, Marathi ministers
> a secretary cannot write so many names.

Close ethnographic observations of armies, common in Persianate texts, were not merely ornate descriptions, giving a litany of names. Mirza Muqim's ability to distinguish different lineages according to their ethnic, regional, occupational, and linguistic markers is curious if one proceeds on the assumption that he was an émigré poet. But this is not surprising at all if we think of him as a regional poet to whom the distinctions between Marathi-speaking Bijapuri courtiers may have been far more recognizable. The long list gives a precise record of those who accompanied Mustafa Khan on the Ikkeri expedition, along with an affirmation of their skills and valor on the battlefield. To further contrast the social diversity within Mustafa Khan's ranks, the poet then turns to a careful appraisal of the enemy, Sivappa Nayak, but with a different tone and purpose. Difference is marked in both cases but for distinct outcomes. The variety of regional clans and ethnicities that fell under and obeyed Mustafa Khan are emphasized to indicate the extent of his political authority. In contrast, the social and cultural differences of those who defied this authority indicate their political otherness. In the latter case, social and cultural difference is exaggerated to highlight who was outside the household, rather than who was included in it. To premodern political observers, what mattered most when producing such representations of political violence was the distance of any figure or social group from a certain authority. As such, in their eyes, the Marathas and nayaka chiefs signified very specific sociological and sectarian entities rather than an anachronistic homogenous, undifferentiated group of Hindus.

In the next few chapters, the poet recounts the exchange of letters and emissaries between Mustafa Khan in Bankapur and Sivappa Nayak in Ikkeri. He uses political insults to demonstrate a familiarity with the enemy's cultural practices. Sivappa Nayak was an enemy not simply because he was an infidel but also because he was an uncouth and uncultured man. Mustafa Khan's insults of Sivappa Nayak are self-explanatory:

> samajh kuch bhī aisī le na pāk tūn,
> huā yūn kī be-sud va bebāk tūn.
>
> you, who have come to think like this, filthy fellow
> you, who have become senseless and disobedient
>
> baṛī khūb khūbī tu hāsil kiyā,
> ke ap sain jahannam men vāsil kiyā.
>
> you think you have done a good deed or two
> but, these shall only ensure your entrance in hell.

Khan Baba's threats and belittling continue in the letter toward the end of which he declares:

> ange dekh tadbīr ap jiyū ke,
> ke bhujte nahīn hain agan ghiyū te.
>
> look ahead to the plan of your death,
> for a blazing fire cannot be put out with ghī (clarified butter).
>
> hove mast bekar pive mūt kon,
> na purā paṛe shīr avadhūt kon.
>
> intoxicated from drinking your own urine,
> and yet, even that is not enough milk for an *avadhūt* like you.

Muqim compares Sivappa Nayak to mendicants who lived on the banks of rivers and consumed human excreta, urine, and the flesh of the dead, an analogy not entirely outlandish. In common Hindustani parlance, *avadhūt* and *aghore* are often used together to identify *aghor panthis*, a religious mendicant order that worships Shiva and is synonymous with filth and impurity, also associated with dark magic and occult practices. The poet portrays his patron as someone familiar with Shaivite sects and ascetics of the Deccan, with the ability to deploy his knowledge of the enemy's sectarian affiliation as a means to put him in his place.

Muqim identified who fell within and who fell outside his patron's authority through a fine sociological profile of both friends and enemies. The repetition of the tropes like believer versus nonbeliever and cultured versus uncultured symbolically marks a political authority that included many diverse constituents. Mustafa Khan's circuit had Marathas like Shahaji and Mambaji, and Afghans like Bahlol Khan, whose names and lineages the poet contrasted against the uncultured social practices of the enemy, Sivappa Nayak. But there was never a moment when, in the social taxonomy of the Persian chronicler or Dakkani poet, that the

Marathas, Indo-Africans, or the nayaka chiefs were grouped neatly according to sectarian difference, with Hindus and Muslims on opposite sides of a political conflict. Rather, Muqim's precise ethnography subsumed different constituents within the patron's world and marked specific distinctions between them to show the limits of his authority.

In the poem's fourth section, the poet summarily describes the siege of Ikkeri, which lasted only five days. After one attack by Mustafa Khan's infantry and cavalry, the fort was shattered. With his defeat imminent, Sivappa Nayak writes to Khan Baba, asking to be forgiven and pleading for peace. The scene begins with the rebellious nayakas losing their senses and Sivappa Nayak expressing regret in a monologue. To articulate his apologies to Khan Baba, he summons a "bilingual letter-writer who knows Persian very well" (*bula bhej apnā du bhāshī dabīr / ke buje jita khūb fārsī zamīr*). Such lines are rare and suggest the poet Mirza Muqim's ability to traverse multiple linguistic registers, a trait perhaps lacking in his Persian-speaking contemporaries. He often observes that some political rivals operated in a language different from his own. Muqim notes each historical actor's choice of language and specificity of speech to capture moments of translation and linguistic overlay that were part of transcending the borders of the Deccan and the Karnatak.

In the rest of this letter, Sivappa Nayak assures Khan Baba that he will no longer make trouble. He urges the prime minister to believe him, pledging never to tread the path of treachery. He asks Mustafa Khan to let bygones be bygones and if he is forgiven, he promises to prostrate himself before the sultan. A messenger delivers Sivappa Nayak's letter to Khan Baba, recounting it verbally. In such moments of reconciliation all the lofty ideals (to destroy infidels, etc.) conventionally repeated at the beginning of heroic texts take a back seat. The preferred form of resolution is to absorb rivals into and under one's political authority. Khan Baba thus promises Sivappa Nayak, "*yahī qaul merā wa mujh shah kā / ke farzand sahī hai tu dargāh kā*" (This is the promise of my king and me / That you are a true son of the court). He honors the messenger with betel nut; the latter then departs to deliver the good news to the nayak. In the meantime, Khan Baba sends a *waqi'a nawīs* (intelligencer) to the sultan who, pleased to hear of Sivappa Nayak's defeat, in turn issues a *farmān* (decree). Sivappa Nayak, delighted at this news, selects the finest gifts and eight lakh *huns* (gold coins) as tribute for the king.

In the second to last scene, we witness Khan Baba's ceremonial reception of Sivappa Nayak at the Ikkeri fort. Khan Baba's speech here is entirely in Persian. This type of code-switching indicates a shift in the political relations between Mustafa Khan and his rival. The language moves qualitatively from threats and insults hurled in the intimate tone of Dakkani in the earlier part of the poem, to a formal language of political incorporation and resolution in Persian in its conclusion. In addition, whereas in the beginning during the confrontation, Sivappa's behavior is aggressive, proud, and insolent, in the moment of political reconciliation, his character idealizes humility and mercy:

utha sar kon nawāb sāhib shiko,
pe chātī lagā ho, kahiyā u guruh.

the honorable Nawab lifted him,
embracing him, addressing him, he said:

safāyī tu bāshad darīn bazm-gāh,
ke kardam ze shafaqat . . . bar tū nigāh.

you must stay pure in this court,
I have taken pity upon you and cleared you of your sins.

rah khūb khūbī tū burd āshtī,
ke bā mā giraftī tā āshtī.

you took the right path, the path of peace,
and you made peace with us.

shawad behtar aknūn hameh kār-i tū,
be har jā ke bāsham nigehdār tū.

now all your works will become better,
everywhere I am, I will protect you.

At the end of this scene, Mirza Muqim gives perhaps a quiet hint to his choice (and skill) in composing in both Dakkani and Persian, an implicit reflection on multilingualism. Describing his patron's generosity, he asks—"*sifat tis sadr ka kahūn kis zabān? / ʿajaib dise dar nazr begumān*" (in which language shall I express this master's traits? / He appears wondrous and incomparable to the eye). Mirza Muqim's and Mustafa Khan's literary sphere was hardly an unmixed, exclusive universe of Persian, but one in which an emerging panregional literary idiom competed for the same circuits of prestige and patronage. Equating the Dakkani language with a homogenous regional identity in south-central India alone fails to explain why such martial works repeat the same conventions for depicting patrimonial power shared across many vernaculars throughout northern and southern India. From the *jangnāma* to *risalo*, the warrior chief is shown across different South Asian martial traditions as a figure who enabled wider participation and adaptation across linguistic zones, inviting multiple communities into his networks.[28] These texts are not intriguing because they show a one-to-one correspondence between region and language; they are intriguing because they emphasize the politics of circulation embodied in a central protagonist shown engaging with multiple languages and moving across cultural and political borders with followers of multiple social backgrounds.

Enemy ethnography in Dakkani poems captures a moment of encounter more intimate and informal than the one represented in Persian chronicle narrations

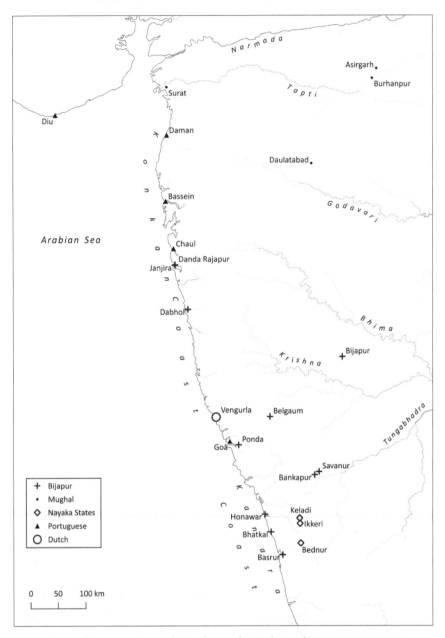

MAP 5. Indo-Africans, Iranians, and Marathas on the Konkan and Kanara coasts, ca. 1650. Drawn by Kanika Kalra.

of political violence and conflict. The contest recounted here unsettles received wisdom and neat typologies of both the patron's identity and the poet's choice of language, form, and content. Mirza Muqim, perhaps an émigré Persian or a Deccani, positioned his patron as a user who deployed two sibling tongues for navigating political, ecological, and cultural borders within peninsular India. To be sure, Mirza Muqim identifies Sivappa Nayak through the common conventions of the conquest poem, as a non-Muslim who stood in the righteous path of Islam. But then he apprehends and incorporates the enemy into the process of reconciliation through a much deeper appraisal of the adversary's cultural cosmology. The practice of code-switching from intimate insults in Dakkani to the negotiation of peace in Persian signals the enemy's absorption into a political authority.

Through such a multivalent portrait, Mirza Muqim signals his patron's place and participation in peninsular India's polyvocal literary ecology. He constructs a second-generation Iranian émigré, moving with his household, friends, and followers away from the city of Bijapur to the highlands of the Karnatak in pursuit of Sivappa Nayak, an enemy with whom he had no language, sect, or ethnicity in common. In the intimate vernacular register, he emphasizes a rival's alterity by marking his uncultanredness, uncleanliness, and insolence. A meticulous appraisal of one's rivals in one tongue, and then the rapid plot twist in the higher linguistic register of Persian constructs a narrative of successful political incorporation into a ghar. The contrast of insult and derision in transregional Dakkani versus the negotiation of peace in cosmopolitan Persian signals the hero's journey from conquest to victory and his ability to not only recognize social differences but transcend them.

NEITHER FRIEND NOR ENEMY: KINFOLK IN THE MARITIME BUREAUCRACY

One of the central goals of this book is to locate the household in the practice of connected histories—the practice of reading across multilingual archives and transcending the fixed geographic conventions associated with them. The foundational sociological unit of the household has remained somewhat invisible in studies that examine large-scale political phenomenon such as interimperial diplomacy, the world of kings, and courtly encounters.[29] State-building elites and monarchical authority have both been examined across South Asian and European sources, oftentimes by focusing on singular figures, reconstructing the history of great men. Such reconstructions partly have to do with the limitations of premodern archives, where the thickest trails of materials often center on individual figures.[30] How, then, do we find the myriad affinal and consanguineal ties that sustained the multiple geographic and linguistic worlds of a household chief? To reconstruct the world beyond and around singular figures, I argue that we read the archive of cultural history, like the vernacular heroic poem *Fathnāma-yi Ikkeri*, alongside and against the archive of social and economic history found in Persian and European documentary materials that reveal the day-to-day administrative lives of relatives, friends, and political competitors.

The recent work of Jorge Flores on Portuguese words generated by indigenous scribes in late eighteenth-century western India has illuminated the possibility of tracing how capaciously indigenous oral genres and cultures of recording influenced representations of contending voices in the colonial archive.[31] Following these studies, I examine actual intersections in European and Persian-language documents that converged on specific conflicts of interest between household and state power. In this section, I continue with the case of Mustafa Khan and his extended household by tracing out how and when different family members utilized their bureaucratic offices to challenge kingly authority. By reading for conflicting voices across Persian and European-language documentary sources, I show how Indic Muslim elites sought to hold bureaucratic offices in perpetuity, thus forging a form of belonging firmly entrenched in the politics of caste.

While the place of the household has remained somewhat invisible in connected histories, the portrait of the court in the vernacular literary archive used by regional specialists also has its limits. Literary narratives such as the *Fathnāma-yi Ikkeri* show the political aspirations of an all-powerful patron at the crossroads of multiple cultural worlds. Endless victories on the battlefields, successful sieges of forts, and the skillful incorporation of rivals narrated in two kindred tongues occlude the everyday operations of elite households that were, above all, sustained by a maze of bureaucratic offices that connected the court to Indian Ocean port cities. The trope of the king as foil to the heroic household chief found in literary narratives was only just partly propaganda. Beneath this literary dyad lay the everyday reality of bureaucratic offices and administrative norms that undergirded the tension between household and kingly power. By cross-reading documentary evidence in Persian, Portuguese, and Dutch from the last few years of Mustafa Khan's career, I show the fraught terrain over which different members of this household sought to consolidate their hold on bureaucratic offices. In a period of contested and overlapping sovereignties during which empire transformed regional politics, granting relatives administrative posts not meant to be held as hereditary turned into sites of contesting power.

It is well known that Indo-Islamic states throughout South Asia's past relied on non-Muslim scribal and learned elites, who held hereditary offices such as *desai* (chief of a *pargana* or division), *deshkulkarni* or, *deshpande* (accountant or record keeper) to collect taxes, govern villages, and perform everyday administrative tasks.[32] In contrast, centrally appointed Muslim "crown bureaucrats," as Hiroshi Fukazawa called them, were rarely assigned positions in perpetuity and were transferred with greater frequency from one appointment to another and regulated much more stringently by the sultan. By studying a Konkani Brahmin family of Patvardhan sardārs in the Ratnagiri district in the eighteenth century, he was among the first scholars to illuminate how the early Maratha state consolidated its control over scattered local chiefs. He showed how, starting in the reign of Shahu Bhonsle (d. 1749), the rise of "new bureaucrats" in the eighteenth century helped assign central offices as hereditary fiefs instead of transferrable ones.[33]

By exploring contentions among relatives holding different bureaucratic offices, I argue that an earlier echo of this pattern can already be found in the first half of the seventeenth century among Indic Muslim elites in the sultanates. Using multilingual archives, I argue for reversing the lens, so to speak, on the familial pasts of Indic Muslim state-building elites. Often simply written out of the history of bureaucracy, caste and social formations are rarely studied in dialogue with the patterns that have long been observed for elite Hindus and their relationship with Indo-Islamic imperial and regional institutions.[34]

The purpose of examining a Muslim émigré household's bureaucratic functions and internal frictions in the seventeenth century is twofold. The period of Mughal suzerainty emboldened the assertion of household autonomy from monarchical power creating the possibility for transforming centrally appointed bureaucratic offices into hereditary occupational ones. The assumption that regional Muslim sultanates were merely "alien ones," where non-Muslims controlled village-level administration, as Fukazawa had shown in his pioneering work on Persian and Marathi documentary materials, leaves out the question of conflicts within and across elite Muslim households appointed to bureaucratic offices and their relationship to kingly authority.[35] Elite Muslim households of peninsular India, such as that of Mustafa Khan, tapped into the very same mechanisms for entrenching social power that non-Muslim elites had—that is, by sustaining themselves as occupational-status or subcaste groups with a hereditary hold over bureaucratic offices. From these critical posts, household members also regulated increasing Luso-Dutch competition in the western Indian Ocean.

THE VIEW FROM VENGURLA

In the 1640s, as members of Mustafa Khan's household dispersed over the Karnatak, they collided with a wider set of changes unfolding across the Indian Ocean. Whereas Syriam (in southwestern Burma or Myanmar) and Hormuz (in southern Iran) fell to the Dutch and English East India Companies in the 1610s and 1620s and Melaka (on the southwest coast of the Malay Peninsula) in 1641,[36] Portuguese power along the Konkan coast survived but was weakened by frequent challenges from the Dutch East India Company, especially through their newly established factory at Vengurla, located just north of Goa. After Bijapur granted the Dutch permission to settle there in 1637, Vengurla was set up under the direct control of Batavia.[37] The factory at Vengurla had a strategic rather than a commercial purpose—namely, hindering movement in and out of Portuguese Goa.[38] Unlike in the case of the factories in Bengal and on the eastern Coromandel coast, precious metals did not flow into this factory. Instead, goods from other parts of the Indian Ocean, such as Indonesian spices (nutmeg, cloves, and mace) and Malayan tin from Melaka, were traded with Vengurla.

Without any assistance from Bijapur and as early as 1621, jointly the English and Dutch unsuccessfully tried to blockade Goa, a blockade resumed by the Dutch in 1635.[39] Although Muhammad 'Adil Shah repeatedly issued orders that exempted the Dutch from tolls in his territories, members of Mustafa Khan's household, who held different bureaucratic offices, disobeyed the sultan and continued to harass the Dutch for payments.[40] While most of the revenues from Vengurla went toward the maintenance of crews at the factory,[41] elite households affiliated with the sultanate of Bijapur were the prime buyers of war supplies—such as saltpeter from the southeastern Coromandel, horses from Masqat, and elephants from Sri Lanka—from this port city facing the Arabian Sea.[42] The case of Vengurla was therefore no different than that of Pulicat on the Coromandel coast between 1610 and 1640, when elite households affiliated with regional courts determined the trajectory of the rivalry between the VOC and Portuguese Goa.[43]

LETTERS FROM AN IRATE SULTAN: THE HOUSEHOLD UNDER ARREST

The movement of different ambassadors in and out of Bijapur made it evident to Dutch officials at Vengurla that they were but one of many suitors at the court. For example, Mustafa Khan's family owned ships that moved between Vengurla and Bhatkal and the Persian Gulf, and, when ambassadors from Safavid Iran arrived in Bijapur, some were brought over on VOC vessels.[44] In 1639, a Safavid ambassador arrived on the Dutch ship *Harderwijk* via Dabhol, stating his principal request was that the Bijapur sultan wage war against the Mughals. Otherwise, he claimed, the Safavid sultan would threaten to destroy all the frigates coming from Bijapur to the Persian Gulf. He added that the tribute paid annually by the 'Adil shahs to the Mughals could instead be paid to the king of Persia![45] The Dutch reported that the Bijapur sultan, for his part, waited and did not answer the Safavid ambassador's request and proposition.

The Dutch chief merchant, Pieter Paets, reported on other European ambassadors who appeared in Bijapur, where the Dutch themselves waited for hours on end for an audience with the sultan. He had a chance to observe the Portuguese ambassador's visit to Bijapur in September 1639. Although the sultan and Mustafa Khan honored this Portuguese ambassador with gifts of a horse, gold embroidered cloth, and a silk veil for his wife, Paets observed that the youngest son of Mustafa Khan did not want to talk to the ambassador, saying that he did not "wish to be either friends or enemies with the Dutch or the Portuguese" (*maer den jongsten soon van den Hartoch en heeft geseijde Portugeesen Ambassadeur niet te spraack willen staen seggende met de Hollanders ende Portugeesen te gelijck geen vijanden segge vrienden*).⁴⁶ Although all the orders granted to the Portuguese during the sultan's father's (Ibrahim ʿAdil Shah II) time were renewed, there appeared to be no consensus within Mustafa Khan's sons and relatives on which Europeans they were going to side with.

In this context of regional family dynamics constantly determining the commercial and political fortunes of Europeans on the coast, Mustafa Khan's nephew-in-law, Muhammad Reza, emerged as a partisan of Portuguese Goa. Early in 1640, in his capacity as havaldār (governor) of Ponda, Reza reprimanded the Dutch for failing to follow diplomatic protocol. In a letter, he chided them for not sending news of the arrival of their new fleet at Vengurla and questioned them about why no one was sent to pay dues to his uncle-in-law, Mustafa Khan. He also kept a close eye on the VOC's negotiations with Goa.⁴⁷ The VOC complained often of the lack of commitment to drive out the Portuguese, who they believed were their weakest naval rival, and did not understand why, despite the promise to do so by the Bijapuris five years before, the Portuguese still managed to burn down the fortress of Mormugão and take its guards as fugitives.⁴⁸ All this time, the commander of the Dutch fleet off Goa's coast, Dominicus Bouwens, wrote separately to the Bijapur king and to Mustafa Khan, insisting that not enough was being done to contain the Portuguese, who, in the early 1640s, continued to have enthusiastic supporters like the havaldār of Ponda.⁴⁹

Bouwens reported to Sultan Muhammad ʿAdil Shah on the activities of Muhammad Reza, whose letters the VOC intercepted at Melaka,⁵⁰ likely believing they could expel the Portuguese entirely from Goa if they had the full backing of his extended family and the sultan of Bijapur. This was similar, in a way, to the alliance they would soon forge with the sultanates of Aceh and Johor in Southeast Asia against the Portuguese in Melaka in 1641. Never a reassuring ally, on June 4, 1641, Muhammad Reza brokered a contract with the Portuguese viceroy on behalf of Sultan Muhammad ʿAdil Shah and his prime minister Mustafa Khan, on the one hand. At the same time, he made a deal with the Portuguese viceroy. Just a few months after the Iberian Union had ended, but before news of its demise had not yet reached Portuguese domains in Asia, both parties promised to set aside previous differences and begin anew.⁵¹ The Portuguese agreed to provide the full support of their fleet to Bijapur while the latter was expected to remove all Dutch residents from the areas in and around Vengurla.

Further, with or without a *qaul* or deed of assurance from the sultan, the contract ensured that Muslim merchants would be allowed to trade in hitherto forbidden items such as elephants, horses, slaves, incense, ginger, and so on. The havaldār's contract also stipulated that the viceroy be allowed to remove the Dutch from Vengurla and all other places on the coast while the contents of their establishment and goods would be kept as loot. Both parties promised to aid each other militarily and each would keep an ambassador in Goa and Bijapur.⁵² Whether or not the Bijapur sultan agreed to any of these articles remains unknown, but in his role as the governor of Ponda, Muhammad Reza now openly declared himself a partisan of the Portuguese even though his maternal uncle, Mustafa Khan, was known to despise them. This was by no means the first time that the havaldār had taken it on himself to represent the sultan and negotiate independently with the Portuguese with the ostensible goal of driving out the VOC.

The second arrest of Mustafa Khan (1642–43), right around the time of his victory over the nayaka of Ikkeri, appears somewhat different when seen through the prism of negotiations between his two feuding *dāmād*—namely, his nephew-in-law havaldār Muhammad Reza and his son-in-law sultan Muhammad ʿAdil Shah. Although the governor of Ponda and his ambitions in the Konkan are never mentioned in Persian chronicles, they are hardly inconspicuous in European-language archives. In one letter dating from February 28, 1642, Muhammad Reza requested that the Portuguese assist him against the Bijapur army, which was making its way to the coast. While some members of the Portuguese state council agreed that any outright assistance to the havaldār would unsettle and provoke the sultan, others did not wish for Muhammad Reza to side with the VOC either. Although the council eventually dodged the request, they concurred that the more there were people rebelling against the ʿAdil Shahi king, the better it would be for Goa.[53]

To trace these multiple layers, we can again look to the unexpected turn negotiations took at the time of Mustafa Khan's second house arrest. On October 1, 1643, the Bijapur ambassador reported that the sultan had taken Mustafa Khan prisoner along with his two sons and Muhammad Reza's father-in-law, Shah Saheb (Xa Saibo). The havaldār feared it would be his turn next, as he was Mustafa Khan's creature (*era feitura sua*). The ambassador requested of the viceroy that Muhammad Reza be given safe conduct, allowing him to come to Goa and from there proceed to Persia or wherever else he wished to go with this family and servants.[54] The council also calculated correctly that since Mustafa Khan and Shah Saheb were known to be close to the Mughals, they might soon be released. Predictably, the Mughal emperor Shah Jahan did eventually intervene and compel the Bijapur sultan to set Mustafa Khan free.[55] While Mustafa Khan was jailed in Belgaum, Muhammad Reza wrote once again to Goa, asking for a safe conduct (*seguro*) to go to Mecca with his family, fearing Sultan Muhammad ʿAdil Shah planned to arrest his entire household. It was pointed out to the council that the havaldār still owed 48,480 xerafins for his plan to throw the Dutch out of Vengurla. Before supporting his escape, it was recommended that this amount be paid back. Besides, the costs of taking Muhummad Reza's family to Surat would likely be prohibitive, not to mention that the Bijapur sultan would then immediately clamor for his return.[56]

Not long after the safe conduct was given to Muhammad Reza, Sultan Muhammad ʿAdil Shah wrote a furious letter to the council on November 16, 1643, in which he asked the viceroy to hand over Muhammad Reza, who had escaped to Goa with a safe conduct. The sultan's letter was described as bad-tempered (*descomposta*) and the meeting minutes noted it was completely out of keeping with the norms of correspondence. The king's letter implicated the havaldār and his maternal uncle-in-law, Mustafa Khan; it runs as follows (in its Portuguese version):[57]

> To the one who resides in great state, [whose] government is full of good fortune, [who is] obeyed by his subjects, luminous in fame and spirit, steadfast in peace, informed of all news, feared, and with power over many, the chosen of the law of the messiah, the whale and lion of the sea, João da Sylva Tello, viceroy of the state of Goa, may he ever be secure and contented, to whom this is written, with love and with pearl-like letters, so that the following may be known:
>
> Despite the fact that Mostafacão did not merit my royal grants and graces, I covered him with them; and when he had them all, he did not know how to benefit from them, and forgetting them he became ungrateful and went about doing bad and dishonest things. And when I was informed of his evil actions and bad works, I became greatly annoyed, and for that reason I had the said ingrate and his sons seized and put in prison, with all the other people who were his dependents and supporters, which included one Mamede Reza, who had the Concão in his charge, which [region] gives much profit to my crown and treasury, and sustains and feeds many people. He being despicable, and rooted in evil and unworthy intentions, and wholly lacking in wisdom, had placed the said Concão and its lands in a poor condition.

Unlike Persianate courtly literature produced by Mustafa Khan's partisans, which cast him as the sultan's wise consul and confidante, documentary correspondence in Persian, Portuguese, and Dutch reveals troubling relationships within this household, including with his most important son-in-law. The sultan expressed alarm at the speed with which Mustafa Khan's kin had entrenched themselves in each office, particularly those of the havaldār along the coast. While the exact reasoning for the arrest has not been given here either, the memory of Mustafa Khan's first arrest in 1635 is implicit in the above letter. Another letter that interpolates the voice of Sultan Muhammad begins by contrasting the equivalence and camaraderie between a community of monarchs, the dynastic line of the ʿAdil Shahi sultans and the kings of Portugal against the insolence of upstart households like those of Mustafa Khan. Here, the king compares the more modest and humble southern Iranian origins of Muhammad Reza and Mustafa Khan negatively to a family of Sayyids (those who claim descent from the Prophet), who he asserts were his true representatives, appointed now as ambassadors to Goa. Shortly thereafter, the rumor of Muhammad Reza's flight from the Konkan coast reached the sultan's ear who urged that he be handed back over to Bijapur:

> There should be no delay in this, and Your Excellency should look to your own well-being, for this is not a matter that brooks dissimulation, and I swear to God almighty that if there is any delay in this, and if Your Excellency does not pay attention to this, you may be certain that no trace of Goa will be left on the ground. So that Your Excellency should do in every way as I say, and should order the handing over of Mamede Reza to my servants and those of my royal state, along with the money, effects and treasury of Mostafacão, and with everything from my royal treasury and

my crown that he has taken. If Your Excellency does not settle this, and act with the rapidity that is appropriate, there will then be problems and dissensions and tumult, all caused on account of Your Excellency, and the Portuguese in Goa, and not on my account, because I have and possess much friendship with the King of Portugal, and on that account I sent Memede Saide there as my ambassador, with whom you can deal in all matters that concern that state, and through whom everything can be negotiated and settled, for it is understood that the increase in the welfare of both states is made up of this. Written on the twenty-first of the month of Xabana [Shaʿban] in the Moorish year of 1053, which is November 4 of the present year of 1643.[58]

The voice of the king interpolated in the Portuguese letter above uncannily echoes Persian *farmāns* issued to Mustafa Khan's nephew-in-law, the havaldār Muhammad Reza, shortly before the sultan's fall out with him, whereby he again threatened to destroy Goa. Addressing Muhammad Reza, the reasons for the sultan's fury in this order were closely connected to deciding the boundaries of the havaldār's everyday functions and duties, and whether or not he could hold this office in perpetuity. The irate sultan recounted in detail how the havaldār, in cahoots with the Portuguese captain, was going beyond the bounds of his prescribed duties and responsibilities for revenue collection and the regulation of ships. He was responsible for ensuring access to goods, horses, and war materials that flowed from the port city factories to inland bazaars and eventually, to the Karnatak war front, but he had now convinced the Portuguese captain in the port city of Chaul to help him enforce additional customs duties on ships belonging to other prominent elite Bijapuri households. The order opened thus:[59]

> A royal farmān issued to the noble, ever vigilant, peerless well-wisher Mirza Muhammad Reza, the havaldār, in charge of the district of Goa, in the year 1041. During these days it was brought to imperial notice [that] a ship from the port of Chaul was prepared for the [title] choicest of nobles, the progeny of the high-ranking, illuminated, servant of Fars, brave in the battlefield, bold, with thousands of favors, of boundless benevolence and the gracious, the exalted *rustam zamān sipāh sālār* [commander of the sultanate] Randaula Khan, and they wanted that this ship [of his] be sent out to other ports. Captain Rewadanda[60] objected to this and going against the agreements and covenants, he instead wanted to cause damage. *Asad ul-bahr*, the viceroy of the island of Goa, claims to be very sincere and friendly, therefore, that well-wisher should send this case to the viceroy and it should be explained to him and [he should be] made to understand that, God forbid, even if the slightest obstruction is made against the ship of the above-mentioned [Randaula] Khan, he [the viceroy] better believe that at the same time Goa would be destroyed, as the entire army is ready. However, you, a well-wisher, agreeable to our *nawāb* [Mustafa Khan], should also show consideration to *Rustam Zamān*. In short, that well-wisher should emphasize and quickly write a letter in the name of the above-mentioned captain, that there should not be the slightest hindrance in the departure of the ships of the said Khan, and that not an iota be left in helping him out.

The six horses that were brought for the government of the said khan were asked to be taxed, and in this way, the above-mentioned captain is aggravating the demand for *zakāt*. Before we ordered this, twenty-five horses are to be treated as exemptions for the government and a notice had to be issued that the captain should not show such a harsh attitude. But instead [of doing so], he made an excuse that if only these [horses] are brought to Dabhol, they would be permitted to pass. What does he mean by this? (*īn lā falāyīn che ma 'ani dārad*), in the port of Dabhol or the port of Rajapur or Goa, the exalted government is exempt from *zakāt* everywhere! In this situation, the above-mentioned captain was making the wrong excuses and wanted to create *fasād* or disturbance. You better believe that this disturbance will cause the destruction of his house [*kharābī-yi khāneh īshān mutazammin ast*].

Therefore, it should be said in this matter, that you, a well-wisher, should warn the above-mentioned captain that he shall make no more unreasonable demands. The above-mentioned captain, as per rule of the past, harshly demanded 28,000 Lārī [Persian coins]. Before the said port was under someone else, but now is under my government, then, how can it be taxed? A letter should be sent to the Viceroy, emphasizing to the above-mentioned Captain, to make no other demands after this warning. Before this 1 percent *Lārī* coin was taken as *zakāt* from merchants and now they demand 10 percent, because of this reason the ports are suffering. What has always been the practice should be continued and it be emphasized that no excessive demands be made, written on 3rd of the month of Jumada I 1051, 10 August 1641.

It appears from this order that the Portuguese captain of Chaul had been sending Bijapuri vessels back and forth, further south to Dabhol, if they wished to be allowed inland without paying any commercial tax. A partisan of the Portuguese, Muhammad Reza decided to regulate ships and goods belonging to other Bijappur-affiliated officials by increasing the *zakāt* or purchase tax, which was supposed to be fixed at a predetermined and uniform rate. This order concerned the ships of the Indo-African Randaula Khan, identified here with the title, *Rustam Zamān*. Persian chroniclers described the volatile fortunes of Randaula Khan over the course of the first half of the seventeenth century, when he was the keeper of the prized saltpeter-producing area around Danda Rajapur. VOC officials in Vengurla often (mis)identified this Indo-African as one of the sons of Mustafa Khan.[61] Described as a houseborn member of the exalted court (*khānazād-i darbār mu 'ālā*), based on his long service, he appears to have been part of Mustafa Khan's extended group of followers during the Karnatak campaigns.[62] Eventually, after a few infractions against his master, Randaula Khan then declared his autonomy, entrenching his kin in Rajapur by monopolizing the gun trade along the Konkan coast. In the order above, Sultan Muhammad 'Adil Shah came to the Indo-African's defense, expressing exasperation at Muhammad Reza's failure to allow the free movement of Randaula Khan's shipments from the Konkan to the hinterland.

Chiding the letter's recipient, the sultan emphasized the transferability of the havaldār's office, reminding him that it had previously been held by another individual and that it could be taken away again. In the ideal type of such "crown bureaucrats" described by Fukazawa, an individual like Muhammad Reza would not have been allowed to foster a long-term connection to a district and could be moved at any time. The irate words of Sultan Muhammad above, however, unveil that exactly the opposite had been unfolding. Kinfolk from Sultanate-affiliated Indic Muslim households, who had governed *mu'āmalā* (crown lands) with heavy trade and traffic, such as those around Ponda, sought to transform their offices into hereditary appointments, a privilege usually only granted to non-Muslims. In the wake of the Mughal conquest in the 1640s, Sultan Muhammad had sought ways to centralize these offices, partly because members of elite Muslim households accessed a range of resources through them.

The right to collect revenues from trade and tax lay at the heart of the sultan's incensed order. This letter points to a much larger pattern in the sultanates. It lays bare how centrally appointed bureaucrats from elite émigré households could entrench the same rights and privileges into their offices usually associated with the positions held by hereditary village-level officials. Throughout the first half of the seventeenth century, centrally appointed havaldārs were reprimanded for intervening in the revenue collection of districts under the authority of hereditary officials such as *desais* and *deshmukhs*, who were directly responsible for sending that revenue to the capital city.[63] By the mid-seventeenth century, émigré Muslim households that had moved beyond the court and capital city mobilized resources in important entrepôts and trading nodes along the Konkan and Kanara coasts, seeking to hold these offices for extended periods, mirroring the practices of non-Muslim bureaucrats defined by the hereditary occupational roles associated with such offices. This familial mobility connecting maritime and land-based resources produced the possibility for émigré Muslim households consolidating a jāti-like occupational status within the regional bureaucracy.

We learn in a letter from Goa to Muhammad Reza that by November of 1644 the governor of Ponda had not, in fact, fled to Mecca with his family after the showdown with the sultan.[64] By the mid-1640s, things seemed to have come full circle with negotiations settled between the sultan, Mustafa Khan, Muhammad Reza, the VOC, and Goa. Between November 1643 and January 1644, through the Dutch broker who went between Rajapur, the factory at Vengurla, and the capital city of Bijapur, Mustafa Khan received numerous gifts, including Chinese porcelain and cloth with brocade.[65] In February 1644, the Dutch, once again drawing a comparison with their experience in other parts of Asia, seemed to think that Mustafa Khan would ask them to join in an alliance against the Portuguese. They received the news that "Mustafa Khan is on the move with a large army and intends to create an alliance between us and the sultan in order to attack Goa with the said army by land and then to make an attack by water, and conquer their forts, and they can imagine nothing else than that this year Goa will be lost just like Ceylon."[66] The fact that Muhammad Reza was under Portuguese protection and not always in agreement with his uncle-in-law Mustafa Khan or the Bijapur king was quite clear to the VOC who therefore tried to keep him placated. In a letter to Muhammad Reza, who seemed to cast doubt on the Dutch naval assistance that had been used to blockade the Konkan coast, we learn of the temporary suspension of hostilities with Goa and obsequious promises to be of service to Mustafa Khan's family.[67]

The archival trail illuminating the whereabouts of Muhammad Reza after this episode peters out, and he presumably spent the rest of his career in Ponda, possibly passing on his office of havaldār to his descendants. The face-off between him and the sultan in the first half of the seventeenth century would set the terrain for many more conflicts between household and state in the second half of the century, the most famous and well-documented being one of another Iranian émigré Mir Jumla Muhammad Sayyid Ardestani (better known simply as Mir Jumla) against the sultan ʿAbdullah Qutb Shah of Golkonda in the late 1650s. After his release from the Belgaum fort and the siege of Ikkeri in 1644, the merchant Martin Portmans was sent to deliver gifts and a message to Mustafa Khan. He was instructed to check on the Portuguese and the English agents of the Courteen Association, which already had their agents in Danda Rajapur and had sent gifts to the court at Bijapur.[68] Although by this time hostilities had temporarily ceased on all sides, Portmans was still instructed to inquire why, despite the full support of the Dutch fleet during times of war, Bijapur had made peace with the Portuguese.[69] In the late 1640s, Mustafa Khan moved southeast toward the forts of Gutti and Senji as the Karnatak conquest moved away from the Konkan and Kanara coasts toward the Coromandel and eastern Indian Ocean. By 1647, the Bijapur army, under Mustafa Khan, who was reported to have reached the domains of the neighboring sultanate of Golkonda in northern Tamil country.[70]

These two strategies, both central to this process of creating ghar, were fraught with challenges. Through a vernacular self-portrait, on the one hand, and the placement of prominent relatives in the bureaucracy, on the other, household power crossed the borders of Hindustan, Deccan, and the Karnatak through multiple kinds of sociocultural and economic negotiations. The story of Mustafa Khan's household is not easily reducible to the narrative of a dominant empire taking over a blank, listless frontier nor the simplistic idea of foreign Muslims accommodating themselves to local—that is, Indic norms. Rather, the polyvocal self-portrait of a figure with ambiguous affinities to imperial and regional rulers emphasized cultural differences within a space as a means to signal his own ability in discerning and transcending those differences. Conflicts within households and among household members over bureaucratic offices shaped the contours of competition between various European powers. We may close the story of the first half of the seventeenth century, when Mustafa Khan's death was reported to the factory at Vengurla in 1648 and the news of his successor was received with caution by Dutch factors.[71] Mustafa Khan's career was the culmination of a longer and consistent pattern in the Deccan of kingly power and succession mediated by elite households. Instead of measuring the absolute value of indigeneity in this elite émigré household, I have traced how the processes of making home generated a politics of place that entrenched competing kin into critical bureaucratic offices that lay between court and port. In the following chapters (4 and 5), I turn to the question of how this tension between household and state was represented in literary observations of marriage and politics, which were produced at the site of regional court capitals, over the course of the seventeenth century.

4

The Adorned Palace
Narrating Ceremony and Relatedness

A book about households would be incomplete without analyzing the cultures of relatedness that make them possible and how these cultures shape politics. Historians of gender across the precolonial world have long confronted and overcome the challenge of deciphering highly structured literary texts in which we find depictions of relatedness, thereby helping us reconstruct familial and gendered pasts.[1] The dynastic household, in different empires across the Islamic world, is one site where gender's constitutive role in imperial politics and empire building has been examined.[2] Most recently, scholars have paid attention to bodily practices and ethical norms with a focus on men's experiences of courtly etiquette.[3] For the eighteenth century, scholars have addressed questions of gender and slavery by moving beyond heterosocial relations and unearthing how slaves and slave selfhoods constituted political power in South Asia.[4]

Drawing on these studies, this chapter examines how relatedness was portrayed in peninsular India's literary traditions in the period before 1700. In it we continue to explore ghar through cultural representations. It focuses on the making of both dynastic and aristocratic marriages and how rituals of consumption, ceremony, and gifting on these occasions were portrayed in different texts. We find the concept of ghar at the center of literary representations that memorialized relatedness. Poets and participants in kinship ceremonies evoked the notion of ghar, an idealized space that could be built on the foundation of marriage, patronage, or fosterage. From Persian chronicles to Dakkani narrative poems and illustrated manuscripts, regional literati conceived of ghar as both a site of volatility and contention that disrupted monarchical power and concomitantly, as a space of celebration, consumption, and hospitality as new household lineages anchored

FIGURE 3. Nusrati, *tarjiʿ-band* (poem with a return-tie) for Muhammad ʿAdil Shah and Khadija Sultana's wedding (ca. 1630s), calligraphy of ʿAli ibn Naqi al-Din al-Husayni Damghani, fol. 2. OR. 13533 British Library, London.

themselves to kingly authority. How were cultures of relatedness represented and what do they tell us about these two contrasting notions of ghar or the home—how it came to be, and who belonged in it—in the period of Mughal suzerainty in peninsular India? This chapter answers this question by putting uncanonized manuscript materials in multiple languages at center stage. It treats different genres in a polyvocal and intermedia archive as embodied objects that do more than just narrate what happened in the historical past. Rather, these sources are a window into myriad social relations between lineages, genders, and ethnicities that underlay ways of belonging and contesting political power in the Mughal frontier.

In doing so, the chapter emphasizes the book's methodological intervention of cutting across literary and nonliterary archives for writing about relatedness and kinship in precolonial South Asia.

The image of the grand wedding portrayed in music, painting, film, and literature throughout South Asia's past and present commemorates the making of households through marriage, or what in kinship studies is called affinity. From writing about these things in devotional poetry to depicting them in the epics, scholars of South Asian literary traditions have argued that every ritual and ceremony associated with this major life event reinforces social norms and hierarchies.[5] Weddings are volatile moments when norms are reinforced and transgressed. A sense of drama lies at the heart of this occasion, no matter where its cultural location is. From a brother taking offense at a marriage proposal for his sister to an aunt being disappointed by a gift from the groom's mother, unsaid frictions reveal the difficulties of creating relatedness between unrelated individuals. Prose, poetry, and material culture from the early modern Deccan turned to the canvas of the grand wedding to celebrate affinity, or what Persianate literati called *khusūr-dāmādī kardan* (to contract affinity by marriage), and other major life stages such as kingly births, circumcisions, and accessions to the throne.

Although such kinship portraits have long been dismissed as mere embellishments, addendums, or distractions from political history, I argue that the patronage bonds between those depicted and those who produced the representations, along with the narrative conventions and polysemic festivity portraits, embody the shifting relationship between monarchical and nonmonarchical power in peninsular India. As I argued in the introduction, kingly power occupies center stage in South Asia's history, especially under the Timurid Mughals of northern India, the subcontinent's largest and longest precolonial dynastic line. This book tells a different story of the Mughals, from the eyes of those who lay beyond the imperial realm. To do so, it must first investigate the valence of kingly power in the south—a region that had long been characterized by decentralized forms of sovereignty—and what happened to these patterns when the Mughals intervened in the region militarily and culturally. How was the relationship between kingship and kinship represented in texts during the period of imperial occupation?

This chapter taps into two very different kinds of texts that both have distinct relationships to "history" and "history-writing." Persian prose chronicles, a genre that necessitated the projection of absolute order and kingly authority, reported on each event of a royal marriage, listing the attendees with their official ranks and visitors who had come from neighboring polities, such as the Mughals and Safavids. Compositions in Dakkani, too, affirm an idealized hierarchy of kingly authority under which different kinds of household chiefs and their kin operated. These works emphasize aristocratic and military households as participants in and patrons of ceremony, spending resources on everyday rituals on par with the monarch. Dakkani poets, although less concerned with listing the names and roles of court members, were also invested in capturing a wedding's sensory and performative canvas, which I reconstruct in the chapter's third part. The latter texts may cultivate a relationship with "historical" events and had different degrees of engagement with figures, dates, and events. But they were part of a larger literary ecology and shaped by concepts, metaphors, and images that constituted poetic craftsmanship.

In terms of sources where kinship narratives can be found, the Deccan offers both old and new textual genres to explore: snapshots of kings as sons and grooms, queens as mothers, daughters, brides, and kingmakers; patrons and elite male household chiefs as in-laws and paternal uncles; and slaves as trusted friends appear intermittently in a mosaic of texts. The cast of characters that occupies center stage in this chapter do not appear in a linear narrative or in chronological archival documents. Persian chroniclers reported on the king's marriages with stock images and topoi, common to this genre across Islamic courts.[6] Beyond Persian prose, narrative poems composed in Dakkani, the panregional literary idiom, contain ceremonial portraits that celebrated the making of affinal bonds. Likewise, when trying to make sense of regional politics, the Portuguese and the Dutch commented on marriages, accessions, and friendships that cut across different lineages.

Literary works depict ceremonies that created relationships between lineages by listing who participated and describing the quality of the gifts, the variety of foods prepared, and itemizing the amount of money spent. The king, often put at the center of these portraits, served as a foil in the narrative, offset against other political actors who partook in and patronized texts that depicted ceremony and ritual. Courtly observers celebrated these occasions partly to allay anxieties about a prospective proposal or assuage fears about political instability and the social standing of different households, aristocratic and dynastic. In this chapter, I examine fraught moments in idealized representations of ceremony in Persianate and European texts, focusing on the tumultuous decades of the 1630s and 1640s, when the Deccan sultanates accepted imperial suzerainty under the Mughals, partially acceding their sovereignty to their northern overlords. Shortly thereafter, a cluster of marriages took place in the Deccan kingdoms of Bijapur and Golkonda, when Sultan Muhammad ʿAdil Shah (r. 1627–56) came to power after a succession dispute.[7] Mughal suzerainty created pressures on the Deccan sultans, allowing more autonomy for the households of aristocratic, military, and hereditary rural chiefs. The extension of Mughal power over the region affected how the Deccan sultans could rule—the rising autonomy of high-status households was one outcome of imperial intervention. In chapter 2, we saw, through everyday documentary practices, how the military bureaucracies of Mughal India and the Deccan sultanates intersected, with provincial households exercising more control over war resources such as soldiers, horses, and weapons. In this moment of overlapping imperial-regional sovereignties, then, independent households engaged in interstate marital relations, not below but almost at the same level as dynastic lines, occasions that thereafter became the subjects of literary and visual representation.

From early modern Europe to the Ottoman, Mughal, and Safavid Empires of the Islamic world, scholars have examined different kinds of rituals, what emotions they engender in participants, and how they shape kingly power.[8] Literary images of ceremonies that created relatedness may be read, as Kaya Şahin argues for the circumcision ceremony in the sixteenth-century Ottoman context, not merely as a sign of a sultan's absolute authority but as competing narratives signaling an underlying fragility and negotiation of power with other elite participants.[9] Public ceremonies took on new significance in the context of interimperial rivalries across the early modern world, and the Mughal-Deccan was no exception to this pattern. Ceremonies that created and celebrated kinship became a moment to flaunt and perform, observe and be observed, receive and be received by visitors, emissaries, and travelers from across the globe.[10] Themes as universal as kingship and as natural as kinship were subjects of textual production at a moment when their very contours looked uncertain and contentious. Contemporary observers mapped social status and relationships of affect and obligation through detailed descriptions of courtly ceremony, consumption, and festivity. Chronicles, poems, and the illuminated manuscripts that commemorated relationships of birth (descent) and marriage (affinity) were also objects that embodied alternative forms of relatedness. For example, the bond between the patrons represented in the texts and the courtly literati and artists who produced them—ties between the observer and the observed—remain implicit in these materials.

The mere fact of documenting these events had a dual effect. That the Persian chronicle form recorded the king's marriages is not at all unsurprising. At the same time, other literary forms, such as the Dakkani narrative poem, were deployed to memorialize the forging of affinal ties with independent aristocratic-military households, a fact that is noteworthy in and of itself. The words composed by poets about wedding rituals were then adorned by multiple calligraphers and paper-makers in luxury ateliers. And yet, twentieth-century scholars, replicating Orientalist interpretations of ceremonial description as either pompous or hyperbolic distractions from the political interpret such occasions as merely symptomatic of the sultan's absolute power or the old problem of court factionalism in peninsular Indian polities.[11] I argue, by contrast, that images of ceremonies commemorating ties between individuals from different social backgrounds unveil the elasticity of monarchical as opposed to nonmonarchical forms of power that marks the seventeenth century, not just in the Deccan but across the early modern world.[12] Examining different kinds of objects enables us to reconstruct a history of relatedness and affinity, at times ungoverned by kings and their consanguine households, a tendency that has defined Mughal studies.[13] Alternate forms of relatedness in different textual genres reveal what Marshall Sahlins calls "mutuality of beings," not created by affinity (marriage) and descent (birth) but by the exchange of gifts, sharing food or commensality, friendship, adoption, patron-client, and teacher-discipleship.[14]

One aim of this chapter is to blur the line between dynastic and family histories, a construct that is as old as the subcontinent itself, a dichotomy handed down by colonial historians and the distinct social settings in which such pasts have been produced.[15] South Asian literary traditions have long offered dual portraits of kingship and kinship that often collapse the difference between household and dynastic power, rejecting distinctions between the political and the familial.[16] Not only is this binary indiscernible in precolonial history-writing, it also appears alien to contemporary observers—poets, chroniclers, bards, and their courtly audiences—who recorded, memorialized, and participated in rituals of relatedness. Literary portraits of the grand royal wedding encompassed a series of rituals: *khwāstegārī* or the proposal, *nāmzadī* or engagement, *nikāh/kat khudāī* or the wedding, *jalwa* or the face-showing ceremony, and *widā'* or farewell. Historians in the twentieth century exorcised these scenes, interpreting them as forms of alliance-building and factionalism, or they dismissed the language as decadent literary tangents from a more central political narrative embedded in each text.[17] And yet, edificatory images of relatedness were not just pointless distractions. They functioned within the narrative structure and ideological imperatives of chronicles, eulogies, and narrative poems. They reveal a terrain of affect on which maternal, filial, affinal, consanguine, master-slave, and patron-client ties were negotiated; they are therefore central to the political, not transgressions from it.

Apart from relations of affinity, how do we go beyond kings and queens to understand other forms of relatedness in the subcontinent before 1700? Evidence for nonkingly historical actors, especially women, slave-poets, and high-ranking servants in the period before 1700 is few and far between. I cull together clues about types of relations between individuals from different social backgrounds from veteran Bijapuri poets like Hasan Shauqi, the rising poet Nusrati, and the renowned Abyssinian slave-poet-emissary, Malik Khushnud. Relationships between master-slave and patron-client are often embedded within ceremonial portraits about members of the royal household. An array of materials offers insight into unlikely affective ties between individuals from different ethnicities, descent, status, and language. Literary representations of optative forms of relatedness reveal how institutional and personal differentiation of service to a ghar overlapped with the boundaries and ties of birth and marriage.

A DISPUTED ACCESSION

We may begin here in the 1620s, a decade when a succession dispute unfolded in Bijapur, after the death of Ibrahim 'Adil Shah II (d. 1627). On the eve of the Mughal conquest, the Deccan sultanates were hardly united; nor were they bereft of internal divisions in order to be able to successfully oppose their northern overlords. At the age of seventeen, Muhammad 'Adil Shah came to the throne at the behest of Mustafa Khan or Mullah Muhammad Amin Lari (whom we encountered in the previous chapter) and Daulat Khan or Khawas Khan, two men who would serve as regents for nine years before a conflict that resulted in the latter being put to death in 1636—an event that has long captured the imagination of political historians.[18] Aside from male household chiefs of different backgrounds, competition between women members of the royal household appears to have played a role in this crisis. The details of Muhammad ʿAdil Shah's accession come from an oft-cited Portuguese document from 1629 that sheds light on Bijapur's tense relations with both the Mughals and the neighboring sultanate of Ahmadnagar.[19] This document appears to be the most detailed Portuguese attempt to make sense of Bijapur's court politics in the 1630s and informs us about the relative ranks of different members within the royal household:

> Ibramo Idalxa died some three years ago, and as he was not on friendly terms at the time of his death with the principal queen called Muluco Jahum [Malik Jahan], the daughter of King Cutubuxa of Telangana; he ordered the putting out of the eyes of the heir called Darmes Pataxaa [Darvez Padshah], the oldest and the legitimate son of the said king and of Queen Muluco Jahú, and left the kingdom to a bastard son by the name of Soltão Mamede, the son of Queen Tage Soltão [Taj Sultan] who had been a lady-in-waiting [*dama do paço*] in the palace, and this Soltão Mamede is [now] in his court in Vizapor, and he is fifteen or sixteen years of age, and he governs through a Persian called Mamedeamym, and now he has given him the title of Mostafacão, and he serves as *Canamaluco* [ʿAin-ul-mulk], which is the post of secretary of state of the king, and he is of the Persian nation, and at the time that Fernão d'Alboquerque was governor [1619-22], this Mostafacão was captain of Ponda and the Concão; and inside the palace, a certain Dolatacão has been placed, who always accompanies the king. He is of the oilmen caste; he was a musician at the time of the father of this King, and today he seems to be more the favorite [*valido*]. He has the king's kitchen in his hands, and the kingdom of this Idalxaa is full of Persians, who are enemies of this *Estado*.

The anonymous Portuguese observer comments here on a rivalry between the two queens of Ibrahim ʿAdil Shah—"the principal Queen," Malik Jahan of the neighboring dynastic house of the Qutb shahs, and Taj Sultan (d. 1633), of more humble social origins, who was a high-ranking servant. His observation reflects preexisting anxieties about women consorts and the roles of their extended kin in court politics, a phenomenon not unfamiliar in the Iberian and Catholic context.[20] The young sultan Muhammad's mother, identified as a lady-in-waiting (*dama do paço*) or a so-called "women above stairs," presided over a rival household and successfully bade for her son to become king. What at first appears as a standard Orientalist framing as a succession dispute between a legitimate and illegitimate heir holds within it an anxiety about high-ranking women consorts forging parallel networks with the potential to undercut kingly authority.

This description of stratification between queens and high-ranking women servants is then supplemented with a comment on what appears to be a power-sharing arrangement between male household chiefs of different social backgrounds: Mustafa Khan, a Persian initially in charge of maritime affairs on the Konkan coast, and Daulat Khan, a low-born former musician of the oil-presser caste who held the position of *valido* (akin to the Duke of Lerma or the Count-Duke of Olivares in a contemporary Habsburg context).[21] The anonymous author gives more complex details both about the court and about relations with the problematic neighbor to the north, the Mughals. Noting competition between the households of the Indo-African Ikhlas Khan and that of the émigré Mustafa Khan, the anonymous observer stresses the relative unimportance of the king to the sultanate's growing control over the coastal areas around Portuguese Goa. The Mughal ambassador arrived in the middle of this succession crisis, further complicating Bijapur's internal political dynamics. The anonymous reporter notes the following about the reception of the Mughal envoy, Shaykh Muhyi-ud-Din:

> this ambassador oppresses them a great deal, and each time he asks for whatever he wants, and he [the ʿAdil shah] is now very tired of being a tributary, for the entire kingdom of the Idalxa can sustain some fifty thousand horse, but he does not actually have that many, and he is a neighbor of this court [Goa], and the entire seafront belongs to him, up to the fortress of Danda, which fortress of Danda is four leagues from our fort of Chaul. According to the peace treaty, this Idalxa is obliged to maintain an official ambassador and entourage in this court, as he in fact does. However, the person who holds the position of ambassador is a Persian and does not carry out his functions correctly.

This report connects stratifications within the house of Bijapur to the oppressive nature of the relationship with the Mughals. By the early 1630s, pressure from the Mughals had increased, leaving the ʿAdil shahs militarily weakened. The document implies, however, that the Bijapur rulers had one continued source of strength, their control over several important ports. What rendered matters even more difficult for the Bijapur sultan was a cross-border interference emanating from the rump state of Ahmadnagar, ruled by Burhan Nizam Shah (r. 1610–31), and an ongoing disagreement among household chiefs about what do with the "bastard son" and heir apparent, Muhammad:

> Between King Idalxa and Nizamoxa [Nizam Shah], who is the Melique, differences remain on account of the fact that they raised up the bastard son [Muhammad], when there was the legitimate one who is the brother-in-law of this Melique, and the brother of his wife the queen, and she has pleaded with her husband on behalf of her brother Darves, the legitimate son to whom the kingdom belonged, saying that her father Ibramo Idalxa had done many unreasonable acts against all the laws in putting out the eyes of her brother Darves Patxah, which he did though he was the true king, and that all that Ibraemo Idalxa had done was on the advice of Mamede Mostafacão, and of Doltacão, and so in any event these two should be expelled from the said kingdom, and that their place should be given to Ecalascão; and that a son of Darves Pataxa should be raised up as king, for he has one who is six years old, and another who is four. But it was never possible to implement this, and after this there was an exchange of ambassadors on the two sides, and things calmed down, and it was

decided that these two kings should be friends, and that the Idalxa would give his help to the Nizamoxa against the Mogores, as they had always done, of fifteen thousand horses for the entire time that the war with the Mogores would endure; and to settle this, another ambassador of the king Nizamoxa came to swear this peace treaty, who was a Persian called Mirza Abulfata, [and] who said that with this his king was content, and that Mamedeamy and Dolatacão should be expelled from his [the 'Adil shah's] kingdom, and that Ecalescão should be given his post of financial intendant of the state as before, and that the Nababo Agaraia [Aqa Raza] should be freed, and that he should be given his place as secretary of state, and when this contract was done, both kings could be friends as they had been before. And all this was for the best, and all the other captains, and regents were content, but as the affair was aimed against these two, Mamedeamym and Dolatocão, they did not let them advance, and as the king is new and incompetent, everything is in a mess.[22]

As the anonymous report makes clear, political alliances did not line up neatly according to ethno-linguistic differences. Its author constructs the category of "Persians" dispersed across two regions of the Indian Ocean in contradictory ways. On the one hand, his dislike for the "Persians" in the 1630s was informed, likely, by the recent Portuguese loss of Hormuz in the 1620s, when various alliances between the Safavids and the English and Dutch East India Companies diminished their hold over the Persian Gulf region.[23] At the same time, however, the presence of Central Asian émigrés in peninsular Indian sultanates was neither homogenous nor uniform; nor did they speak from a single standpoint vis-à-vis other social groups. As the observer notes, the Persian ambassador of the neighboring Nizam shahs, Abu'l Fath, had refused to condone the actions of the émigré Mustafa Khan, urging that he be expelled along with his ally, Daulat Khan, a courtier of the "oilman caste," of more modest background, who would later be executed.

The narrative shift here from examining rivalries between a hierarchy of queens within the palace to commenting on the sultan's dependency on these multiethnic elite households is corroborated by Persianate texts, albeit with a markedly different attitude toward revealing internal hierarchies in the royal household. We may compare the Portuguese report to Zuhur ibn Zuhuri's chronicle *Muhammadnāma* (The book of Muhammad); he was a close friend of the aforementioned Persian Mustafa Khan, a figure to whom he and several other mid-seventeenth-century chroniclers dedicated their work and who, along with queen Taj Sultan, steered the accession of Muhammad 'Adil Shah.[24] Unlike the anonymous Portuguese reporter, Zuhur muted the hierarchies among the competing queens, adhering to the genre's standard king-centered and providential framework.

Simultaneously echoing and contradicting the anonymous report, Zuhur recounted the role of palace women in this succession dispute as propitious and inevitable. But he chose not to mention the rank nor the pleas of the disaffected queen Malik Jahan and her blinded son, Prince Darvish. Instead, he devotes considerable care and attention to elevating the status of the queen mother Taj Sultan (whom the Portuguese identified as a high-ranking servant), describing her as the chaste and virtuous matron (*tāj ul-mukhaddarāt*), who presided over a great retinue within the palace in the final years of Ibrahim ʿAdil Shah's reign.[25] Zuhur borrows the overarching frame to explain Muhammad ʿAdil Shah's birth, the selection of wet nurses, and the accession to the throne by borrowing a narrative template from Abu'l-Fazl's Mughal chronicle, *Akbarnāma*.[26] Zuhur begins by recounting the queen mother Taj Sultan's astonishment at her infant son's miraculous refusal to take to the breast of many wet nurses and his eventually selecting a certain Jiji Man as his nurse, a woman who came from a reputed family that had long served the house of Bijapur.[27] He edifies the queen mother and the head wet nurse, reaffirming the bid to make Muhammad heir to the throne, disregarding the claim of the elder son of Ibrahim ʿAdil Shah.[28] In another narrative echoing the Portuguese report, in the same chapter Zuhur then turned to his patron, the Persian Mustafa Khan or "Khan Baba," and how he shared duties with the aforementioned Daulat Khan/Khawas Khan. Despite acknowledging Daulat Khan's skills in managing state affairs, he derogatively calls him *ghulām ghūl* or a demon servant, being far less generous toward him than the anonymous Portuguese observer had been.[29] Declaring his allegiance to Mustafa Khan, Zuhur recounts changes after Ibrahim ʿAdil Shah's death, including the often-discussed civil war that followed and that necessitated that the young Muhammad hand over all important matters of governance to the Persian prime minister.[30]

Persianate and European observers commented on kinship and stratification within the Deccan courts and its elite households and how these hierarchies shaped moments like kingly birth, accession, and marriage. These different textual traditions generated histories that at once echoed each other and diverged from each other in their concerns. Persian chroniclers and European observers made sense of status differences between queens, sons, and courtly elites in different ways. To Portuguese and Dutch observers, household stratification appeared familiar, as they drew analogies with equivalent positions and familial norms in their own contexts. They invented a vocabulary for comprehending indigenous forms of relatedness with great specificity and at other times, flattened out status differences by measuring indigenous households against European modes of the familial. Chroniclers also made strategic choices in naming relatives and the status of particular actors—such descriptive choices often reveal the chronicler's own affinities to particular patrons in court.

The anonymous Portuguese report (ca. 1620) and Zuhur's *Muhammadnāma* unveil three overarching themes that would characterize the relationship between rulers and elites in the Deccan courts in the seventeenth century. First, pressure from the northern imperial overlords transformed the already tenuous grip of monarchs in the south. Courtly elites, whether male office-holding elites or high-ranking women in the royal household, determined how, when, and who would be king. Second, marriage within and outside dynastic lines would anchor elite households into monarchical authority. Third, the focus of this chapter's subsequent sections are representations of these events that unveil contestations, disputes, and disagreements between household and monarchical state forms while also shedding light on other forms of relatedness, such as those between patrons and poets and those between the adopted and the enslaved.

A PRINCESS AND HER POETIC CIRCUIT

Within the longer context of his disputed accession to the throne in the 1620s, Muhammad ʿAdil Shah came of age just as his closest advisors negotiated suzerainty under the Mughals in the 1630s. A series of weddings took place between 1631 and 1633.[31] These affinal ties did not merely align the Deccan kingdoms with each other; they also augmented the autonomy of semi-independent households vis-à-vis kingly power. Sultan Muhammad ʿAdil Shah's marriages to the sister of a neighboring sultan, on the one hand, and to elite women from courtly families, on the other, suggest that the seventh Bijapuri ruler succeeded in making alliances and consolidating power. But differing narrations of these events suggest otherwise. Conflicting accounts of the marriage events reveal the fragility of affinal ties and the uncertain grounds on which kingly authority stood.

The most notable of these tied the ʿAdil shahs of Bijapur and the Qutb shahs of Golkonda, the Deccan's dynastic houses, to each other for the last time in the seventeenth century. Out of a total of four marriages of sultan Muhammad ʿAdil Shah mentioned by contemporary chroniclers, three were with the daughters of aristocratic households. The one marriage into a royal household, with Princess Khadija Sultana, the sister of the Golkonda Sultan, ʿAbdullah Qutb Shah, is the most well recorded of these events. Muhammad ʿAdil Shah married the daughter of his maternal uncle, Sayyid ʿAbd al-Rahman Husayni[32] and he married the daughter of another courtier; this was celebrated in the Dakkani poem, *Mezbanīnāma* (The book of hospitality), a festive narrative poem examined in this chapter's last section. Shortly after negotiating peace with the Mughals, the Bijapur sultan married Taj Jahan Begam, the daughter of Mustafa Khan (d. 1648), the aforementioned Persian prime minister who helped broker the peace deal with the Mughals. This wedding was a celebrated affair that sealed the new arrangement of imperial suzerainty negotiated by Nawab Khan Baba, such that on the wedding day, ambassadors from Iran and Hindustan rode in front of the groom, the Bijapur king.[33] To make sense of the politics of affinity, I analyze these unevenly distributed, idealized, and conflicting narrative sources about these weddings. Despite the king being placed at the center of the wedding narratives, I show how chroniclers expressed the subordination of monarchical authority by signaling how the king became a son-in-law (*ba takht-i dāmādī girafte*) to an ever-increasing number of nonroyal households.[34] As scholars have suggested, the Persian chronicle form and its narrative conventions, as convincing as they may be, must be read for their conspicuous gaps and silences.³⁵ The celebratory wedding image in this genre, long dismissed as mere pomp and hyperbole, leaves much unsaid. These elisions sit uncomfortably around the obviously observable evidence of unequivocal kingly authority. The portrait of the king becoming a son-in-law is just as much about the cast of characters who sought to control the king and, if possible, unseat him altogether through new affinal bonds.

Before turning to narrations of Khadija Sultana's wedding to Muhammad 'Adil Shah, we may ask who was this queen, bride, and sister to reigning Deccan kings? And what do the multisited journeys of this elite Shi'i woman tell us about her bonds with a wider circuit of friends, servants, and slaves? Khadija Sultana, also known as Haji Bari Sahiba, wielded considerable influence in regional politics and effectively ruled Bijapur as regent between 1646 and 1656. Persian chroniclers often crystallize depictions of high-ranking women like Khadija Sultana, creating virtuous portraits of them as beholden to fraternal and affinal ties to elite men, husbands, brothers, or fathers who were king. Present-day scholars (and the Persian chroniclers they follow) emphasize Khadija's role as a sister and a bride to two competing and tenuously allied regional kings.³⁶ However, contemporary observers commented on this young bride's interventions in political decisions soon after her marriage to the Bijapur sultan. After arriving in Bijapur, the Golkonda chronicler Nizamuddin Ahmad observed Khadija's role in counseling her husband, Muhammad 'Adil Shah, and sealing the fate of the aforementioned Khawas Khan:

> After coming to the 'Adil Shahi palace, the queen turned her attention towards the behaviors and actions of that court and saw that the conditions were not to her own taste and disposition [*mutawajjih auzā'i wa atwār-i ān bārgah shud wa tarz-i ānjā rā muwāfiq-i tab'i 'ālī-i khud nadideh*], the 'Adil shahs should take control of the kingdom by removing those who were disobedient [*ahl-i tasallut wa tughyān rā dafa' numāyad*]. The queen reported back the news of that court to her brother ['Abdullah Qutb Shah] with the hope that he would help remove these rebellious ministers.³⁷

In Ahmed's account of this affair, Khadija Sultana served as adviser to her husband, counseling him throughout on how to remove enemies within the household (*dushman-i khānegī*) and how to manage affairs through good politics (*tadbīr*). Ahmed suggests that Khawas Khan accused Mustafa Khan of being pro-Mughal. Although he does not clarify whether Queen Khadija Sultana also favored a compromise with the imperial overlords, he does reveal that the queen's goals converged with those of the Persian Mustafa Khan. A nested power arrangement under the Mughals allowed for more autonomy for courtly elites while ensuring that the sultanates reached their largest territorial extent by expanding into the Karnatak region.

Apart from being instrumental in the power struggle of the 1630s, Khadija Sultana's long career as a patron of a polyvocal literary circuit remains less known, as do her bonds with male literati whose verses would memorialize her wedding to the Bijapur sultan. While mediating relations with the Mughals and Europeans, Khadija Sultana patronized a circuit of regional poets who traveled with her in 1633 as part of her wedding party and journeyed with her in 1661 across the Indian Ocean to Mocha when she departed for the hajj. We find clues about her abiding interest in retellings and translations from Persian into Dakkani. One poet, Kamal Khan Rustami, who composed the *Khāvarnāma* (ca. 1649), cited Khadija's wish to translate the renowned Persian masnavī (ca. 1426) of Ibn Husam, on the battles of Imam ʿAli and his companions, into Dakkani.[38]

Her most enduring friendship and bond was with the celebrated Indo-African Sunni Muslim poet, Malik Khushnud, who composed a Dakkani poetic work called *Jannat Singār* (ca. 1647), which was implicitly based on Amir Khusrau's Persian *Hasht Bihisht* (Eight paradises).[39] An Abyssinian slave in the Qutb Shahi court, he resided in Hyderabad much of his life. Malik Khushnud was sent to guard Khadija Sultana's dowry when she moved to Bijapur in the early 1630s. His poetic works allude to the slave-poet's friendships with two patrons—in particular, Khadija Sultana and the Iranian minister of Golkonda, Mir Muʾmin Astarabadi (d. 1625).[40] Beyond what we know about his allegiance to these patrons, we have very few biographical details about this poet. In a comprehensive study of his oeuvre, Sayeeda Jafar observed that Khushnud speaks of his unfree status as a slave and prays for his freedom through these words:

jo hove ruh jīyū tan mein merā shād / kare khāliq tumare kin son azād

my soul rejoices in this bodily form / from which the creator may set [it] free[41]

Like many enslaved Indo-Africans in the Deccan before him, Khushnud rose in status and eventually served as a diplomat between the Deccan courts, earning repute as a poet in Khadija Sultana's literary circuit.[42] Further clues about Malik Khushnud's career, his role as an emissary, and his bond with Khadija Sultana reveal a friendship that cut across status, descent, and blood ties.

The queen and the slave-poet were bound by the two homes they shared, grew up in, and moved to. Hyderabad was the queen's natal ghar and the adoptive ghar of Malik Khushnud. As a member of Khadija Sultana's circuit, Khushnud moved with her to Bijapur but frequently returned as an ambassador to Hyderabad, where he had spent much of his youth. After recounting Khadija Sultana's pivotal role in the struggle between Mustafa Khan and Khawas Khan in the 1630s, the chronicler Nizamuddin Ahmad reports that ʿAbdullah Qutb Shah sent a letter to congratulate Muhammad ʿAdil Shah for removing enemies of the household (*dushman-i khānegī*). In return, to mark the occasion and thank his brother-in-law, the Bijapur sultan sent Malik Khushnud as ambassador to Hyderabad. In a narration of this embassy, the chronicler Ahmed notes:

Malik Khushnud, who was one of the great servants of this exalted court, had been in charge of the golden palanquin of *bilqīs zamān* [Khadija Sultana], having been given as part of her dowry along with other servants and eunuchs [*ū ra dākhil-i malikān wa khwāja sarāyān jahez kardeh*]. He served the queen so well and was close, kindred to her that he acquired distinction, earning a rank higher than other eunuchs [*az khwājaha-yi dīgar imtiyāz be ham resānideh būd dar khidmat-i malika-i 'ālamīyān qurb wa manzilat zyada yāfte*]. On this occasion, he brought with him a chain of elephants and six horses as gifts. When he reached the area near the city, he was honored more than past ambassadors [*bā ū ta 'zīm wa takrīm namūdeh*]. Lords and eunuchs from the capital city came to welcome him and brought him to the king's exalted throne, where he was honored. The king gave him the house of Narayan Rao, a *majmū 'adār* who had passed away and served the court. Every time king called on him, Malik Khushnud was honored and treated with great respect [*har waqt ū rā be hūzūr-i ashraf be talab farmūdeh nawāzish mī kardand*]. After some time, Malik Khushnud returned to Bijapur along with the Dakkani poet Mullah Ghawasi, with some gifts from the king.[43]

Malik Khushnud's ascent in the Deccan courts was partly a consequence of his friendship with Queen Khadija Sultana. Describing their relationship as kindred, proximate (*qurb*), the slave-poet prospered in his role as a regional emissary. Khushnud himself appears to have straddled two status groups—eunuchs (*khwājasarah*) and poets (*shā 'ir*)—but he managed to set himself apart from other high-ranking servants. At the same time, he circulated in a wider community of roving regional poet-ambassadors, alongside figures like Mullah Ghawasi, who sought patrons for their verse while delivering diplomatic messages across the Deccan courts.

Further clues about Khadija Sultana's literary investments in artists and literati from different social backgrounds can be found in the material objects produced, circulated, and gifted between Bijapur and Golkonda to commemorate her wedding. In February of 1633, a young Nusrati (a poet whom we will encounter condemning the Mughals and Marathas in chapter 5), penned a celebratory *tarjī'-band* (poem with a return-tie) on the occasion of Khadija Sultana and Muhammad 'Adil Shah's wedding. Nusrati's words were put to paper and ink in an illuminated manuscript by a second-generation Iranian calligrapher, 'Ali ibn Naqi al-Husaini al-Damghani, whose renowned father had adorned inscriptions on the iconic Ibrahim Rauza, the tomb of the previous ruler Ibrahim 'Adil Shah II. During Khadija Sultana's regency, Nusrati would later also compose his celebrated Sufi poem, *Gulshan-i 'Ishq* (ca. 1658), in which he also commented on her patronage and her role in the politics of the two sultanates.

The physical manuscript and poetic composition in Nusrati's earliest work commemorated the forging of affinal ties across the two dynastic lines. Here, once again, the metaphor of ghar or home, a measure of affect and belonging, tied two dynastic households and their members to city, place, and dominion. Thus, Nusrati began by first praising Sultan 'Abdullah Qutb Shah, who came from the city of Hyderabad, marking his descent from the city and a good home (*hyderabad nagar kā/sū sharaf kīch achī ghar kā*). He then described his sister, the young Khadija, as the Deccan's pride, skilled in affairs of the home (ghar) and the world (*jag*),[44] also evoking her lineage and ties to place:

hain sū asad var kī maryam / dukhtar-i shāh mukarram
sū dakkan kī nikū makdam / khātūn-i hashr kī mahram

she who is the Mary of lion (sons) / daughter of the illustrious king
keeper of the Deccan's good repute / chosen among the gathering of great women[45]

In this composition, Nusrati welcomes the brother and sister, Sultan ʿAbdullah Qutb Shah and Khadija Sultana of Golkonda, to Bijapur. Through Dakkani's distinct phonetics, Nusrati captures aural and visual qualities of the ceremony—the banquets, the sounds, the processions of armies, the dancing, the gifts, and the receptions. The manuscript's adornments and design match the visual qualities signified by the words in verse. Its eclectic margins and illuminations suggest that the unique poet-calligrapher collaboration created the manuscript as a gift for the great wedding, a part of the new bride's dowry, indicating that both artists were part of a luxury workshop with access to many talents and templates, under the patronage of Princess Khadija Sultana.

The occasion of a wedding between two dynastic lines produced artistic-literary partnerships that cut across lines of ethnicity and language and across different material mediums. This manuscript of twenty-eight folios produced for Khadija and Muhammad's wedding embodies the interactions of a network of individuals from different social milieus—namely, regional Muslim poets, Iranian émigré calligraphers, and their royal patrons. Persian-speaking Iranian migrant calligraphers wrote out poetic works in the regional literary idiom, Dakkani, possibly from drafts or copies of the poetic works in dialogue with the poets who composed them.[46] Through Nusrati's ode to the princess's wedding, memorialized in an expensive manuscript, a portrait of Khadija Sultana emerges—as a consumer and patron of multitalented and multiethnic literati before and after her wedding, on the one hand, and as political advisor to the two regional sultans, her husband Muhammad ʿAdil Shah and her brother, ʿAbdullah Qutb Shah, on the other.

A RELUCTANT PROPOSAL

And yet, when Khadija's much anticipated wedding linked the dynastic houses of Bijapur and Golkonda, it was not without disagreement. The marriage proposal unfurled during a time when the Mughals were threatening the very existence of the Deccan sultans. Zuhur's *Muhammadnāma* from Bijapur and Nizamuddin Ahmad's *Hadīqat al-Salātīn* from Golkonda offered parallel portraits of this wedding bracketed by chapters that recast Mughal imperial occupation. Describing affinal ties in a moment when the actual physical borders of regional kingdoms were uncertain presented a contradiction for provincial Persian chroniclers. Affinal bonds would not ensure the regional integrity of peninsular India's Islamic courts. The potential political advantages of this interdynastic marriage were not at all apparent to contemporary observers, which explains why the narrations concerning this proposal vary considerably from one chronicler to another.

Zuhur and Ahmed preface accounts of Khadija Sultana's wedding by first casting an eye on the changing relationship with the Mughals. A standard form of rhetoric among provincial commenters was to size down the imperial overlords, a theme we saw in the previous chapter. Portraits of consumption and celebration at weddings followed narratives of Mughal humiliation, where the imperial rulers were reported (and imagined) to have retreated in defeat. Golkonda's Nizamuddin Ahmad, for instance, contrasted famine and death in the Mughal frontier city of Burhanpur at the time of Emperor Shah Jahan against the prosperity of the Deccan kingdoms. He evoked the protection of the twelve innocent Imams (*i'mmah-i ma'sūmīn*) to protect the residents (*ahl-i īn bilād*) of the lands of Telangana (*mumlikat-i tilangāna*) from all disasters and unfortunate events.[47] In Bijapur, Zuhur also inverted Emperor Shah Jahan's successful invasion of the south in the 1630s, framing it as a misguided and unethical war with fellow Muslim polities. Shah Jahan, therefore, returned to Daulatabad. He stopped his troops from entering Bijapur out of respect for followers of the religion of the Prophet and the realization that Muslims should not go to war with each other (*shāh jahān pās-i dīn-i khair ul-mursalīn dāshte nemīpasand ke musalmānān bā yek dīgar jang kunand*).[48] Chroniclers then contrasted the unjust character of Mughal rule with the generosity of the Deccan sultans toward each other and toward their subjects as more ethical and more just. The image of the grand wedding and consumption rituals followed immediately after such portraits of war and destruction of an external enemy. As the imperial army marched toward the Deccan sultanates' northern borders, projecting regional unity and solidarity through celebratory kinship portraits was not just a symbolic move. It stood in marked contrast to what we saw in the second chapter whereby regional states adopted imperial institutional mechanisms for pansubcontinental military recruitment and identification practices. In effect, regional states were starting to look like their enemy. Emulating Mughal institutions, such as horse branding, could be used to check the growing power of provincial elites within peninsular India. Despite these actual overlaps, the chronicle form created an ideological opposition far starker by juxtaposing it with ceremonial wedding portraits that projected regional resilience and solidarity.

And yet, there were limits to this rhetorical interregional affinity between the two dynasties of Bijapur and Golkonda even within chronicle representations. The marriage of Khadija Sultana to Muhammad 'Adil Shah marked both the beginning and the end of an "ancient custom of relations" (*nisbat i-qadīmī*) across the Deccan sultanates.[49] As the last exogamous, interdynastic marriage between the two houses, it followed an old pattern across the regional sultanates that had been developed since the sixteenth century.[50] Golkonda chronicler Nizamuddin Ahmad, citing previous marriages between the two dynastic houses, began by acknowledging that there was indeed a custom (*mirāsim*) of close relations (*nisbat-i qurbatī*) between the two lineages (*dūdmān*), for they had often come together (*muwāsalat*) through marriage.[51] Shortly after coming to the throne, Muhammad ʿAdil Shah sent two ambassadors, Shah Abuʾl Hasan and Shaykh Rahim, with the proposal for Khadija to her brother, the sultan of Golkonda, ʿAbdullah Qutb Shah. Ahmed informs us that the Bijapuri ambassadors

> reminded the Qutb Shahi sultan of the relations of [the] unity [*nisbat-i-itihād*] and friendship and love [*rābteh yegānegī wa wadād*] he had had with the ʿAdil shahs. Upon hearing these worlds from the chamberlain [*hujjāb*], ʿAbdullah Qutb Shah answered, as God was willing. The sultan said what our ancestors had done in the past was good. His most trustworthy and close advisors advised the king. He answered this question but covered his words with a garb of silence [*be kiswat-i-sukūt wa libās-i mutarz betarāz-i khāmushī*]. From the way the king expressed his words and from his countenance, the wise chamberlain understood it to be proof of his agreement with the proposal. The ambassadors went back to Muhammad ʿAdil Shah and told him of the nature of the circumstances in great detail, expressing the truth of the facts with the hope of opening the doors of marriage [*abwāb-i muwāsalat*]. When this fortunate and joyous news reached Muhammad ʿAdil Shah, he was pleased. Such good tidings [*navīd farrukh afzāyī*] and the hope of this gain took away the [Bijapur] king's sadness, as this occasion would strengthen the arms of his kingdom, which had grown weak due to challenges from enemies, for now his kingdom would be stronger.[52]

Ahmed's cautious reconstruction of the proposal gives the reader pause. He dissuades us from accepting affirmations of a natural unity and a friendship between the Deccan sultans that preface the narration. The chronicler proceeds with a degree of ambiguity, not quite revealing the Golkonda sultan ʿAbdullah Qutb Shah's answer. Eventually, he concludes that this marriage strengthened the groom and the house of Bijapur more than it did Golkonda, the prospective bride's natal home. But it was doubtful whether this alliance would ensure political stability at a time when regional sultans were faced with two choices—either accept Mughal suzerainty or commit to fighting their northern rival together. Ahmed's account suggests that a regional political unity was easy to imagine but far more difficult to commit to in practice. Given his allegiance to the Qutb shahs, the chronicler was responsible for making his king appear all-powerful at all times. Instead, Ahmed notes that his king's response, veiled with silence rather than an enthusiastic acceptance, betrays his vulnerability. In signaling ʿAbdullah Qutb Shah's reluctance, Ahmed reveals a sense of foreboding that undergirded affinal bonds. Rather than guaranteeing a natural alliance and political certitude, kinship forged through marriage brought with it the possibility of unraveling the monarchical form all together.

The uneasiness around Muhammad and Khadija's marriage comes alive when considered through another chronicler, Zuhur ibn Zuhuri, writing from the vantage point of the groom. In contrast to Ahmed's cryptic narration, which suggested the proposal was not wholeheartedly accepted, Zuhur presents a narrative of outright refusal and coercion. Recounting how negotiations of the engagement (*kat khudāī*) began, he notes:

> when 'Abdullah Qutb Shah heard Muhammad 'Adil Shah's proposal for his sister [*khabar-i khwāstegārī-yi ham-shīra wālānizād-i khīsh*], he did not want to send her away as he loved her more than his own life and saying no, he apologized. The king [Muhammad 'Adil Shah] came to know this and called upon Nawab Khan Baba and Khawas Khan and told them that 'Abdullah Qutb Shah wished to take a step in an opposing direction [*qutb shah mī khwāhad qadm dar rah-yi khilāf nihād*] and lose his entire kingdom in one breath. It is necessary to send the victorious troops to Golkonda to destroy them and make 'Abdullah Qutb Shah obey the world-obeying emperor.[53]

Unlike Ahmed, who is reticent in this regard, Zuhur constructs the Bijapuri sultan as an imperial overlord presiding over his regional neighbor, echoing the relationship of vassalage that the Deccan sultans had with the Mughal Empire. In this imagined hierarchy, Muhammad 'Adil Shah and his advisors could reprimand 'Abdullah Qutb Shah and paint him as misguided and naive. Only after the prospective groom threatened to send his army, out of fear and helplessness, did the prospective bride's brother accept the proposal. Zuhur's rendition right away blurs the boundary between the affective and the familial, on the one hand, and the political, on the other. A gendered and hierarchical portrait of the two sovereigns emerges with the bride's brother subordinate to the groom. This political equation is then contrasted with the more intimate affective bond of the bride, as a beloved sister to her brother. According to Zuhur, 'Abdullah Qutb Shah used the excuse of brotherly love to reject the marriage proposal and avoid becoming a political subordinate to the neighboring sultan, his future brother-in-law, Muhammad 'Adil Shah.

That Persian chroniclers constructed narratives to one-up rival rulers is nothing new.[54] Marriage portraits frequently appear in this textual genre but have been dismissed as mere corollary to alliance politics, another way of affirming the sovereign's absolute power. And yet, to contemporary observers like Ahmed and Zuhur, marriages were hardly natural or inevitable. Affinal ties were rarely absolute indicators of kingly power despite the rhetorical overtures to naturalness that framed such representations. Rather, contemporary observers treated such occasions with a degree of caution and, in Zuhur's case, even suspicion.

It should come as no surprise, then, that both chroniclers followed up their conflicting reports of the marriage proposal with images of abundance, consumption, and courtly ritual before and during the wedding. Here the wedding canvas moves to a wider circuit of courtly participants. In the performative scenes that dramatized court ritual, descriptive terms emphasize the status, as well as the degree of trust and loyalty, of those who attended the wedding, and what role each actor played in the ceremony. The two chroniclers echo each other's narratives in describing the sequence of public rituals that consecrated the marriage. From Bijapur, the groom's (*dāmād*) older sister departed for Hyderabad to deliver the formal proposal and gifts along with Murari Pandit, the Brahmin chief of armies (*sipah sālār*), and an Abyssinian general, Husayni Habz Khan, who had served the crown since childhood. These men were like house born sons (*khānazād*), a portrait that would change quickly after the so-called civil war.[55] On the way back from Hyderabad:

> Mir Fasihuddin Muhammad, who was known for his great talent and abilities, was selected to take the queen's palanquin to the ʿAdil shahs. He was given two Turkish horses with adorned saddles and silver stirrups. The king gave this responsibility to Mir Fasihuddin Muhammad along with a *tankhwāh* of eighty thousand. Shaykh Muhammad Tahir, a high-ranking learned religious scholar, also received special gifts with two horses, to go along with the queen's palanquin. Another person that he chose was Qazi Ahsan, known as the *qāzī* of Mecca, a very famous scholar and a member of the *majlis*, to go on this journey. Sayyid Babu, a general, and Makhdum Malik with four hundred cavalry, along with followers, all were given gifts and accompanied the bride's palanquin.[56]

Listing which nobles had the honor of visiting the bride's brother, ʿAbdullah Qutb Shah, Ahmed concludes the wedding festivities that stretched over a month and a half from June to July of 1633. After the formal acceptance of the proposal (*khwāstegārī*) and gift-giving, the city of Hyderabad was decorated in order to receive the groom's party. Both chroniclers concluded their accounts of the wedding of 1633 with descriptions of festivity, ceremony, and consumption.

Following the chronicle form's convention of reporting, the description of the royal wedding's courtly participants is named; the ranks of officers, itemizing lists, and the amount of dowry (*jahez*) and bride price (*mahr*) given. After the proposal for Khadija Sultana and Muhammad ʿAdil Shah was accepted and the preparations began, Nizamuddin Ahmad plots the bridal party's journey within and eventually outside of Hyderabad to Bijapur, noting audiences held with the bride and her brother, Sultan ʿAbdullah Qutb Shah:

> On the twenty-sixth of Shaʿban the bejeweled palanquin of the queen plus twenty *khāssa* palanquins and a hundred and fifty other palanquins with servants, elephants, horses, and camels, with ministers and nobles, they went outside the capital city. At the end of the night, ʿAbdullah Qutb Shah met the elder sister of Muhammad ʿAdil Shah to bid farewell to them, giving her and all the ladies of the *haram* so many gifts. The palace was lit up with lamps and lights, and ʿAbdullah Qutb Shah then returned to the capital city. The value of the dowry was five lakh *hun* and all the expenses of the celebrations were around fifty thousand *hun*. . . .
>
> All the celebrations took one and a half months and were continued day and night at different places. In the middle of the month of Ramadan, the entourage of the Queen set off for Bijapur and two thousand infantry were sent. When they were close to the border of ʿAdil Shah, high ranking generals and nobles who had accompanied the Queen's entourage, returned back to the Qutb Shahi territories. When

the Queen's entourage entered the Bijapur kingdom, they reached Gulbarga, where Ikhlas Khan, the *mir jumla*, along with four thousand cavalry came to welcome them and kiss the queen's throne; in return, she presented him with special gifts.[57]

Ahmad concludes the wedding narrative with poetic images of rituals. The first of these is *jalwa* or the face-showing ceremony, a well-known custom in the Deccan (*rūsūm wa qā'ida-i jalwe ke dar dakkan muta'ārif ast*). The final image of the night of the union (*shab-i wasl*), when the royal bride and groom consume the marriage, the chronicler concludes with the following distich (*qit'a*):

lailatu'l-qadr būd ān shab-i wasl / ke namūdand mehr-o-māh qirān
bud dar khurramī be az nawrūz / ān shab-i faiz bakhsh nūr afshān
gul-i 'ashrat sabāh-yi 'id ān shab / chīd az bazm-gāh sad dāmān

The night of the union was the night of power / with the sun and moon conjunction,
more joyful than the day of Nowruz / that bountiful, luminous night
on the morning of that night, flowers of delight / were picked from that banquet

With these words, the wedding portrait of Khadija Sultana of Golkonda and Muhammad 'Adil Shah concludes, moving on to matters of war with the Mughals. The 1630s marked merely the beginning of Khadija Sultana's long itinerancy between Hyderabad and Bijapur. After 1646, when the Bijapur sultan fell ill, she would rule as regent for ten years until her adopted son 'Ali 'Adil Shah II came of age. Her regency had a lasting effect on the final years of both sultanates, including on the ability of the English, the Dutch, and the French to function on the Coromandel coast. In chapter 6, we will see that, in the 1670s, Khadija's political career would require frequent trips between the two capital cities to negotiate with several contenders, including the chiefs of military households, such as the much-maligned Indo-African Siddi Jauhar (d. 1665?), the Maratha Shivaji Bhonsle (d. 1680), and the Miyana Afghan Bahlol Khan, all of whom sought to carve out autonomous strongholds in the military campaigns of the 1660s in the Karnatak.[58]

A FEAST OF WORDS: CONSUMPTION AND AFFINITY IN A REGIONAL IDIOM

One such household was that of Muzaffar Khan, whose daughter married Muhammad 'Adil Shah of Bijapur shortly after his wedding to Khadija Sultana. This final wedding of the 1630s was memorialized, not in the Persian chronicle form but in a narrative poem composed in Dakkani. The Bijapur sultan would give the title *khān-i khānān* (lord of lords) to his father-in-law, Muzaffar Khan, an act that would infuriate Mughal emperor Shah Jahan, since the title was reserved for high-ranking imperial nobles.[59] Like his contemporary Mustafa Khan Lari (d. 1648), the aforementioned Nawab Khan Baba, whose daughter also married the Bijapur sultan, Muzaffar Khan was a second-generation Persian who led Bijapur's campaigns in the Karnatak in the late 1630s. Both weddings were reported in contemporary chronicles and narrative poems. In a telling reversal of the gender and lineage hierarchies in these marriages, the chronicler Zuhur, for instance, noted that the groom-king had made the father-in-law Nawab Khan Baba proud (*mufakhkhar wa mubāhī gardānīdand*) by asking for his daughter's hand, rather than the other way around.[60] Under imperial suzerainty, aristocratic-military household chiefs in regional courts interlocked themselves with kingly authority. Just as Mustafa Khan was the patron of a polyvocal literary circuit that included chroniclers like Zuhur, who wrote in Persian, and Muqim, who wrote in Dakkani, we may surmise that Muzaffar Khan commissioned Hasan Shauqi to compose *Mezbānīnāma* on the occasion of his daughter's wedding to the sultan.

Now the question remains why a text was commissioned in Dakkani, rather than simply being recorded into a Persian chronicle, to commemorate yet another wedding of the Bijapur sultan to a household lord. We can only turn to internal clues and themes within the text to understand the social, literary, and political purposes of the *Mezbānīnāma*. Dakkani textual traditions, in the romance genre, offered images of spending, consumption, wealth.[61] Drawing on that tradition, I argue that *Mezbānīnāma* draws the audience's attention to the material resources necessary for celebrating and forging new households. The fact that this work was composed in the panregional literary idiom of Dakkani to commemorate the king's marriage with the daughter of a second-generation émigré household raises questions, once again, about how we read representations of "Iranians" beyond Persian in the Deccan courts, particularly in portraits of consumption and celebration that drew on Indic and Persianate imagery. As I showed in chapter 3, such representations were not anomalous. Unsurprisingly, and as with other new social groups not associated with regional languages but rather with the high register of Persian, émigré households asserted their political claims to the region by deploying a well-established idiom that drew on recognizable Perso-Arabic forms infused with an Indic vocabulary. These works code-switched between different linguistic registers particularly to show the resolution of political and military conflicts.[62]

Commemorating a wedding between the royal lineage of Bijapur and the household of Muzaffar Khan, Hasan Shauqi's *Mezbanīnāma* (ca. 1630s) is a rare, versified work and one of the earliest texts to focus on a nonmilitary historical event. It falls in line with the leitmotif of *bazm* (meaning feast, assembly, or festivity) in Persian literature, the counterpart to war or *razm*.[63] In the next chapter, we follow Nusrati's ʿ*Alināma*, which adopted the latter frame of battle or fighting within which the poet embedded a broader political commentary. In contrast to war, the festive poem draws on a different set of images, aesthetics, and metaphors to depict courtly life.

Images of feasting and consumption on the occasion of a wedding emphasized the ability and capacity to bear expenses (*kharchīyā*) on innumerable objects, materials, rituals, and ceremonies that sacralized affinity. Shauqi details *kharchā* or spending, an image running throughout the *Mezbānīnāma*, in all its physical forms—coins, gold, silver—resources that made the consumption and enjoyment of food, drink, carpets, clothing, jewelry and therefore a grand wedding possible. With the objective of illustrating consumption, poets mobilized a range of motifs legible to courtly audiences to capture the wedding feast's sounds, sights, and smells. To do so, they devised original metaphors, a critical foundation of Persian poetry, while adhering to strict rules of form and literary convention.[64] It goes without saying, then, that readers listen to the poem's literary and aesthetic qualities first, rather than seek in it a straightforward, instrumentalist purpose of merely legitimizing the patron. Below, I follow the narrative sequence and describe the composite sensory and linguistic canvas of the *Mezbānīnāma*, reconstructing images of spending and objects of consumption that sacralized affinity in the regional idiom. Throughout the poem, I examine how Shauqi played with Indic vocabularies within a Perso-Arabic poetic to highlight Muzaffar Khan's polyvocal spheres of patronage, which evolved alongside those of the sultan, his new son-in-law.

In terms of its structure, the *Mezbānīnāma* consists of three short chapters or sections (*bāb*). In the first, the Bijapur sultan, Muhammad ʿAdil Shah, titled the friend of God (*khudā kā khalīl*) and the Prophet's successor (*nabī kā khalīfā*), presides over an assembly, giving gifts to people in preparation for the party (*majlis ārāstan wa bakhshish kardan sultān muhammad mardmān rā mezbānī-i khud*). In the second, he mounts his horse to tour the city of Bijapur (*dar bayān-i shahar gasht sawār shudan sultān muhammad ʿādil shah*).[65] The groom's party reaches the bride's home, where Muzaffar Khan (the bride's father) makes preparations to welcome them. In the third and final scene, a great feast is hosted at the wedding party and a dowry is given for the daughter of Nawab Muzaffar Khan (*dar bayān-i mehmānī kardan sultān muhammad ʿādil shah rā wa dādan-i jahez-i dukhtar-i nawab muzaffar khān*).

Shauqi begins with the usual convention of praising God and the sultan. These sections are brief and, within a few lines into the poem, he turns to the task before him. He once again begins with the metaphorical and spatial notion of *ghar* and the adorning of this place for a grand feast:

> *suniyā mein ke shah ghar badā kāj hai / ke jis kāj kā khalaq muhtāj hai*
> *jahāndār ne mezbānī kariyā / usse nāvon mein shādmānī dhariyā*
>
> I heard there was a great work at the king's house
> A work on which all of creation depended
>
> The possessor of the world was to host a feast
> One that would instill joy and delight to his name

The notion of home or ghar appears in narrative poems with both the *bazm* and *razm* leitmotif, but for distinct purposes. For Nusrati in the *ʿAlīnāma*, political conflicts threatened the very integrity of the home, a space of belonging, the building block of the state. In the bazm poem, the home or ghar is a site of poetic and aesthetic adornment and celebration. The groom's home and the bride's natal home are interlinked through the poet's description of procession, assembly, gifting, and feasting. Shauqi constructs a portrait of the preparations for the king's house, drawing the listener's attention to sensory objects of adornment and decoration. The verses capture the visual, experiential, and aural qualities of consumption items and decorated spaces, from latticed chalices (*mushtabik mane jām*) to water basins (*hauz khāne*) filled with perfume (*ghāliyah*).

For seventeenth-century courtly listeners, the interplay between the alliteration of words and the physical characteristics of each object would have resonated with the experience of seeing the elaborate preparations for the king's wedding being made across the city of Bijapur. Consider for instance, Shauqi's description of light and candles, objects revered for their myriad qualities in Persian poetry:[66]

> *lage maum bātiyān kanchan ke lagan / kanchan ke lagan nau ratan ke gagan*
> *yatā maum kharchīyā apas kāj kon / na kaun rāj kharchīyā apas rāj kon*
>
> the wick of candles like gold / gold like nine jewels of the skies
> so much was spent for candles on this occasion / no other king had spent as much in his realm[67]

The ability of kings to bear expenses for lighting candles in public spaces such as mosques featured in inscriptions across the Islamic world.[68] The two meanings of the *tatsama*-Sanskrit loanword *kanchan/kānchan* in this verse refer to the visual quality of golden light but also to the shimmering of thousands of lit candles being compared here to moving dancers.[69] In the single manuscript of the *Mezbānīnāma*, in this line the letter ʿ*alif* has been omitted to adhere to the poem's meter. Shauqi appears to be playing on both meanings of the word, *kanchan* (dancers) versus *kānchan* (gold), to bring alive the visual and tactile qualities of thousands of lit candles. Shauqi uses an Indic vocabulary to name objects and substances associated with festive courtly ceremony, a pattern that continues in the rest of the poem, when describing flowers, foods, and drinks at the wedding party.

The poet turns to worldly images of money, the ability to spend (*kharchā*), giving *bakshīsh* (presents) to subjects, *sone hor rupe* (gold and money) to courtiers, and so forth, placing them in a broader geographic imaginary.[70] When the court gathers around the king in the poem's second chapter, Shauqi once again turns to gifting, in the form of gems and horses from across the world, and its role in connecting the king (*shah*) to the people (*log*) and to the lords (*mīr wa mirzā*), placing an emphasis on the scale of expenses and transregional spaces where things were acquired:

> *huā kharch us kāj kon beshumār / sunere rupere hazārān hazār*
> *jadat hor jawāhir yatā kuch diyā / jo ūs dekhte khalq hairān rahiyā*
>
> the expenses on that task were infinite / thousands upon thousands of gold coins
> so much gold and precious jewels were given / leaving all of mankind astonished[71]

kite la 'l wa nīlam wa marmar kite / diyā bhī jawāhir sau bartar kite
firangān wa kurdī diyā turbatī / jabnī alemānī wa maghribī
sau dībāye rumī wa chīnī parend / sau tāzī wa turkī malūkān pasand
'arabī 'irāqī wa turkī turang / sau balkhī bukhārī wa khatlī surang

So many rubies, sapphires, and marble / giving many such sublime precious stones
Franks, Kurds, Turbati / German and Maghrebi
Hundreds of Rumi brocades and Chinese silks / Tazi, Turki, the choicest from all lands
Tazi, Turki, Arabi, Iraqi horses / A retinue of Balkhi, Bukhari and chestnut [horses.]

yatā kharch pānān huā rāj kāj / na sone mein dekhiyā kad mein rām rāj
diyā khalq kon dān hor pān le / diyā pān hor dān hor mān le[72]

so much was spent in the kingdom / such that even Ramraj had not seen in his dreams
giving mankind so much food and drink / in return, gaining honor and respect

Here again, historical referentiality in the poem is apparent through two images—one of material prosperity based on the acquisition of a variety of luxury items; the other of an ideal kingly authority. The image of enumerating people and goods from distant lands was common across narrative poems in regional literary idioms, mediating between images borrowed from the Persian, cosmopolitan sphere to the regional, listing foods, décor, and dress specific to the Deccan.[73] The second image that Shauqi plays with is of Aliya Rama Raya, the Aravidu chief of the erstwhile Vijayanagara Empire, who was defeated by an alliance of the Deccan sultans at the so-called Battle of Talikota in 1565, an event that the poet also commemorated in his previous work, the late sixteenth-century poem *Fathnāma-yi Nizām Shah*.[74] The Vijayanagara ruler, identified as Ramraj, became a stock literary image with historical referentiality in the Deccan's Persianate texts over the course of the seventeenth century, deployed to symbolize both an incomparable kingly authority and an existential rival of the Deccan sultans. The figure of Ramraj operates as a symbolic measure for a peerless patron-king who could spend and devote enormous resources to ceremony and ritual.

The *Mezbanīnāma*'s final portrait captures the groom's arrival at the wedding feast hosted by Muzaffar Khan. The poet begins by placing the groom and father-in-law relationship into the frequently used image of King Solomon and his wise minister, Asaf, while likening the bride and groom to the moon (*chānd*) and the sun (*sūr*). Objects of consumption that were part of the dowry (*jahez*) solidified this new affinal bond between the king and the lord and now father-in-law, Muzaffar Khan:

sulaimān kon āsaf ne mehmān kiyā / 'ajāib gharāib bahut kuch diyā
diyā chānd kon sūr ke sāt kar / diyā nūr kon nūr ke sāt kar
aqīq miyānī kīre martabān / sau la 'l badakhshān kīre kīfdān
nabātāt mein hor jamādāt mein / diyā khūb tar jo athā zāt mein
khatay ghulāmān halqa begūsh / sau chīnī kanīzān zarbaft push[75]

Asaf hosted Solomon as a guest / giving all things wonderful and strange
giving the moon to the sun / uniting light with light
jars full of carnelian / boxes full of rubies
filled with sweetmeats and stones / giving all that they possessed
with Scythian slaves, rings in their ears / with female servants in gold-embroidered dress

The vivid portraits of consumption of food, clothing, and gifts mark the status of the poem's nonkingly patron and reputation within a wider community while still keeping the monarch as its main protagonist.

At the final banquet in the bride's home, the poet turns his attention to food and commensality, motifs that embody the poem's central theme of hospitality. The practice of eating together and appreciating a meal seals the affinal bond between the king and the lord's households. Shauqi sketches images of different foods, capturing the experiences of wedding guests from far and wide who encountered unfamiliar and familiar tastes, smells, and sights at the feast:

> *huā bār sufra shahr-yar kā / milāyā log sab ār kā bhār kā*
> *kiyā bārdārāye darya-i shukoh / zalebiyān ke jāle wa halwān ke koh*
> *sau biryān wa bughra wa qalya subās / sau machliyān ke khandre andre ke rās*
> *bilīmbū wa nimbū wa sirkā masīr / sau jughrāt wa na'na' wa pudina panīr*[76]

> the king's table was abundant / people met from far and wide
> as majestic as the sea of glory / coils of *jalebī*, mountains of sweetmeats
> the smell of biryani, pastries, fried pilafs / varieties of fish, rows of eggs
> pickled limes and lemons / cream and mint and cheese

A wider transregional circuit of courtly audiences at the wedding marveled at the taste of new ceremonial foods, such as *pān* or betel-nut, which had long fascinated travelers visiting the subcontinent:

> *jite mīr wa mirza khurāsān ke / rahe dekh hairān tabaq pān ke*
> *sunaharī rupahrī supāriyān ko dekh / jite pān khāte son sāriyān ko dekh*[77]

> all the great lords from Khurasan / were astonished seeing the trays of betel
> beholden to gold and silver-tinted betel-nuts / looked astounded at all upon tasting it

With such descriptions of mouth-watering dishes, music, the ornamented dresses of dancers, and adornments across the city of Bijapur, the poem invites its listeners to experience the celebration's aural and visual delights. Shauqi ends the poem with the standard poetic convention of self-exaltation (*ta'allī*) with a reflection on the poetic form and its unique ability to capture the wedding's rich sensory stimuli and the consumption rituals that sacralized affinity. He remarks that neither register nor book (*na daftar mein pāvein na andar kitāb*) could have recorded this event in the way verse could. In other words, administrative documentary genres used in the royal treasury for inventorying countless vessels of gold and silver (*zuruf-i zar-o-sīm*), shining porcelain (*nichal ghoriyān hor faghfuriyān*), and chests (*sandūqān*) could not transmit the sensory and aesthetic effects of these objects on guests at the wedding as effectively as his poem. It was the poet alone who could immortalize it with a feast of words, memorializing the bond between the king and the lord:

> hidāya magar dhan kirāmāt son / kifāyat kiyā us muhimmāt kon
> qalm kardan rās sab bāns ke / siyāhī daryā kāghaz ākās ke

> gifting with miraculous wealth / capturing the qualities of this important [event]
> I wrote gathering all sticks from earth / using the sea as ink and skies as my paper

The *Mezbanīnāma* is a meditation on poetic craft at the intersection of two linguistic worlds, the Indic and the Persianate. Shauqi mobilizes words, metaphors, and well-known Indic motifs in the masnavī form to represent a grand wedding's festive sensorium. Objects of consumption and ritual were described with attention to their physical and tactile qualities, and the motifs of home, spending, adornment, and food were utilized to capture the theme of hospitality. The wedding's reception by transregional visitors and audiences emphasizes the expression of tastes, sounds, and smells, inviting the poem's readers to inhabit the celebration and its sensory delights.

Why were these grand weddings of the 1630s represented in the panregional literary idiom of Dakkani alongside Persian? I would argue that unlike in the late sixteenth and early seventeenth centuries, when such aristocratic marriages into the dynastic line were also common,[78] in the period of Mughal suzerainty, the composition and patronage of Dakkani works was no longer limited or exclusive to sultans. Scholars have focused on the celebrated illustrated manuscripts in Dakkani, such as the *Kitāb-i Nauras* (Book of Nine Essences) of Ibrahim 'Adil Shah II and the *divān* (collection of poems) of Muhammad Quli Qutb Shah (d. 1612), often interpreting these two golden age works as reflective of a kingship ideology rooted in the Deccan's syncretic or local culture.[79] Shortly thereafter, aristocratic-military elites from diverse social backgrounds patronized the regional literary idiom, once reserved for the royal dynastic line alone. Dakkani literary representations, whether of festivity or war, were marking boundaries of kinship, language, and status. It should come as no surprise, then, that second-generation Persians, such as Mustafa Khan and Muzaffar Khan, and Afghan military household chiefs (as I show in chapters 3 and 6) deployed the narrative poem genre in the regional idiom to represent their political claims.

CONCLUSION

As I noted in the introduction, extant textual genres pose certain limits for writing a history of relatedness before 1700. This chapter has stitched together portraits of affinity culled from a mosaic of texts by tracing representations of a series of marriages that took place in the Deccan sultanates in the 1630s. Likewise, from these moments, we have drawn out auxiliary circuits of friendship and patronage between, for instance, elite women patrons and slave literati, to reimagine expressions of relatedness between individuals of different status. Placing new genres, such the regional narrative poem, alongside more standard ones, such as the Persian chronicle at the chapter's center, had a twofold purpose. First, I argued that the users, listeners, and audiences of these two linguistic registers intersected and expanded over the course of the seventeenth century. Second, I showed that affinity was memorialized through images of feasting and consumption, a fundamental activity within courtly life. The multiple social locations of hospitality included the adorned palace with the king's assembly, a public procession through the city of Bijapur, and the bride's natal home in Hyderabad.

Moving beyond the usual Persian prose chronicles and European accounts required us to abandon the desire for a sequential narrative history and instead turn to the affective and sensory articulations of affinity and relatedness in the narrative poem. The *Mezbanīnāma* is part of a rare but sizable body of texts that decenter the Persian chronicle, revealing a new set of patrons and listeners. But these texts have largely been dismissed as sources, given the difficulty of extracting straightforward political history from them. Turning to the linguistic layers of the *Mezbanīnāma* shows the familiar pattern of Sanskrit-Indic vocabularies deployed within Persian forms used to portray a consumption culture that lay at the heart of the politics of relatedness.

In South Asia, the Mughal dynastic line has long captured the imagination of political historians and literary scholars with an overwhelming focus on the kingly figure and its corollary—the consanguine household—wherein blood and descent through a male ancestor takes primacy over all other forms of kinship. The Persian-language chronicle is the paradigmatic textual genre from which histories beholden to the consanguine have been periodized and narrated. However, as this chapter shows, the dominant form of writing history, *tārīkh*, is one among a constellation of materials available to us to refract the story of the king and his consanguine household. Along with narrative poems in the panregional literary idiom, we find clues about alternative notions of relatedness and kinship, unbound between the two extremes of blood or fiction.

Together, these texts reflect a larger political shift unfolding in the seventeenth century, that of new, hybrid nodes of political power—namely, elite household chiefs—anchoring, undercutting, and redefining the monarchical form. This was done, as the next chapter will show, to capture the divergence between kingly and household power. Redefining what changed about the meaning of ghar in the regional capital and casting their gaze to sites of conflict across the peninsula, Persianate literati set aside the chronicle form and embraced alternate modes of literary expression to comment on the political uncertainties of their present and the place of households in state power.

5

At Home in the Regional Court
Critiquing Empire

The meaning of the term *ghar* changed a great deal from the first to the second half of the seventeenth century. Learned elites articulated the political stakes of this term in the Muslim courts of the Deccan, the south-central plateau of peninsular India. A shared religion, Islam, and a transregional language, Persian, had rarely produced harmony across northern and southern Indian Muslim courts, a pattern that continued in the seventeenth century as military conflicts and diplomatic confrontations intensified.[1] The Mughals loomed large in the imagination of people far removed from the capital city of Delhi who had never set foot in the imperial realm. This chapter shows how two poets from regional courts resentfully admired the empire's strength while, on other occasions, contemplating the possibility of the Great Mughals unraveling all together. Persianate Muslim courtly literati, nonimperial subjects who resided in the Deccan, participated in a shared ecumene that stretched from Iran to India and was ruled by many different monarchs. Despite living outside imperial domains, these observers formulated the most evocative criticisms of the Mughals at a time when they showed no sign of retreating. Making sense of imperial power encompassed expressing emotions such as envy, resentment, suspicion, scorn, and anger toward it.

In this chapter, I interpret two largely unexamined martial works by Persianate Muslim literati from the regional court of Bijapur—narrative poems written in the masnavī form.[2] These works represented ghar as a political category, using it to formulate an ethical critique of the problems of patrimonial power, understood as a perpetual balancing act or a game of chess between household and state. One meaning of ghar was loyalty toward two lineages of service, first the king and then the household. According to these poets, both regional and imperial kings violated the moral and ethical criteria for righteous and just rule, as

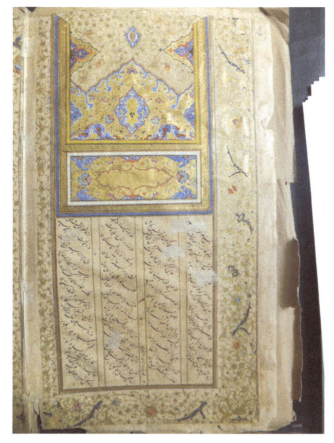

FIGURE 4. Hakim Atishi, ʿĀdilnāma (The book of ʿĀdil, ca. 1630s), fol. 2, Ms. P. 4300. YSR Reddy State Museum, Hyderabad, India.

had the aspiring elite household chiefs who now sought to be kings. Provincial Persianate literati expressed their political views through well-established literary templates discussing how kingly power stood on shaky grounds in the seventeenth century—it faced challenges from regional elite families, regardless of whether or not they were Iranians, Marathas, Habshis, or Afghans. Poetic critiques went beyond the Mughal dynasty to encompass a whole host of political players—namely, patriarchal heads or household chiefs whose increasing autonomy threatened kingly sovereignties.

The first work, written in Persian by Hakim Atishi, ʿĀdilnāma (The book of ʿĀdil), was composed and compiled between the years 1628 and 1637, and the second, written in Dakkani by Nusrati, ʿAlināma (The book of ʿAli), was completed in the 1660s.[3] Serving in the courts of consecutive Bijapuri sultans, Muhammad ʿAdil Shah (r. 1627–56) and his son ʿAli ʿAdil Shah II (r. 1656–72), Hakim Atishi and

Nusrati's poetic milieu intersected in the 1650s at a time when Persian and Dakkani poets vied for patrons beyond sultans. Together, the ʿĀdilnāma and ʿAlināma act as bookends for tracing Mughal suzerainty's narrative arc from the perspective of literati in regional courts. Composed at different times and in different languages in the Bijapur sultanate, both texts comment on the shifting terrain of defining ghar in peninsular India under Mughal occupation.

Hakim Atishi, or Muhammad Amin, was a Shiʿi Muslim, the son of a certain Hakim Shamsuddin ʿAbdullah. His family hailed from Basra (present-day Iraq) but moved to Shiraz and then later to Lar (in Fars province, southern Iran). Traveling from Hormuz in the Persian Gulf to the port of Dabhol on the Konkan coast in southwestern India, Atishi arrived in the Deccan in the 1620s, making the city of Bidar (in present-day Karnataka state) his home for the next thirty years.[4] He wrote several masnavī; the martial poem, ʿĀdilnāma, accounts for the early years of sultan Muhammad ʿAdil Shah's reign (1627–56).[5] Like many skilled émigré Persian courtiers before him who made their home in southern and northern India, Atishi's itineraries also followed well-established networks of circulation and patronage across the Indian Ocean.[6] These migrants brought with them not just literary skills and an experiential knowledge of kindred Islamic courts but also a rubric for observing power relations in the interconnected worlds around them. Atishi thus dramatized Bijapur's complicated relationship with the Mughals that resulted in a short-lived alliance against the Nizam shahs of Ahmadnagar (ca. 1490–1636), followed by a fallout and a series of battles and negotiations between the ʿAdil Shahs and the Mughals. From the first half of the seventeenth century, then, the ʿĀdilnāma presents the years just before and after the negotiations with the Mughals that culminated in the historic deed of submission of 1636, when the Deccan sultanates ostensibly gave up their sovereign status and ceded to nominal imperial rule.[7]

The second work, ʿAlināma, begins with Maratha warrior chief Shivaji Bhonsle's famed encounter with Bijapuri general Afzal Khan (d. 1659) and goes on to cover relations with the Mughals, with the poet reflecting on the different household lineages' role in reshaping imperial and regional monarchical sovereignties. It was composed in the late 1660s, when multiple semi-autonomous provincial elite lineages openly contested regional sultans and posed formidable challenges to Mughal Delhi. This martial poem's author, Nusrati (d. 1674?) arguably one of the most celebrated Dakkani poets from Bijapur (both during his lifetime and later), received recognition during the reign of Sultan ʿAli ʿAdil Shah II (r. 1656–72).[8] Although only a few biographical insights can be gleaned from Nusrati's work, we know that he came from a family of soldiers who had served in Bijapur's army for generations and who were followers of the Deccan's most famous Chishti saint, Khwaja Banda Nawaz Gesudaraz (d. 1422).[9] A Sunni Muslim theologian with a deep knowledge of the Qurʾan and Hadith, Nusrati was also perhaps one of the earliest practitioners of the so-called *sabk-i hindī* or "Indian style" poetics in Urdu.

Examining this poet's reflections on the diglossia between Dakkani and Persian offers another way of deepening literary scholars' critique of the pejorative and ahistorical term, *sabk-i hindī*, which referred to premodern Persianate works produced in the Indian subcontinent as below canonized works in classical Persian.[10]

What is at stake in comparing texts in two languages and the ways in which two authors perceived shifting senses of belonging in the Mughal Empire's distant provinces? In the last twenty years or so, regional specialists of South Asia have emphasized the need to examine multilingual literary texts for their political, social, and aesthetic contexts and functions.[11] Instead of fixating on Persian texts for extracting the political history of Muslim-ruled dynasties, scholarly work on Mughal north India has illuminated the interactions between transregional cosmopolitan languages such as Persian and Sanskrit, and between Persian and other regional vernaculars, showing in particular how non-Muslim literati engaged, observed, and made sense of Mughal power.[12] Such comparisons have collapsed the easy correlation of premodern languages with fixed religious, linguistic, and regional identities.[13] Several regional histories of the period from 1500 to 1800 that examine martial works have shown how adaptation across linguistic zones drew multiple communities into new courts and networks.[14] In contrast to the study of multilingualism in Mughal north India, the Muslim courts of peninsular India, despite their greater linguistic and social heterogeneity, have largely been studied through Persian texts.

My aim in this chapter is to contribute to the larger scholarly conversation on multilingualism by making two arguments. First, by examining provincial Muslim critiques of imperial power in transregional Persian and panregional Dakkani, I emphasize the dynamic history of intrasectarian political critiques within South Asian Islam, wherein Muslim literati held Muslim-ruled dynasties accountable to the standards of proper political conduct. Second, I show that the cross-pollination of political critiques in these two languages was grounded in their long histories of circulation across the north and south. As the previous chapters have demonstrated, the linguistic spheres of individual elite patrons were rarely exclusive and unmixed. Cultural production in both Persian and Dakkani sought to make sense of the fusing of north and south, along with the movement of elite household chiefs across these fragile political borders. This portrait contradicts the prevalent idea of associating regional vernaculars exclusively with a local or regional identity. Examining a shared poetic form in both Persian and Dakkani undergirds the circulatory regimes inherent in the making of premodern literary cultures. It rejects straightjacketing language into identity, as Francesca Orsini has shown, a frame that had developed in the earliest colonial and nationalist literary histories that downplayed northern Indian Urdu's early relationships with Dakkani, Gujri, and other regional idioms.[15]

Recent investigations of Persianate narrative poetry and prose[16] view these textual traditions as part and parcel of a constellation of inherited literary tropes and metaphors modified to the realities of different contexts; they therefore urge more empathetic readings.[17] As has been argued in many different literary contexts, we cannot impose neat modern-day genre distinctions on the capacious heterogeneity within the masnavī form.[18] And, at the same time, literary and aesthetic borrowings in Persianate poetry cannot be decoupled from its inherently political concerns, whether about poetic practice or contemporary rulership. Together, a literary-historical analysis reveals how early modern literati apprehended power, witnessed change, and sought to explain these historical changes by mobilizing the tools, vocabularies, and conventions of an established literary form. To this end, Atishi's and Nusrati's poetic representations capture the transition and tensions between monarchical authority and the crystallization of regional households in the seventeenth century.

Unlike the Persian chronicle, constrained by the obligation to report on events (or at least to pretend to report on them), poetic dramatizations of contemporary events both make possible and preclude certain ways of reading. These textual genres do not always attest to the chronicle's truth claims; nor can such representations be read to index the dates, battles, and names found in prose histories. Rather than reading martial works merely for narrative history, it is worth reading them for how poets recast well-known narratives about events unfolding in their present to declare a political viewpoint.[19] Thus, the two poetic texts at the heart of this chapter ask this question: what did an early modern empire mean for those who lived beyond its borders?

The chapter examines articulations of ghar in the politics of literary patronage and as a category of belonging that transformed in the wake of imperial rule. In the first part, I examine each poet's reflections on poetic craftsmanship and the defenses of their aesthetic and linguistic choices as they sought to secure patronage under new household chiefs. In literary circuits across premodern South Asia, poets and literati dealt with a crisis of validation and self-worth, a theme shared in Persianate literature from the Deccan.[20] While Atishi reflected on competition with other Persian-speaking literati, Nusrati discussed the linguistic tension between Persian and Dakkani. He declared his goal of recounting contemporary events in a lesser tongue—a topic I have addressed elsewhere and briefly revisit here as another form of political meaning-making.[21] The problem of literary competition inexorably tied to the politics of securing patronage permeated the content of these poetic works.

In the second part of the chapter, I examine representations of ghar as a political category that encompassed different kinds of patrimonial power. Both poets addressed the growing challenge that regional rulers faced from different household lineages—from émigré Central Asian Muslim aristocrats to Maratha warrior chiefs who fought for political autonomy in the shadow of imperial suzerainty. In the third part of the chapter, I trace how the two poets emplotted the Mughals on a tenuous political spectrum replete with other familiar constituents, including

Iranians, Habshis or Indo-Africans, Marathas, and Portuguese. I examine representations of selected household chiefs by interrogating the affective vocabularies and the contrasting language of social difference that poets used for laying out criteria for belonging to ghar, laying out how poets transitioned from advice to invective toward the Mughals over the course of the seventeenth century.

The fact that the Mughals were fellow Muslims meant very little to either Atishi or Nusrati. Sectarian, linguistic, and cultural commonalities between empire and its margins held little importance for Atishi, who assessed both the Mughals and the Deccan sultans through the rubric of kingly righteousness and just rule. As an émigré poet, Atishi thought in more transregional terms about empire's pitfalls. Writing in the late 1620s, he observed a rivalry between ruling kings and a series of "minister-favorites," who held high-ranking positions in court and on whom regional sultans depended for governing newly conquered territories.[22] By contrast, in the second half of the century, regional courts swelled with many more possibilities of power beyond these lesser grandees and court ministers. Our second poet, Nusrati, writing in the 1660s, articulated an unapologetic disaffection for the Mughals, decrying threats to kingly power from many independent, regional household lineages, including the Marathas and the Indo-Africans. To make sense of challenges from former vassals, soldiers of fortune, and friends who had become rivals, Nusrati did not mince his words and turned eulogy into invective.

PAYING HOMAGE TO MASTERS: POETIC GENEALOGIES AND THE ART OF COMPLAINING

Martial works are not mere histories about a finished past from which the modern historian can extract a narrative. To read them as such would belie the narrative poem's overarching ethos and multiple layers, including its central concern with form and literary technique. Paying homage to previous poets was one common practice across Persianate works.[23] Both Atishi and Nusrati deployed this standard practice, of acknowledging literary giants before them, in order to reveal political allegiances with their friends, call out their rivals, and affirm an intellectual community in the present. In this section, I examine how poets placed themselves within a line of literary figures in a longer classical tradition while attempting to indicate the novelty of their compositions; I also examine what their declarations tell us about how the politics of patronage created senses of belonging to a ghar.

In their authorial confessions, Atishi and Nusrati engaged in the common practice of citing the great masters of classical Persian poetry—Nizami, Hafiz, Firdawsi, and Saʿdi. But both poets infused into the stock image of paying homage to a received literary tradition details about who their true friends and patrons in court were while calling out imposters and enemies. To examine the politics of paying tribute to the masters, we may begin by turning to Hakim Atishi's authorial confession first. More than a third of his ʿĀdilnāma covers a range of subjects, from advice to kings (hidāyat or pand) and exempla (hikāyāt), to illustrate various moral lessons on giving up material things, worldly impermanence, not being greedy, living righteously, and so forth, all of which then shape the poet's critique of the Mughals and their kingly power that appear in the narrative poem's later chapters.[24]

Atishi begins his composition by expressing his professional frustrations and personal anxieties around the poetic memories of the great Persian masters. His foremost lament is on the problem of plagiarism in his industry about which he expresses grief at the outset and on many pages thereafter. We may empathize with premodern literati's anxieties, which are not unlike present-day academic ones. In a world of intellectual exchange and dialogue, rivalries inevitably revolved around perceived and actual instances of unacknowledged borrowing or rehashing of someone else's words—a concern that plagued Persianate literati working within strict constraints of form and language.[25] Without naming a rival poet but needing to distinguish himself from other Central Asian émigrés to secure patronage, Atishi locates the root of this problem not only in an individual's moral degeneracy but in the bigger trend of riff raff, third-rate, thief poets (sukhan duzd) coming to Hindustan from Iran. He sets himself apart from his unnamed rivals because he wishes to uphold the qualities of righteousness and wisdom and disregard gossip. To illustrate the plagiarism problem, Atishi utilizes the image of the world of poetry as a marketplace to recount a story (qissa) about a thief poet who came to India hoping to set up shop and sell his wares. He informs his readers sarcastically that this thief poet came from the world of stupidity to give pearls in Hindustan (sukhan duzdī az ʿālam-i ablahī / be hind āmad az bahr-e gohar dahī). Atishi was not the only one with a complaint against this particular plagiarist who had a reputation for stealing others' verse.[26]

In between such moments of anxiety about poetic craftsmanship, he imparts ethical advice to his peers and colleagues on how to be a good poet. For example, seeking the master poets was one way for the struggling poet to cure himself of the plagiarism problem, since reading the classics would lead the wayward in the right direction. Thus, in both the prologue and epilogue, while paying homage to the great masters, Atishi counsels the aspiring poet to turn to Nizami, Saʿdi, and Firdawsi to learn poetry's secrets. However, what first appears to be stock verses eulogizing these figures quickly transforms into veiled insults targeting the current Bijapur sultan and a place where the poet asserts his affinities for new patrons, in particular, his benefactor Mustafa Khan Lari, the Iranian prime minister, whom we already met in chapter 3.

This shift of allegiance from king to household chief comes alive when Atishi discusses the greatest innovator of martial poetry, Firdawsi (d. 1019), and the poetic memory of his relationship with Sultan Mahmud of Ghazna (d. 1030).[27]

He begins by praising Firdawsi, who wrote thousands of timeless verses making legends about the dead eternal.[28] As was well known, Sultan Mahmud of Ghazna had failed to recognize Firdawsi's talent and give him credit (and pay him) for his monumental work, a narrative that became part of poetic memory across the Persianate world.[29] Atishi took this well-worn trope a few steps further, using it to complain about the reigning Bijapur sultan, Muhammad ʿAdil Shah (r. 1627–56). By calling Mahmud of Ghazna a breaker of covenants (*paimān gusil*), he casts doubt on his own reigning king's birth:

*be nā pāk zādeh nadārīd umīd / ze zangī be shustan na gardad safīd
na būd shah-i ghaznīn ze pusht-i pedar / ke firdawsī az vey be shud shikwe-gar*

do not have hope from a bastard / for washing a *zangī*[30] cannot turn him white
the sultan of Ghazna was not from his father / that's why Firdawsi complained about him

By directly referencing Mahmud of Ghazna's bastard status, Atishi's implicitly points to the disputed lineage of the current Bijapur king whose birth was at the center of courtly intrigue and a disputed accession in the 1620s around the time of death of the previous ruler, Ibrahim ʿAdil Shah II's, a moment already examined in chapter 4. Atishi expresses his dissatisfaction with Sultan Muhammad, who, like Mahmud of Ghazna, failed to recognize the talents of great poets. By evoking the example of Mahmud of Ghazna's vizier, Ahmad Maymandi (d. 1032), who was the first to recognize Firdawsi's genius, Atishi declares his allegiance to the current prime minister, Mustafa Khan Lari.[31] Drawing a temporal parallelism, Atishi mentions a past sultan and poet to draw an analogy between himself and the current sultan of Bijapur. Noting how he labored for six months to compose the *ʿĀdilnāma*, Atishi beseeches Mustafa Khan, a true customer of poetry, openly stating his disaffection with Sultan Muhammad ʿAdil Shah and declaring a newfound allegiance to the minister and his extended household:[32]

be nām-i tū dar pardah-yi madh-e shah / namūdam jahān ra pur az mehr-o-māh[33]

In the guise of praising the king, in your name / I showed the world a path with sun and moon

Atishi therefore draws on the well-known history of the sultan's failure to recognize Firdawsi's talents to claim his own current allegiances in court. However, making such declarations also came with dangers and so, by doing this, Atishi distinguishes himself from Firdawsi and his iconic work, the *Shāhnāma* (*The Book of Kings*), which recounts rivalries between fictionalized kings and heroes. Despite praising Firdawsi for immortalizing the dead, Atishi laments that writing about the dead is better (and perhaps safer) than writing about the living, because the former would remain unaware of your poetry (*bovad mordeh behtar az ān zindeh tan / ke ghāfil bovad az adā-yi sukhan*).[34] Later innovators of martial poetry thus saw themselves as surpassing Firdawsi, the creator of the *Shāhnāma* and its imagined stories. By writing about the living, like Amir Khusrau and other poets who had declared how they had departed from Firdawsi, Atishi too saw himself as taking greater risks by going beyond storytelling toward recording actual events, contemporary historical actors, and the politics of his own times.[35]

Nusrati's work in the second half of the seventeenth century likewise addresses the theme of professional competition but his poetic competitors were composing in the imminent panregional literary idiom, Dakkani. Persianate literati debated what it meant to memorialize contemporary events and emulate Persian classics such as Firdawsi's *Shāhnāma* in Dakkani, in a derivative linguistic register. Unlike Atishi's anxieties, which centered on compatriot Persian émigré poets, Nusrati's authorial confession reveals tensions between these two tongues while reiterating a similar, measured appraisal of Firdawsi.

In the *ʿAlīnāma*'s preface, Nusrati first turns to the task of thanking his intellectual interlocutors who encouraged him to take on the challenge of recording the present in lowly (*haqīr*) Dakkani.[36] While Nusrati pays homage to his patron, Sultan ʿAli ʿAdil Shah II, who was also a prolific Dakkani poet, he goes beyond merely praising the sultan to express his gratitude toward literati friends. Such gestures of gratitude for interlocutors and friends were not unlike the acknowledgement sections of scholarly monographs in modern times. Through the simple task of saying "thank you," Nusrati self-consciously reveals his intellectual community and political affinities. Among his contemporaries and those whom Nusrati held in the highest regard was Nurullah Qazi, an Iranian poet-historian who had just completed a chronicle titled *Tārīkh-i ʿAli ʿĀdil Shāhī*, covering the early years of the reign of ʿAli II, who urged him to write a new kind of history.[37] Recognition from learned friends lent Nusrati credibility in his position as official chronicler, a position that had never before been assigned exclusively to a Dakkani poet.

In comparison to Persian, Dakkani had less prestige in Bijapur and Golconda's literary circuits, and poets writing in this literary idiom often emphasized the fact that their respect was hard-won. To valorize the skill of bilingualism, Nusrati points to himself, declaring that the truly gifted poet must have skills in both Persian and Dakkani. Moreover, he had nothing but an attitude of condescension for those who could not appreciate verse about contemporary politics, calling those who had dismissed it in the past jealous and ignorant (*hasīdān jāhilān*).[38] Modifying the mirror motif to refer to the mutually enriching relationship between these two tongues, Nusrati makes the case for polyphonic verse:

> *agar koi ho mʿanigar wa ārasī /padhe razmiya hindī wa fārsī*
> *agar hai u kāmil samajh ka dhanī /to is yek te hue do hunar son ghanī*
> *ke donon kī khubī mujh ankhiyān men ān / khulāsa nikāliya hun khush maye chān*[39]

if someone is intelligent and a mirror
let him read poems of war in *hindī* and *fārsī*
he shall be enriched with two sets of skills
my eyes have the vision of both [languages]
for I sieve goodness from both

A true connoisseur would appreciate any literary idiom in any recognizable poetic form. A poet-historian who could think in multiple tongues drew on received templates, eventually hoping to surpass his predecessors in both theme and content.

Like other Persianate literati before him, after discussing linguistic choice, Nusrati also returns to the sensitive question of originality by paying homage to the great masters. Anointing the ʿ*Alināma* as the *Shāhnāma-i dakkan* (The book of kings of the Deccan), Nusrati evokes the distressing memory of Firdawsī's disappointment with Sultan Mahmud of Ghazna, declaring that the great master's soul would forget its grief and delight (ʿ*ajab kiyā hai firdawsī pāk zad / apas gham besar ap kare ruh shād*) from reading the ʿ*Alināma*, a skillful emulation of his classical work.[40] Like Atishi, who paid homage to the canon, before him, Nusrati also contrasts the *Shāhnāma*'s imagined stories and plots with the actual events and battles fought by Mahmud of Ghazna (r. 998–1030) and his kinsmen, events and battles that Firdawsī left unrecorded.[41] Nusrati's ʿ*Alināma* stands out because it focuses on the tumultuous present and takes the risk of representing current historical actors. At a time when so many new players claimed to be kings, deploying the genre of the martial poem to create heroes was a particularly fraught endeavor. For the poet-historian, casting nonkingly contenders as heroes from much humbler social backgrounds was a tricky exercise. Poets were declaring the high stakes of representing contemporary rulership, acutely aware that decentering kings and replacing them with nonkingly aspirants could pose problems for their own livelihoods. Memorializing the living rather than the dead was, therefore, a dangerous undertaking.

To be sure, demonstrating that one knew the canon and locating oneself within a poetic tradition was essential for building a reputation and finding an affiliation with a ghar. But such received images were then modified to observe, judge, and take a position on contemporary politics—the other ambition of narrative poetry. Both poets' authorial confessions reveal how the poetic terrain of the Persianate was contested with debate about which themes and tongues were worth recasting into well-established templates. In self-reflective moments, Atishi and Nusrati unveiled their intellectual and professional communities and their complaints about unappreciative audiences and shady colleagues. At first glance, these two seventeenth-century works appear to merely eulogize kings and dynasties. I have argued that much more lies within, including avowing linguistic choices, calling out competitors and friends, signaling the risk of talking about politics, and announcing why their compositions should stand out. Now, I turn to unpacking how the two poets constructed the politics of ghar in their uncertain present by casting their critical gaze on the mighty Mughals, as well as more intimate friends turned rivals, over the course of the seventeenth century.

THE POET-COMMENTATOR: HOUSEHOLD POLITICS AS A GAME OF CHESS

At first glance, page after page of kingly praises in both the *'Ādilnāma* and *'Alināma* may lead us to regard the texts as unexceptional, no different than myriad other Persianate martial poems in masnavī form. But underneath the layer of customary verses about a monarch's valor, wisdom, fairness, and justice, both Atishi and Nusrati pause to look upon the unruly world around them and reflect on the fact that, in such times, kingly virtues no longer count for much.[42] As we saw before, Atishi admitted that singing the sultan's praises was, in fact, a cover for eulogizing his true patron, the prime minister Mustafa Khan. By the second half of the seventeenth century, the cast of nonkingly lineages carving out independent power circuits exploded. Nusrati was preoccupied, even alarmed, by the emboldened autonomy of Marathas, Indo-Africans, and Afghans, all of whom had long operated within peninsular India's courts. He compared the current volatile political landscape to a game of chess where the rules were constantly changing. He coined new words and analogies to define the various meanings of political loyalty, which, at the time, seemed to have no enduring criteria.

Both the *'Ādilnāma* and *'Alināma* captivate the reader not because they present us with a minefield of new facts about well-known historical events, but for their many telling silences and everything that the two accounts leave unsaid. In the *'Ādilnāma*, for instance, Atishi does not mention Bijapur's infamous civil war that took place in the late 1620s to early 1630s between three courtiers of distinct lineages—the *habshī* or Abyssinian Khawas Khan, the Maratha Brahmin Murari Pandit, and the Iranian Mustafa Khan Lari—and that resulted in the deaths of the first two and the latter's ascendance in court, an event much discussed in political histories.[43] Likewise, chronicles from this period typically mention the deed of submission that was negotiated with the Mughals in 1636, but Atishi does not. Omissions of major political negotiations in the heroic verse genre meant to valorize regional sultans alerts us to multivalent functions of such representations. Poetic representations offset the reality that the Deccan sultans were ceding sovereignty to imperial overlords. Given the roughly eight-year period during which the *'Ādilnāma* was composed (1628) and compiled (1637), prior to the civil war but after the acceptance of Mughal suzerainty, the poem's hero in each chapter depends entirely on who was winning at that particular historical moment.[44] Considering the relationship of verse with contemporary historical contexts, we need to accept that although such representations may be exaggerations, they nonetheless were meaningful to those who produced them and they therefore offer insight about the context within which they were produced. Despite the historicity of the events and figures depicted in premodern works, the inversions of political reality in these representations may unsettle the positivist historian. And yet, these inflected portraits of power allow us to ask the question—to what extent was Mughal rule accepted and admired across distant regions of seventeenth-century South Asia? The observations of Deccan's poets answer: to a very limited extent. According to them, imperial overlords could neither be trusted nor excessively admired. By composing anti-imperial works at a time when the Mughals dominated every corner of the subcontinent, contemporary actors rejected the inevitability of imperial authority.

Falling within the long continuum of ethical literature in Persian, what Mana Kia has called the "*adab/akhlāq* complex," the *ʿĀdilnāma* weighs in on moral dilemmas understood through the shifting grounds of patron-client relationships.[45] Imparting ethical advice throughout the narrative, Atishi first counsels his new patron and well-wisher Mustafa Khan on good governance, prudence toward one's friends, generosity toward subjects and, last but not least, the patron's duty to appreciate (or adequately compensate) the poet for his labor.[46] At different points in the narrative, Atishi praises Khawas Khan and Mustafa Khan with the well-worn image of the wise, insightful minister (*dastūr-i roshan nazar*) who imparts good governance (*tadbīr*) by counseling the king, a role he prays will last forever.[47]

Signaling the growing tension between kings and households, Atishi eventually wields the wise minister image to diminish the Bijapur sultan's authority. He addresses his patron Mustafa Khan, endowing him with a stature above the regional sultan and anoints him with the title of the Deccan kingdom's protector (*nigehdār-i mulk-i dakkan*).[48] Mustafa Khan led negotiations with the Mughals who likewise regarded the prime minister as indispensable and as the one who adorned the king's throne (*be sar hamnashīn sāz tāj-i mahī / muzaiyan kon takht-i shahenshāhī*).[49] The poet goes so far as to say that out of great respect the imperial army and its commanders bowed before the prime minister, thus momentarily dissolving the hierarchy between a Mughal commander and the Bijapuri prime minister (*nishastand bā yek digar ān chunān / ke zāhir nabūd farqī ān dar miyān* [they sat beside each other, as if there was no difference between them].[50] By altogether removing the regional sultan from Mughal-Deccan diplomatic negotiations, Atishi paints the regional household chief as equal in status to the Mughals. He imparts old conventions of representing kingly virtues on new nonkingly patrons, casting household chiefs as direct negotiators with imperial power, operating without the intervention of regional sultans. It would still be a few more decades before the Deccan's political terrain shifted from sultans to nonkingly households that, in turn, would curtail Mughal presence in peninsular India.

In the second half of the seventeenth century, we witness a far more resolute break from charismatic kingly authority, a process that unfolded in tandem with

Mughal entrenchment in the south. Thirty years after Atishi, Nusrati commented on an altogether different political landscape, choosing to make sense of it in the lesser literary idiom of Dakkani. In his times, a greater number of players—from Afghan military households to former Indo-African slaves who commanded their own militaries to Maratha warrior chiefs—now made claims to sovereignty. But, alternating careful praise and critique was not enough to capture this brave new world where anyone could be king. A far more irreverent mode of expression was employed to express how one's most familiar friends and kin had become strangers and even bitter rivals.

Unlike the celebratory seventeenth-century Marathi literary works and triumphant Mughal chronicles in Persian, Nusrati's work offers an uncensored evaluation of late seventeenth-century Mughal-Deccan politics written, if you will, from the perspective of the losing side (that of the Deccan sultanates).[51] Nusrati writes about his understanding of historical change and his verdict on politics in contemporary times. Indicating to his audience that he "is about to explain the end of kingship in the Deccan" (katā hun atā bāt ik kām kī / dakhan kī shahī kī saranjām kī), he first draws a portrait of an unpredictable, riotous chess game where conventional rules and strategies are suspended. ʿAli ʿAdil Shah II's ascension to the throne in 1656 came with the bleak realization summed up in these lines:

> nanhe aur bade the so sab bad nihād / achāle u chāron taraf se fasād
> mukhālif te aksar munāfiq hue / muwāfiq bhi kayī na muwāfiq hue
>
> Small and big were all wicked / creating discord from all four sides
> Opponents became enemies / those who agreed became disagreeable[52]

In this new game of chess (navī shatranj kī bāzī), the king faced most difficult choices, since everyone around him played the same moves but with unexpected twists that violated the rules of the game. Nusrati begins by describing changes in politics as a game of chess, noting:

> jine liya sake khel yūn apne hāt / sake kar ū lelāj par piyād ko māt[53]
>
> he who is able to seize this game in his hand / like al-Lajlaj, he could checkmate as a pawn

Evoking the tenth-century Arab chess theorist and chess master, Abu'l-Faraj Muhammad ibn ʿUbayd Allah al-Lajlaj (or "the stutterer/stammerer") (d. 970), Nusrati decries the fact that the game's age-old strategies, which so few had managed to master, were now being turned upside down.[54] As the verse above notes, these were times in which the most insulting form of defeat, where the pawn delivers a checkmate to the king, was not just an unsurprising outcome, but a likely one. In this new game dushman (enemy) and dost (friend) were two sides of the same coin with an equal opportunity to turn on the king. One had to tread with great caution in such times. This dialectical relationship between friendship and enmity, trust and betrayal, and familiarity and estrangement shape Nusrati's subsequent narratives in the ʿAlīnāma about contemporary political encounters. His observations of the Maratha warrior chief Shivaji Bhonsle, the Indo-African military commander Siddi Jauhar (d. 1665?), as well as high-ranking Mughal generals such as the Kachawaha Rajput Jai Singh (d. 1667), inverted contrasting affective terminologies to capture a fractious political landscape where an ever-increasing number of pawns now claimed to be kings.

FROM ADVICE TO INVECTIVE: ON EMPIRE AND ITS DISCONTENTS

When do wisdom, advice, and words of praise turn into invective and insult? When those closest to you become enemies. Poets observed the actions of aristocratic and military households that had long been tied to monarchical power but were now seeking to carve out independent domains. Atishi and Nusrati's works embody this core transformation that took place over the course of the seventeenth century. Both poets put the martial poem's form and content to the task of representing the uncertainties faced by monarchical power by composing a new set of heroes and villains. Above, I showed the transition in the century's first half from the minister-favorite figure to a much larger playing field of semi-autonomous household lineages that threatened regional sultans at the same time they were negotiating with imperial power. The Mughals came to represent different things to different actors over the course of this century.

Persianate narrative poems capture the long transformation in the meaning of the term ghar and what it came to signify as the Mughals marched south, which was at times negative. At the beginning, poets would describe the empire as an object of begrudging consternation, then patronize it as a sort of wayward kin in need of a scolding, and finally by defining it as a diabolical entity that deserved only opprobrium and derision. The term *Mughal* was understood best in contrast to its antonymic signifier *Deccani*, the meanings of which simultaneously widened in the second half of the century. Regional poets writing in the 1630s or 1660s refused to accept Mughal ascendancy and instead sought to explain the fragility of the empire's universal ambitions and the uncertainties it had brought on multiple societies.

Let us turn again to Hakim Atishi and the question of what belonging to a ghar under the Mughals in the early years of imperial suzerainty from the 1620s to the 1640s meant. A reluctant admiration and a sense of obligation toward the Mughals crumbled as alliances with the Deccan sultanates broke, treaties were violated, and disputes over territory intensified. Still, rather than admonishing them outright, Atishi imparted measured moral advice to all rulers, Mughal and Deccani alike, framed through the idiom of *nasīhat* or *pand* (advice).[55] At the level of their poetic compositions, Persianate literati in the Deccan sought to invert imperial suzerainty's punitive terms that had been put upon the region, which included measures such as paying tribute, reading the *khutba* (sermon) in the Mughal emperor's name, and regulating the ranks and titles of the regional nobility.

Thus, Atishi's text begins with a degree of deference and filial devotion that the Deccan sultans professed toward Mughal rulers, starting with a period of unity when Bijapur and Delhi delivered a final blow to the nearly extinguished neighboring sultanate of Ahmadnagar (ca. 1490–1636). With a clear recognition of and awe before imperial power, the poet admires the Mughal army's magnificence by composing many verses eulogizing the Mughal emperor Shah Jahan (r. 1628–58).[56] Atishi both unsettles hierarchies between regional and imperial sovereigns and at the same time holds imperial power accountable to an obligation to protect its subordinates. He begins by inverting the hierarchy between the king of Lahore (*shahinshāh-yi lahor*), who was lower than the Deccan sultan (*bādshāh-i dakkan*). Then, expressing a filial devotion to empire through an idiom of kinship, he recasts this relationship as one between a father and a son (*chū ū bābā bāshad man ū rā pesar*). Together, the two would last with certainty as long as the son, the Bijapur sultan, fulfilled his obligation to pay taxes to the father, the Mughal emperor (*pedar gar ze farzand khwāhad kharāj / musallam shavad har do rā takht-o-tāj*).[57] This idealized image of filial devotion marked multiple dramatizations of letters exchanged between the Mughal emperor Shah Jahan and the Bijapur sultan Muhammad ʿAdil Shah, according to which both rulers agreed to a mutually beneficial bond.[58] In an initial arrangement in the late 1620s, the two sides agreed to divide the lands above and below the River Krishna.[59] Thus, the Bijapur sultan instructed his army to follow a righteous path and give half of the conquered lands to the Mughals with respect and without any war or conflict, for this was the way of Muslim rulers.[60]

Shortly thereafter, however, the imperial masters fell in Atishi's eyes, as the Bijapur-Mughal alliance that had extinguished the Nizam shahs of Ahmadnagar collapsed in the 1630s. For the remaining narrative, Atishi's assessment of the Mughals turns dour; many battles, embassies, and negotiations ensued and many promises made were quickly broken.[61] In scenes of renewed armed conflict with the Mughals, he comments on their *kaj ravī* (crooked ways), *makkārī* (cunning), and *makr-o-fareb* (deceit), as well as on Shah Jahan's tendency to give ambiguous, two-faced answers.[62] The Mughal emperor, now belittled and addressed by his given name of Khurram, held grudges (*kīneh*), which was unbecoming of a king who sought universal legitimacy.[63] According to Atishi, Shah Jahan had showed gratitude outwardly for Bijapur's help defeating the Nizam Shahs, but in private the king remained ungenerous and wished to take over both kingdoms.[64]

Referring to Shah Jahan as the great man who broke the treaty (*chunam gasht peymān shikan ān janāb*) and consistently failed to keep promises, Atishi warns the Mughal sovereign that even honey turns to poison for those who are weak in keeping their word (*kasī kū buvad dar jahān sust ʿahd / khurad zahr peyvaste barbād-i shahd*).[65] The poet concludes by imploring the Mughal king, "why does the wise man go on the path / going on which he is overcome by regret" (*chera mard-i dānā be rāhī ravad /ke az raftan-i khud pashīmān shavad*).[66]

Then, after many verses imparting moral maxims to the Mughal ruler on how to be righteous and just, Atishi pauses to admonish himself for giving advice:

> khāmosh ātishī īn che pand ast pand / kas īn guftagū rā na dārad pasand
> kanūn bar sar-i dāstān bāz kard / ke āmad sar-i nām zīn gham be dard[67]
> be silent, Atishi! What's with all this advice?
> no one is fond of this talk of yours
> go back to the story now
> for the story itself is tired of your advice!

Here, Atishi breaks away from the main narrative as a kind of aside, where he is both self-evocative and self-referential, admitting to his audience that interrupting the story of Mughal-Deccan politics flouts narrative norms. But this digression is absolutely necessary in times when kings themselves are breaking the norms for ethical rule and the poet has to step in, as a political observer, to share what righteous and just rule means. It should not come as a surprise, then, that Atishi concludes all his narrations of battles and diplomatic negotiation with pronouncements on the Mughal Empire's moral degeneracy, followed by advice on how to correct such behavior in the advice mode of *pand* or *nasīhat*. Such multivocal narrations therefore serve to unify the text's prescriptive/didactic purposes with its other goal of recording political events.

Across the Persianate world, scholars have long recognized how the *adab/akhlāq* complex offers fertile ground for reading the political, not merely as symptomatic of context but as unfolding within the text's responses to its own conditions of production.[68] Atishi was not writing an ethical treatise nor composing his verse within the mirror for princes genre. Early modern literati and their audiences rarely drew such neat distinctions that are so clearly delineated in modern scholarship.[69] The heroic-historic masnavī could simultaneously encompass *hikāyāt* (exempla), *madh* (eulogies) for regional household chiefs, and advice for or criticism of reigning monarchs. The *ʿĀdilnāma*'s stakes and content transformed over the roughly eight years during which it was compiled and composed with themes fusing it together to record new events and encounters unfolding at different points in time.

The poet's turn to nonkingly patrons occurred at the same moment that regional contenders were vying for their own power when Mughal power had itself weakened regional kings. Provincial Persianate literati tried to make sense of what it would mean to pledge symbolic allegiance to Delhi, have Mughal soldiers permanently encamped across the River Krishna, and pay tribute to imperial overlords. The signifier *Mughal*, a term the Mughals themselves never used, took on new meanings over time for observers like Atishi and Nusrati, who located themselves within conflicting imperial identities. As subjects of a shared Perso-Islamic ecumene, Atishi's verse was, of course, no different than his Persian-speaking courtly compatriots in Mughal north India. What, then, made his observations on empire any different? For one, as we just saw, that to Atishi the Mughals were hardly beacons of harmony. To this outsider on empire's margins, promises broken with those who were weaker violated the very criteria for universal sovereignty. The Mughals could not be trusted or relied on but nonetheless had to be tolerated for the sake of political survival. It would be another few decades before a more negative assessment of the Mughals and a far more dystopic vision of empire emerged from the pens of Dakkani literati.

Along with growing political and military conflicts, the choice of language itself allowed for a more scathing evaluation of the empire. In the century's latter half, then, appraisals of imperial power were no longer measured or careful. In fact, words to apprehend the Mughals were not selected with caution; they were meant to hurt, reprove, and castigate. Entanglements with imperial power in any part of the early modern world cannot be understood without their predictable corollary—the explosion of corporate groups within imperial territories or, as in our case, provincial household lineages residing beyond imperial domains that challenged kingly authority.[70] Nusrati mapped the Mughals onto a contentious political landscape now littered with many familiar contenders. He compared the Mughal-Rajput general Mirza Raja Jai Singh and the Mughal emperor Aurangzeb (d. 1707) with homegrown, intimate foes such as Shivaji and Siddi Jauhar. From famous battles in recent memory to the destruction of the great port city of Surat and innumerable fort sieges across the Hyderabad-Karnatak, Nusrati drew up a map of places and people impossible to pin down as friend or foe, loyal or disloyal, confidant or traitor.

A critique of empire and its fragility came alive in Nusrati's verse many decades before the disintegration of imperial order in the eighteenth century.[71] Familiarity served as the basic criterion through which he gauged each actor's character and pronounced the requisite moral judgements. Those who had once been the closest advisors, trusted vassals, or sworn themselves as kin protected by the sultan deserved the most extreme invective. For instance, Shivaji and the Siddi Jauhar, hailing from lineages that had long been attached to the 'Adil shahs of Bijapur, were the most familiar and, consequently, deserved the maximum scorn. On the other hand, Mughal generals such as the Mirza Raja Jai Singh and Shaista Khan (d. 1694), strangers from the outset, deserved a different kind of criticism, as did players much further afield, such as the Portuguese and the Dutch. As a learned political observer, Nusrati imparted wise counsel, but he also chose to berate, launching his invective against and censure of those who had dared to revolt against kingly power.

Let us briefly revisit the chronology of events in the 1660s before turning to how they were narrated in Nusrati's verse. When Mughal emperor Aurangzeb returned to Delhi from the Deccan, the War of Succession among princes temporarily paused attempts to conquer the southern Indian sultanates in 1657–1658. At the same time, provincial household chiefs who previously served regional sultans now appealed to the Mughal emperor, making promises to protect newly conquered imperial territories in the northern Deccan and on the Konkan coast.[72] In 1659, Shivaji killed Afzal Khan (d. 1659), a general who was sent by the Bijapur sultan ʿAli ʿAdil Shah II to capture or kill him—an iconic event embedded in both popular and scholarly retellings. After the Mughals subsumed all territories north of the River Krishna and Shivaji's domains near the region around Pune, armed skirmishes between the Mughals, Marathas, and Deccan sultans were suspended for a few years. In 1663, Shivaji attacked Aurangzeb's maternal uncle and new Mughal viceroy to the Deccan, Shaista Khan and his encampment, sacking the Mughal port city of Surat in early 1664, an event that caught imperial authorities and European mercantile observers off guard.[73] With Mirza Raja Jai Singh's arrival in the Deccan in 1665, a new set of negotiations unfolded between Bijapur, Golkonda, Shivaji, and the Mughals, with each side forging cross-cutting alliances to undercut the other.[74] All these events lie at the *Alināmā's* center, but instead of following a neat chronology, Nusrati moves in and out of recent memories to events unfolding in the poet's present, collapsing distinctions between different temporalities and plotting historical actors onto his larger cognitive map—that is, by setting the stage for a chess game about the politics of ghar.

We may begin by following how the poet depicted Siddi Jauhar, also known as Salabat Khan, who first swore allegiance to but later revolted against ʿAli ʿAdil Shah II.[75] Narrative histories and modern representations have recounted a sequence of events from the time ʿAli II chose Siddi Jauhar to capture Shivaji at Panhala fort, to the moment when he turned coat and rebelled around the year 1661. But beyond what really happened, how did contemporary observers understand this encounter between an Indo-African elite slave-general, a Maratha warrior chief, and the Bijapur sultan? Nusrati gives meaning to this conflict by fitting each character into a vocabulary of difference and affinity with respect to the larger problem of kingly authority's uncertainty. In a world of tenuous solidarities, it should come as no surprise that physical, cultural, and sectarian differences were fair game for recasting enemies, who had once been loyal vassals.

The narration of Siddi Jauhar's revolt also illustrates how a household head from a prominent social group, Indo-Africans, who had long been integrated into southern India's political and social fabric,[76] could be simultaneously understood as both deeply familiar and a political Other, depending on the observer's ideological agenda. In such premodern encounters, honor was rarely a static, normative category because its valence changed according to what was at stake among opposing social groups.[77] In other words, honor came from without, emergent from what a particular historical actor did in relation to others, rather than being inherent in any individual or group. For instance, in the case of Siddi Jauhar, we witness him going from honorable to dishonorable in the course of just a few months. On March 9, 1660, Siddi Jauhar interceded on behalf of the Bijapur sultan to enlist support from Gondaji Pasalkar, a *desai* from the Muse valley near Pune, for his military campaigns against Shivaji. When he mediated Bijapur's relationship with several other such Maratha hereditary subordinate territorial chiefs, a series of honorific titles (ʿumdatu 'l-wuzrā-yi ʿuzzām zubdatu 'l-umarā-yi kirām / the most trusted of ministers and finest among the greatest nobles) precede mentions of Siddi Jauhar in Persian administrative documents.[78] Even our poet, Nusrati, casts this trusted former slave as a "devoted friend of the people and of soldiers" (ra ʿāyā kā Mukhlis / sipāhī kā yār)[79] when sultan ʿAli ʿAdil Shah II first anointed Siddi Jauhar with an honorable title, Salabat Khan, and praised him for offering to lay siege to Panhala fort, where Shivaji was hiding.

However, shortly thereafter these honorific titles transform into biting insults. Recalling that Siddi Jauhar had taken over the *jāgīr* of Karnul after revolting against his master, the Bijapuri commander ʿAbdul Wahab, Nusrati condemned Sultan ʿAli ʿAdil Shah II's hasty decision to pardon him.[80] He disagreed with the king's tendency to forgive so easily and ignore this troublemaker's faults (*apas sāf dil sāt shah be khilāf / use phir nawāze khatā kar mu ʿāf*).[81] When he rebelled against the Bijapur sultan, Nusrati used a contrast of phenotypes, a premodern colorism of sorts, to capture the shift in Siddi Jauhar's political loyalties. As soon as the Indo-African rebelled, the poet used his physical attribute of dark skin to heighten his otherness. Word reached the king that Siddi Jauhar had turned into a *bāghī* or bandit. At this point, the poet declared:

> siyah rū te ich thā ū ghadār / jiyā thā honth zāgh-i murdār khwār
> kavā nā thī us son anast kise / sadā thag pane kī ich thī gat usse
>
> black face! It was he who was the traitor,
> his lips red like a raven gorging on dead corpses
> no one liked him one bit
> for he only knew how to inveigle

Decrying Siddi Jauhar's decision to negotiate with Shivaji, Nusrati admonished the Indo-African general for smearing his own name and sinking his household (*dubāyā āpas nām-o-nāmūs-o-ghar*).[82] This euphemism of the home or *ghar* that appears consistently throughout the ʿAlināma, connotes two meanings: on the one hand, it refers to each regional chief's own lineage and extended household; on the other, it alludes to being brought up in the king's court but revolting against the very home that has nurtured you. Later in the ʿAlināma, Nusrati laments in a qasida about Siddi Jauhar's rebellion the following: those who had been reared in the king's court (*shāh ke ghar*) had turned into rebels, with sedition the only skill known to such lost souls (*nawāziyā shah ke ghar ho athā shah son phir bhāgī / na thā bin fitna angīzī fan us gumrāh utangal kā*).[83] This dismay at betrayal from one's closest and very own is what drives Nusrati's suspicion of nonroyal regional elites who defy kingly authority. The poet turns praise into invective as political circumstances shift by heightening phenotypical difference to express the loss of honor and a sense of betrayal from a former slave and trusted vassal.

For Nusrati, no figure exemplifies this attitude of ingratitude and disloyalty more than the Maratha warrior chief Shivaji Bhonsle, whose family had once served under the ʿAdil shahs of Bijapur. According to Nusrati, Shivaji sowed the seeds of sedition (*tukhm-i fasād*) in the Deccan and was the reason fighting began between the Deccan sultans and the Mughals (*bade bādshāhān mai pādhya ladāyī / dakkan aur mughalān ke dar miyān*). Mapping Shivaji onto a wider canvas of contentious politics, from the Franks to the Mughals, the poet exhorts:

> *bhariyān thā sab us zāt makrūr yū / dise ādmī rūp ban nasl deo*
> *dikhā de tū tuk apnī talbīs kon / lage vird la haul iblīs kon*
> *firangi te thā kufr mai at ashad / kare dīn son dushmanī sakht bad*
> *na is qatl-i hajj te ʿibādat nahnī / haram main bī sonpadhe tu thā kushtanī*
> *sadā sahībān son namak bar harām / kiyā nit namak khārīyān kār kām*[84]

> An essence filled with cunning
> He appeared to be a man but was actually a devil
> Show your disguise now!
> In the way we say *la haul*, and the devil escapes
> He is a worse disbeliever than the Portuguese
> The greatest enemy of faith
> And yet, the reason for him tending towards murder is not worship
> For you were caught killing even in the house of god
> You had always been a *namak harām*
> Killing even those who were loyalists

Here, Nusrati judges Shivaji according to a broad universal criterion: not being a believer in any faith. Among those who lacked this trait were the Portuguese, the greatest unbelievers according to Muslims, and against whom all other rivals were measured, referring here to their attempts at disrupting the pilgrimage to Mecca. The problem with Shivaji was that he managed to surpass even the Europeans, not because of any special allegiance to one faith but because of his merciless behavior toward everyone. As Nusrati saw it, the fact that Shivaji was a non-Muslim was not what underlay his proclivity to kill. At the end of this verse and many other narrations throughout the poem, the poet returns to the very old concept of eating one's salt—*namak harāmī*—of someone who has violated an allegiance and is guilty of breaching the trust of a former friend. The measure of loyalty was relative, rather than absolute, and at its center lay the problem of deep familiarity and intimacy. Those who were the most familiar and dared to turn coat deserved maximum disdain and were caricatured in terms of ethnic, sectarian, or physical difference. Just like the known quantity and formerly loyal Indo-African Siddi Jauhar, whom Nusrati had no qualms denigrating in terms of his physical features, the very familiar Shivaji failed the measure of being true to any one faith. His complete disregard for religion, rather than his affinity for one, is what Nusrati chose to highlight in this instance. Standard measures of recognizing social difference, whether through skin color or faith, were often underscored in moments of political conflict with the most familiar rivals.

And yet, the seventeenth-century narrator was hardly oblivious to pointing out sectarian difference and using it to frame a political rivalry polemically, which begets the question of *when* such narrative choices were made.[85] We may extend here the argument that Cynthia Talbot has made for intersectarian encounters in southern India in preceding historical periods. She argued that constant competition among warrior elites shaped their shaky claims to legitimacy and necessitated marking boundaries or the production of ethnicity against an outsider or other.[86] By the seventeenth century, we are no longer dealing with a clearly defined encounter of first-time rivals, such as those elucidated by Talbot in medieval Andhra (southeastern India) in the fourteenth and fifteenth centuries. Under Mughal suzerainty in the seventeenth century, peninsular India's variegated ethnolinguistic elites had accumulated a long, layered memory of past encounters and were well known to each other. After 1650, we witness a reappropriation of old tropes and binaries to articulate politics in a context of deep familiarity and relatedness. Household chiefs from different ethnic and linguistic lineages who had long known each other now cut across southern India's sultanates and imperial north India, necessitating validation or rejection of each group's ascriptive identity. By the time Nusrati was writing in the mid-1660s, very familiar contenders—Iranians, Indo-African, Marathas, and Afghans—were part of one seamless, coconstituted continuum of politics in a shared ghar.

Another narration in the *'Alināma* that illuminates sectarian difference is the famed encounter between Mirza Raja Jai Singh and Shivaji.[87] In Nusrati's framing of this incident, sectarian affinity subsumes or contradicts one's political loyalty. To open this episode, the poet draws out scenes, such as that involving Mughal emperor Aurangzeb appointing Mirza Raja Jai Singh to the Deccan, and then recounts the historic siege of Purandar and the treaty negotiated after it in 1665, which reduced Shivaji's domains.[88] Nusrati dramatizes Shivaji's political calculations first in a monologue and then as a conversation with Jai Singh. With an imperial victory over Purandar fort inevitable, the Maratha commander sees his house burn down from all sides (*dikhiyā do taraf te lagī ghar ko āg*), reckoning with the fact that the Mughals would not spare him (*mughal son to main sakht kitā hūn khod / ke le gad muje chup nā devenge chod*).[89] To save himself, Shivaji implores Jai Singh that very little would be achieved by arresting him. Instead, the Maratha commander makes a proposal to the Mughal-Rajput:

kadhein fauj-i dihlī kī is shān son / chalī thī nā yūn sāz-o-sāmān son
rakhein bait merī to kyā kar ke fan / yadī le ke detā hūn mulk-i dakhan . . .
dikhāyā hathelī mein aisā behisht / lagī bāt tajvīz mein khūb resht[90]

Delhi's army have come here with great pomp and glory
What will you get out of capturing my house?

But, what if I give you the kingdom of the Deccan?
Approving this talk, [Shivaji] thus showed [Jai Singh] paradise in the palm of his hand

The premodern poet's compelling words here may at first lead the modern reader to pick a side regarding what really happened in these contentions. It should come as no surprise that generations of scholars have sought to determine the truth value of such representations—that is, whether Shivaji wished to defend the Deccan against the Mughals or whether he welcomed the imperial overlords with open arms.[91] But premodern narrative constructions, even if more or less accurate, are unlikely to provide straight answers. For they only provide suggestive evidence for the political and ideological positions of who it was who was telling the story of these conflicts in the seventeenth century. Rather than reflecting each historical actor's true intent, Nusrati's construction of Shivaji's and Jai Singh's meeting unveils the shifting terrain of ghar at a time when provincial familial lineages threatened charismatic kingship. Whether the literate observer was a partisan of a regional household chief or not, they could not deny the latter's growing ability to undercut ties between dynastic powers.

Nusrati thus declares how Shivaji's ability to manipulate Jai Singh led the latter to break the Mughal alliance with the ʿAdil shahs of Bijapur. Shivaji's ability to manipulate Jai Singh stained the Mughal name (*sivāya ne mughal son katak kar jo kām / diyā dāgh thā leke nāmūs-o-nām*) while compromising the Kachawaha Rajput's primary obligation to the Mughal imperial household.[92] In this instance, Nusrati chooses to emphasize sectarian difference, naturalizing a solidarity between two vastly different kinds of non-Muslims—Shivaji, a Maratha Bhonsle peasant-warrior and Jai Singh, a Mughal-Kachawaha Rajput.[93] We saw earlier that when compared to the Franks or Europeans, the Maratha warrior chief was cast as the greatest of unbelievers, unequivocally disloyal to all faiths, willing to murder even in the house of God. But moments later, when citing Shivaji as the primary reason for friction among great kings, Nusrati heightens his sectarian otherness. The Maratha commander's newfound solidarity with a Rajput general thus undercuts the latter's primary political loyalty to the Mughal crown. Nusrati closes this episode with moral lessons on the dangers of greed (*tamaʿ*) and how greed can destroy one's own. Ethnic and denominational differences thus carry more value when political hierarchies appear to be under threat.

And yet, when we take the case of the Bhonsle household more broadly, there are no natural solidarities. Nor is there a well-defined stance for or against the Bijapur crown. For instance, Nusrati was far more generous toward Shivaji's half-brother, Ekoji, who remained a vassal of ʿAli ʿAdil Shah II and would soon establish the Maratha court at Tanjavur after displacing its *nayaka* rulers in 1675.[94] As the son of Shahaji Bhonsle (d. 1664), who had served the ʿAdil shahs of Bijapur and was one of the wisest ministers at court (*ekoji jo shahjī kā farzand thā / vazīrān mein nāmī khirdmand thā*), Nusrati lauded Ekoji's bravery (*mahābalī*) and prudence (*samajhdārī*), which made him far superior to his insolent half-brother.[95] Premodern literati certainly mobilized an idiom of difference (physical, sectarian, ethnic) to delegitimize some actors and elevate others.

The intimate diagnosis of major regional households, whether Marathas or Indo-Africans, was the prism through which Nusrati made sense of the changing meanings of ghar. Mughal suzerainty opened up space for more and more regional contenders to participate in territorial expansion while strengthening their own domains. The dramatizations of confrontations, such as those between regional kings and provincial household chiefs examined above, bring us to the poet's assessment of the Great Satan among them all—the Mughals—and to the question, what did Nusrati think of the mighty imperial masters who indirectly caused the rise of contending household states? The filial bond articulated in Atishi's work thirty years earlier vanished in the decades of continuous war in the late seventeenth century. At the outset, Nusrati, too, conceded to and was in awe of the Mughal army's scale and size. He began by observing their weapons and armor, listing Mughal soldiers' ethnicities, places of origin, castes, and lineages. But shortly after sizing them up, he devoted page after page for sizing them down, expressing an incisive critique of all things Mughal. Empire actually meant a set of panimperial behaviors and vices, shared across its highest and lowest ranks, building an overall morally degenerate and fickle entity called "Mughal."

At first, like Atishi looking north earlier in the seventeenth century, Nusrati expressed wonder at the enormous Mughal army marching toward the Deccan. He beheld the sight of the mosaic of people who made the rank and file of Mughal soldiers. All these different levels of personnel, from the common soldier to the high-ranking noble, together constituted the idea of Mughal-ness. But empire's moral degeneracy would compromise the enormous breadth of human and material resources at its disposal. An imperial army with universal ambitions, drawn from across the world, failed to compensate for the empire's unethical moral conduct:

> katā hun itā fauj dehlī kī bāt / chalī thī dil pe kis dhāt sāt
> ke kis fauj kon dekhne mai samaj / dise na kise inteha hor apaj
> mughlān kate mulk wa kayī shahar ke / kate hind wa koyī māvarānnahr ke
> chaghtai qizilbāsh uzbeg balī / qandahārī kate balkh hor kabulī
> . . .
> fareb un ke fan men badhā burd hai / janam jag jā iblīs shāgird hai
> nichī jin mai aslā murawwat kī bū / karen us pe bad jis te nek un pe hue
> thikāna īch duniyā ko māder kahen / chupa laudh zāhir kon khwāhar kahein
> badī bāp saun apnī mirās jān / birādar ka khūn shīr māder pehchān
> dekhen kuch hai jān fāidah āp ko / nā chode sageh bhai aur bāp kon
> . . .
> rohille katak zāt ke the ūvatt / zabardast panjābīyān dil ke ghatt
> bahūt rāo rāne athe raj ke put / ghurūrī son shaitān jhagde pe bahūt[96]

> now I say a bit about the Delhi's army,
> and how it set out with a mission in its heart

upon seeing this army, one understands,
it appears it has no beginning nor end

say, Mughals came from many cities and kingdoms
say, some from Hind, others from Transoxiana

the bravest Chagtai, Qizilbash, Uzbeg
Qandahari, Balkhi, and Kabulis
. . .
in any challenge, deceit is their art,
for ages, the devil has been their student

they do not have even a little stench of compassion,
they do bad to those who do good to them

to show the world, they'll call someone their mother
hiding their lust, they'll call a girl their sister

to mistreat their father is hereditary,
to them, the brother's blood is like mother's milk

when they see their own benefit
they won't even spare their brother nor father
. . .
Rohillas, with an essence of deceit,
formidable Panjabis, cowards at heart

many Raos, Rane and Rajputs
devils full of pride, ready to fight

Nusrati observed the different kinds of people, places, ethnicities, and lineages that constituted the abstract idea of "Mughal."[97] From Central Asia to Hindustan, distant regions and ethnic units defined the panoply of people that fell under the term *Mughal*. But Nusrati very quickly stripped the Mughals of their universal, cosmopolitan grandeur by uniting the empire's diverse subjects through pan-Mughal vices of deceit, lying, cheating, ruthlessness, and killing relatives. Despite ethnic, regional, and linguistic variety, certain inherent traits of disloyalty, untrustworthiness, and treachery were shared across the highest and lowest imperial levels.

For instance, Nusrati seized every opportunity to take a jab at the War of Succession, which had transpired among Mughal princes in 1657 and 1658, an event that was then part of popular memory. He belittled an empire whose sons for the sake of their own gain did not spare their own fathers and brothers (*dekhen kuch hai jān fāidah āp ko / na chode sageh bhai aur bāp kon*). The imperial trait of betraying family manifested itself in different ways at the empire's more humble echelons. Hailing from different parts of Hindustan and Transoxiana, the whole empire was united by the quality of *fareb* or the quality of lying and inveigling others. The Mughal army was strong in numbers and weapons, but treachery was the primary strategy through which it won fleeting loyalties during diplomacy and war. Mughal greatness thus had its limits, and even while acknowledging empire's ability to encompass so many different kinds of people, observers on the margins mistrusted it.

Going to the very top of the imperial chain of command, Nusrati cast Mughal emperor Aurangzeb (r. 1658–1707) as a spineless, gullible character. In one portrait of the moment when Shivaji plundered the imperial port city of Surat in 1665, we find the beleaguered Mughal emperor consulting his incompetent officers who had failed to protect the empire's most important gateway to the Indian Ocean. Surat, with the whole world's wealth and goods, was the city where merchants from across land and sea resided (*rahein bahr-o-khushkī kī tujjār jān / mile bast-i ʿālam mein jo nayīn so dhān*). Shivaji cast his gaze on the port that had blessed the lands of Hind (*levein hind nit faiz us te nol*), making plans to capture it.[98] After describing Surat's riches, Nusrati then dramatizes its plunder and destruction, the news of which was delivered to the Mughal emperor Aurangzeb. On hearing the bad news, the emperor clenches his teeth with his fingers and bites his lips hard in anger (*pakad apne dānton main hairat son bont / kahīyā chābnā sakht gusse se hont*) and realizes that the only way to cleanse the lands of that rascal (*zamīn us harāmī se karnā hai pāk*) is to turn to the ʿAdil Shahi sultan for help.[99] Nusrati deliberately changes the dominant image of the Mughal emperor as universally all powerful and formidable into a hapless sovereign who, lost in neurotic monologues, appeals to much smaller neighboring sultans to deal with a formidable political rebel.

It should come as no surprise, then, that Nusrati's appraisal of the Mughals also entails a complete disregard of their claim to be fair Muslim rulers. Just as we found no consistency in the poet's criticisms of regional non-Muslim contenders like Shivaji, who were sometimes judged based on sectarian difference and at other times cast as antithetical to all faiths, the Mughals also receive no special treatment simply because they were fellow Muslims. In one such appraisal, Nusrati begins with the usual insults when comparing Mughal and Deccani armies:

> *mughal āke avval jo lāt khāte hain / dakhan kī ladāyī te kachū āte hain*
> *yek yek maut ke waqt farzand kon / kahīn yād rakh pūt is pand kon*
> *dakhan pur moham huī tū sutt rozgār / ke zanhār nayīn phir ū āne ke thār*[100]

> The Mughals come here to get their asses kicked
> But they evade a fight with the Deccan
> At each and every moment of death
> Remind our sons of the following advice
> Set yourself upon the important task of defending the Deccan
> Such that they [the Mughals] never have the nerve to return here

"Mughal" here is synonymous with unmanly (*nāmard*) and a trickster (*hīleh-gar*). In one dramatization of an alliance between the ʿAdil shahs of Bijapur and the Qutb Shahs of Golkonda against the Mughals, Nusrati compares the Mughal army's invasion of the Deccan with the failed attempt of Abraha, the sixth-century Abyssinian Christian king, who attempted to destroy the Kaʿba, alluding to the Qurʾan's well-known chapter:[101]

madad un jise āp be shak karein / bashar kyā hai jo is ko komal kare
kīyā mār gard āp thā jis vakīl / abā bīl ke hit son ashāb-i fīl[102]

those who God helps without a doubt,
what is man, for he can never weaken [God's] help

the enemies, of those whose advocate is God, turn to straw
in the same way the flight of birds pelted stones at the companions of elephants

Abraha and his army, the companions of elephants (*ashāb-i fīl*) were miraculously pelted by a flight of birds (*abā bīl*) as they invaded the Hijaz. Similarly, the Mughals were bound to lose against the Deccan's armies because God was not on their side. Like Abraha, the Mughals had a much larger army, but the Deccan was exalted and revered in a manner similar to Mecca and would remain protected through divine intervention.

Nusrati appropriated literary topoi repeatedly deployed in conquest narratives across the Islamic world to dramatize encounters with non-Muslims.[103] He took the Abraha image a step further to strip much more formidable, fellow Muslim sovereigns of their claim to be just rulers, as the imperial masters had already lost credibility in the eyes of contemporary observers by invading the Deccan sultanates.[104] It would not be an exaggeration to say that Nusrati saw nothing redeeming in the Mughals when he declared:

kabal waqt par yū ich kām āyenge,
mughalān son zāt apnī dikhlāyenge.
nā 'āqil hai hargez himāqat kon chod,
jo gurgī kon sehrabandī sar ko chod

at the hour of need, only we can help them
then, the Mughals will show their true colors
for they're unintelligent and will never let go of stupidity
instead of on their head, they wear the groom's veil as their pajamas!

Writing within a shared discursive heritage with a universal criterion for just kingship, Nusrati disagreed with contemporary Indo-Persian authors who valorized the Mughals as ethical, righteous rulers. From the perspective of this provincial observer, the empire was impaired by remaining oblivious to its own weaknesses.

CONCLUSION

These words, meant to implore the Mughals, reveal how masnavī shifted from praise and eulogy to critical advice and invective as the terrain of belonging to a ghar changed within the course of a century. When imperial suzerainty first begins in the 1620s, we hear Atishi's measured words for reforming the Mughals. In the latter half of the century, when imperial occupation indirectly facilitated the rising autonomy of regional household chiefs, Nusrati's invective reflects anxieties about the rapid reversal of political hierarchies and unsettling of the status quo caused by the presence of the empire in a distant region. Both poets, in recounting contemporary events, assert the fragility of all things Mughal by questioning war's moral and ethical implications in their uncertain times, and their role in unsettling senses of ghar. What starts first as ambivalence then becomes deep mistrust and even disdain for mighty imperial overlords—this is how those on the margins, who were still very much within the extended Mughal imperium, made sense of what they observed was wrong with empire.

Counternarratives about imperial and regional power were not merely untrue and exaggerated representations in which poets played with tropes and words. Among the many layers in this textual tradition, I have here followed the ʿĀdilnāma and ʿAlīnāma for political meaning-making and tracing the evolution of the politics of place. In some ways, a literary archive's formal constraints and limits prevent us from tracking the sequence of events that led to the Mughals annexing peninsular India in 1687 or telling the story of a single ethnolinguistic group, narratives that can be easily constructed from Persian chronicles and European travelogues. Instead, I mapped out what changed about the politics of ghar in the seventeenth century and in which words this change was represented. What the martial poem offers is a profile of the many emotive responses to imperial power and what iconic events meant to contemporary observers. Our two Bijapuri poets honed their art in the long and continuous tradition of martial poetry by producing portraits of different kinds of political problems—first, the crisis of dealing with poetic competition and second, the tension between kings and households.

Reading a literary archive for compositional techniques and tropes is indispensable for interpreting texts as rich and capacious as the ʿĀdilnāma and ʿAlīnāma.[105] While being less focused on the literariness of these materials, in the first part of this chapter I investigated how poets used standard tropes and images for declaring their political affinities, professional anxieties, and courtly allegiances, all of which were tied to senses of belonging to a ghar. Next I showed how the martial poem served as an ideal medium for creating a new set of heroes and villains in a raucous political landscape. Persianate literati memorialized political encounters, deploying appreciable poetic forms in Persian and Dakkani, partly to distinguish the political category of the Deccan from the Mughals, but mostly to make sense of what was changing about the nature of power in their times. Regional poets emphasized their difference as nonimperial subjects and either embraced new nonroyal patrons (as Atishi did) or grew alarmed by household lineages that were growing distant from monarchical authority (as in the case of Nusrati). Innovations within this form, in proximate linguistic registers, were perhaps another means to oppose and outdo, literally and militarily speaking, deeply familiar, similar, and intimate rivals.

From provincial Persianate Muslim literatis' vantage point, claims to Mughal greatness were not entirely untrue, but they were, at least at times, vastly overblown and exaggerated. Despite being in awe of empire's military strength, regional critics hardly looked up to the Mughals as legitimate rulers, as righteous Muslims, or as beacons of *adab*. They gave new meaning to existing affective terminologies for loyalty and betrayal, familiarity and estrangement, as well as sectarian difference to plot imperial power onto a wider canvas of contentious politics, as nonkingly figures made claims to political power in the seventeenth century. These intrareligious fault lines and debates within Islamic South Asia enable us to move away from the task of constantly restoring the Mughals to a preconceived idea of "India" or telling the story of a quaint, syncretic precolonial society, which the empire partly helped sustain. In a period of imperial suzerainty, the meanings of empire-building and territorial domination were contested, not just militarily, but through words, metaphors, and narrations that revealed the contingent meanings of loyalty and the uncertain grounds on which regional and imperial sovereignties stood in the early modern period.

It is worth reiterating here a point emphasized in the book's introduction. The tensions between a purportedly all-powerful kingly authority and non-royal household lineages is a pattern as old as South Asia itself. No matter which region of the subcontinent or which era we consider, the household, or what Sumit Guha calls the "locus of sociopolitical organization,"[106] as the fundamental basis of property inheritance and social reproduction, persisted regardless of which dynasty held power. So, what changed about this relationship in the age of imperial consolidation and how did historical actors diagnose or perceive this problem across different units of time and space in South Asia? Persianate Muslim elites in the Deccan courts represented the political vicissitudes of their own times by casting moral judgments and declaring what was right and wrong in one's quest for power, a very old theme in ethical literature across the Islamic world.[107] In doing so, the words and images in these poetic compositions revealed the fragility of political identities and the contingent articulations of loyalty to a ghar at a time when kings and households contended over sovereignty.

Although old and new political histories have tracked the chronological sequence of battles, treaties, negotiations, and alliances that led to an inevitable Mughal conquest, often by meticulously following the Persian chronicle's certitudes, our task here was to investigate a literary archive that illuminates what these political events meant to contemporary observers.[108] Entering the story of Mughal-Deccan relations from a different textual register—poetic counternarratives that represent the tension between kingly and household power—refracts the narrative of imperial inevitability and regional decline that pervades the seventeenth century.[109] Poetic works reveal how a different set of actors—regional elite poets and household chiefs—eclipsed sovereigns, interlocking northern and southern India's political structures by articulating the stakes for political identities (Mughal versus Deccani and so forth) and the loyalties they were supposed to represent.

The late seventeenth century, far from being a moment of origin, was a moment of accumulated layers of familiarity and the culmination of old patterns, a time to settle scores with the deepest, most intimate acquaintances. Rather than being an inaugural moment when the self-professed Maratha Hindu Shivaji collided with the perennially Other Muslim sultans of Hindustan and the Deccan, this was a time when well-acquainted historical actors, who belonged to the same political ghar, contended over what it meant to be a Mughal, Deccani, Maratha, Habshi, and Afghan. To diagnose all these players in the cantankerous present, instead of their more common practice of giving advice and counseling, Muslim poets turned praise into invective to declare their political allegiances and ideological agendas.[110] Pathologizing intimate rivals required the use of sectarian, phenotypical, and gendered language to heighten a sense of difference with those who were familiar and too similar to oneself. Rather than shy away from the controversial vocabularies of sectarian and ethnic difference, poets wielded such emotive language as a form of political meaning-making. My analysis pays attention to when and why an idiom of difference was used to construct crucial representations of friends and enemies. I show how premodern literati mapped a range of groups onto a political spectrum by turning to the language of difference and affective binaries to make sense of their most familiar rivals.

One of the primary aims of this book is to bridge the distance between studying the court and the state by transcending different textual genres that have been used to reconstruct separate kinds of South Asian pasts. In order to do so, we have to raise the question about the reception, the possible audiences, and the social setting within which poetic works such as those of Atishi and Nusrati circulated. Across Persianate societies, the martial poem became a powerful medium that complemented chronicles about contemporary events while also engaging with the burden of tradition from Firdawsi onward. The first and most immediate audiences were, of course, other courtly literati, to whom both Atishi and Nusrati made references as either interlocutors or rivals. The martial poem and its central topoi—of all things related to the battlefield—may also suggest Dakkani's role as a language that circulated in sites of military engagement, going beyond Persian's learned courtly circuits, limited to capital cities of empires and regional sultanates. Chroniclers often reported that martial poems or *fathnāma* were commissioned and written at encampments after military victories, suggesting that the social setting of Dakkani was analogous to similar oral genres in Bundeli and Marathi.[111] Using the regional idiom thus enabled a palpably different and much more biting criticism of imperial rule that reached a wider audience than Persian's elite register.

During the seventeenth century, just as the Mughal frontier reached the Coromandel Coast in southeastern India, the sociological profile of regional elite lineages challenging kingly authority also changed—from Iranians to Marathas, Indo-Africans, and Afghans—all of whom occupied center stage in martial works. In a fraught political landscape, provincial literati redefined the meaning of disloyalty and betrayal, fitting distinct groups into shifting definitions of what it meant to be a Mughal and a Deccani or both. In the next chapter, we will enter the closing decades of the seventeenth century, where social elites from the Deccan encountered merchants, weavers, and companies entangled in the economy of the southern Coromandel coast and the wider world of the Indian Ocean.

6

From Battlefield to Weaving Village
Disciplining the Coast

Historians narrate the story of kings and households in the Mughal empire's peripheries through the neat sequential rhythms of high politics, partly because this is where the most commonly used sources—Persian court chronicles, diplomatic correspondence, and European travelogues—invariably lead the historian.[1] But such narratives of kingly ideologies, interelite alliances, rivalries, and collaborations, the stuff of political history, ignore the breadth of human and natural resources spread across land and sea that make empires and their agents work, an argument made by social historians of southern India for later historical periods as well.[2] How did elite household chiefs, subordinates of the Deccan courts that were now firmly under Mughal suzerainty, encounter actors who operated along Indian Ocean coasts? How did a moving agrarian warfront transform the lives of ordinary subjects when the imperium first extended to its farthest reaches? And finally, what kinds of artifacts help us reconstruct these alternate pasts?

To answer these questions, this chapter moves from battlefield to weaving village, turning to interstatus and intercaste negotiations that sustained state-making activities when an imperial-regional order edged toward the seas. By the 1660s, the Mughal-Deccan warfront moved to distant villages in the Karnatak lowlands, where weavers spun and wove cloth, to busy market towns in coastal provinces where merchants bought and sold commodities like cotton, silk, rice, saltpeter, and tin. Likewise, thousands of enslaved men and women were shipped from port cities like Teganapatnam (present-day Tamil Nadu) to Jaffna (northern Sri Lanka), where vessels from Bengal, Malacca, and Aceh anchored to unload goods and people subject to inspection by officials like the havaldār or governor/port keeper, who deducted his share from the tolls levied on such commodities.

In the previous chapter, we saw how critiques of the Mughal Empire evolved in regional courts over the course of the seventeenth century. In this chapter, we reverse the lens, looking on courts and courtly actors from the vantage point of their socioeconomic interactions and transactions unfolding in a coastal economy. Elite poets like Atishi and Nusrati, sitting in the inland capital city of Bijapur, penned horizontal critiques of their coreligionist Mughal overlords, princes, and rank-holding officials, observing how imperial intervention emboldened regional household claims to political power. The stakes for defining place, community, and belonging under imperial suzerainty and during interhousehold rivalry heightened as a warfront closed in on distant coastal regions abundant in economic resources. In regions far removed from court capitals, household chiefs encountered forms of resistance from more vertical social encounters with occupational groups positioned at the middle and bottom of economic life. As this chapter will show, the meeting of an agrarian warfront with a subregional coastal economy involved negotiations wherein sultanate-affiliated household chiefs relied on existing social hierarchies in coastal economies to sustain their networks. It focuses on one of the earliest encounters of the Mughal-Deccan warfront with the southern Coromandel coast that precipitated long-term processes of regional autonomy,[3] which lasted well into the eighteenth century, when independent states emerged from the processes of imperial conquest.

The chapter proceeds in two parts and includes a cast of characters whose journeys from the court to the coast are visible in a range of literary and documentary artifacts. In what follows, I move between vernacular literary traditions and the Dutch East India Company's (VOC) archives to reconstruct internal political conflicts within the Deccan sultanate of Bijapur, its competing households, and their encounters with the southern Coromandel's mercantile and weaving communities in the areas near Senji in the second half of the seventeenth century.[4] Of these two types of materials, VOC documents, along with all the other varieties of company archives (whether French, English, or Danish), have for decades served as the basis for writing Indian Ocean history before colonialism, telling the familiar story of European expansion in Asia or its more recent avatar of European-Asian diplomacy and cross-cultural encounters in the early modern period.[5] By contrast, textual traditions in regional Indian languages rarely make an appearance in these so-called global histories, partly because their audiences are limited to literary scholars and regional specialists.

In what follows, I go about asking a different set of questions from these materials. First, I urge (when possible) that Indian Ocean historians first read incommensurable textual genres in regional languages to open up the vastly different cultural and intellectual conceptual frameworks of precolonial actors whose roles in the political economy are simultaneously visible in European archives. Second, I build out from the long tradition in social history (and later on in postcolonial studies) of examining non-European actors and their voices in European sources[6] by interrogating the interpolation, translation, and constitution of indigenous documentary forms in maritime archives that predate colonialism by a century. Juxtaposing vernacular texts with VOC documents, contemporary yet incommensurable materials, reveals a variety of interdependent spheres of influence—the court, the battlefield, the port city—within which households reshaped the imperial and regional states around them.

In the first part of the chapter, I reconstruct the broad political changes unfolding in the sultanate of Bijapur when the imperial-regional warfront moved toward the Coromandel coast, starting in the 1650s.[7] Here, I juxtapose archival documents from the VOC to reconstruct the regional political economy alongside a poetic observation of political change, Nusrati's last narrative poem, called *Tārīkh-i sikandarī* (History of Sikandar, ca. 1672), composed in Dakkani. In this work, Nusrati portrays the rivalry between two contending regional households— the Miyana Afghans and the Maratha Bhonsles—who occupied center stage in imperial-regional politics in the second half of the seventeenth century. The poet deployed the conceit of the house—the ghar—to make sense of intimate, kindred lineages competing with each other and against the larger backdrop of regional kingship's dissolution. This poetic commentary uses tropes of difference to represent a battle between the Miyana Afghan ʿAbdul Karim Bahlol Khan (d. 1678) and the Maratha Shivaji Bhonsle (d. 1680). As we saw in chapter 2, through the earliest deposit of administrative documents like the muster roll, both the Miyana Afghans and the Maratha Bhonsles had served in the armies of the Mughal Empire and the Deccan sultanates. In this chapter, we find these groups consolidating their autonomy from kingly power. ʿAbdul Karim Bahlol Khan's grandfather had served under Khan Jahan Lodi (d. 1631), a five thousand-rank *mansabdār* who defected from the Mughals and fled briefly to the Deccan.[8] The Bhonsles were one among many Marathi-speaking families that inhabited western India, ranging from warrior groups to holders of hereditary grants who held village-level positions under various Muslim rulers.[9]

Both new and old scholarship has often looked on these two groups as cultural others, framing this moment exclusively through the prism of identity and indigeneity.[10] The understanding usually goes that Muslim Miyana Afghans were foreigners, while the Hindu Maratha Bhonsles were Deccanis, indigenous to peninsular India and thus the true defenders of this space against the Timurid Mughals of northern India.[11] However, such a simplistic modern binary was not how seventeenth-century observers themselves understood the place of these contenders in contemporary politics. As I show through an analysis of the *Tārīkh-i sikandarī*, the poet Nusrati laid out a moral definition of ghar to which both contenders belonged. We return to the idea of the home in this chapter, where ghar refers to the political category of the Deccan and includes multiple household lineages.[12] Writing toward the end of his life in the 1670s, with the dissolution of the Deccan sultanates imminent, Nusrati considered the moral stakes of the duty to protect the house that one's ancestors had served for many generations. Judging the Miyanas' and Marathas' place within a shared ghar, Bijapur's foremost political observer never professed simplistic syncretism to suggest these social groups were not mutually exclusive; nor did he suggest that they always got along with each other. Nor, ultimately, did he claim the two groups were existential, essential opposites. The poet resolutely defined and marked their differences to demonstrate the intimate space of ghar, which multiple households had inhabited for generations and were morally obliged to serve.

In his previous works, such as the 'Alināma, Nusrati had already reflected on the Marathas and the Indo-Africans, and how and why they belonged to the political category of the Deccan. As we saw in the previous chapter, he had thought through terms such as watan (homelands) and mulk (domains), the meanings of which were transformed radically with the arrival of the Mughals in the south. In the twilight of his career and to make sense of the place of Marathas and Afghans in contemporary politics, Nusrati expanded on these ideas with ghar or house/home, a conceptual space that undergirded the language and tropes of sectarian difference that had been common across Persianate and Indic texts for centuries.[13] He saw the Marathas and Afghans not merely as Hindu and Muslim, but rather as two kindred rivals who belonged to the same home,—namely, the Deccan. While studies have examined how the Marathas were memorialized in contemporary Marathi-textual genres like bakhar, lavani, and powada,[14] all these texts were part of a broader literary ecology produced alongside other contemporary genres, such as Dakkani masnavī. Together, these texts illustrate the competitive arena within which both Hindu and Muslim households in the seventeenth-century Deccan operated, seeking textual legitimation of their competing claims to political power.

The third part of the chapter then journeys with the close associates and kinsfolk of this poem's protagonists to the southern Coromandel where they encounter new social groups operating in a coastal economy. Looking at the physical features of southern India on a map, we see that the southern Coromandel is where the black and red soil regions of the Deccan plateau end (where the capital cities of the Islamic sultanates of Bijapur and Golkonda were located) at the city of Tiruvannamalai in present-day Tamil Nadu. It consists of multiple river basins, port cities, and in general a geographic heterogeneity that has shaped economic and social life for centuries.[15] Flanked by the continuous mountain ranges of the Western Ghats and the discontinuous Eastern Ghats, its coastal plains run from the convergence of the eastern and western Indian Oceans at the subcontinent's southernmost district, Kanyakumari, also known as Cape Comorin. The area between the two coastal cities of Cape Comorin and Chennai encompasses multiple subcoastal regions divided by distinct bayheads and commodities produced around them, ranging from pearls and cotton to rice.[16] Moving north on a map from the subcontinent's southernmost point in Cape Comorin, where the Pearl Fishery Coast begins and ends at the port city of Tuticorin, we can then

MAP 6. Indo-Africans, Marathas, and Indo-Afghans on the southern Coromandel coast, ca. 1680. Drawn by Kanika Kalra.

follow the Ramnad coast that reaches up to Point Calimere, also known as Koddaikarai. The Pearl Fishery and Ramnad coasts enclose the Gulf of Mannar and Palk Strait, which connect southern India to the Jaffna peninsula in northern Sri Lanka. Moving north from Point Calimere to Chennai lies the area between the Rivers Kaveri and Palar, which both flow east toward the Bay of Bengal where this chapter's narrative concludes and its characters converge. Between the deltas of these two rivers from south to north lie the port cities of Nagapattinam, Porto Novo, Cuddalore, Pondicherry, and St. Thomé. All are located south of the city of Madras or Chennai, where Bijapur-affiliated households, coastal merchants, and weaving communities converged in the seventeenth century's second half (See map 6).

How did Bijapuri subordinates encounter the southern Coromandel's variable coastal and human ecology? To answer this question, the chapter considers the dealings of ʿAbdul Karim Bahlol Khan's close associate Sher Khan Lodi (d. 1681)[17] with the southern Coromandel's well-established mercantile Sunni Shafiʿi Maraikkayar, Tamil-speaking Muslims, and Tamil and Telugu-speaking upper-caste Hindu merchant communities. The latter had long served as suppliers of European companies and negotiated with them by financing capital to regional weaving castes such as the *kaikkolar, devangulu, and sale*, who circulated across the Karnatak lowlands around the port cities of St. Thomé, Teganapatnam or Cuddalore, Porto Novo, and Nagapattinam (See map 3).[18] Sultanate-affiliated agents like Bahlol Khan and Sher Khan Lodi, who propelled the warfront into the northern Tamil country, had much in common, sociologically speaking, with the region's Tamil- and Telugu-speaking "portfolio capitalists."[19] At different ends of peninsular India, these very different kinds of merchant-warrior groups had long combined their commercial, military, and political interests through the institution of revenue-farming, working at the edges of monarchical state-forms.[20] In some ways, the Miyanas had much to learn from the dominant social groups of the northern Tamil country who had been entrenched in the coastal economy for far longer.[21] The episode examined in this chapter unveils the resilience, portability, and shared mutual understanding between different kinds of portfolio capitalists. These premodern elites transcended differences of region and language to preserve existing ways of doing business, which entailed entrenching inequalities and preventing social discord. To reconstruct the complex web of transactions between actors from these distinct social locations, I read their voices in Persianate documentary forms that were translated into the Dutch East India Company's (VOC) archives. Markedly different from their primary form and functions, translated indigenous documents interpolated in the VOC archives were constituted by the negotiations between regional provincial household chiefs, coastal merchants, and weaving castes, with the latter two groups having a long history of collaboration, borrowing, and conflict.[22]

This chapter has two goals. First, in keeping with the book's larger objective, it moves away from canonized Persian chronicles and published European accounts, the usual suspects that historians often use to tell rise and fall narratives of political entities such as the Dutch East India Company and the Deccan sultanates, or of individual actors and various high-ranking officials in the French, Dutch, and English East India Companies. One could easily recount a straightforward narrative history about interelite machinations by sketching the serialized biographies and political fortunes of elites like Sher Khan Lodi or Shivaji. Indeed, since the early twentieth century, historians have done just that by following the truth claims of well-known early nineteenth-century Persian chronicles, such as Ibrahim Zubayri's *Basātīn us-Salātīn*, supplemented with published and translated European accounts, such as those of the French governor of Pondicherry, Francois Martin's *India in the Seventeenth Century*. But pairing these two historical genres offers only a top-down perspective of a far messier portrait. For instance, Martin's account is unsurprising in singing the praises of figures like Sher Khan Lodi and the Miyanas who were known partisans of the French.[23] While it offers great detail about interelite negotiation, where Martin's considerable disdain for Brahmins is obvious, almost entirely absent from the account is how these elites dealt with ordinary subjects whose lives were transformed in the wake of war.[24]

Relying on Persian chronicles and published European accounts risks reifying premodern political power and stripping it from its broader social realities.

This chapter turns to a very different body of literary and archival ecologies to find such voices and a different vantage point. It does so by connecting the Persianate with the Indian Ocean, two historiographical fields that are difficult to put into dialogue with each other.[25] It brings the growing field of Persianate studies, largely limited to the analysis of literature, into conversation with well-known and old debates about caste and labor stratification along the Indian Ocean littoral,[26] aspects of social history that have, at times, been lost in our quest to restore the virtues of courts, kings, and other elite actors, particularly in the Deccan. Conversely, it builds on recent interventions in cultural histories of the early modern Indian Ocean that investigate the constitution of Company documents but that rarely venture to read them against and alongside the subcontinent's literary traditions generally associated with land-based political formations.[27] For all the claims to write imperial history in a local register, in recent studies based on European sources, the images of non-European actors and concepts are only partly visible against the more vivid portraits of the conflicts between different officials within the Company hierarchy.[28] Calls to write microhistories of the global can only be fulfilled by placing conceptual and philosophical viewpoints expressed in literary modes, no matter how unfamiliar and disorienting these may be for audiences in the West, alongside and against the far more legible and conventional European Company archive that has become a euphemism for the "global."[29] By juxtaposing literary and documentary artifacts, I reconstruct a world where solidarities between elites from vastly different cultural backgrounds and status groups were indeed commonplace. But, these moments of interelite collaboration entailed a mutual recognition of shared socioeconomic interests, renewing commitments to preserve the existing social order. The convergence of portfolio capitalists, whether Persianate Bijapuris or the diverse merchant-warriors of the northern Tamil country, required the disciplining of nonelite social groups, in this case the weavers of the southern Coromandel coast. I argue that narratives of harmony and elite sociability across lines of religion and language are only one part of how power worked in premodern Indian society. Divisions across status groups and caste were just as important in bringing the interests of multireligious and multiethnic elites together.

AN AGRARIAN WARFRONT ARRIVES AT SEA

In political histories, the years between the 1650s and the 1670s are often underanalyzed, usually being explained away as symptomatic of sultanate decline and Mughal ascendance in peninsular India. And yet, the evolutionary perspective of dynastic change and kingly ideologies produced in capital cities elides what happened in the aftermath of iconic events and in relation to other historical figures who journeyed away from these centers during this period. For instance, the Siege of Hyderabad in 1657 and the infamous defection of Mir Jumla Muhammad Sayyid Ardestani (d. 1663) to the Mughals from the Golkonda sultanate in 1655 are seen as symptoms or premonitions of the eventual decline of the Deccan sultanates in 1686–87.[30] However, even as Mir Jumla joined the imperial camp, he left behind an intricate network of fortified provincial strongholds, like Gandikota and Gutti in the Karnatak, which continued to thrive under other sultanate-affiliated military commanders in the 1660s and 1670s, who once again tapped into the coastal economy to finance, clothe, and feed moving armies. Shortly after the Mughal prince Aurangzeb renewed attempts to subsume the regional sultanates before returning north to fight his brothers in the War of Succession (ca. 1656–61), provincial household chiefs incorporated portions of the Karnatak into their networks, pushing their boundaries to the largest territorial extent.

The period of imperial suzerainty invigorated an old pattern of state formation in southern India when different "co-sharers in the realm," who controlled a cache of agrarian and military resources, periodically challenged kingly authority.[31] In the last quarter of the seventeenth century, from within this political milieu, the most sustained and durable threat to the Mughal Empire would emerge from peninsular India, the Marathas, who would subsume all other contenders. What was the political and economic landscape inhabited by the Maratha Bhonsles and their competitors, the Indo-Africans and the Miyana Afghans, between the 1650s and 1670s? In this section, I reconstruct a portrait of Bijapuri politics at two geographic endpoints: from the port-city of Vengurla on the Kanara coast of western India facing the Arabian Sea, where political changes in the capital-city were observed, to the port cities of Teganapatnam and Nagapattinam in the southern Coromandel, where these households asserted their autonomy from kingly power.

European observers in Vengurla tried to make sense of several contradictions in Bijapuri politics in this period. As Sultan Muhammad ʿAdil Shah (r. 1627–56) fell ill, his wife, Queen Khadija Sultana, referred to with the honorific "Old Queen Bari Sahiba" (*oude Conninginne Bari Sahib*), ruled Bijapur until her adopted son (*aengenomen zoone*), ʿAli ʿAdil Shah II (r. 1656–72), grew old enough to assume the throne.[32] In these interim years, she frequently clashed with contending elite households, including the Marathas, the Indo-Africans, and the Miyanas, even seeking the assistance of Mughal overlords to discipline them.

The English and the Dutch held similarly condescending views of the aging queen who lay at the center of court politics. Now in her twilight years, her wedding to Muhammad ʿAdil Shah had been celebrated and memorialized in multiple linguistic registers (see chapter 4). Representations of her regency have shaped the imagination and the misogynist undertones of both the earliest and most recent postcolonial appraisals of this queen. It is here that that we find the earliest images of the Deccan sultanates as kingdoms in decline, caught between an ineffective queen, a debauched nobility, and a feeble king,[33] the earliest echoes of which we find in the words of the English factors Henry Revington and Randolph Taylor, who wrote in 1659:

> It was beleivd and told us by Rustum Jemah himself, who is much the Englishes freind, that hee should have binn sent this years against Goa, as formerly hee hath bin, but the Queene suspects him to bee her enemy, and so indead hee is; which leads Us to another subject, as worthy of your consideration as the former. The person that is cald King of this country is knowne to bee the bastard of this Queenes husband, and she, notwithstanding that, would have the crowne setled on him; but some of the Umbraures of this country, knowing him to bee spuriously begotten, will not give him homadge and refuses to goe to court; and these are Rustum Jemah (Rustam Zaman), Bull Ckaune [Bahlol Khan] Shawgee [Shahaji] and Sevagy [Shivaji]; which latter lyes with an army to the no[rth] ward and commands all alongst, the cost from the upper Choul unto Dabull; against whom the Queene this yeare sent Abdle Ckaune with an army of 10,000 horss and foote; and because she knew with that strength hee was not able to resist Sevagy, shee councelld him to pretend freindshipp with his enemy; which hee did.[34]

It appears that the *mutabanná* (adopted) status of ʿAli ʿAdil Shah II, which the English called here "spuriously begotten," as such unrecognized in Islamic law, was partly brought into question to delegitimize this succession in Bijapur and make the case of Mughal annexation of the Deccan. However, to counter these claims and resist Mughal pressure, Bijapuri chroniclers, although silent on the identity of ʿAli's birth mother, went to great lengths to publicly acknowledge Khadija Sultana's adoption of and deep affection for the infant ʿAli II three days after his birth, which was sufficient to legitimize the adoption.[35] While the English spoke of Bari Sahiba contemptuously as a "mercenary Queene," the Dutch, on the other hand, although grudging the exorbitant costs and scale of arrangements needed for her sea voyage, were convinced that facilitating this powerful and renowned queen's passage to Mocha would make them famous not just in Golkonda but also in other Muslim kingdoms like Hindustan and Persia.[36] At the same time, they blamed her *geldsuchtig fantasien* (money-minded fantasies) for the unrest and instability in Bijapur and its inland regions.[37] In April 1661, the Dutch resident at Vengurla described what was happening at Bijapur court to the governor general Joan Maetsuycker, as recruitment negotiations and preparations were made for Bari Sahiba to set sail for Mocha (on the Red Sea coast of Yemen).[38] Anxieties swelled about what would happen in Bijapur after her departure with predictions that troubles with Shivaji, who had recently held captive the English captain Henry Revington in Danda Rajapur, would resurge.[39]

Before she set off for Mocha, Khadija Sultana made numerous overtures to mediate between Shivaji Bhonsle, Bahlol Khan Miyana, and Siddi Jauhar Salabat Khan, but none of her attempts succeeded because, as the Dutch saw it, no one had any genuine feelings toward nor did they trust each other (*waer wel een vrede maer met geen oprecht gemoet alsoo malcanderen niet vertrouwen*).[40] Given that the relationship with her adopted son ʿAli ʿAdil Shah II was a subject of constant intrigue, the queen sought on numerous occasions to neuter threats made to him by contending with household chiefs through both violence and negotiation. In a detailed observation of the relations between the Bijapur crown and its contending households, the Dutch reported on what happened in the aftermath of Siddi Jauhar Salabat Khan's siege at Panhala fort against Shivaji in 1660. As they put it, these strange happenings and great changes in Bijapur's government were difficult to put into writing (*'t vreemt gewede en de grote veranderinge in dese tegenwoordige regering binnen dit ryck zijn naulyck op 't papier te brengen*).[41] While Shivaji was seen as a troubling rebel, a dirtbag (*een kwele rebel/een vuilenroop*), and as a free-standing leader (*de vrijbovensten*)[42] whom the lords of the kingdom were trying to defeat, it was not entirely clear to VOC observers what to make of the positions of military household chiefs such as Siddi Jauhar and Bahlol Khan, whose rapid movements from court to coast they observed:

> Salabat Khan desires to get an increased portion of power in Bijapur. He says he will set off for Kanara and that he wants to blackmail Venkatapa Nayak to get forces and money from him in service for the kingdom. However, Bahlol Khan, who is an important enemy of Salabat Khan, tried to discourage this plan completely, saying to the king that he himself could serve as a way to scare off the *nayak* at least in Bankapur, which has a large fort, and where a flourishing trading city lies. Bahlol Khan is also in charge of this city. He advised the king to stay in Bankapur until this whole situation came to an end, ensuring him that he would earn at least four lakh *pagodas*.
>
> The king attempted to appease Salabat Khan, but Bahlol Khan warned him not to do so. Bahlol Khan's reasons give more credibility to the king. Even though he did not fully side with either, the king considered their proposals for a long time. Salabat Khan noticed that the king had no intention to do what he proposed. For that reason he returned to his previous lands, unhappy that the king did not give in to him. We have not heard any further news about where he is residing now. The above-mentioned king ʿAli ʿAdil Shah is advancing with an army toward Bankapur and Kanara, but Bahlol Khan along with his followers wanted to catch up with his Majesty, to welcome him, and explain to him all the necessities. However, when the king arrived the army was attacked from the fortress, and they tried to seize power in Kanara. The king had to hide himself and was greatly shocked.
>
> This has made the king resolve to turn back to Bijapur; we hope to get to know soon what will happen. There are strong rumors that Bahlol Khan was actually the one who set up this attack from the fort, in revenge for the death of his brothers who had been murdered by the queen [*de geruchten lopen sterck dat Bullolchan dit verraet, tot revengie van zyne breeders doot, die door toe doen van de Coninginne vermoort is, in 't berck gestelt heeft*].[43]

Queen Khadija Sultana's departure from Bijapur was, therefore, timely, strategic, and very likely even dangerous. The voyage was undertaken in the wake of her plot to murder the Miyana brothers on the one hand and the infamous episode of sending Afzal Khan to kill Shivaji in 1659 on the other. Some years after she was gone, on November 5, 1664, the forlorn sultan ʿAli II described receiving the news of his mother's well-being from Governor Cornelis Speelman, as "the opening of my heart with joy like a rose that opens at dusk" (*zijnde mijn hart van blijdschap open gegaan gelijck een roos inden avont stond doet*).[44] Such words of filial devotion contrast with the main objective of ʿAli II's letter, which was to admonish Bahlol Khan Miyana and his associates, who had reached the port city of Teganapatnam. In his letter, the king assured the VOC that he had ordered Bahlol Khan and his associates to be in their service. He urged Bahlol Khan to ensure that his port keeper and all other Muslim captains maintain peace with the Company, so that commerce would improve in the area.[45] Indeed, the king's pleas fell on deaf and defiant ears. In the next ten years, until the late 1670s, the Miyanas would carve out their autonomy by expanding their interests on both land and sea, in Bay of Bengal shipping and in controlling the production of cloth in areas around Senji.

But the Miyana Afghans were hardly unique in looking out at the seas. Before they arrived in the Karnatak, the Maratha Bhonsles had already sought ways to establish themselves in the hinterlands of the port cities south of Madras. Members of all these households found themselves split between two subregions in a position to negotiate directly with the king in Bijapur in the Deccan proper at one end, and the various post-Vijayanagara *nayaka* states in the Karnatak. While Shivaji stayed near the hereditary lands of the Bhonsles near Pune (present-day Maharashtra, western India), his father Shahaji (d. 1664) moved between Bangalore, Tanjavur, and Madurai during the 1650s.[46] Reports from the factory of Vengurla recounted Shivaji's invasion of Bardes (a district north of Goa) in 1667, where recalcitrant *desais* refused to acquiesce and accept the authority of the Bhonsles.[47] Following in their footsteps, ʿAbdul Karim Bahlol Khan and his kinfolk, based at first in Miraj and Bankapur (central Karnataka), described as a great trading entrepot, would incorporate the southern Coromandel's port cities of Teganapatnam and Porto Novo in the late 1650s. At the same time that Shahaji began raiding the nayakas of Tanjavur and Madurai in Tamil country, Bahlol Khan laid siege to the port city of Teganapatnam after taking over Porto Novo. Trade in these port cities came to a standstill, where the Bijapuris, both Miyanas and Bhonsles, were seen as unwelcome guests (*een schraepende gast*). Rumors circulated that the nayakas of Tanjavur and Madurai, deeply suspicious of each other, were entirely unwilling to combine their forces to oust the Bijapuri household chiefs from Senji province. The 1650s to the 1660s were marked by rapidly shifting alliances, with Shahaji regularly raiding Tanjavur and the Madurai nayaka contemplating whether to come under the protection of Bahlol Khan.[48] Observing that the Madurai and Tanjavur nayakas were unwilling to ally with Shahaji to oust ʿAbdul Karim Bahlol Khan from Senji, VOC officials noted that trade might return to normal despite low-level fighting remaining constant in the region.[49]

As these interhousehold rivalries moved from Bijapur in the Deccan into the southern Coromandel, new demands and pressures transformed the coastal economy. As inland wars raged near Tanjavur and Nagapattinam, the price of rice, which was produced and shipped into the southern Coromandel's port cities from Bengal and Orissa, skyrocketed.[50] Another significant outcome of the Mughal-Deccan wars was the slave trade across the Palk Strait and the Gulf of Mannar, which, along with textiles, became particularly important to sustain the warfront in the Coromandel, emerging as one of the most profitable ventures, not just for the VOC but also for Bijapuri and later Mughal-affiliated subordinates who taxed slave purchases in the Coromandel at a much higher rate than other goods.[51] Periodic wars and small-scale conflicts produced a feedback loop that regularized the supply of slaves from the Karnatak lowlands. With more frequent famines, people died or fled the region. In 1661, when Shahaji Bhonsle was left in the Karnatak to occupy Tanjavur, the whole area was depopulated, leaving the port city of Nagapattinam desolate:

> With continuous destruction of the land, people flee every day, this war will need time to come to a natural end, before things can go back to normal. The main and only advantage of these troubled times in this province is the slave trade. Because of these internal wars near Nagapattinam, a large number of slaves have arrived. Both groups are taking prisoners of the enemy and selling them on the market, who are then taken to Jaffnapatnam.[52]

On June 25, 1661, it was reported that around 3,695 slaves died of hunger before they could be shipped to Jaffnapatnam. From this same shipment, some were skilled weavers, including entire enslaved families—men, women, and children from weaving castes—were sold and shipped to establish cloth production areas in Jaffnapatnam (in northern Sri Lanka) that would be exclusively controlled by the VOC.[53] As early as 1654, the Bijapuri Indo-African Khan Muhammad had stipulated the terms of VOC trade in cloth, indigo, saltpeter, tin, and grains in the lands near Senji, subject to a tax of 2.5 percent, while the purchasing of enslaved men and women was taxed at 15 percent. Any enslaved person who fled would be arrested by the local *kotwāl* (*cauterbael*, police chief) and promptly returned to the VOC.[54] From the enslaved displaced by war and famine to the imports of nonprecious metals like tin, and Coromandel's prized export trade of cotton textiles—household chiefs sought to control the movement of commodities that not only fed, clothed, and armed imperial-regional armies, but also financed their day-to-day expenses. This coastal ecology was very different from what we saw in chapter 2, the resource-scarce regions of the northern Deccan, where Mughal soldiers had first encamped in the first few decades of the seventeenth century, in the landlocked arid districts of Khandesh, Berar, Aurangabad, and Telangana.

Bijapuri-subordinates in the Karnatak, whether Marathas, Indo-Africans, or Afghans, all tapped into preexisting economic networks to increase their autonomy from monarchical authority and the royal household, which was of little relevance on the coast. Two of the most prominent families—the Maratha Bhonsles and the Miyana Afghans—operated between the ends of a warfront that stretched from Bijapur to Cuddalore, alongside others such as the Indo-Africans Siddi Jauhar Salabat Khan (d. 1665) and Nasir Muhammad (d. 1680).[55] All these groups attempted a shared set of strategies, ranging from frequent raids and sieges, the implementation of tolls at choke points across land and sea, monopolies on the movement of certain commodities, and the standard practice of using one European power against the other to compete with each other.[56] The twin viewpoints of their activities near the capital city versus the southern warfront unveil the markedly similar ways that provincial household lineages functioned, irrespective of their ascribed sectarian, linguistic, or cultural identities. The Miyanas were following the same mechanisms with which the Bhonsles had combined their longer presence in the western Deccan with new opportunities for political autonomy as military commanders in the Karnatak. Indeed, as the next section's examination of a literary text will show, these two groups appeared more alike, kindred, and coeval even to contemporary observers than our modern-day minds would like to imagine. It is not as if cultural differences between the Miyanas and Bhonsles were not observed at all. On the contrary, contemporary observers marked, exaggerated, and emboldened these differences by using absolute contrasts of good versus evil, loyalist versus betrayer, and of those who were one's own and those who became strangers. All these striking binaries were subordinate to an ethical and moral concept of a shared home/house or ghar, to which these rival households belonged.

RECASTING HOME: MIYANA AFGHANS AND MARATHA BHONSLES IN DAKKANI VERSE

If we were only interested in rise and fall narratives, we could consult reams of archival documents from various European trading companies to index the claims of previous historians and fill gaps to build thicker narrative histories. But, when all is said and done, what did these political and economic changes mean to contemporary observers in the seventeenth century? How did they make sense of the place of Miyana Afghans and Maratha Bhonsles in the Deccan? To answer this question and to reconstruct the affective frameworks of the material conditions described above, I now turn to a very different body of evidence, which we encountered in previous chapters, martial works in Dakkani, the Deccan's panregional literary idiom. The text under consideration is Nusrati's last work, the *Tārīkh-i sikandarī* (History of Sikandar, ca. 1672), which sought to capture this complex political moment.

Before proceeding to its content, first, a word on the text itself. Rising linguistic and religious nationalism of the early and mid-twentieth century and disciplinary divides have heavily shaped the print history of Nusrati's *Tārīkh-i sikandarī*. The historicity and politics of these representations, as I will show, are difficult to subsume under a modern binary of perpetual harmony or hostility between Hindus and Muslims. While Anglophone and Persophone historians and literary scholars have largely ignored the *Tārīkh-i sikandarī*, it has had a long and contentious afterlife in regional scholarship within the subcontinent in the highly politicized fields of Urdu, Hindi, and Marathi studies, where its historicity continues to be discussed to the present-day.[57] As a rare text closest to the earliest part of Shivaji's career, it captivated a generation of twentieth-century vernacular scholars who were deeply invested in finding, editing, and processing manuscripts. Its numerous editions in the twentieth century were an outcome of sharing materials among Hindi-, Marathi-, and Urdu-speaking scholars across India and Pakistan.[58] And yet, as the disagreements expressed in the introductions to the *Tārīkh-i sikandarī* make clear, the text offered slippery grounds for settling scores on contentious questions about sectarian, ethnic, and linguistic origins that plague the two modern nation-states today. The text was understood by neatly categorizing its language, script, and form, according to modern sectarian identities, with each edition raising the question of where and to whom the *Tārīkh-i sikandarī* belonged. For instance, the literary scholar Suresh Dutt Awasthi, emphatically claimed it for Hindi studies by extracting Nusrati's use of Sanskrit *tatsama* words throughout the poem. As was a common practice among modern scholars seeking the earliest origins of Hindi and Urdu,[59] Awasthi brushed aside questions of *lipi* (script, in this case, the use of Perso-Arabic) and the poem's rhymed couplet form (masnavī), according to which, he claimed, the text had been miscategorized as belonging to Urdu studies. Script and form, he argued, were less relevant than the quality of the poet's language.[60] Further, disciplinary divides between historians and literary scholars have led to disputes about the historicity of such martial works, which are often seen as the domain of literary scholars who studied them for their aesthetic and literary conventions alone. In contrast to Persian chronicles, Nusrati's various works do not offer the modern historian clear dates, events, and neat sequential narrations; for this reason, they were seen as mere addenda to what was already known about political history.[61] For our purposes here, the first step in making sense of the *Tārīkh-i sikandarī* is to decouple its historicity from the politics of the postcolonial present and the rigid modern disciplinary divides that separate literature from history.

The debates among polyvocal scholars in the twentieth century show how the stories from these texts are received, not just in academic circuits, but in popular culture, film, theater, and television today. The contrasting silence on the *Tārīkh-i sikandarī* within Anglophone and Persophone circles, the cloister of professional history writing, versus its prevalence, wide circulation, and visibility in regional-language intellectual circuits, speaks to the divergent social settings in which history and collective memory are produced in South Asia.[62] It should come as no surprise that vernacular texts such as the *Tārīkh-i sikandarī* that transcend the divide between history writing and memory have reached much broader audiences than

Persian-language texts, both then and now. This gives us more reason not to dismiss them as outside proper forms of writing history but to study them for making sense of place, community, and belonging in premodern South Asia.

The politics of place at the heart of the *Tārīkh-i sikandarī*, which preoccupied the text's polyphonic twentieth-century editors, articulates a mode of belonging impossible to fit into modern-day searches for origins and territorial notions of space and sovereignty. As I show here, the text both reifies categories of difference and then collapses them completely, testing received definitions of "Deccani" versus "foreigner," rendering moot the age-old question of who belonged and who did not belong. Nusrati located the antagonism between the two protagonists—ʿAbdul Karim Bahlol Khan and Shivaji—in a shared foundational idea of home, house, dwelling, habitation, or ghar that fitted into larger spatial concepts such as city (*shahr*), village (*gāon*), dominion (*mulk*), and homeland (*watan*). He upheld and highlighted the differences between members of this ghar. At the same time, he saw these antagonistic members as inextricably linked, morally bound to protect, conserve, and reproduce a space that their lineages had inhabited for generations. The semantic field of relevant terms for place and community in the *Tārīkh-i sikandarī* illustrates a house defined by relationships built on shared activities amongst its members, not merely by blood or ascribed sectarian, linguistic, and social identities. The poet deploys an identarian language to construct contrasting portraits of self and other, of Afghan versus Maratha, which are all contained within the idea of the house. He used the concept of ghar to make sense of overlapping regional and imperial sovereignties. Nusrati asked—what did it mean to belong to peninsular India, a space that had been the ghar inhabited by so many different kinds of communities at a time when its internal limits were being contested and redefined?

For an answer to this question, let's first lay out the standard political narrative about the 1670s. The *Tārīkh-i sikandarī* is intriguing not because it proves something about what we already know about the rise and fall of court factions in the Deccan sultanates in this decade. Rather, it holds the reader's attention for all the well-known truths it censors and all the historical figures it excises, inverts, and caricatures! Along with Bhushan's *Shivrajbhusan* (ca. 1673) in Brajbhasha, the *Tārīkh-i sikandarī* is part of a larger ecology of texts when nascent household lineages sought to claim and construct new narratives to project themselves as righteous rulers in the 1670s.[63] As we saw earlier, already in the 1650s and 1660s, kingly authority had largely receded, and household lineages occupied center stage in Mughal-Deccan politics. By the time of its composition in the early 1670s, shortly after the death of Sultan ʿAli ʿAdil Shah II (d. 1672), a struggle unfolded between the Maratha Bhonsles, the Indo-Africans, and the Miyana Afghans in Bijapur.[64] As we saw earlier in VOC records from Vengurla and Nagapattinam, members from each household were split between the capital city of Bijapur in the Deccan and recently acquired holdings in the Karnatak. The Indo-African brothers Khawas

Khan, Ikhlas Khan, and Nasir Muhammad (all sons of the aforementioned commander Khan Muhammad, who was murdered in late 1658)[65] rallied against Bahlol Khan Miyana, his uncles and sons, and a close associate and well-known figure, Sher Khan Lodi, who had moved down to Cuddalore in the late 1650s.[66] The Maratha Bhonsles moved between their hereditary holdings near Pune, with Shivaji and his half-brother Ekoji engaging frequently in conflict around Tanjavur.[67] Nasir Muhammad and Sher Khan Lodi fought a months-long war to control the southern Coromandel in 1676.[68] Shortly thereafter, Shivaji would decisively defeat Sher Khan Lodi, after the latter's master ʿAbdul Karim Bahlol Khan died in 1677.[69]

Throughout the seventeenth century, a common strategy for these provincial household chiefs was to use the Mughals by offering them the Deccan as a bargaining chip to oust the other. When ʿAbdul Karim Bahlol Khan had the Indo-African Khawas Khan executed in 1676, the latter had been negotiating with the imperial overlords to cede Bijapur's territories to them.[70] Shortly thereafter, in 1677, Bahlol Khan would himself make the same offer to cede Bijapur to the Mughals to help defeat Shivaji.[71] After Shivaji's coronation in 1674, the Miyanas would lose their possessions in the Coromandel, with figures like Sher Khan Lodi submitting to Shivaji and retiring to the court of the nayakas of Ariyalur.[72] But these well-known political maneuverings, which trace how the Marathas won and the Miyanas lost are neither discernible nor verifiable in a text like the *Tārīkh-i sikandarī*.[73] The more salient question that this representation raises is what did these individuals—ʿAbdul Karim Bahlol Khan and Shivaji—and the categories they purportedly represented (Afghan versus Maratha/foreigner versus Deccani/Muslim versus Hindu) mean to contemporary observers?

The *Tārīkh-i sikandarī* was, partly, an exercise to make the Miyanas legible to contemporary competitors and elite audiences. This heroic portrait of a nascent household was made in Dakkani, instead of Persian, to affirm the Miyanas' rightful place in panregional politics. The portrait of the political economy that I sketched at the beginning of this chapter shows the tumultuous relationship between the Miyanas, Indo-Africans, and Bhonsles and the Bijapur sultan ʿAli ʿAdil Shah II and his mother, Bari Sahiba, with the latter making numerous attempts to discipline all these households. When Nusrati composed the *Tārīkh-i sikandarī*, the Miyanas' claim to Bijapur was shaky and made amid intense political and economic competition. As stated above, rumors had been circulating that the queen had one of the Miyana brothers killed.[74] At the same time, in the Karnatak, the Bhonsles first and the Miyanas next began carving out autonomous domains by drawing on coastal resources along the southern Coromandel. It is not at all surprising that given the uncertain place of the Miyanas in Bijapuri politics, the poet so frequently evoked the ethos of *ghaza* (holy war), fashioning Bahlol Khan as a *ghāzī*.[75] In scenes on the battlefield when in dialogue with his soldiers, Bahlol Khan deployed the language of holy war (*ghaza*), martyr (*shahīd*), and apostate (*murtadd*). Such evocations positioned the Miyanas as defenders of the Deccan vis-à-vis the non-Muslim Bhonsles as well as the region's competing Muslim households like the Indo-Africans Siddi Jauhar Salabat Khan (d. 1661) and the brothers Khawas Khan (d. 1676), Ikhlas Khan, and Nasir Muhammad (d. 1680), some of whom fiercely opposed the Miyanas.

The *Tārīkh-i sikandarī* refers obliquely to the aforementioned historical events, and it is not worthwhile to simply mine this text for already well-known facts. For example, although it portrays the Battle of Umrani in 1673, fought between 'Abdul Karim Bahlol Khan and the Maratha commander, Pratap Rao,[76] the latter historical figure does not appear in the poem at all. Instead, his master, Shivaji, occupies center stage. The poem consists of seven chapters, the titles of which are in Persian, while the chapters contain Dakkani narrations of events. Each chapter includes portraits of a series of assemblies, from the court, the city, to the battlefield, where the poem's hero—'Abdul Karim Bahlol Khan—receives honors, mounts his horse, and consults with a gathering of his army's advisors, military commanders, and soldiers, before finally going off to war. The poet uses devices such as absolute contrasts and insults to create a binary between the hero, 'Abdul Karim Bahlol Khan, and the villain, Shivaji Bhonsle. He deploys aggressive and playful language, but underneath this discourse of rivalry and absolute otherness simmers the problem of deep familiarity, intimacy, and cohabitation between these two protagonists who shared much in common, including a sense of belonging to the same ghar.

The poet opens by evoking the omnipresence of God in the *hamd*, laying out the reasoning, time, and place of the work's composition.

> *bahan hār hai jis zamīn par jo khūn*
> *bahe kiyūn nā huve sabab kuch zabūn*
>
> the land in which blood flows
> to speak, of the reasons that it was shed,
> ...
>
> *kahan hār yū Tārīkh-i sikandarī*
> *lage jis kī guftār yūn sarsarī*
>
> I say this history of Sikandar
> with such brevity of speech
>
> *sahas hor āsī par jo the tīn sāl*
> *kare yek men bar sab zamāne ne hāl*
>
> one thousand eighty three
> on a moment in that time
>
> *jo mulk-i dakkan men huā shāh-i nau*
> *libās āp duniyā kare tāzah nau*
>
> when the new king came to the throne
> in the Deccan kingdom, the world adorned itself anew[77]

Images of gratuitous violence, blood being spilled on land, heads being crushed on the battlefield, entire cities burnt to the ground, reservoirs and lakes filled with the dead, were typical of the *razm* topos and its sensorium. But these images were not just poetic exaggerations; they also reveal Nusrati's broader concern with and lament for the human costs of war. To make sense of war's repercussions, the poet accorded a range of meanings to spaces of belonging such as ghar, mulk, and watan, and what it meant to lose them. *Mulk-i dakkan* in the above verse, for instance, refers to the kingdom of the Deccan, where the child king Sikandar ʿAdil Shah had just ascended the throne of Bijapur (r. 1672–86). In other scenes, mulk could be decoupled from kingship and have other meanings such as realm, region, and dominions.

The politics of place that lie at the heart of the *Tārīkh-i sikandarī* also speak to the role of Nusrati's oeuvre, more broadly, in the larger literary transition between Persian and Urdu. Sunil Sharma has traced changes in classical Persian poetry with *shahr-āshob* elements, originally an appellation for a beautiful beloved in a lyric poem, which could include praise for an idealized city and its kingly patrons. This later turned into the *shahr-āshob* (the disturbed city) poetic tradition of classical Urdu of the eighteenth-century when poets lamented and satirized the Mughal Empire's political decline, offering bleak images of urban life.[78] Nusrati's work sits in the middle of these two literary moments and provides a bridge between Persian (celebratory) and Urdu (morose) cityscapes. He begins by first praising the city of Bijapur, which was both a *jogi kā math* (ascetic's monastery) and the *shahr-i islām* (city of Islam) and then contrasts it with a portrait of loss, and the city's unrelenting destruction and desolation. Locating Bijapur in the larger spatial unit of watan, the poet grieves the destruction of its neighborhoods and that his own homeland had become a stranger to the world (*nagar sut chaliyā be jatan / huā jag kon bigānā apnā watan*).[79] He addresses the reader/listener as a metaphorical traveler, taking them through sites of destruction in progressively larger urban scales going from neighborhood (*nagar*) to small settlement (*basti*) to city (*shahr*), located in broader conceptual units, starting with the house or ghar and moving to *mulk-i dakkan/mulk-i hindustān*, dominions of the Deccan/Hindustan, which are paired as two distinct entities.

According to the poet, the actions of and relationships between kindred people caused the destruction of a shared space of belonging, the house. Nusrati has a charge sheet, of sorts, listing the morally questionable actions of those around him. Excessive greed that caused houses to disintegrate (*hawas thī jo har kun kon ghar ghar judā / ke honā shahī ke apen kad khudā*) (covetousness in each split house from house / each considered himself king and God alike).[80] Here, ghar is identified as singular household units that together constitute a unified whole. The image of the house could refer to a physical space under threat that needed to be defended with one's life (*jo sevat pade ghar peh mushkil sabab / to jīyūn kharch kar ghar yū rakhna hai tab*).[81] Similarly, multiple dominions were understood relationally, from the Deccan to Mughal Hindustan, as they together partook in experiences of war and violence. For instance, the poet painted an image of a smaller, empty ghar or house, lying unadorned and uninhabited in a desolate mulk. Placing the dominions of the Mughals within a larger community of mulk, Nusrati thus laments that there were no means to buy lamps for the house (*mughal kā mulk te uste aisā ujād / divā lāne kā nayīn hai jiyūn ghar ko chār*).[82]

The relationship between words for spaces and words referring to people comes to the fore when Nusrati sets up contrasting portraits of the two protagonists—Bahlol Khan and Shivaji. The poet explains that each *nasl* or lineage was morally tied to the house owing to its generational service. The poem's first battle scene begins by inverting the reality of Bijapuri politics. In this image of a gathering with his ministers and courtly elites, Bahlol Khan is showered with praise and adulation by some of his archrivals, including the Indo-African Khawas Khan, whom he had murdered shortly thereafter.[83] Khawas Khan acknowledges that Bahlol Khan's lineage and renown are spread across transregional kingdoms and cities from the Deccan to Delhi:

> *dharyā jab te nawāb nāmī te dāb*
> *khatā khān bahlol khānī khitāb*
>
> the weight of his name became apparent
> he whose title was Bahlol Khan
>
> *dakkan ke tū yek mulk kā hai vazīr*
> *vale dil men dehlī ke nayīn tis nazīr*[84]
>
> you who is a minister of one of the Deccan kingdoms,
> but, its known that there is no one like you even in Delhi

Multiple terms identify the title of Bahlol Khan with a lineage (*nasl*) and *ajdād* (ancestors), who were dispersed across Hindustan and the Deccan. Noting the bravery of three generations of the Miyana household, Nusrati thus writes:

> *tun potā hai us khān bahlol kā*
> *na thā hind men mard tis tol kā*[85]
>
> that you, who are the grandson of that Bahlol Khan
> who no other man in Hindustan could match

Generational service was one criterion for any lineage's claim of belonging to a ghar. But this service could be reason for both praise and trenchant criticism, as it was tied to the enduring idea of eating the salt of one's master (*namak halālī*). Shivaji's lineage, like Bahlol Khan's, was also famous across these dominions but for all the wrong reasons. According to Nusrati, the problem with Shivaji was not that he was a congenital other, but that he was considered a kindred or relative (*apan/apein* or one's own—that is, someone who belonged to the same, shared ghar). The poet marks him as a fellow kinsman destroying the very house that had nurtured him, referring to the long service of the Bhonsles under the sultanates:[86]

> ke jis ghar te jīkoī badyā ho ange
> pachen tod ne phir vahī ghar mange
>
> the very house from where he has risen,
> breaking that very house from the back
>
> ziyān kār kon kuch na us sūd hai
> padyā ghar to apein bhī nābūd hai[87]
>
> there is no profit in bad deeds
> if the home breaks, even one's own become no one

Generational service placed a moral obligation on members of the ghar to serve and protect it. Lineages could be of two kinds, those that were loyal and those that had a history of mistrust and betrayal. Nusrati evaluated the place of the Miyanas and the Bhonsles vis-a-vis the Bijapur crown, evoking the familiar dyads of loyalty and betrayal, virtue and dishonor, believer and nonbeliever, which he had also utilized in his earlier work, 'Alināma (ca. 1665). Unlike the previous work, the Tārīkh-i sikandarī was composed at a moment when regional sovereigns were no longer relevant. Nusrati overcame the challenge of creating a portrait of the Miyanas, as defenders of the ghar in the absence of a king by placing them in undeniable proximity to and intimacy with the Marathas who belonged to the same house.

Like he did in the 'Alināma, he turned once again to the moral binary of namak halālī versus namak harāmī to locate Bahlol Khan and Shivaji's shared place in the house. In the absence of a king, the moral obligation for staying true to one's salt or namak was no longer tied to a lord or master, but to the remembered pasts of each lineage, its renown, and its reputation in the realm. While Bahlol Khan put his life and wealth on the line to do great deeds and always sought to eat the king's salt (bade kām par kharch apas jān-o-māl/mange nit namak shāh kā khāne halāl) and was the true claimant of Delhi (ke hūn dil men dihlī kā mein da 'wa-dār), Shivaji was someone who had learnt to eat harām since birth (sikhīyā hai janam charke khāne harām) and the one who harbored thoughts of breaking the house (dharyiā yū jo ghar todne kā khayāl).[88] A common, shared sense of belonging by the Miyanas and Afghans to the house may explain why the poet hardly used any words signifying the ethnic or linguistic profile of these two groups throughout the poem. Both the common Hindustani terms pathān, which refers to Afghans as a group, and the term ghanīm or enemy, which was frequently used to refer to Marathas in Indo-Persian texts, are used sparingly throughout the composition.[89] Rather than distinguishing them through these ethnographic terms, the poet judges them through a common rubric of loyalty, placing them on an equal footing to protect the integrity of their shared ghar.

In the poem's final battle, Bahlol Khan speaks to his troops, instructing them on the art of war by drawing an analogy of Deccan politics with the Mughal War of Succession a momentous event memorialized across multiple literary traditions of the subcontinent.[90] By drawing parallels between regional and imperial politics, Nusrati once again reaffirms the inherent kinship between Bahlol Khan and Shivaji, even as he casts them as polar opposites. This chapter of the poem begins with the hero Bahlol Khan addressing his soldiers affectionately as friends (*yārān*), evoking a spirit of camaraderie and friendship among his soldiers (*har yek dil men yārī ke guftār ache*) on the battlefield.[91] Listening to the fears about Shivaji among his troops, he calls upon them by evoking a famous incident from the Battle of Samugarh that had unfolded on May 29, 1658, between the Mughal princes Aurangzeb (d. 1707) and Dara Shikoh (d. 1659).[92] According to Nusrati, Shivaji was the equivalent of Aurangzeb while Bahlol Khan stood for the figure of Dara Shikoh. This correlation would seem bizarre not just to modern-day readers, but probably to seventeenth-century listeners like the Mughal emperor Aurangzeb himself, who had long considered Shivaji his mortal enemy. Nusrati deliberately inverted and inserted this analogy to reaffirm the kinship between the Miyanas and the Marathas. Recounting the memory of this battle, Bahlol Khan exhorts his troops:

>*sune soche nawāb yū bāt kahe*
>*ke tumnā kon yārān yū ma'alūm hai*
>
>*ke dārā kon ā shāh-i aurang son*
>*padī thī ladāyī so sondal ke jiyūn*
>
>*athā shāh dārā jo hātī savār*
>*padiyā jiyūn ghaluliyān kā chondhar te mār*
>
>*na liyā tāb utar gaj tarang jiyūn chadiyā*
>*lagyā fauj kon tab ke khāssa padiyā*
>
>*huī pal men us dhāt lashkar kī mod*
>*ke nayīn lad sake phir kabhī fauj jod*
>
>upon hearing this talk, the Nawab thought and said,
>oh, friends! for you all know
>
>that Princes Dara and Aurangzeb
>had gone to war with their armies
>
>when Dara was riding his elephant
>surrounded by canon on all sides
>
>unable to withstand, he dismounted his elephant
>that particular moment cost his army
>
>in a flash, the tide turned against his army
>never again would it come together to fight[93]

Dara Shikoh had descended from his elephant at the Battle of Samugarh, and his troops mistook his fleeing elephant as a sign of the prince's death. This tactical mistake flipped the battle's outcome in prince Aurangzeb's favor.[94] Reference to this famous tipping point from a recent battle was more than just a lesson in military strategy; it was also a means of illustrating the correspondence and moral similarity between different sets of political players across the Deccan and Mughal Hindustan. But, crucially, by comparing political competition between princely brothers within the Mughal dynastic line to the Deccan's households that did not share blood, language, or affinal ties, Nusrati constructs a bond between the Miyanas and Bhonsles grounded in their service to the same house or ghar. Through such an unbecoming analogy, he casts the Miyanas as the Deccan's rightful defenders against the claims of an intimate opponent like Shivaji, whose family had been equally, if not more, entrenched in service to regional sultans.

To sum up, then, what is the significance of the *Tārīkh-i sikandarī*? As a premodern text that lives today, like its Marathi and Brajbhasha counterparts, it is debated among scholars who write in Indian languages and their vernacular reading publics in the subcontinent. By contrast, in Persophone and Anglophone scholarly spheres, the text is largely invisible. However, in both scholarly worlds, its historicity and the question of belonging falls into an easy binary of communalism versus syncretism. Rather than rationalizing premodern actors' actions, freezing the frame on a resolutely contradictory representation of difference rejects both paradigms, where premodern actors are either never motivated by divisions of sect, caste, and language or they are completely and only driven by them. The *Tārīkh-i sikandarī* collapses the fixed meanings ascribed to political identities. The poet emphasizes the ubiquitous and enduring concept of ghar, which held together different social groups in a single arena of competition, bound by generational service. The text answers the perennial question of who belongs and who does not belong in unexpected ways, by both marking the social differences between groups and then collapsing these binaries within the spatial concept of the house.

The material stakes sketched at the outset of this chapter show how the dissolution of regional kingship and the rise of household lineages depended on the exploitation of new economic resources, connecting the drylands of the northern Deccan plateau with the rich cotton- and rice-producing regions of the Karnatak coastal plains. In the second half of the seventeenth century, southern India's political landscape was awash with deeply familiar and intimate political rivals. Nusrati observed the changes wrought by Mughal overlordship on the sultanates, which resulted in more autonomy for aristocratic-military-agrarian households, a familiar pattern in peninsular India. He commented on the conflicts between soldiering groups such as Afghans, who had circulated in the armies of northern and southern India vis-à-vis warrior-peasant groups who held a combination of hereditary village-level occupations and official military positions such as the Marathas, who had a much longer presence in the Deccan. Nusrati saw the two groups as political kin united by their generational service and judged them through a common moral standard of the obligation to protect their ghar.

But, interelite rivalries, memorialized by court poets and chroniclers, are only one leg of a much longer journey that connected the Deccan to the wider Indian Ocean world. Right around the time Nusrati composed the *Tārīkh-i sikandarī*, the kith and kin of Bahlol Khan and Shivaji had already begun venturing toward the Coromandel coast, subsuming post-Vijayanagara nayaka polities and acquiring new territories where they encountered an unfamiliar set of economic networks and resources—namely, myriad social groups that made possible freight trade of tin, rice, and participated in the production of textiles that were shipped across the Bay of Bengal. Bahlol Khan Miyana would send his close associate, Sher Khan Lodi, down to the southern Coromandel from his initial posting in Bankapur to Valikondapuram, twenty-five miles from the port city of Cuddalore or Tegenapatnam. Similarly, aside from his father in Bangalore, Shivaji's half-brother Ekoji—someone our poet Nusrati spoke of with great admiration—was sent by the Bijapur sultan to oust the *nayakas* of Madurai from Tanjavur in 1676.[95] The region that fell under these Bijapuri subordinates, south of the city of Chennai (Madras) and north of Koddaikarai or Point Calimere, was not a blank frontier, but encompassed multiple competing occupational groups who had long mediated relations between inland polities and various European companies.[96]

How did these coastal communities encounter Bijapur-affiliated actors seeking new resources to sustain the Mughal-Deccan warfront and with whom they shared very little in common culturally? As the subsequent discussion will show, Bijapuri subordinates found their political and economic interests converging with and, at times, tamed by the coast's dominant mercantile groups. By supporting preexisting fault lines of caste and status in the littoral economy, realigning with the mercantile elites of the northern Tamil country was key for securing their growing autonomy from kingly authority in the Deccan and shaping the Mughal Empire from the Coromandel coast.

AN ACT OF KINDNESS OR WEAVERS' REVOLT?

Before we delve into the minutiae of an episode that unfolded in the 1660s and 1670s between Bijapuri subordinates, regional merchants, cotton weavers, and the Dutch and French East India Companies in the southern Coromandel, it's worth laying out the stakes of this discussion. One of the foremost questions that confronts historians of premodern India is how the subcontinent's vibrant political economy was subsumed by the English East India Company in the late eighteenth and early nineteenth centuries, thus paving the way for European colonialism.[97] The textile industry has often been the battleground on which this debate unfolds.[98] Historians locate the moment and causes of decline in the Indian subcontinent before or on the eve of European conquest, when relationships between textile producers, merchants, and the state transformed.[99] Much of this modern historiography draws on the English East India Company and its well-preserved records across India to answer the question of economic decline.[100] The role of both precolonial merchants and political elites, as well as the question of whether or not they aided or abetted the rise of European companies, is of significance to this debate.[101]

Vijaya Ramaswamy was one of the first historians, in her now classic study *Textiles and Weavers in Medieval India*, to connect the social worlds of weavers in the centuries before colonialism with larger political changes.[102] She did so by examining the earliest (and most difficult) set of Tamil and Telugu inscriptional evidence from medieval south India. Ramaswamy unearthed references to taxes levied on both merchant groups and head weavers (members of the community who had risen to become intermediaries) or both. She showed hierarchical relationships within and across these groups, arguing that production came to be controlled by the figure of the "broker/middleman," who would then later become henchman for European companies, preserving their and his own economic interests while impoverishing producers.[103] While recognizing a palpable shift in these group's social relations from the heyday of the Vijayanagara Empire in the sixteenth century to the era of the English and Dutch companies, Ramaswamy hinted that changes in social stratification, whereby head weavers rose among weaving castes, emerged owing to a combination of new factors. The growing demand for new kinds of textiles, technological shifts, and changes in state patronage of trade particularly occurred because of the expansion of the Islamic sultanates of southern India into the northern Tamil country in the second half of the seventeenth century.[104] The moment of cross-status group and intercaste conflict I examine in this final section picks up this puzzle by turning to how Persianate elites, subordinate to the Deccan sultanates and the Mughal Empire, dealt with weaving castes and intermediary mercantile groups involved in the southern Coromandel's textile trade.

In what follows, I show that precolonial political elites were not unique in drawing on preexisting inequities to further their own interests, even if their means for disciplining other social groups were far more restricted and circumscribed than what came much later under the English East India Company in the eighteenth century. Bijapuri households aligned themselves with regionally dominant mercantile groups, forming networks that cut across differences of language, caste, and region to discipline artisans in a coastal economy. All these elite actors had successfully combined the advantages of revenue-farming with commercial interests to strengthen their autonomy from monarchical forms. European companies had long negotiated with these famed indigenous portfolio capitalists to establish their operations across the Indian subcontinent. Often heralded as the harbingers of early modernity in South Asia and hailed for moving across multiple political and ecological boundaries, these elites also had to consolidate control over human and nonhuman resources to accumulate wealth. Cementing existing hierarchies strengthened their networks and undercut the monarchical state forms they were nominally affiliated with at the intersections of the sultanate and nayaka worlds.

In some ways, then, the alignment of Bijapur-affiliated Miyana Afghans with Tamil- and Telugu-speaking merchants of the southern Coromandel in the 1670s was part of a longer pattern. Even in the 1640s, after the fortunes of the Chandragiri kings waned, the Telugu-speaking Balija merchant and the VOC chief broker Chinanna Chetti established himself as a close aid of the Golkonda sultanate's most prominent Iranian courtier, Mir Muhammad Sayyid Ardestani (d. 1663), who had a variety of investments in diamond mining, textiles, and tin trade across the Bay of Bengal.[105] The artificial separation of the Deccan sultanates and the nayaka kingdoms belies the fact that their political economies were strikingly alike, as were the structural relationships of mercantile and military households to kingly power in them.

In 1672, the French East India Company acquired a settlement in Pondicherry, south of which lay the ports of Devanampattinam or Teganapatnam, and Porto Novo, which had fallen under Bijapur in the 1640s and encompassed inland textile-producing regions previously held by the nayakas of Senji.[106] More than a decade before the French, the Dutch East India Company had taken the port city of Nagapattinam from the Portuguese in 1658, supplementing their more well-established ports of Masulipatnam and Pulicat, which were located in the northern Coromandel coast and which fell under the authority of the Golkonda sultans.[107] The southern Coromandel region was notable because of the relative autonomy and resilience of non-Company traders, whether those were the Maraikkayar Muslims or independent Indo-Portuguese merchants, a pattern from the late sixteenth century that remained the norm even in the period under consideration, irrespective of the fortunes of political dynasties.[108]

In areas south of Point Calimere, Tamil-speaking Maraikkayar Muslims affiliated with the Marava Setupatis of Ramnad, along the Fishery and Ramnad coasts, had allied with the Dutch to counter the Portuguese-Parava alliance.[109] The Maraikkayar Muslim commercial elites traversed multiple linguistic registers, particularly with their use of Arwi or Tamil written in Arabic script.[110] In the second half of the seventeenth century, this mercantile community circulated in regions north of Point Calimere, where they ran operations alongside Telugu- and Tamil-speaking Hindu merchant intermediaries. To the chagrin of Dutch observers, non-Company actors with investments in trade endured in the areas north of Nagapattinam up to Madras. For the VOC, this subregion remained a volatile source of profits, even when its administration was transferred to the government in Ceylon.[111] Here, Bijapur subordinates such as Sher Khan Lodi, serving under Bahlol Khan Miyana, established their household (*huijshouden/huijsheid*) and close associates (*maagschap*) in the village of Valikondapuram, where they had to deal with established local merchants and weaving populations who had long operated in the littoral economy.[112]

If we are to take representations in published European accounts at their word, we might get the impression that there were no underlying frictions between Bijapuri subordinates, such as Sher Khan Lodi and local merchant groups, to say nothing of the weaving communities concentrated in the cotton-growing districts around Coimbatore, Madurai, Ramanathapuram, and Tirunelveli. Indeed, this is certainly the portrait we get from the first French governor general of Pondicherry, Francois Martin (d. 1706), whose account can easily be mined to narrate straightforward biographies of several of the figures discussed in this chapter such as Shivaji, Sher Khan Lodi, and others. In June of 1676, when the French requested that Lodi seize a ship that had arrived at Teganapatnam from Manila, Martin wrote, "I was myself doubtful as to whether my proposal would be accepted. Sher Khan prided himself on keeping his word. He was particularly careful with merchants in this respect being desirous of attracting them to trade in his territories."[113] And in June 1678, when Lodi's defeat by Shivaji was imminent, the French governor lamented:

> The master of Ariyalur received Sher Khan with his customary warmth and hospitality. Ekoji and the other Hindu princes offered to take him into their service, but he rejected their proposals as they did not appear to enjoy his confidence. Sher Khan was the only person who could have upheld the authority of the Moors of Bijapur in these parts. He was respected by the local people. Had he possessed sufficient forces, he may have been able to teach a lesson to all these Hindu rulers.[114]

Martin's observation of the kindness extended by the nayakas of Ariyalur to Lodi was unsurprising, as was the French governor's lament for the waning fortunes of a crucial ally who had enabled the French Company to acquire its first settlement at Pondicherry. But these words of praise raise unresolved questions about Lodi's dealings and circulation beyond elite circles. Why did Bijapuri subordinates like Lodi have to be "particularly careful with merchants"? And who exactly were "the local people," whose lives were transformed by the incorporation of Bijapuri military elites, such as the Miyanas and Maratha Bhonsles, into the southern Coromandel?

To answer these questions, we need to turn to the years that led up to the siege of St. Thomé in September 1674. St. Thomé, in the southern Coromandel, was the town where the fabled tomb of Saint Thomas the Apostle was located. The Golkonda sultanate took it over from the Portuguese in 1662; given its importance to the Catholic church, the French Company sent Admiral De la Haye to take over this city in 1672.[115] It was the only other port city that the French acquired; however, they would soon be ousted from it by the Dutch who then handed it over to the Golkonda sultan in 1674.[116] It was in the middle of the negotiations with the French over St. Thomé that the Dutch captain Martin Pit and his secretary Nicolas Ruijser were sent to visit Sher Khan Lodi on February 15, 1674.[117] The details of this twenty-three day journey, covering short trips between many villages, towns, and port cities over a distance of a hundred and twenty miles, recorded the day-to-day conversations with Lodi, along with translations of many of his letters and the responses of other port officials and local merchants. It also included the highly sought-after documentary outcome of these negotiations—three original *qauls* or deeds of assurance from Lodi, along with their translations—which assured that the French would be forbidden from transporting more weapons and ammunition into Pondicherry and St. Thomé.

By the 1670s, the Miyanas had tapped into the trade of multiple commodities, especially the import trade of tin from Pegu (in southern Burma), selling this everyday metal along inland routes dotted with markets that went north toward the Deccan. In addition, they transported rice along the Coromandel coast and, above all, engaged in the production and then the export of textiles from this coast to Southeast Asia. Sher Khan Lodi ensured the movement of commodities from coast to court; his other responsibilities included policing disruptive Europeans— the French in Pondicherry, the Danes in Tranquebar, and the Dutch in Nagapattinam. While preventing drunken brawls between squabbling French and Dutch messengers was not at all difficult for Lodi, matters at sea posed an altogether different challenge.[118] Along the coast, Miyana shipping was caught between the standoff between the French and the Dutch over St. Thomé.[119] In one letter to the VOC, Sher Khan Lodi complained that among the ships belonging to his master Bahlol Khan, which sailed to and from Malacca, one had been forbidden from returning to Porto Novo. Lodi explained that Bahlol Khan suffered losses as the ship had to stay in Malacca through the winter; he implored the Dutch governor to send a letter for its return.[120] The ship's *nakhoda* or captain, a certain Khan Mahmud, an associate of Bahlol Khan and Sher Khan Lodi, had purchased the ship in Malacca, in defiance of the VOC. To continue pushing Lodi to abandon the French, the Dutch held back Miyana ships coming into Porto Novo and Teganapatnam from Malacca.[121]

When the Miyanas first arrived in the lands near Senji, questions immediately arose as to which groups fell under their authority. After protracted negotiations with the Dutch, Sher Khan Lodi would issue a *qaul* to limit French presence in St. Thomé, copies of which were sent to his archrival, the governor of Senji, Nasir Muhammad, as well as to the Danes in Tranquebar, the English in Madras, and the local merchants of Porto Novo. Nasir Muhammad's father, Khan Muhammad, had granted the VOC terms of trade in the lands near Senji. Sher Khan Lodi's *qaul* did not list very specific clauses about the terms of trade, nor was it accompanied by any supporting document from the Bijapur sultan to affirm its validity. While Lodi was identified at the outset as the great governor of the portion of Bijapur's inland areas and as the havaldār of the trading city of Porto Novo, (*groot Gouverneur van een deel der beneden landen van Visiapour en den Habaldaar der Coopstadt Porto Novo*), within the *qaul* we do not find terms to clarify his affiliation or status as a representative of the Bijapur sultan. Lodi thus directly addressed Anthonio

Paviljoen, governor and director of the Coromandel coast. The *qaul*'s first part consisted of a description of events in the recent past, the first two sieges of St. Thomé, the visit of Captain Pit and Secretary Ruijser to Valikondapuram, and where things stood at the moment. The rest of the document listed Lodi's promises about what actions would be taken to oppose the movement of French ships, preventing them from acquiring new war supplies in Pondicherry and letting them keep what they already had in store while stopping the Dutch from transporting war supplies via his lands. Lodi concluded his qaul with phrases of placation and promise to not break his word (*dat ick belove naar behooren te zullen achter voegen zonder dat daar aan in het minste niet zal gebreeken*).[122] The document was reproduced and identified as "his written commitment [*schriftelijk verbetenisse*] via the Caul, as they call it, in their style of writing and described in the Tamil language [*na haar stijl van schrijven en beschreven in de Malabaarse taal*]."[123] While the written form in Dutch attested that it followed the qaul template, the document's content was orally transmitted, not in Persian but in Tamil and Telugu. Sher Khan Lodi spoke in the first person as himself in the *qaul*. His promise was mediated by multiple scribes and translators, working at the intersections of vastly different chancery practices and linguistic worlds. We may imagine the double mediations this document underwent before taking its final form in the VOC archives. Lodi likely had scribal staff proficient in Persian, Tamil, and Telugu who narrated and explained these official orders to Company clerks. In its writing and content, it held together the politics of repute that Francois Martin had spoken of, and a recent memory of the fragile relationships that Bijapuri subordinates like Lodi had forged with the local merchants and weaving communities of the regions near Senji.

Before turning to the politics of Lodi's qaul, it's worth digressing to first understand the purpose and functions of this document type. Whether in the context of the Sultanates or the nayaka kingdoms of the Kannada and Tamil-speaking regions, maritime historians have mined thousands of such qaul for their content to mark changes in commercial and political relations, but without any reflection on this interpolated documentary form's purpose and content across southern India's multiple linguistic registers.[124] One function of the qaul, which Prachi Deshpande recently examined in the context of the Marathas, was to deal with issues of land and agrarian resources.[125] Definitions of the term *qaul* and its auxiliary document types can be found in Persian and Urdu scribal manuals that were continuously in use as late as the nineteenth century, particularly under the Nizams of Hyderabad (r. 1724–1948) who, like the Marathas, inherited sultanate and Mughal-era bureaucratic practices.[126] A word of Arabic origin, *qaul* literally meant speech or utterance (*bāt, sukhan, bachan*), or acknowledging the fact of an agreement; in plainer terms it could also mean "dictated by" (*ʾan qaul*).[127] In the late eighteenth and early nineteenth centuries, two separate definitions of this term endured. One definition of qaul was a written document issued by an authority for a temporary grant of land that was being prepared for cultivation (*qaul ek wasīqah-yi kāghazī ka nām hai jo mu'ta-yi muqtadir kī jānib se ek ghair mustaqill 'atā kī nisbat zamāne-yi salf mein likh diyā jātā thā*).[128] When ruling kingdoms changed, qaul could be continued or annulled—it was common for the signatures of previous grantors to be erased from the document and previous arrangements broken. Under the Hyderabad Nizams, the inherent volatilities and uncertainties of the agrarian qaul were even recounted in popular lore—it was said that any person to whom this document was issued often rode their horse facing backward to make sure that another individual was not following them with a different qaul in hand, annulling their own![129]

In the seventeenth century, as the Mughal warfront subsumed territories in northern and western Deccan, many Persian qaul were issued in the name of hereditary officials, the village accountants and headmen (*deshpande, deshmukh*), to continue agrarian relationships and functions they already had under the Deccan sultans.[130] With standard phrases, these documents described the conditions—for instance, that these lands had been conquered and what should be done—that said groups should continue to cultivate their own lands (*mahal wa makān-i khudh ābād būdeh*) and make an effort to increase cultivation (*talāshī numāyand ke zirā'at wāfir shavad*).[131] Offering the assurance that no one should destroy these areas, it affirmed that, as per regulations, the villages' tax-exempt status granted in previous times would continue (*bar dīhā-yi in'ām-i deshmukhī az qadīm ast beqarār ābād numūdan*).[132]

A second use of the term *qaul* was in the context of treaties identified as *qaul wa qarār-nāmeh, ahad-nāmeh* or *tah-nāmeh* concluded between various powers, such as the Nizams with Tipu Sultan of Mysore, or with the Marathas and the English East India Company, descended from similar earlier iterations in the seventeenth century that recorded the fact of diplomatic or political negotiations.[133] The countless seventeenth-century qaul translated into the VOC's archives inherit elements of these two divergent functions, the agrarian deed of assurance regulating relationships with the state and the treaty between individuals and states. Coastal qaul held onto its agrarian predecessor's inherent volatility, what Deshpande calls "the fragility of the *kaulnama*'s assurances," handed out amid the uncertainties of military conflict and shifts in political power in port-cities and their hinterlands where multiple sovereignties overlapped and collided.[134] The role of mercantile communities, which are not always directly visible in the agrarian version, are very much apparent in maritime qaul.[135] Mercantile groups shaped the relationships between agrarian state-affiliated agents such as Sher Khan Lodi, who were seeking out ways to tap into the profits of cloth production in the southern Coromandel. The efficacy of a qaul that would regulate commercial and diplomatic ties on the coast depended on the support of mercantile groups and their preexisting relationships with cultivators and craftsmen. In light of these broader definitions and functions of the qaul, the translations of this document type found in the VOC archives begin to make sense. The question of Lodi's reputation among regional merchants that the French governor Francois Martin had raised can now be examined through his relationships with merchants and weavers that underlay the qaul of 1674.

Not long after it was issued, a flurry of correspondence followed Pit and Ruijser's visit to Valikondapuram, discussing whether the qaul was being followed by all parties, along with accusations and counteraccusations of each side not honoring its word.[136] Lodi, various officials of the VOC and the Danish East India Company, and local merchants went to great lengths to affirm its validity across the three port cities of Porto Novo, Teganapatnam, and Nagapattinam. But the motives for doing so were far less clear. Part of the problem lay in the divergent understandings of what the qaul's objective was, what it was meant to do, and what was at stake for each party involved. In one letter, Sher Khan Lodi balked at the Dutch governor's incessant requests to throw an addendum into the qaul. The governor wanted Lodi to add a clause to send his own guards out to spy on the French in Pondicherry. Irate at their request, Lodi reminded Anthonio Paviljoen that the qaul was no less than a formal agreement to which new points could not be added on a whim long after it had been issued with a fixed set of terms.[137] Besides, he pointed out that putting the two embittered and quarreling nations (the French and the Dutch) in one place would only lead to more problems. If something went wrong, the Dutch governor would then "blame me for this fighting and aside from the blame, this would give me a bad name" (*de onlust en beschulding van zijn Edele op mijn zal comen, buijten mijn schult aan moeijte ende een quadienaem zoude geraaken*).[138] He added that nothing new could be learnt about what the French were up to, apart from what his associates in Teganapatnam were already reporting. The qaul was more than enough to prevent the French from acquiring supplies.

Part of the insecurity, as the two visitors Pit and Ruijser articulated, stemmed from the VOC's anxieties about the Miyana household's well-known partisanship toward the French. They observed how the household's position stood in stark defiance of regional sultans who had been generally favorable toward the Dutch for decades. Lodi, in particular, was not only fond of the French but believed they would do great things with their future power in the East Indies as they were known for their progress in Europe (*hij de Franken zeer genegen was, die hem groote dingen van haar toekomst macht in Oost Indien ende haar progresse in Europa had die genaamt*).[139] However, as we noted earlier, the Miyanas' inclination toward the French had more to do with their troubled relationship with the queen-regent of Bijapur, the wife of Muhammad 'Adil Shah (d. 1656) and the princess of Golkonda, sister of 'Abdullah Qutb Shah (d. 1672), Khadija Sultana. The queen had departed for her sea voyage to Mocha on a Dutch ship, shortly after conspiring to murder one of the Miyana brothers, part of her many attempts at disciplining defiant households, whether the Maratha Bhonsles, Miyana Afghans, or Indo-Africans.[140]

But the Bijapur sultan and his mother were of little relevance on the coast. Here, Bijapur's sovereignty itself was represented and dispersed among its competing households, which sought to control forts and ports across the Karnatak. As such, they were one among many other contenders, including diverse communities of merchants who had their own recent experiences of operating at the edges of kingly authority. The most significant response to Lodi's qaul came from a collective of coastal merchants hailing from communities that had served as intermediaries between European companies and the nayaka polities of the northern Tamil region and in southern Andhra long before the arrival of Bijapuris.[141] Captain Pit and Secretary Ruijser met with the merchant collective the morning after their visit with Lodi in Valikondapuram, giving them a copy of the qaul. Together, this collective then sent a letter affirming their decision to support Lodi's injunctions against the French. The merchant collective was diverse and multiethnic.[142] The multireligious and multilingual profile of the names in this collective indicates the convergence and mobility of a range of mercantile communities at the intersections of the Tamil and Telugu-speaking regions, north of the Kaveri River delta, circulating along the southern Coromandel coast. It included Muslim Tamil-speaking Maraikkayars, with personal names in Arabic and status titles to indicate *periya* (great) and *pillai* (son/child of a king) in Tamil—for example, Periya Nayina (Nia) Pillai Maraikkayar. Status titles were granted to prominent individuals by rulers—for instance, to the Maraikkayars by the Setupatis of Ramnad when they took on important roles on the Madurai coast in areas south of Point Calimere.[143] In the second half of the seventeenth century, Marraikayyar Muslim merchants moved their operations all the way up to Porto Novo and Teganapatnam. Venturing further north, they drew on their long experience dealing with European companies on the Fishery and Ramnad coasts to fill roles as translators and scribal intermediaries between the VOC and Bijapuri officials in port cities north of Nagapattinam. Indeed, a copy of Lodi's qaul was also sent to a certain Sayyid Marraikkayar, who was regarded as an important scribe in the city of Porto Novo.[144] Alongside the Maraikkayars, the merchant collective consisted of Tamil and Tamil-speaking Hindu merchants, similarly identified with status titles such as *reddi*, which might indicate village headmen or land-holding agricultural subcastes along with the broad term for merchant communities in south India, *setti* or *chetti*.[145] The list of names in this merchant collective concurs with what Cynthia Talbot has argued regarding similar titles for names in inscriptions from medieval Andhra, which cannot be understood as equal to modern-day understandings of caste. Status titles cut across differences of sect, region, and language, indicating instead the broad occupational, functional, and earned affiliations of individuals.[146] The merchants of Porto Novo who organized themselves into a unified group to respond to Lodi's qaul had a shared set of economic interests rather than any hereditary or kinship links. They were unified by the occupation of buying and selling goods and their shared dealings with local kingdoms and European companies.

The Dutch governor urged the merchants of Porto Novo to be vigilant about preventing the movement of supplies into St. Thomé, a city that was still living under "the violence of the French criminals" (*het geweld van de Frans gewelden-aers*).[147] He reprimanded them for letting two boats loaded with rice reach the city. The merchants' letters, although obsequious in tone, insisted that this had not happened on their watch and that they had always respected the Company by offering it help and protection throughout. They added the explanation that the French were cunning thieves and animals and could have hijacked the boats at sea (*de Francen bezendige rovers en dieren sijn, zo kunnen ze ook wel iets ten zee kapen*).[148] They acknowledged receiving Lodi's qaul and affirmed that they would follow it, but Captain Pit and Secretary Ruijser were not entirely convinced the merchants would do so. Pit and Ruijser observed that the traders appeared to be complying to the qaul not because the VOC had itself given them sufficient reason to do so, but because of the obligation they felt toward Sher Khan Lodi, from whom they had received many acts of kindness (*ook niets over gegeven hebben dat onredelijk is, maer aff de Heer Sher Khan Lodi door zijn uit budige genegentheijt die zij menig maal in verschiede occasie tot haer heeft betoont*).[149]

So, what exactly were these "acts of kindness"? For an answer to this question, we must go back a few years and see what underlay the issuing of Sher Khan Lodi's qaul in 1674, which we will do from the vantage point of those who inhabited the very bottom of the regional political economy, the *kaikkolar* (*kai* meaning hand, *kol* referring to a kind of weaving shuttle used then) weavers of the Senji region. The *kaikkolar* were one among many weaving castes, traditionally identified as left-hand castes in the Tamil country.[150] They appear to be at least one of the weaving communities that inhabited the areas around Valikondapuram, where Sher Khan Lodi's household settled.[151] Much has been written about intercaste conflict and cooperation within south India's system of social organization, between the so-called *idangai* (left-hand, mercantile-warrior and artisans) and *valangai* (right-hand, primarily agricultural communities, tied to the land) castes in the late eighteenth and early nineteenth centuries, particularly with regard to how such relationships fared under European companies.[152] The case at hand—the dispute between Bijapuri elites, Porto Novo merchants, and weaving castes in the early 1670s—was, in some ways, less bound to the left-right-hand dichotomy, which had to do with certain ritual privileges in public spaces, the allocation of honors, and status rankings in temples. The Tamil-speaking Shafi'i Sunni Muslim Maraikkayars, for instance, do not map onto the left-right binary although, because of their common economic interests, they may have often allied with Tamil- and Telugu-speaking upper-caste Hindu merchants on either side of this dichotomy at different times and places. The multireligious and multilingual merchants in the Porto Novo collective who responded to Lodi's qaul were more unified by their interests as a status group that cut across sectarian lines, which stood in opposition to those of the weaving castes.

As sultanate-affiliated Muslim elites, the Miyana Afghans were not new in trying to establish a foothold on the Coromandel coast; as such, Lodi's encounter with the weavers of Valikondapuram was not without precedent. The Miyanas were following the same routes charted by Golkonda's celebrated Iranian courtier Mir Jumla in the 1640s and later by the Bijapuri Indo-African Khan Muhammad in the 1650s, all of whom sought access to the Bay of Bengal and its resources to sustain the sultanates' expanding boundaries in the wake of Mughal suzerainty.[153] Since the early 1660s, during the Karnatak war campaigns, Sher Khan Lodi's contemporary from Golkonda, Reza Quli Beg or Neknam Khan (d. 1672), gained notoriety in the northern Coromandel not just for policing Europeans but also for disciplining weaving castes in Madras and Pulicat on numerous occasions. VOC officials made comparisons to the situation in Pulicat, which fell under Neknam Khan's and Golkonda's authority, with the regions south of Madras falling under Lodi and Bijapur's control. In the port city of Pulicat, a large number of weaving groups had moved out of the city because of Neknam Khan's disciplinary actions. The heads of caste (*hoofden der castas*) traveled to the court in Hyderabad with a letter, waiting for months without an audience with the Golkonda sultan. In response to this attempt to voice their grievances, Neknam Khan jailed the head weavers and forbade the residents of Pulicat from buying provisions from the VOC.[154] Similar disputes unfolded in the regions south of Madras in 1670, where Bijapuri-affiliated Miyana Afghan interests converged with those of regional merchants, causing a weaver's revolt that brought all trade to a standstill.

When the weavers around Senji first expressed their grievances, the object of their complaints was not Lodi as such, but the merchants (identified with the broad term *chetti*) who had been the VOC's suppliers for a long time. The weavers decided to no longer use the merchants as intermediaries and instead tried to deliver their linen directly to the VOC, despite lacking the capital and means to do so. In the port city of Teganapatnam, the revolt took an ugly turn when one weaver committed suicide to encourage his allies from giving into the Chettis (*eene der wevers, goetwilligh hadde laten doden, om sijne medestanders daer door aen te moedigen datse hare strenge omtrent de Chittijs zouden blijven vast houden, dat onder die wevers voor een onverbreecklijknent wert gehouden*).[155] When Lodi arrived on the scene on behalf of his master 'Abdul Karim Bahlol Khan, he sought to monopolize the advancing of capital directly to the weavers, removing both the Muslim and non-Muslim Tamil- and Telugu-speaking merchants from their intermediary role altogether and forcing the cotton weavers into a contract to supply cotton cloth directly to him.[156] The standoff brought trade to a standstill in the three port cities of Teganapatnam, Porto Novo, and Nagapattinam. With inland production inexorably intertwined with what was happening at sea, the Dutch attempted to block Miyana shipping across the Bay of Bengal, anticipating that this would bring Lodi to the negotiating table. The strategy worked. With their ships from Malacca and Aceh unable to reach Teganapatnam, the Miyanas incurred a significant loss of income. As a result, Lodi arrived at the Dutch lodge one morning and agreed to crush the weavers' revolt instead and make them return to supplying the merchants. Although the Dutch appear to take credit for ending the tripartite standoff by pushing Lodi toward this humiliation, the decision to preserve the old way of doing business would prove advantageous for Lodi, local merchants, and the VOC, but not for the weavers.[157]

The negotiations and realignments that preceded the qaul of 1674 therefore essentially preserved the existing status quo by maintaining regional merchants' role as the VOC's sole suppliers. It was this "act of kindness" that had obliged the Porto Novo merchant collective to implement Lodi's qaul of 1674 to limit the movement of supplies to the French without any protest or objection. That these negotiations cut across lines of sect, region, and language is an unremarkable pattern for precolonial southern India. More intriguing, within these interelite realignments, the interests of Persianate brokering elites on the one hand and those of an intrasectarian collective of regional merchants on the other, intersected in preserving socioeconomic hierarchies, a pattern worth examining in other parts of the subcontinent's coasts. Although the voices of weaving communities are often difficult to find in this early period, on the rare occasions they do appear, particularly through interpolated indigenous documentary genres such as the qaul found in Company archives, they tell a story of how resources were redistributed at a moment when different sovereignties collided at the intersections of an agrarian warfront and a subregional littoral economy. The triangular relations of the groups that labored on the Coromandel coast with various Bijapur and Golkonda brokering elites along with dominant regional merchant castes unveils the messy mechanisms that underlay interelite solidarity, rather than an essential and pregiven quality of harmony, tolerance, or absolute opposition.

CONCLUSION: COMPARING SOCIAL EXCLUSION ACROSS REGIONS

A celebrated feature in scholarship about South Asia before the British is that premodern, elite, economic, and political realignments cut across differences of language, status, ethnicity, and sect; however, I suggest that in an era unbound by the nation-state form and its attendant identities this is somewhat unremarkable. Instead, I examine the underlying mechanisms of interelite alliances, which simultaneously depended on sustaining entrenched inequities of status and caste. No different from the agents of other state formations throughout global history, members of corporate groups asserting their autonomy from both the regional (Deccan) and imperial (Mughal) kingly authority had to tap into existing socioeconomic hierarchies in coastal regions to sustain their networks. The case study here, of the negotiations of military households alongside mercantile and artisanal groups in the Deccan-Karnatak, merits a comparison of the study of social hierarchies across different regions of early modern South Asia. Divya Cherian has demonstrated how in eighteenth-century Marwar interelite and intra-elite competition actually resulted in the cleaving out of a larger Hindu upper-caste dominance in the eighteenth century.[158] Unlike Rajasthan in northwestern India, where the harsh climate of the Thar Desert created more centralization, the regulation of natural resources, and forms of coercion under various Rajput lineages,[159] the Deccan-Karnatak frontier, with its greater social and ecological diversity, created long periods without a singular centralized power, thereby necessitating that social elites forge cross-cutting ties that could encompass more than one religious or sectarian group. And yet, these realignments also preserved status hierarchies in this region.

To put it plainly, whether premodern elites were good or bad, heroes or villains, or better than what came later—that is, European colonialism—is a less interesting question for the postcolonial historian to ask. Starting with these modern binaries speaks more to our present-day anxieties than to the task of reconstructing the imperfect actions of historical actors in times past, along with an unwitting elision of marginalized voices.[160] The question of belonging in South Asia, across different time periods, can therefore never be decoupled from the study of social exclusion and inequality.

I showed how contested ways of belonging emerged at the intersections of the court and the state and between literary and documentary ways of being. Bridging these modern binaries this chapter is also an experiment with method, sources, and disciplines, as it connects literary studies with social history and historical sociology. The cantankerous itineraries from the capital city of Bijapur to the port city of Teganapatnam reveal the coconstitutive and interdependent spheres of state and court at the intersections of which household and state operated.

One of the defining tropes of seventeenth-century peninsular India is the region's inevitable incorporation into Mughal Hindustan and the role of ethnic court factions in either resisting or facilitating this endeavor. The journeys of this chapter from Bijapur to Cuddalore, moved past political histories often fixated on the question of identity, by transcending the divide between literary and nonliterary ways of being, the court versus the state, the agrarian versus the maritime, and the cultural versus the economic. Court factions were not a deviation from a supposedly centralized kingly authority; rather, that imperial suzerainty only heightened the relative autonomy of households from kingly authority, an old pattern of state formation in the south. Whether it was the Miyanas, the Indo-Africans, or the Maratha Bhonsles, household lineages operated in similar ways. In this context, seventeenth-century observers like the poet-historian Nusrati judged political contentions between households through a shared rubric of all belonging to the same house or ghar. Bijapur's premier court poet, even as he excoriated Shivaji, emphatically highlighted the proximity and intimacy of his patrons, the Miyana Afghans, with the Maratha Bhonsles.

While modern intellectuals have often used such uneasy premodern representations to resolve present-day anxieties about identity, I show that these sites of contradiction reveal how politics and political concepts were expressed in Indian vernaculars by both mobilizing recognizable tropes of difference and then collapsing them altogether. Juxtaposing the vernacular literary expression of premodern Indian politics with the portraits we find of the same protagonists in European Company documents creates space to transcend the social worlds of courts and states and the discrete archival molds these spheres have left behind for historians to make sense of. Although Persian sources have often been paired with European travel accounts and Company documents, examples of placing vernacular literary texts against the so-called "global" archives of "European expansion in Asia" are far fewer.[161] When we turn to Company documents, we find members of elite households transcending differences of language, region, sect, caste, and status, but not for the sake of upholding an idealized syncretism. The social and economic transactions of Bijapuri affiliates such as the Miyana Afghans with Tamil- and Telugu-speaking Muslim and non-Muslim merchants, on the one hand, and the weaving castes of the Coromandel, on the other, suggest a far more pragmatic orientation toward existing differences of caste and status, which was to keep such hierarchies intact and undisturbed.

7

Postscript

Forgetting Households, Making Dynasties

Spatially, this book began at the site of the military barrack scattered across gateway fortresses like Asirgarh and Daulatabad in the center of the Indian subcontinent, where thousands of imperial soldiers encamped before marching south toward the tip of the peninsula. From the imperial encampment, we first moved westward with elite households, tracing their conflicts over agrarian and maritime resources on the Konkan and Kanara coasts. We then stopped at the courts of Bijapur and Hyderabad, where contemporary poets tried to make sense of an imperial occupation, creating literary representations of the tension between household and monarchy in seventeenth-century politics. Finally, we ended up as far south as the weaving villages around the port city of Nagapattinam, looking out at the Bay of Bengal, where household elites navigated divisions of status and caste, mobilizing commercial resources for war-making and preserving the social order. Temporally, the book's journeys have stayed within the limits of the seventeenth century, during which household and monarchical sovereignties overlapped, intersected, and contested each other.

We will conclude its journey in the small town of Savanur (present-day Karnataka) in peninsular India in the 1840s, more than a hundred years after the dissolution of the Deccan sultanates. In the twilight years of the Mughal Empire, a man named Nawab Dilir Jang Bahadur returned to his home in Savanur after many years of exile in the city of Pune (present-day Maharashtra). Writing petitions and pleas to various English East India Company officials, Dilir Jang hoped to resolve bitter ongoing feuds with many of his nieces, nephews, and the widows of his brothers and half-brothers, holding onto the hope that he would be restored as the legitimate heir to this small "princely state," which now fell under Company suzerainty. The story of this Sunni Muslim Miyana Afghan family is recounted in a Persian text called the *Tārīkh-i Dilīr-jangī* (History of Dilir Jang, ca. 1847) by Muhammad ʿAzimuddin, an Arcot-born bureaucrat who had worked for fifteen years as a scribe for the English East India Company.[1]

How did this text written in the early colonial period remember a household's journey across the Mughal frontier in peninsular India more than a century before? The author combined two major modes of writing and curating the past: the court chronicle or *tārīkh*, the most common Perso-Arabic literary form of writing history; and the anthology or *majmūʿa*, a collection of copied letters, treaties, petitions, and revenue lists of and about particular lineages. By combining narration and curation, two forms of remembering the distant past and contemporary events, the author grappled with a larger anxiety, how to continue to write about the political in familial terms.[2] ʿAzimuddin's attempt to renarrate Savanur's past was part of a global phenomenon of transitional literature responding to early colonial attempts to categorize indigenous forms of knowledge, which included grappling with the question of what qualified as proper dynastic history versus what did not.[3]

One way to make sense of the momentous transformations of the eighteenth century is to turn to how colonial officials and administrators rewrote the precolonial past in their own self-image. Recent readings have meticulously examined how the precolonial past in different regions of the subcontinent was reframed—from the first political agent of the English East India Company in Rajasthan, Colonel James Tod (d. 1835), who wrote *Annals and Antiquities of Rajasthan* (ca. 1829), to Alexander Dow (d. 1779), who wrote the monumental *History of Hindostan*, to Alexander Forbes Kinloch (d. 1865), who wrote *Rās Mālā: or the Hindoo Annals of the Province of Gujarat in Western India* (ca. 1856).[4] In this postscript, by going beyond colonial accounts in English, I turn to one of the innumerable histories that indigenous intellectuals continued to write in Persian as well as in various vernaculars well into the colonial period. The authors of these texts meditated on the meanings of belonging, still turning to the motif of ghar or house. Through a text like the *Tārīkh-i Dilīr-jangī*, I explore, following the aforementioned studies of English colonial writing that show how a radical shift in the writing of history took place in the early colonial period, the question that Manan Ahmed Asif has asked of this period—namely, "what is the past that remains visible after the annihilation of one's present?"[5]

The choice to conclude the book with a postscript that examines a much later text reflecting back on the events and places examined in its preceding chapters is twofold. The first stems from the desire to make sense of how households were remembered and endured in various forms of writing history in the nineteenth century. Transitional authors tried reconstructing the precolonial past in the colonial present by restating the relevance of the family to political history. Second, the book's itinerary from one social site to another across peninsular India—from the military barrack to the adorned palace—are in some ways mirrored in the themes recounted in early colonial texts like the *Tārīkh-i Dilīr-jangī*. With Company rule firmly in place and the Mughal Empire of little or no relevance, the memory of these sites served as a canvas within the text through which the author told a story about household power. Finally, part of the aim here is also to consider the limits of the method of connected histories, placing sources in multiple languages from vastly different philological and philosophical contexts in conversation with each other. When viewed from the vantage point of the early colonial period, the question of what is visible about the precolonial past was irrevocably linked to how colonial knowledge forms had transformed indigenous practices of writing history.

In the tiny town of Savanur in the first half of the nineteenth century, our author Muhammad ʿAzimuddin was but one of many historians across early colonial South Asia attempting to make sense of their unbecoming present by remembering many different pasts. Like his predecessors, following the Perso-Arabic chronicle tradition, he stuck to defining power in past times in the familial idiom. And yet, in refusing to succumb to romance when writing about contemporary events, he made striking distinctions between familial and dynastic pasts and what it meant to write these as separate kinds of historical narratives. He reflected on the family as an object of narration at a moment when Company rule had effectively subsumed all political competitors, deciding which lineage was a mere family and which deserved to be a dynasty. Indeed, the very term for indirectly-ruled, "princely states" in the nineteenth century, signaled an unrealized and unfinished political formation, remnants of precolonial forms of sovereignty allowed to endure but without a dynastic king. In the early decades of the nineteenth century, intrafamilial conflict was complicated by the interference of the Governor's Council in Bombay and Calcutta and a long line of political agents of the English East India Company who kept a grip on patrilineal succession, adoption, and inheritance, a pattern common across minor kingdoms in early colonial South Asia.[6] Combining the chronicle form, which had long been used to invent the origins of dynasties, with the *majmūʿa* or anthology of documents, which made household claims to power legible, our bureaucrat-historian-author sought ways to continue narrating power through the familial idiom of ghar when recording the latter was becoming a less worthy subject for writing narrative history.

The modern anxiety involved in separating family history from dynastic histories, as we saw in the preceding chapters, was a dichotomy irrelevant to premodern textual traditions. The trope of ghar or house, evoked so often by the seventeenth-century poet Nusrati, had framed politics within the intimate, familial register. Why, then, did the writing of history in the nineteenth century come to be equated with only dynastic history? At the dawn of colonialism, Persianate literati were still being commissioned to reassert the legitimate origins of various lineages at precisely the moment when the English East India Company positioned itself as the only heir to Mughal imperial sovereignty. Reflecting on these times,

Muhammad ʿAzimuddin chose to divide his text into two parts: in the first, he traces the *khāndān* or family's journeys across Mughal Hindustan and the Deccan; in the second part, he explains his reasons for composing such a work at a time when volatile and violent intraclan feuds had shifted the fortunes of his patron, Nawab Dilir Jang, necessitating a rewriting of Savanur's past.

In this postscript, I reconstruct three temporalities embodied in three sequential images of the house in the *Tārīkh-i Dilīr-jangī*: the "burnt house," signifying the author's immediate present in the first decades of the early nineteenth century; the "remembered house," covering political relations in the eighteenth century; and the "eminent house," which is about the distant past in the seventeenth century when households were integral to state-making. My reading here begins in the middle of the text, where the author's present is recounted in a section that includes the authorial confession, rather than at its chronological opening, where the authorial confession is typically found, which, in this case, is set in the distant past.

I first examine ʿAzimuddin's curious authorial confession that appears more than halfway through the *Tārīkh-i Dilīr-jangī*, where the act of forgetting households and making dynasties begins. In the first half of the text, in contrast to his declaration halfway through it about separating the distant past from the present, the author begins by constructing a memory of itinerance, tracing the footsteps and longer histories of Afghan circulation across Mughal Hindustan and the Deccan sultanates in the seventeenth century. He then moves on to representing Savanur's political relations with other contemporary regional polities such as those connected with Haider ʿAli and Tipu Sultan of Mysore (ca. 1761–99) and the Peshwa government of the Maratha Empire (ca. 1751–1818), marking the boundaries of intermarriage, interdining, and sectarian purity with these regional competitors in the late eighteenth century. In the second part, ʿAzimuddin narrates various intrafamilial or interlineage disputes, illustrating how "the family feud" came to define the late eighteenth and early nineteenth centuries, when Company rule had restricted and transformed the terrain of kinship.[7]

The *Tārīkh-i Dilīr-jangī* is but one example of many late Persianate texts from different regional contexts across early colonial India that tries to make sense of the eighteenth century's momentous political transformations. And yet, modern historians often consider such texts as either apocryphal or not as great as the canonized Persian chronicles of the sixteenth and seventeenth centuries. These texts are reflections on well-established forms of writing and curating the past that were called into question in the early colonial period. For example, in one political history of Savanur, a twentieth-century historian faults the text's author, Muhammad ʿAzimuddin, for failing to adhere to neat chronologies and for messing with the facts. And yet, political historians continued to rely on such texts to extract the sequential narrative of events among the major eighteenth-century political players such as Tipu Sultan of Mysore, the Peshwas, and the Nizams of Hyderabad (ca. 1724–1948), while diligently purging their legendary and anecdotal portions.[8]

As this chapter will show, the gaps, inventions, and split temporalities within this text index a much larger reflection on a dilemma that came into its own in the early colonial period: How to write the family in and out of history? The dichotomy between the familial and the political was not irrelevant to the way ʿAzimuddin reimagined political power in the early colonial period. Marking the familial as opposed to the political produced two seemingly contradictory outcomes in a text like the *Tārīkh-i Dilīr-jangī*. On the one hand, the familial frame remained capacious; it continued to enable real and imagined notions of ghar that transcended differences of religion, language, and ethnicity. On the other hand, in the period of early colonialism, anxieties about both caste endogamy and sectarian purity within communities also produced far more circumscribed definitions of belonging to a house. As the chapter will show through the *Tārīkh-i Dilīr-jangī*, and in other such late Persianate texts, we also begin to see the earliest iterations of the politics of *sharāfat* or respectability, defined in and through caste, which would come to define Indic Muslim elite identities along sectarian lines in the wake of the Revolt of 1857.[9]

THE BURNT HOUSE

Writing about his patron's changed fortunes in the mid-nineteenth century, Muhammad ʿAzimuddin begins his authorial confession by lamenting all that was left of his patron's house(hold) was a piece of hay from a burnt house (*az khāna-yi sukhte kāhī*) and a lone brick from a ruined monument (*az ʿimarat-i munhadima kheshtī*).[10] He evokes this image of the burnt house when recounting a recent incident. Some faithful palace guards had recently prevented Nawab Dilir Jang's nieces and nephews from robbing the little jewelry and money left in the treasury. In an ideal world, these nieces and nephews, who were the house-born sons or blood relatives and children of the heads of this family (*sāhebzādegān* and *khānezādegān*), would have been treated with the same respect according to the sons of dynastic kings (*shahzādegān*). According to ʿAzimuddin, the thieving progeny had done little to accord such respect from posterity and were unworthy of being written into history as dynastic heirs. And yet, for more than ten chapters (*aurang*) of the *Tārīkh-i Dilīr-jangī*, ʿAzimuddin remains silent. He holds back his critique of a disobedient new generation at the mercy of the English East India Company, all of whom had played a part in setting aflame the house of Savanur. It isn't until the book's final chapters that ʿAzimuddin reveals his position, laying out the reasons for the house burning down in the present.

Sighing with sadness for the state of his own times, in this confession he first signals the shift in temporality before writing the final five chapters that recount the present. He alerts his readers to the text's two distinct temporal parts, noting that he is finished writing about the long past (*tawāmir-i māzī*) and would now speak of the news of ensuing and future events (*bar akhbār pur ayandeh*) as a means to restore the facts about the family that had been lost in some stories.[11]

To understand how the familial anxieties that plagued ʿAzimuddin's times shaped the craft of narration and curation, it's worth recalling the uncertain conditions of Nawab Dilir Jang's exile in Pune, where he had lived for six years, prior to his return to Savanur in 1825. Nawab Dilir Jang was expected to report frequently to the government of Bombay and the acting collector in Dharwar on his plans to return home, which he was granted permission to do in 1819 after the death of his elder brother, Munawwar Khan, who incidentally left behind a wife who was six months pregnant. Interrupting narrations of these recent events, ʿAzimuddin diligently copies relevant documents and correspondence to and from the English East India Company, translated into English from Persian and Urdu and vice versa—for instance, from William Harrison, the acting collector in Dharwar, to index the veracity of his narration of his patron's claim to rule.[12] Given his vocation as a professional scribe, the author affirms the need to prepare documentary forms accurately, as one problem afflicting Savanur's administration at this time was bad scribes and counterfeit writing (*khat-i jaʿlī*), even making an example of a few wayward, prodigal scribes, whom the author names and shames.[13]

After copying and curating selected documents, ʿAzimuddin then returns to the narrative about his patron's troubles in the decades before he completed the *Tārīkh-i Dilīr-jangī*. The elder brother Munawwar was known to have been careless with managing finances; disagreements between the two brothers led to the younger Dilir Jang's departure. Politically isolated, ridiculed, and forgotten by the people of Savanur and all his paternal relatives, Dilir Jang set off for Pune along with his wife and most loyal servants and friends. He took out loans to sustain himself, relying on the generosity of those who proved more loyal than his real uncles and brothers (ʿ*amm-i haqīqī wa birādarzādī*). In asides within such narrations about family feuds, ʿAzimuddin goes to great lengths to emphasize how the English East Company admired his patron's character, praising his moral fortitude and respectability with the maxim "*har ja sharāfat ast / dalil az rafāqat ast*" (where there is respectability, there is friendship). Despite the Company's appraisal of the Nawab Dilir Jang's character as respectable and righteous, which made it seem like he had gained its steadfast approval, his patron remained anxious about the likelihood of his return home to Savanur.

The news about the impending birth of another nephew troubled Dilir Jang, who was urged to be patient and wait in Dharwar, where the acting collector patronizingly told him to stay optimistic and patient (*az khairiyat-i khud lutf farmā bāshand*). But Dilir Jang remained worried, and he even sent a few of his trusted men back to Savanur to watch over his sister-in-law giving birth to check whether the baby was a boy or girl and to make sure the palace servants did not switch or exchange the infant.[14] Answering the nawab's prayers, the infant turned out to be girl. But, by the time he returned to Savanur, he was confronted by more opposing relatives, nieces, and nephews from other brothers who opposed his claim to rule. Despite these trials, Dilir Jang gained permission from the Company to sort out a great mess of judicial and administrative matters and make decisions about what to do about members of his extended relatives with absolute independence (*khud mukhtāriyāt-i mutlaq*), without consulting the government of Bombay. He was, for instance, allowed to withhold the monthly pensions of his disobedient nieces and nephews unless or until they gave a *zamānat* or guarantee for good behavior and not cause future troubles.[15] The nawab's authority to discipline the family here stands in contrast to and is superseded by the larger frame of the Company's inescapable control over the political and having granted him such authority. The image of the burnt house therefore captures the contradictions of Savanur's present when this small state's ability to exist depends entirely on the Company's decision to allow policing the squabbling relatives within it. From the authorial confession, therefore, we learn that the Company's strict grip over all matters political shaped the terrain on which intrafamilial disputes unfolded.

THE (RE)MEMBERED HOUSE

From this halfway section, which contains the authorial confession where 'Azimuddin reveals the reasoning for his composition, we can work our way back to the beginnings of *Tārīkh-i Dilīr-jangī*. The aforementioned anxieties and the image of the burnt house captured the tumult of the most recent decades before 1847, setting up a contrast for remembering the house in the previous century. In the ten chapters that precede the authorial confession, 'Azimuddin describes political relations between Savanur and other neighboring rival polities. The metaphor of the burnt house that 'Azimuddin identifies with his patron's recent family troubles in the first half of the nineteenth century contrasts with his retrospective on the (re)membered house, when political ties with competing states were held together through a vocabulary of kinship in the eighteenth century.

Under the Company's watchful gaze, the family feud had come to determine an elite household's terms of either survival or complete extinction. 'Azimuddin begins narrating the relevant events of the eighteenth century as a way of reflecting on the crisis of his family in the present. He begins by imparting moral maxims about the futility of revolting against the family's elders (*akābir-i khāndān*), a lesson which he applies back to previous eras—for example, two generations prior, to the year 1752. In this example, he writes about when one Khaliq Miyan and Rasul Miyan unsuccessfully rebelled against their brother and the man who was next in line to be ruler, Nawab 'Abdul Hakim Khan (d.1795), they were paraded around town on a donkey with their faces blackened. 'Azimuddin concludes narrations of many such episodes in the eighteenth century by admonishing family members' split loyalties and misguided actions with the common Hindustani proverb— *dhobhī kī gadhī huī ghar kī na ghāt kī* (a rolling stone gathers no moss)—evoked by the author in a curious feminine version (*gadhī* instead of *gadhā*).[16] This literally means, "the washerman's donkey has no home, neither at the house [ghar] nor the washing steps,; this idiomatic phrase conveys the sense of contempt and judgement reserved for those who fail to remain loyal to one's house. When retelling numerous succession disputes, ʿAzimuddin continues to reflect on the dangers of one's own and the problem of revolting against one's own.[17] He held a mirror to familial bonds, often seen as being expressions of a natural sense of duty and obligation towards one's kin. And yet, the author understood family ties to be the most fragile of social relations, the quickest to unravel and often proving the most destructive. Throughout the *Tārīkh-i Dilīr-jangī*, he revisits the theme of succession and fratricide across different generations in the Miyana household, persuasively making the case that blood lines and agnatic descent offered uncertain foundations for sustaining the house.

These internal family feuds stand in stark contrast to other iterations of the familial in the text's preceding ten chapters on the eighteenth century. Rewriting past political encounters in a language of relatedness, ʿAzimuddin devotes his attention to narrating Savanur's bonds with various eighteenth-century polities. Here, he references other previously well-known chronicles while also curating copies of documents to index his own retelling. The first set of political ties were with rulers, such as the Peshwas and nayakas of Keladi and Bidnur, who shared no obvious commonalities of blood, sectarian affiliation, or marital ties with Savanur. ʿAzimuddin affirms that these ties were based on obligation and service alone and were, at times, more resilient than those Savanur had with contemporary coreligionists. The second set of political ties were undergirded by affinal or marital bonds and carried implicit expectations of caste and commensality that defined the boundaries of a house within and against coreligionists. The latter included the competing, neighboring Indic Muslim households that surrounded Savanur, such as those of Haider ʿAli and Tipu Sultan of Mysore and the Nizams of Hyderabad. As in the case of the internal family feud within the Miyana household, defining the boundaries of intermarriage and interdining with affinal coreligionists was often volatile and created insufficient conditions for maintaining political unity.

To write about the eighteenth century, he then turned to numerous examples of cross-cutting alliances between Savanur, the Peshwas of the Maratha Empire (ca. 1751–1818), and the nayakas of Bidnur and Chitradurg (ca. 1499–1763), which were imagined as akin to and, at times, even stronger than family. If those within the household cannot be trusted, those completely outside it held out some hope for sustenance. It is well known that by the mid-eighteenth century, Savanur ceded territories to the Marathas and fell under the protection of Balaji Rao Nana Saheb Peshwa (d. 1761) in the second half of the eighteenth century, episodes that ʿAzimuddin sums up by referencing previous chronicles.[18] He begins a summary of these events in the mid-eighteenth century first by copying the entire *sulahnāma* or peace agreement (ca. 1756), detailing the revenues of Savanur's villages, districts, and hamlets ceded to the Peshwa government.

After curating diplomatic documents that affirmed Savanur's vassalage to Pune, he then turns to explaining how this alliance managed to forge a different kind of house all together. He thus describes the *garm jūshī* (love) and *bagal gīrī* (embrace) between Nawab ʿAbdul Hakim Khan and Nana Saheb. According to ʿAzimuddin, the latter's first wife, Kupa Bai (Gopikabai) apparently gave birth to her son Madhav Rao in Savanur, whom the Nawab loved dearly. The Nawab of Savanur took care of Nana Saheb's wife and son in the same way a paternal or maternal uncle would of his daughter or a brother would of his sister (*chūnānche ʿamm wa pedar wa khāl wa birādar nisbat be dukhtar wa khwāhar be-nuzūl midārand wa marʿī mifarmūdand*). Even after many years of returning to his *watan*, Madhav Rao, remained like a nephew to the Nawab, whom he continued to call maternal uncle (*ʿammū-yi khāl* or *māmā*).[19]

Casting past political relations as durable familial ones sets up a contradiction throughout a text like the *Tārīkh-i Dilīr-jangī* because ʿAzimuddin's central claim is, indeed, that familial ties are the ficklest and most troubles originate from them. By stating the common expectation from one's family, in this case, that an uncle take care of his nephew or niece as if they were his own children, ʿAzimuddin is addressing his present audiences, Nawab Dilir Jang's nephews and nieces who, at this very moment, were proactively contesting and undermining their uncle. To frame the bond with Nana Saheb's wife and son as exemplary, therefore, presented a lesson for those who were currently engaged in defying their maternal uncle. Rather than being anomalies or mistakes in writing a linear history, in this way, ʿAzimuddin's representation of split temporalities of how the family used to be as opposed to how it is now actually read purposefully against each other, demonstrating the moral meanings of the house to his immediate readers.

This remembered kinship with Nana Saheb's family is extended to others, including the nayakas of Keladi, with whom the Miyana nawabs of Savanur did not share any sectarian, religious, and linguistic commonality. Like the wife of Nana Saheb, ʿAzimuddin describes the emotional bond between Nawab ʿAbdul Hakim Khan and the Keladi queen, Viramma of Bidnur (d. 1763), the widow of Basavappa Nayaka II, who was ruling at the time until her adopted son, Chennabasavappa Nayaka, came of age.[20] Alluding to her regency, while echoing portraits of her that had been repeated in other Persian chronicles such as Mir Husain ʿAli Khan Kirmani's *Nishān-i Haidari* (ca. 1802), ʿAzimuddin regarded her as a woman with a man's temperament (*an zan-i mard sīrat wa mardānagī sarīrat*).[21] Speaking of the affinity between Bidnur and Savanur, he notes that Viramma wished well for the Nawab and nurtured the seed of true friendship and devotion toward him (*dil-i khīsh mamlu mīdāsht wa tukhm-i sadāqat wa ʿaqīdat dar mazraʿ dil-i khīsh mikāsht*), with the hope that he would come to her aid when she was in need. The queen regent of Keladi was an equivalent ruler to the Nawab, who was obliged to her in the same way that one would be toward a close relative. This sense of obligation toward the Keladi queen however, spelled trouble for the Savanur Nawabs, as it raised the ire of Mysore's Haider ʿAli (d. 1782) and his ally, the raja of Chitradurg. Again, ʿAzimuddin sutures these widely known cross-cutting eighteenth century alliances into his broader diagnosis of the household and the state in the past and present.

In contrast to the portrait of enduring ties with the Peshwas and Keladi nayakas, ʿAzimuddin offers a much more cynical appraisal of Savanur's ties with its coreligionists, the Nizams of Hyderabad and Haider ʿAli and Tipu Sultan of Mysore. In the second half of the eighteenth century, the relatively small state of Savanur faced military threats from larger regional states, including from the Peshwa government to the north and from Haider ʿAli and Tipu Sultan in Mysore to the south. Events, battles, and treaties of this period have been narrated many times in political histories written since the late eighteenth century.[22] Narrations of these well-known political events are revealing for other reasons, too, such as the portrayal of ceremony and everyday social practices. It is here, when the author tries to make sense of the family formed through affinal ties within a community that anxieties about sectarian purity and commensality come to the forefront. The occasion of memorializing a major wedding between Savanur and Mysore afforded ʿAzimuddin the opportunity to highlight social practices that demonstrated the distinctiveness of his patron's household.

As we saw in chapter 4, in the chronicle form, the canvas of a wedding served not merely as an ornate description that digressed from its more central narrative of battles and treaties, but as commentaries integral to the making of fraught affinal ties. More than a century later, ʿAzimuddin continued to draw on the chronicle form's wedding as topos for a different purpose. As a means to emphasize status differences between competing Indic Muslim households, through a wedding narration, he elaborated on the everyday politics of caste that came into play when two families became interlinked through marriage. Meeting standards of hospitality was one measure for gauging an elite household's reputation. Weddings and their rituals that created new households were sites for expressing violations of custom and obligation, critical for preserving the standards for being a respectable Muslim family. Therefore, the author of an early colonial chronicle-anthology like the *Tārīkh-i Dilīr-jangī* worked with the familiar topoi of the wedding—its preparations, food, and ceremony—to represent political relations. In his descriptions of wedding celebrations, ʿAzimuddin uses the politics of caste and cleanliness to mark respectability within and among competing Indic Muslim households. After several confrontations over the course of two decades, Nawab ʿAbdul Hakim Khan and Haider ʿAli sought to deter war by marrying their sons and daughters to each other, most notably in two celebrated weddings in the 1770s. The Nawab's daughter Nawaz Begam married Karim Saheb, the second son of Haider ʿAli and the latter's daughter, Sultan Begam, married ʿAbdul Khair Khan, the Nawab's son.[23]

For the second wedding, the ruler of Savanur, the groom's father, traveled to the outskirts of Mysore where Haider ʿAli, the bride's father, came to receive him. Up to this point, ʿAzimuddin had described the two rivals, now soon to be kin, as two seeds of an almond in a single shell (*mānand badām do maghaz alal ittisāl*). He then describes the scale of preparations, the elaborate palace decorations, and how the wedding guests began to be served the finest dishes prepared by the best cooks from Delhi and Hindustan. All this effort was made to give the groom's side no excuse to blame the bride's father or complain about their hospitality. Alas, despite the extravagance, a mistake happened. This mistake not only ruined the *zauq* (taste) of ʿAbdul Hakim Khan but also laid bare an uncleanliness characteristic to the house of Haider ʿAli and disappointed the ruler of Savanur. The wedding feast laid out and put before the groom's father smelled delicious and looked exquisitely cooked, but something was wrong. Taking the first bite, the Nawab noticed the food had been cooked in unclean vessels, which had not been sufficiently scrubbed by applying the technique of coating them with tin (*qalʿī*).[24] In contrast to the way things were done in Mysore, back in his own kitchen in Savanur, vessels were kept fresh by coating them with tin every single day. If the tin coating had been applied on the cooking vessels properly, the food would have tasted just right.

As if the disappointment of dining from unclean vessels was not enough, another incident followed that reveals to the reader how the bride's side (Mysore) did not meet the criteria for respectability. To make up for and remedy the first embarrassment, Haider ʿAli sent over a servant with a set of fine hookahs to the Nawab's chambers, shinier than gold and silver and scented with rosewater and musk to the groom's father. Right before the hookah's pipe touched the Nawab's lips, he saw smoke twirling in the air, and he threw the pipe down to the floor. His facial expression turned dour as he interrogated the hookah carrier. He saw that instead of fresh coals, stale ones wrapped with leather were burning, producing noxious smoke. Whether the polluting leather was placed in the hookah on purpose or not, the narrative serves to mark distinctions of cleanliness between the two households. As a result of this incident, Haider ʿAli was embarrassed again and apologized profusely to the groom's father, trying his best to make it up so that the guests could trust him again. Despite these embarrassing incidents, the weddings between Savanur and Mysore continued, with great attention paid to the cleanliness in lavish preparations.

The image of the groom's father coming into contact with smoke from burning an unclean substance like leather serves a larger purpose. The Nawab's disgusted response to the possibility of bodily pollution from inhaling the smoke from a piece of burning leather implicitly carried a critique of the bride's household. By critiquing the patriarch Haider ʿAli's carelessness regarding standards for food preparation, ʿAzimuddin sought to emphasize the difference between these two elite Muslim households that, on the surface, might seem indistinguishable.

For a modern reader, such narratives about dining taboos that violated standards of hospitality can come off as facetious embellishments unthinkingly affixed to the more important narrative of political relations. However, the passages that emphasize the cleanliness of one elite Muslim household vis-à-vis another reveal how social distinctions and boundaries were marked. The politics of caste included standards of cleanliness and dining that highlighted the ethnic difference between the current rulers of Mysore, Haider ʿAli (a Sunni Muslim soldier of fortune with unknown origins) and Savanur, founded by one line of the Sunni Muslim Miyana Afghans, who had long served as soldiers in Deccan and Mughal armies. The narratives about cleanliness and hospitality worked in tandem with anxieties that lay at the heart of the uneasy affinal ties forged between Mysore and Savanur in the eighteenth century.

Shortly after narrating these awkward wedding incidents, ʿAzimuddin further emphasized the differences between Mysore and Savanur. On the eve of the invasion and looting of Savanur, an old confidant and childhood friend of Haider ʿAli, Laʿl Khan, dissuaded him from proceeding with battle. He warned that most of the great nobles of Savanur served in Mysore's army while their wives and families were still in Savanur. Repeating an old trope of intra-Afghan solidarity, Laʿl Khan noted that these relatives were bound by feelings of brotherhood for other Afghans (*birādarī wa hamdīgarī-i qaum-i afghānhā*) and had affection and respect for ʿAbdul Hakim Khan.[25] If all the Afghans united (*hameh-yi qaum-i afghān yek dili wa yak zabān shawand*), Mysore was bound to lose. It is against this imagined ethnic solidarity that the troubling violations of caste and commensality in the wedding narratives must be read. Through such narratives, ʿAzimuddin constructed the criteria through which he could distinguish the respectability of two elite Sunni Muslim households, both of which came from relatively modest soldiering backgrounds.

This image of Afghans on different sides of a political fight uniting to turn the tide of major battles goes back several centuries to the time of the Mughal emperor Aurangzeb and still earlier to the time of the Deccan sultanates in the seventeenth century, when chronicles first constructed this trope.[26] Finally, in the first third of *Tārīkh-i Dilīr-jangī*, ʿAzimuddin begins with narratives memorializing the seventeenth century when the journeys of households at the edges of states first emerged, journeys that have taken us in this book across peninsular India.

THE EMINENT HOUSE

So, finally, what did the distant past of the seventeenth century mean to someone like Muhammad ʿAzimuddin composing a Persian chronicle-cum-anthology in the nineteenth century for his little-known patron, Nawab Dilir Jang Bahadur? In the very beginnings of the *Tārīkh-i Dilīr-jangī*, we find a sweeping genealogical account starting in the sixteenth century, when the *akābir-i khāndān* (greats of the household) first emerged journeying across the Mughal frontier and into peninsular India. The author tells us that his patron Nawab Dilir Jang asked him to compile a history of Savanur's ancestors from an array of scattered and separate histories and write them anew in a sequential, colorful manner. The first *aurang* (chapter 1) thus begins with a *shajara* (family tree) going back to the earliest ancestors of the Miyana Afghans who settled in the watan of Hindustan, where they held a *jāgīr* for seventeen years.[27] After the fourteenth generation, in the time of the Mughals (*timuri bādshah*) and under Emperor Humayun (r. 1530–40), they came to hold the title of *malik* or lord. It was during the reign of Sher Shah Sur (r. 1537–45) that they earned the titled *nawāb* (variously translated as vice regents, governors, or lieutenants) and came to be held in the highest regard by kings. When describing the sixteenth and seventeenth centuries, 'Azimuddin expresses a nostalgia for the relationship between households and states in the distant past with the following Urdu verse:

> *mu'tamad milti hai shāhon kī jo hote hain rafīq*
> *sab ko milti hai par aisī hawā jawānhā kahān*
>
> those who become friends receive the trust of kings
> no longer can it be found, where have such youthful winds gone?

The twenty-second descendent, 'Abdul Khan Bahadur, became minister of the lands of the Deccan at borders of the Karnatak (*wazīr-i mumālik-i dakkan ke mahdūd-i karnātak ast*). 'Azimuddin describes the multivalent itineraries of the family line: while some sons joined the Mughals, others entered the service of the Sultanates. Here, the recounted narratives follow the templates of the mirror-for-princes genre, attaching moral lessons to actual historical events that conclude with the lesson that monarchs cannot function without the wise consul elite householders. For instance, on the eve of the Mughal invasion of Bijapur in the 1670s, the author explains how 'Abdul Rauf Khan made a peace deal with the Mughal emperor Aurangzeb.[28] 'Azimuddin follows this narrative about how integral the Miyana household was to Bijapuri sultans with a well-known story about how they also helped the Mughals. He recounts how Prince Muazzam Khan, one of the Mughal emperor Aurangzeb's disaffected sons, was persuaded to return to his father by 'Abdul Rauf Khan (who, as a result, earned the title of Dilir Khan Bahadur). In constructing these household memories, 'Azimuddin draws heavily on preexisting chronicles, such as Kirmani's *Nishān-i Haidari* (ca. 1802), a text he acknowledged using as a reference and one in which such narratives about the household's ancestors are also recounted.[29]

A final legacy of the Mughals and the Deccan sultanates, as the author explains, was the production and collection of books and manuscripts about these preceding political formations that ended up in household libraries in the early nineteenth century. This preexisting knowledge implicitly shaped an early colonial chronicle-anthology like the *Tārīkh-i Dilīr-jangi*. Thus, in the final chapters, we learn that Nawab Dilir Jang's library received many manuscripts from Bijapur and Hyderabad, confirming the circulation and transfer of many renowned materials into elite libraries in the early nineteenth century.[30] 'Azimuddin's patron's love of learning and deep knowledge of the Arabic and Persian languages, and prose and poetry in general meant he was constantly seeking authentic and original manuscripts. In this portion of the work, the author acknowledges that a learned Sufi from Bijapur even sent a copy of Ibrahim Zubayri's *Tārīkh-i Bijāpūr* (which he titles *Hasht Bustān-i Tārīkh-i Bijāpūr* or the Eight gardens of the history of Bijapur [ca. 1802]) to Savanur. This was one of the key texts consulted to learn about the previous kings of the Deccan and it shaped how the author composed the early chapter of the present work, much like the Nawab himself, who benefited from reading such well-known chronicles. In the early colonial period, manuscripts moved across libraries in peninsular India, echoing the itineraries of households that had in past centuries moved across the same landscape,—from the military barrack in its central plateau to the weaving villages on its coastal plains.

The purpose of concluding a book about the seventeenth century with a reflection on the meaning of ghar and what it means to write its histories more than a century later is twofold. The burnt house in the present, the remembered house in the immediate past, and the eminent house of the distant past all constituted how 'Azimuddin conceptualized the place of household and state in historical time. He was looking back at the time when elite households mattered to dynastic power— that is, as opposed to his time, when they were being actively forgotten at exactly the moment when dynastic histories were becoming separated from family histories. This postscript presents what was visible to 'Azimuddin—namely, a refraction of the book's preceding chapters on the seventeenth century. In other words, what was discernable about the household's role in state power to early nineteenth century authors was inexorably conditioned by ruptures in the early colonial present.

PRECOLONIAL IMPERFECTIONS AND THE POSTCOLONIAL PRESENT

This book began as an inquiry into the place of the household in connected histories.[31] Raising the question of historical method here was also a way of reflecting on the book's larger stakes and the interdisciplinary fields in which it intervenes. The central question before us was how to reconstruct the role of the subcontinent's most enduring form of social organization—the household—across vastly different linguistic and philosophical archives, as well as geographic units. Poems, administrative documents, chronicles in South Asian languages share no obvious linguistic or common epistemic ground with European Company archives. To me, the salient question in connected histories is not so much the mutual legibility of any body of materials, for their philological and philosophical worlds are indeed mostly separate and mutually exclusive. Rather, a more interesting direction one can go with them is to show how together they illuminate proximate geographies and units of circulation within which premodern power functioned. Thus, through our analysis of both a battle poem and Company archives we saw how soldiers, poets, and household chiefs moved across shorter distances from one social site to another, competing, contesting, disputing with one another, linking the central plateau to the Kanara coast and the Raichur Doab to the northern Tamil country. Tracking everyday mobilities across more proximate geographies of circulation thus helped us move away from the usual sites where we tend to look for connections, such as the world of diplomats, courtly circulation, and overlapping high literary cultures.

Tying the ambitions of social history to the practice of drawing from sources in multiple languages, whether through textual traditions in indigenous languages or European archives, this book has, above all, presented the case for an unromantic portrait of premodern power. Students of South Asia, in the United States and elsewhere across the world, are now better acquainted with the subcontinent's colonial and postcolonial pasts, as a range of disciplines—whether literary studies, anthropology, or history—have all embraced the critique of Orientalism. One of the generative questions emerging from postcolonial studies, still insufficiently explored, is how to make sense of everything that existed before Europe? The radical rewriting and pulverizing of indigenous texts in the colonial period is a process echoed in our postscript here, through the reflections of Munshi Muhammad ʿAzimuddin in his *Tārīkh-i Dilīr-jangi*.[32]

But the alternative to the critique of colonial knowledge cannot be that premodern South Asia was a land bereft of competition, conflict, and social hierarchies or that all identities before colonialism were necessarily fluid. Belonging somewhere in the vertical hierarchy of a ghar was a form of privilege. Social historians have long argued that elite power must be examined not merely as a question of identity and representation, but also as it related to other actors, whether commercial elites or laboring groups, a question that deserves closer examination in the sixteenth and seventeenth centuries when the subcontinent's largest precolonial and most enduring empire was intact and improvising its institutions very far from the so-called center.[33] Over the course of the book's chapters, we traversed different social sites across peninsular India, where cross-status interactions are most visible—spaces where elite households participated, constituted, and undercut state institutions.

The Mughal Empire occupies a complicated position in the public life of the postcolonial nation-states that constitute South Asia today.[34] Given the rise of ultranationalist movements that seek to erase every imprint of Islam in the modern Indian republic, it should come as no surprise that scholarly work has successfully restored Mughal greatness by emphasizing this Sunni Muslim Turko-Mongol empire's capacious forms of cultural patronage, its ability to rule over subjects from various different religions, ethnicities, and linguistic worlds, and most importantly, its role in defining a sense of belonging.[35] As this book shows, nowhere else is the empire's role in shaping the politics of place more clear than in peninsular India, a region that was never fully incorporated into the imperial domains. Here we found that contestation and disagreement, as much as accommodation and borrowing, lie at the core of belonging to a ghar or house. That the story of Mughal presence in southern India is not one of happy harmony need not be lamented. But, by emphasizing the conflict and contestation inherent in it, we can observe how the empire transformed and built on regional patterns of sovereignty, producing debates about imperial power.

Working at an empire's edges meant moving along with different kinds of households across nodes and sites of interaction with the state and focusing on how social relations transformed when an imperial and regional war front first started expanding. Starting in the 1620s, the book began by first turning to the untold story of naming ghar in caste (the foundational building block of households) and various other identifications in the Mughal Empire. When provincial elites first fell under the northern Indian Mughal Empire's shadow, at the site of the military barrack at the northmost limits of peninsular India, household and state encountered each other. At these interconnected networks of checkpoints and forts, social identifications were written, recorded, and interrogated, bringing a state scribe into conversation with the humble soldier affiliated with households from many different sectarian, ethnic, linguistic, and regional backgrounds.

In chapter 2, by shifting the question of identity to identification, I argued for the utility of using documentary fragments for writing the social history of caste, rather than turning to frozen representations of elite power and identity in court chronicles. In these terse materials, a pointillist portrait of everyday interactions and bureaucratic processes that held down a massive military occupation showed how social categories were created, used, and defined by ordinary actors. In chapters 4 and 5, just as regional sultanates were falling under the Mughals in the mid-seventeenth century, we stopped at regional courts, which remained a key site for producing a critique of imperial rule. In Bijapur and Hyderabad, from the 1630s to the 1660s, we heard the voices of émigré and regional poet-political commentators who formulated the earliest and most trenchant critiques of the imperial occupation. These observers saw provincial households making claims to power, thereby unsettling the criteria for belonging to ghar. In the adorned palaces of regional capital cities, dynastic and aristocratic marriages, births, and circumcisions continued to be celebrated, where participants in public ceremony once again evoked the notion of ghar, an idealized space that could be built on many forms of relatedness, such as marriage, slave patronage, and fosterage. In chapters 3 and 6, we moved beyond courts to the coasts of peninsular India, where, through case studies of interactions between Iranian, Afghan, and Maratha households, we saw two kinds of bottom-up perspectives on elite power—from intra-kin competition, on the one hand, which threatened the very survival of regional rulers, to realignments along lines of status, on the other, which conserved economic hierarchies in the coastal economy. I showed that in an era unbound by the nation-state form and its attendant identities based on religion, region, language, gender, and ethnicity, such interelite solidarity is entirely unremarkable; and by interrogating the underlying mechanisms of these affinities, we saw how social order was preserved.

The general scholarly focus on the Mughal heartland in northern India has meant that reigning imperial rulers continue to organize extant scholarship on the empire. Recent studies have usefully moved toward a social history but are still firmly located in Delhi or the northern Indian plains more broadly. By contrast, in peninsular India, scholarship has either focused on courtly and literary cultures or on political history, leaving unanswered the question about the social constitution of power. To recover an unromantic picture of elite power, the space between the household and the state offers one possible site for the study of precolonial social history, particularly in peninsular India, where diverse physical and human geographies have for centuries produced weak monarchical states and a continuous and fraught pattern of corporate groups as cosharers in sovereignty.

Given vexed political debates in the postcolonial present, the Mughal historian today must apparently try to prove whether this premodern political formation and its rulers were good or bad.[36] The notion of good Mughals and bad Mughals remains pervasive, as recent popular histories readily embrace this trope for the Muslim rulers of the Deccan as well.[37] One way of making the Mughals Indian has been to affirm their proximity to or affinity with non-Muslim groups, languages, traditions, and sects in the subcontinent. And yet, this paradigm still leaves us with the problem of origins that begins with the fundamental otherness of Islamic polities (in this case Mughal and the Deccan sultans) often cured by taking on local flavor or adopting preexisting cultural norms.[38] The focus on Mughal pluralism has often overshadowed the dynamic story of intrareligious and intrasectarian critique within various communities across South Asia, which recent work has usefully undone.[39] Despite bringing to light the polyglot Mughal world, an integrationist model leaves out the problem of competition and contention within the senses of belonging created by South Asian Islam. Both narratives in part draw on persistent colonial and nationalist discourses that frame the empire as a monolithic imperial entity by exclusively examining the rise and fall of dynastic kings, who in turn are cast as either the paragons of syncretic culture or conservative rulers guided by Islamic orthodoxy.

It goes without saying that the Indian subcontinent has for centuries been the ghar of many kinds of people, languages, ideologies, religions, and communities. On the eve of colonialism in the eighteenth century, it was the Mughal Empire that played the single biggest role in integrating the subcontinent's distant, heterogenous regions, which, in turn, did their part in transforming imperial ambitions. Stepping outside Delhi and the Hindi heartland requires putting the Mughals at the center of the discussion about caste in circulation and internal mobilities in early modern India. The Sunni Muslim Mughals have largely been left out of the discussion about their role in shaping the history of caste mobility partly because the history of the subcontinent's most enduring social variable, particularly in the periods before 1800, is purportedly one of and about Hindus.[40]

This book's chapters offer an itinerary with stops at different social sites, where we can see the internal and external interactions of household power and caste circulation with state institutions. If and when possible, this book interrogates not just the representations of elite power in courtly literature but also its everyday workings and interactions within and across social classes in surviving documentary genres, the body of evidence traditionally generated by the state. Whether by tracking the movement of a vast panoply of soldiers in the imperial military or through case studies of intraclan conflicts within elite households, this book urges that histories of the subcontinent's most salient social feature of status and caste need not be erased in the well-meaning effort to restore Mughal greatness. If anything, the best reason to make the Mughals "Indian," as the late historian M. Athar Ali observed decades ago, is that they were firm believers in caste and efficient enforcers of social hierarchy.[41] By moving across different social sites where we see the practices and meanings of social identities in circulation, it may also be possible then to bridge the divide between the world of the court versus the state, a dichotomy naturalized in recent studies of both the Mughal north and peninsular India.

Like any other category, the rich history of South Asian Islam long before colonialism deserves closer scrutiny for its innumerable contradictions in a story replete with disagreement and debate. If we want to move away from either exaggerating or minimizing the significance of sectarian difference in the precolonial world by talking to or against the Indic versus the Islamicate paradigm, then contending with political meaning-making and debates within either of these categories may also be useful.[42] There is therefore no denying that for seventeenth-century provincial Muslim observers, the Mughals were, indeed, a troubling presence, especially in peninsular India. Rather than shying away from the earliest trenchant critiques of the empire, it is worth listening to the dissenting voices that diagnosed how imperial ambitions transformed the meanings of belonging and altered politics and institutions.

NOTES

1. THE HOUSEHOLD IN CONNECTED HISTORIES

1. Abu'l-Fazl, *The History of Akbar*, ed. and trans. Wheeler M. Thackston, vol. 8, 369–82.
2. Rao Bahadur and C. S. Srinivasachari, *A History of Gingee and its Rulers* (Madras: Annamalai University, 1943).
3. Janaki Nair, "Beyond Exceptionalism: South India and the Modern Historical Imagination," *Indian Economic & Social History Review* 43, no. 3 (2006): 324–25. As Nair shows, the category of "south India" has operated as an eternal exception to attest to the normativity of northern India across many different historical periods, a persistent convention in the subcontinent's historiography, including that having to do with the Mughals and the Deccan sultanates.
4. Manan Ahmed Asif, *The Loss of Hindustan: The Invention of India* (Cambridge, MA: Harvard University Press, 2020), 1–27.
5. Sanjay Subrahmanyam, *Empires between Islam and Christianity, 1500–1800* (Albany: State University of New York Press, 2018), 4–5.
6. Pamela Kyle Crossley, Helen F. Siu, and Donald S. Sutton, eds., *Empire at the Margins: Culture, Ethnicity, and Frontier in Early Modern China*, vol. 28 (Berkeley: University of California Press, 2006), 3–11.
7. Peter Perdue, *China Marches West: The Qing Conquest of Central Asia* (Cambridge, MA: Belknap Press, 2010); Jane Hathaway, *The Arab Lands under Ottoman Rule, 1516–1800*, 2nd ed. (London: Routledge, 2020).
8. Paolo Sartori, "Seeing Like a Khanate: On Archives, Cultures of Documentation, and Nineteenth-Century Khvārazm," *Journal of Persianate Studies* 9, no. 2 (2016): 233–34; James Pickett and Paolo Sartori, "From the Archetypical Archive to Cultures of Documentation," *Journal of the Economic and Social History of the Orient* 62, nos. 5–6 (2019): 793; Sumit Guha, "Rethinking the Economy of Mughal India: Lateral Perspectives," *Journal of the*

Economic and Social History of the Orient 58, no. 4 (2015): 554; Sanjay Subrahmanyam, "Writing History 'Backwards': Southeast Asian History (and the Annales) at the Crossroads," *Studies in History* 10, no. 1 (1994): 137–39.

9. James C. Scott, *Seeing Like a State: How Certain Schemes to Improve the Human Condition Have Failed* (New Haven, CT: Yale University Press, 1998), 1–2. For a South Asianist engagement with Scott's *The Art of Not Being Governed: An Anarchist History of Upland Southeast Asia* (New Haven, CT: Yale University Press, 2009), see Indrani Chatterjee, *Forgotten Friends: Monks, Marriages, and Memories of Northeast India* (New Delhi: Oxford University Press, 2013), 1–35.

10. Crossley, Siu, and Sutton, eds., *Empire at the Margins*, 3.

11. We may extend Talbot's paradigm for examining social identity through inscriptions to later periods of premodern South Asia. The fragmentary documentary records and literary sources produced in the circulatory regimes of the Mughal frontier in peninsular India may also be understood as "materially embodied records of practice." See Cynthia Talbot, *Pre-Colonial India in Practice: Society, Region, and Identity in medieval Andhra* (New Delhi: Oxford University Press, 2001), 13–17.

12. Feminist historians like Indrani Chatterjee and Ruby Lal laid the foundations for examining how monastic, lay, and royal household generated expansive categories of belonging and identity within imperial formations. See Indrani Chatterjee, *Forgotten Friends*, 36–80 and (as editor) *Unfamiliar Relations: Family and History in South Asia* (New Brunswick, NJ: Rutgers University Press, 2004), 3–45. See also Ruby Lal, *Domesticity and Power in the Early Mughal World* (Cambridge: Cambridge University Press, 2005).

13. Claude Markovits, Jacques Pouchepadass, and Sanjay Subrahmanyam, eds., *Society and Circulation: Mobile People and Itinerant Cultures in South Asia, 1750–1950* (New York: Anthem Press, 2006), 1–22; Thomas De Bruijn and Allison Busch, eds., *Culture and Circulation: Literature in Motion in Early Modern India*, vol. 46 (Leiden: Brill, 2014), 1–20; Keelan Overton, *Iran and the Deccan: Persianate Art, Culture, and Talent in Circulation 1400–1700* (Bloomington: Indiana University Press, 2020), 3–49; Finbarr Barry Flood, *Objects of Translation: Material culture and medieval "Hindu-Muslim" encounter* (Princeton, NJ: Princeton University Press, 2009), 3–5.

14. Sebouh Aslanian, Joyce E. Chaplin, Ann McGrath, and Kristin Mann, "AHR Conversation How Size Matters: The Question of Scale in History," *American Historical Review* 118, no. 5 (2013): 1431–72.

15. Marshall Hodgson, *The Venture of Islam*, vol. 3, *The Gunpower Empires and Modern Times* (Chicago, IL: University of Chicago Press, 1974); Abbas Amanat, ed., *The Persianate World: Rethinking a Shared Sphere* (Leiden: Brill, 2018), 1–62; Richard Eaton, *India in the Persianate Age 1000–1765* (Oakland: University of California Press, 2019), 3–10; Nile Green, ed., *The Persianate World: The Frontiers of a Eurasian Lingua Franca* (Oakland: University of California Press, 2019), 1–74; Emma J. Flatt, *The Courts of the Deccan Sultanates: Living Well in the Persian Cosmopolis* (Cambridge: Cambridge University Press, 2019), 17–24; Mana Kia, *Persianate Selves: Memories of Place and Origin Before Nationalism* (Stanford, CA: Stanford University Press, 2020), 13; Kevin Schwartz, *Remapping Persian Literary History, 1700–1900* (Edinburgh: Edinburgh University Press, 2020), 29.

16. Jerry H. Bentley, "Sea and Ocean Basins as Frameworks of Historical Analysis," *Geographical Review* 89, no. 2 (1999): 215–24.

17. For a critique of this first generation of economic histories of the Indian Ocean between 1500–1700, see Sanjay Subrahmanyam, *The Political Economy of Commerce: Southern India, 1500–1650* (Cambridge: Cambridge University Press, 1990), 1–9.

18. For a critique of recent trends, see Sanjay Subrahmanyam, "Hybrid Affairs: Cultural Histories of the East India Companies," *Indian Economic & Social History Review* 55, no. 3 (2018): 419–38.

19. In an early rich interdisciplinary exploration of this concept, ghar was fixed into the modern-day linguistic state of Maharashtra, with scholars recognizing the difficulty of applying anthropological theories of "fictive kinship" in making sense of the historical evolution of Marathas. See Marina Yu. Lomova-Oppokova, "Marathas: The Role of Kinship Relations in the Social and Political Life of Maharashtra," 185–98; Irina Efremova, "Delimiting the Ghar in Socio-Cultural Space," 41–57; A. R. Kulkarni, "'The Jedhe Gharane (The House of the Jedhes)," 173–84. All these chapters are in *Home, Family and Kinship in Maharashtra*, ed. Irina Gluškova and Rajendra Vora (New Delhi: Oxford University Press, 1999).

20. Pradip Kumar Datta, ed., *Rabindranath Tagore's The Home and the World: A Critical Companion* (London: Anthem Press, 2005).

21. Ellen Barry, "Families Feud over Delhi Estates," *New York Times*, September 9, 2014, https://www.nytimes.com/2014/09/10/world/asia/families-feud-over-delhi-estates.html.

22. For proverbs on ghar, see S. W. Fallon, *Hindustani-English Dictionary of Idioms & Proverbs* (Banaras: Medical Hall Press, 1886), 87–90.

23. Sumit Guha, *Ecologies of Empire in South Asia 1400–1900* (Seattle: University of Washington Press, 2023), 18–43.

24. Jaya Tyagi, *Engendering the Early Household: Brahmanical Precepts in the Early Grhyasutras, Middle of the First Millenium B.C.E.* (Delhi: Orient Longman, 2008), 346–48.

25. John T. Platts, *A Dictionary of Urdu, Classical Hindi, and English* (London: W. H. Allen, 1884), 932.

26. Platts, *A Dictionary of Urdu, Classical Hindi, and English*, 485–86.

27. Munis D. Faruqui, *The Princes of the Mughal Empire 1504–1719* (Cambridge: Cambridge University Press, 2012), 262; Rosalind O'Hanlon, "Kingdom, Household and Body, History, Gender and Imperial Service under Akbar," *Modern Asian Studies* 41, 5 (2007): 889–923. Recent examinations of documentary evidence have shown a long view of how one agrarian household was tied to multiple empires across time in central India. See Nandini Chatterjee, *Negotiating Mughal Law: A Family of Landlords across Three Indian Empires* (Cambridge: Cambridge University Press, 2020), 25.

28. Crossley, Siu, and Sutton, eds., *Empire at the Margins*, 27–112.

29. Sumit Guha, *Beyond Caste: Identity and Power in South Asia, Past and Present* (Ranikhet: Permanent Black, 2016), 117–18.

30. For various usages of these terms in the eighteenth century, see Mana Kia, *Persianate Selves*, 36–44. See also Bernard Lewis, "Watan," *Journal of Contemporary History* 26, no. 3 (1991): 523–33.

31. A. R. Kulkarni, "The Deshmukh watan with Special Reference to Indapur," *Indian Historical Review*, 3 (1976), 289–300; Frank Perlin, "State Formation Reconsidered: Part Two," *Modern Asian Studies* 19, no. 3 (April 1984): 431; André Wink, *Land and Sovereignty in India: Agrarian Society and Politics under the Eighteenth-Century Maratha Svarājya* (Cambridge: Cambridge University Press, 1986), 157–250.

32. Sumit Guha, *History and Collective Memory in South Asia, 1200–2000* (Seattle: University of Washington Press, 2019), 114.

33. Gijs Kruijtzer, *Xenophobia in Seventeenth-Century India* (Leiden: Leiden University Press, 2009), 1–17, 256–64.

34. Chatterjee, *Forgotten Friends*, 36–80.

35. Abu'l-Fazl, *The History of Akbar*, vol. 8, 129, 383, 401.

36. The shared intellectual geography of these two historians is evocatively described in Ahmed, *The Loss of Hindustan*, 129–42.

37. P. M. Joshi and Haroon Khan Sherwani, eds., *History of the Medieval Deccan*, vol. 1, *Mainly Political and Military Aspects 1295–1724* (Hyderabad: Government of Andhra Pradesh, 1973), ix.

38. M. Z. A. Shakeb, *Relations of Golkonda with Iran* (Delhi: Primus Books, 2017); Muzaffar Alam and Sanjay Subrahmanyam, "The Deccan Frontier and Mughal Expansion, Ca. 1600: Contemporary Perspectives," *Journal of the Economic and Social History of the Orient* 47, no. 3 (2004): 357–89; Keelan Hall Overton, "Introduction" to *Iran and the Deccan: Persianate Art, Culture, and Talent in Circulation 1400–1700*, (Bloomington: Indiana University Press, 2020), 3–76.

39. Joshi and Sherwani, *History of the Medieval Deccan*, vol. 1, 358.

40. Haroon Khan Sherwani, *History of the Qutb Shahi Dynasty* (Delhi: Munshiram Manoharlal, 1974), chapters 6 and 7; John F. Richards, *Mughal Administration in Golkonda* (Oxford: Clarendon Press, 1975): 34–51; D. C. Verma, *History of Bijapur* (Delhi: Kumar Brothers, 1974): 195–213; Richard M. Eaton, *Sufis of Bijapur 1300–1700* (Princeton, NJ: Princeton University Press, 1978), 177–201; Jadunath Sarkar, *History of Aurangzib*, vol. 4 (Calcutta: M. C. Sarkar & Sons,1919), 41–42.

41. Velcheru Narayana Rao, David Shulman, and Sanjay Subrahmanyam, *Symbols of Substance: Court and State in Nayaka Period Tamil Nadu* (New Delhi: Oxford University Press, 1992); Markus Vink, *Encounters on the Opposite Coast: The Dutch East India Company and the Nayaka State of Madurai in the Seventeenth Century* (Leiden: Brill, 2017), 17–23; Lennart Bes, *The Heirs of Vijayanagara: Court Politics in Early-Modern South India* (Leiden: Leiden University Press, 2022), 1–46.

42. V. J. Adams Flynn, "An English Translation of the Adab-i 'Alamgiri" (PhD diss., Australia National University, 1974), letters 54–60, 206–26.

43. Burton Stein, "State Formation and Economy Reconsidered," *Modern Asian Studies* 19, no. 3 (1985): 387–413.

44. Dilip Menon, "Houses by the Sea: State-Formation Experiments in Malabar, 1760–1800," *Economic and Political Weekly* (1999): 1995–2003; David Washbrook, "South India 1770–1840: The Colonial Transition," *Modern Asian Studies* 38, no. 3 (2004): 479–516.

45. Sanjay Subrahmanyam, "Aspects of State Formation in South India and Southeast Asia, 1500–1650," *Indian Economic and Social History Review* 23, no. 4 (1986): 357–77.

46. Sunil Sharma, *Mughal Arcadia: Persian Literature in an Indian Court* (Cambridge, MA: Harvard University Press, 2017), 1–15; Allison Busch, *Poetry of Kings: The Classical Hindi Literature of Mughal India* (New York: Oxford University Press, 2011), 136–65; Audrey Truschke, *Culture of Encounters: Sanskrit at the Mughal Court* (New York: Columbia University Press, 2016), 1–26.

47. Simon Digby, "Before Timur Came: Provincialization of the Delhi Sultanate through the Fourteenth Century," *Journal of the Economic and Social History of the Orient* 47, no. 3 (2004): 333–39.

48. Sumit Guha, "Bad Language and Good Language: Lexical Awareness in the Cultural Politics of Peninsular India, 1300–1800," in *Forms of Knowledge in Early Modern Asia: Explorations in the Intellectual History of India and Tibet*, ed. Sheldon Pollock (Durham, NC: Duke University Press, 2011), 49–68.

49. Catherine Asher and Cynthia Talbot, *India Before Europe Second Edition* (Cambridge: Cambridge University Press, 2022), 1–24.

50. Rao, Shulman, and Subrahmanyam, *Symbols of Substance*, 242–304; Richard M. Eaton and Philip Wagoner, *Power, Memory, Architecture: Contested Sites on India's Deccan Plateau, 1300–1600* (New Delhi: Oxford University Press, 2013), 323–28.

51. Subrahmanyam, *The Political Economy of Commerce*, 62–77.

52. Sanjay Subrahmanyam, *The Portuguese Empire in Asia 1500–1700*, 2nd ed. (Chichester: Wiley-Blackwell, 2012), 72.

53. Jorge Flores, *Unwanted Neighbors: the Mughals, the Portuguese, and their Frontier Zones* (New Delhi: Oxford University Press, 2018), 1–31.

54. Philip J. Stern, *The Company-State: Corporate Sovereignty and the Early Modern Foundations of the British Empire in India* (New York: Oxford University Press, 2011), 3–16.

55. Subrahmanyam, *The Portuguese Empire in Asia*, 167–69.

56. As was pointed out decades ago, intrafamilial conflicts shaped the outcome of Luso-Dutch relations as well as those of other European states in maritime Asia. See Sanjay Subrahmanyam, "The 'Pulicat Enterprise': Luso-Dutch conflict in South-Eastern India, 1610–1640," *South Asia: Journal of South Asian Studies* 9, no. 2 (1986): 17–36.

57. Geoffrey Parker, "Crisis and Catastrophe: The Global Crisis of the Seventeenth Century Reconsidered," *American Historical Review* 113, no. 4 (2008): 1053–79; Macabe Keliher, "The Problem of Imperial Relatives in Early Modern Empires and the Making of Qing China," *American Historical Review* 122, no. 4 (2017): 1001–37; Anthony Reid, "The Seventeenth-Century Crisis in Southeast Asia," *Modern Asian Studies* 24, no. 4 (1990): 639–59.

58. Samira Sheikh, "Aurangzeb as Seen from Gujarat: Shi'i and Millenarian Challenges to Mughal Sovereignty," *Journal of the Royal Asiatic Society* 28, no. 3 (2018): 559.

59. Nizamuddin Ahmad, *Hadīqat al-Salātīn*, ed. Syed 'Ali Asghar Biligrami (Hyderabad: Islamic Publications Society, 1961), 121 (hereafter *Hadīqat*); Hakim Atishi, *'Ādilnāma*, fol. 74, fol. 76.

60. *Hadīqat*, 105, 107, 121, 127; Zuhur ibn Zuhuri, *Muhammadnāma*, MS. 26, Bijapur State Archaeological Museum, Bijapur, fol. 77, fol. 79, fols. 133–34.

61. Zuhur, *Muhammadnāma*, fol. 133; *Hadīqat*, 106. For instance, Deccan chroniclers favorably described the revolt of the Mughal Afghan noble, Khan Jahan Pathan, former governor of Khandesh and Burhanpur, against Shah Jahan in the late 1620s, condoning his attempt to seek refuge in the rump state of Ahmadnagar.

62. V. J. Adams Flynn, "An English Translation of the Adab-i 'Alamgiri" (PhD. diss., Australia National University, 1974), Letter 65, 239–40.

63. Subah Dayal, "Making the 'Mughal' Soldier: Ethnicity, Identification, and Documentary Culture in Southern India, c. 1600–1700," *Journal of the Economic and Social History of the Orient* 62 (2019): 875.

64. Iftikhar Ahmad Ghauri, "Organization of the Army under the Sultanates of the Deccan," *Journal of the Pakistan Historical Society* 14, no. 3 (1966): 148–50.

65. Munis D. Faruqui, *The Princes of the Mughal Empire, 1504–1719* (Cambridge: Cambridge University Press, 2012), 1–23.

66. Wink, *Land and Sovereignty in India*, 51–65.

67. Kulkarni, "The Jedhe Gharane," 175.

68. Similar instances of intrafamilial conflicts have been examined in the eighteenth century by Sumit Guha, "The Family Feud as Political Resource in Eighteenth-Century India," in Chatterjee, *Unfamiliar Relations*, 73–94 and Prachi Deshpande, "The Marathi Kaulnāmā: Property, Sovereignty and Documentation in a Persianate Form," *Journal of the Economic and Social History of the Orient* 64 (2021): 583–614.

69. Hiroshi Fukazawa, *The Medieval Deccan: Peasants, Social Systems, and States, Sixteenth to Eighteenth Centuries* (New Delhi: Oxford University Press, 1991), 15–18.

70. The Khopades had remained loyal to the Bijapur sultans primarily to oppose their rivals, the Jedhes, who rallied behind Shivaji (d. 1680), as shown in the work of A. R. Kulkarni ("The Jedhe Gharane," 175–179) and André Wink (*Land and Sovereignty*, 176–177, 157–205).

71. In chapter 3 of this book, I explore how members of émigré Persian households attempted to consolidate their hold over the office of the havaldār, adapting the practice of entrenching occupational roles.

72. Ganesh Hari Khare, ed., *Persian Sources of Indian History* (*Aitihāsik Fārsī sāhitya*, hereafter *P.S.I.H.*) (Pune: Bharata Itihasa Sanshodhaka Mandala, 1934–61), vol. 2, 26. See the nine letters between the Khopades of Ambade, Bhor-Poona and Sultan Muhammad 'Adil Shah.

73. *P.S.I.H.*, vol. 2, November 4, 1655, from 'Ali 'Adil Shah II to Kedarji, 27.

74. *P.S.I.H.*, vol. 2, undated *arzdāsht* of Kedarji to 'Ali 'Adil Shah II, 28–30.

75. Ibid.

76. *P.S.I.H.*, vol. 2, March 1660, 30. See also V. S. Kadam, "Forced Labour in Mahārāṣṭra in the Seventeenth and Eighteenth Centuries: A Study in Its Nature and Change," *Journal of the Economic and Social History of the Orient* 1 (1991): 55–87. Mughal emperor Aurangzeb's order, renewing the Khopades' appointment in subsequent decades, makes no mention of this preceding feud with Khandoji. It urged the *watandārs* to convince the residents not to flee and continue cultivating their lands that had now fallen under the imperial realm. See *P.S.I.H.*, vol. 2, three documents from Aurangzeb dated ca. 1665, June 17, 1665, and November 30, 1665, 32–34.

77. The Bijapur sultan issued several such *farmāns* to garner support for Siddi Jauhar's campaign, including to the Pasalkar household of the Muse valley, near Pune. *P.S.I.H.*, vol. 2, 72–73. Shivaji would successfully break Siddi Jauhar's siege of Panhala in 1660.

78. Sumit Guha, "Patronage and State-making in early modern empires in India and Britain," in *Patronage as Politics in South Asia*, ed. Anastasia Piliavsky (Cambridge: Cambridge University Press, 2014), 104–22. For traditional and revisionist approaches to patrimonial power, see Stephen P. Blake, "Returning the Household to the Patrimonial-Bureaucratic Empire: Gender, Succession, and Ritual in the Mughal, Safavid and Ottoman

Empires," in Peter Fibiger Bang and C. A. Bayly eds., *Tributary Empires in Global History*, (London: Palgrave Macmillan, 2011), 214–26 and John F. Richards, "Norms of Comportment among Imperial Mughal Officers," in *Moral Conduct and Authority: The Place of Adab in South Asian Islam*, ed. Barbara Metcalf (Berkeley: University of California Press, 1984), 255–89.

79. I elaborate further on Nusrati's engagement with the concept of ghar in chapter 5.

80. Indrani Chatterjee and Sumit Guha, "Slave-Queen, Waif-Prince: Slavery and Social Capital in Eighteenth-Century India," *Indian Economic & Social History Review* 36, no. 2 (1999): 165–86; M. Z. A. Shakeb, "The Black Sheep Tribe from Lake Van to Golkonda," *Itihas: Journal of the State Archives Andhra Pradesh* 3, no. 2 (1975): 60–65; Sanjay Subrahmanyam, "Connected Histories: Notes towards a Reconfiguration of Early Modern Eurasia," *Modern Asian Studies* 31, no. 3 (1997): 735–62; Indrani Chatterjee, "Connected Histories and the Dream of Decolonial History," *South Asia: Journal of South Asian Studies* 41, no. 1 (2018): 69–86.

81. Guha, *Beyond Caste*, 117–41.

82. For a critique of the overemphasis on long-distance travel, see Dipti Khera, "Arrivals at Distant Lands: Artful Letters and Entangled Mobilities in the Indian Ocean Littoral," in *The Nomadic Object: The Challenge of World for Early Modern Religious Art*, ed. Christine Göttler and Mia M. Mochizuki (Leiden: Brill, 2018), 577–78.

83. Kären Wigen, "Mapping Early Modernity: Geographical Meditations on a Comparative Concept," *Early Modern Japan* 5, no. 2 (1995): 4, 7.

84. Guido van Meersbergen, *Ethnography and Encounter: The Dutch and English in Seventeenth-Century South Asia* (Leiden: Brill 2021).

85. Case studies of Yacama—for example, an early seventeenth-century Telugu Velugoti lineage warrior chief who settled in the northern Tamil country, and Citakatti or 'Abd al-Qadir, a Tamil Maraikkayar Muslim merchant with networks spread between the Marava state of Ramnad and the Gulf of Mannar who opposed the Dutch East India Company's ambitions—illuminate a consistent pattern of elite households shaping state-formation not at the center of dynasty but at the periphery. See Rao, Shulman, and Subrahmanyam, *Symbols of Substance*, 242–304. This utility of starting from so-called peripheries in periods of transition was shown by Sanjay Subrahmanyam in "The Tail Wags the Dog: Sub-imperialism and the *Estado da índia*, 1570–1600," in *Improvising Empire: Portuguese Trade and Settlement in the Bay of Bengal* (New Delhi: Oxford University Press, 1990), 137–57.

86. Guha, *History and Collective Memory in South Asia*, 61–62. In the present, for instance, in the republic of India (and at various points in postindependence Pakistan, Sri Lanka, and Bangladesh), the specter of "family dynasties" running political parties elicits public scorn, since the parties are often accused of being run as personal fiefdoms, antithetical to the ideals of liberal democracy.

87. Jerome Duindam, *Dynasties: A Global History of Power, 1300–1800* (Cambridge: Cambridge University Press, 2016), 4.

88. Julia Adams, *The Familial State: Ruling Families and Merchant Capitalism in Early Modern Europe* (Ithaca, NY: Cornell University Press, 2005), 13–37.

89. For a critique, see Indrani Chatterjee's introduction to *Unfamiliar Relations*, 3–45.

90. Michael Szonyi, *The Art of Being Governed* (Princeton, NJ: Princeton University Press, 2017), 1–22.

91. Jane Hathaway, *The Politics of Households in Ottoman Egypt: The Rise of the Qazdaglis* (Cambridge: Cambridge University Press, 2002), 3–16; Amy Aisen Kallander, *Women, Gender, and the Palace Households in Ottoman Tunisia* (Austin: University of Texas Press, 2013), 1–50; Helen Pfeiffer, *Empire of Salons: Conquest and Community in Early Modern Ottoman Lands* (Princeton, NJ: Princeton University Press, 2022), 57–96.

92. James Casey, *Family and Community in Early Modern Spain: The Citizens of Granada, 1570-1739* (Cambridge: Cambridge University Press, 2007), 1–7; J. Adams, *The Familial State*, 13–37; Thomas M. Safley, *Family Firms and Merchant Capitalism in Early Modern Europe: the Business, Bankruptcy and Resilience of the Höchstetters of Augsburg* (New York: Routledge, 2019), 1–31.

93. David Sneath, *The Headless State: Aristocratic Orders, Kinship, Society, and Misrepresentation of Nomadic Inner Asia* (New York: Columbia University Press, 2007), 39–64, 181–204. Sneath's work offers a critique of how modern scholarship mistranslated kinship terms as "race" and "ethnicity." However, it does not address the precolonial state's role in creating these categories, opening up the possibility of investigating how ethnicity was differentiated through identifiers of place, residence, occupation, region, and language. Following Sneath, studies have shown how postnomadic empires, borrowing from Chinggisid social engineering practices of incorporating warbands, tied itinerant mounted horseman to rulers through administrative and institutional mechanisms rather than hereditary lines of descent. For the subcontinent, this model has been applied to the study of caste, emphasizing the processes and practices of forming social identities, rather than viewing it as a timeless, static structure of South Asian society. For an application of this critique to Turani aristocratic orders in early Mughal India, see Ali Anooshahr, "Mughals, Mongols, and Mongrels: The Challenge of Aristocracy and the Rise of the Mughal State in the Tarikh-i Rashidi," *Journal of Early Modern History* 18, no. 6 (2014): 559–77. See also Jos Gommans, "The Warband in the Making of Eurasian Empires," in *Prince, Pen, and Sword: Eurasian Perspectives*, ed. Jeroen Duindam and M. van Berkel (Leiden: Brill, 2018), 316–20, 324–25, 335–36. This was also how Afghan and Rohilla identities were reconstituted during Afghan regional (Rohilla) and imperial (Durrani) state formation in the late eighteenth and early nineteenth centuries (see Jos Gommans, *The Rise of the Indo-Afghan Empire, c. 1710-1780* [Leiden: Brill, 1995]). Citing Ira Lapidus's work on North Africa and the Middle East, Guha notes that kinship among leaders of war bands was of secondary importance during conquest because warring groups deployed other incorporative bonds to absorb new groups. See *Beyond Caste*, 73–74.

94. Ali Anooshahr, *Turkestan and the Rise of Eurasian Empires: A Study of Politics and Invented Traditions* (New York: Oxford University Press, 2018), 1–6, 114–38.

95. Kathryn Babayan, *The City as Anthology: Eroticism and Urbanity in Early Modern Isfahan* (Palo Alto: Stanford University Press, 2021), 1–29.

96. Nandita Prasad Sahai, *Politics of Patronage and Protest: The State, Society, and Artisans in Early Modern Rajasthan* (New Delhi: Oxford University Press. 2006); Ramya Sreenivasan, "Rethinking Kingship and Authority in South Asia: Amber (Rajasthan), ca. 1560-1615," *Journal of the Economic and Social History of the Orient* 57, no. 4 (2014): 549–86; Tanuja Kothiyal, *Nomadic Narratives: A History of Mobility and Identity in the Great Indian Desert* (Cambridge: Cambridge University Press, 2016); Divya Cherian, *Merchants of Virtue: Hindus, Muslims, and Untouchables in Eighteenth-Century South Asia* (Oakland: University of California Press, 2022), 1–40.

97. Kumkum Roy, ed., *Looking Within, Looking Without: Exploring Households in the Subcontinent Through Time, Essays in Memory of Nandita Prasad Sahai* (Delhi: Primus Books, 2015).

98. Going still further ahead in time, for the period after 1800, scholars of modern and colonial India analyze the family within its stationary regional, linguistic, or sectarian units—the Bengali, Tamil, or Muslim family—within the limits of the nation-state of India. See Mytheli Sreenivas, *Wives, Widows, and Concubines: The Conjugal Family Ideal in Colonial India* (Bloomington: Indiana University Press, 2008); Rochona Majumdar, *Marriage and Modernity: Family Values in Colonial Bengal* (Durham, NC: Duke University Press, 2009).

99. Guha, *Beyond Caste*, 19; Peter B. Evans, Dietrich Rueschemeyer, and Theda Skocpol, eds., *Bringing the State Back In* (Cambridge: Cambridge University Press, 1985). For a reason to not study states, see Daud Ali, *Court Culture and Political Life in Early Medieval India* (Cambridge: Cambridge University Press, 2004), 5–7.

100. Jadunath Sarkar, *History of Aurangzib*, vol. 4, 5. Sarkar also made the analogy "what Gaul was to Julius Caesar as a training ground for the coming contest for empire, the Deccan was to Aurangzib," in *Studies in Mughal India* (London: Longmans, Green, 1920), 36. See also Muzaffar Alam, "The Zamindars and Mughal Power in the Deccan, 1685–1712," *Indian Economic and Social History Review* 11, no. 1 (1974): 89; Satish Chandra, "The Deccan Policy of the Mughals—A Reappraisal," *Indian Historical Review* 4, no. 2 (1978): 334–35 and "Some Considerations on the Religious Policy of Aurangzeb during the Later Part of his Reign," *Proceedings of the Indian History Congress* 47, no. 1 (1986): 369–81; John F. Richards, "Imperial Crisis in the Deccan," *Journal of Asian Studies* 35, no. 2 (February 1976): 238–40; Shireen Moosvi, "The Mughal Empire and the Deccan: Economic Factors and Consequences," *Proceedings of the Indian History Congress* 43 (1982): 365–82; Zakir Hussain, "Aurangzeb's First Viceroyalty of the Deccan: A Reappraisal," *Proceedings of the Indian History Congress* 70 (2009–10): 310–17. Despite overlapping mechanisms of rule, a Mughal-based centricity pervades both regional and imperial historiographies, and much of the story we know, especially of the seventeenth century, is one of Mughal ascendency and Deccan sultanate decline. See Haroon Khan Sherwani, *History of the Qutb Shahi Dynasty* (Delhi: Munshilal Manoharlal, 1974), chapters 6 and 7; John F. Richards, *Mughal Administration in Golkonda* (Oxford: Clarendon Press, 1975): 34–51; D. C. Verma, *History of Bijapur*, 195–213; Richard M. Eaton, *Sufis of Bijapur*, 177–201; J. Sarkar, *History of Aurangzib*, vol. 4, 41–42.

101. Abhishek Kaicker, *The King and the People: Sovereignty and Popular Politics in Mughal Delhi* (New York: Oxford University Press, 2020); Chatterjee, *Negotiating Mughal Law*.

102. Farhat Hasan, *Paper, Performance, and the State: Social Change and Political Culture in Mughal India* (Cambridge: Cambridge University Press, 2021).

103. Ramphal Rana, *Rebels to Rulers: The Rise of Jat Power in Medieval India, c. 1665–1735* (Delhi: Manohar, 2006), 111–18. Several recent studies from other parts of the subcontinent have demonstrated the utility of studying regional-level documentary evidence in tandem with broader imperial patterns. See Farhat Hasan, *State and Locality in Mughal India: Power Relations in Western India, c. 1572–1730* (Cambridge: Cambridge University Press, 2004). Imperial-regional suzerainty also changed the ethnic composition of *zamīndārs* on the eve of colonial rule, as shown by Bernard S. Cohn, "The Initial British Impact on India: A Case Study of the Benares Region," *Journal of Asian Studies* 19, no. 4 (1960): 418–31.

104. Marika Sardar and Navina Haider, *Sultans of Deccan India, 1500–1700: Opulence and Fantasy* (New York: Metropolitan Museum of Art, 2015).
105. Eaton and Wagoner, *Power, Memory, Architecture*, xxi–xxv.
106. Eaton, *India in the Persianate Age*, 1–18.
107. Emma J. Flatt, *The Courts of the Deccan Sultanates*.
108. Roy Fischel, *Local States in an Imperial World: Identity, Society, and Politics in the Early Modern Deccan* (Edinburgh: Edinburgh University Press, 2020).
109. Farhat Hasan, *Paper, Performance, and the State*, 121–31.
110. G. H. Khare, *P.S.I.H.*, vols. 1–3.
111. Prachi Deshpande, *Scripts of Power: Writing, Language Practices and Cultural History in Western India* (Ranikhet: Permanent Black, 2022); Guha, *Beyond Caste*, 117–42; Frank Perlin, "The Pre-Colonial Indian State in History and Epistemology: A Reconstruction of Societal Formation in the Western Deccan from the Fifteenth to the Early Nineteenth Century," in *The Study of the State*, ed. Henri J. Claessen and Peter Skalnik (Berlin: De Gruyter Mouton, 2011), 275–302.
112. Dayal, "Making the 'Mughal' Soldier," 891–93.
113. For north India, the earliest studies focused on court factions in eighteenth-century Delhi and in the south, scholars have examined multiple iterations of ethnic conflicts between Westerners and indigenous factions in the Deccan sultanates across different time periods. See Satish Chandra, *Parties and Politics at the Mughal Court, 1707–1740*, 4th ed. (Delhi: Oxford University Press, 1959); M. Athar Ali, *The Mughal Nobility under Aurangzeb*, rev. ed. (Delhi: Oxford University Press, 2001); Haroon Khan Sherwani, *The Bahmanis of the Deccan* (Delhi: Munshiram Manoharlal, 1985), 151–73; Richard M. Eaton, *Social History of the Deccan 1300–1761: Eight Indian Lives* (Cambridge: Cambridge University Press, 2005), 59–77. More recent evaluations emphasize the continuity of premodern categories (*dakkanī* vs. *gharībān*) with modern religious identities (Hindu vs. Muslim); Kruijtzer, *Xenophobia in Seventeenth-Century India*, 103.
114. For the evolution of this problem of the study of the Mughal state versus the court, see the two introductions by Muzaffar Alam and Sanjay Subrahmanyam, eds., *The Mughal State 1526–1750* (New Delhi: Oxford University, 1998) and *Writing the Mughal World: Studies on Culture and Politics* (New York: Columbia University Press, 2011). See also Sanjay Subrahmanyam, "The Mughal State—Structure or Process? Reflections on Recent Western Historiography," *Indian Economic & Social History Review* 29, no. 3 (1992): 291–321.
115. For reading chronicles against the grain and supplementing them with other types of materials, see Sunil Kumar, "Bandagi and Naukari: Studying Transitions in Political Culture and Service under the North Indian Sultanates, Thirteenth–Sixteenth Centuries," in *After Timur Left*, ed. Orsini and Sheikh, 89–98. For broader comparisons of the chronicle form, see Sholeh A. Quinn, *Persian Historiography across Empires: The Ottomans, Safavids, and Mughals* (Cambridge: Cambridge University Press, 2020), 1–19; Blain S. Auer, *Symbols of Authority in Medieval Islam: History, Religion and Muslim Legitimacy in the Delhi Sultanate* (London: I. B. Tauris, 2012); Ali Anooshahr, *Turkestan and the Rise of Eurasian Empires: A Study of Politics and Invented Traditions* (New York: Oxford University Press, 2018), 1–6; Jyoti Gulati Balachandran, *Narrative Pasts: The Making of a Muslim Community in Gujarat, c. 1400–1650* (New Delhi: Oxford University Press, 2020), 20–24; Sumit Guha, "Empires,

Languages, and Scripts in the Perso-Indian World," *Comparative Studies in Society and History* (2024): 1–27.

116. Green, *The Persianate World*, 4.

117. For earlier periods of South Asia's past, the utility of working across literary and nonliterary archives has most recently been show in the groundbreaking work of Manu V. Devadevan, *The "Early Medieval" Origins of India* (Cambridge: Cambridge University Press, 2020), 1–26.

118. Helen Creese, "Judicial Processes and Legal Authority in Pre-Colonial Bali," *Bijdragen tot de taal-, land- en volkenkunde* 165, no. 4 (2009): 515–50 and "Balinese Babad as Historical Sources: A Reinterpretation of the Fall of Gèlgèl," *Bijdragen tot de Taal-, Land- en Volkenkunde*, 147, nos. 23 (1991): 236–60.

119. Studies of South Asian vernaculars and Persianate literature could benefit by extending the concept of "worldmaking" as elaborated by Ayesha Ramachandran, *The Worldmakers: Global Imagining in Early Modern Europe* (Chicago: University of Chicago Press, 2015), 6–10.

120. On various scholarly positions regarding the intersections of microhistory and global history, see John Paul Ghobrial, "Moving Stories and What They Tell Us: Early Modern Mobility between Microhistory and Global History," supplement, *Past & Present* 242, no. 14 (2019): 243–80 and in the same special volume, "Introduction: Seeing the World Like a Microhistorian," 1–22; Francesca Trivellato, "Is There a Future for Italian Microhistory in the Age of Global History?" *California Italian Studies*, 2, no. 1 (2011); Tonio Andrade, "A Chinese Farmer, Two African Boys, and a Warlord: Toward a Global Microhistory," *Journal of World History* (2010): 573–91. On the relevance of "place-based research" to global history, see Lara Putnam, "The Transnational and the Text-Searchable: Digitized Sources and the Shadows They Cast," *American Historical Review* 121, no. 2 (2016): 397, 401.

121. Allison Busch, *Poetry of Kings: The Classical Hindi Literature of Mughal India* (New York: Oxford University Press, 2011); Orsini and Sheikh, *After Timur Left*, 1–44.

122. Sharma, *Mughal Arcadia*, 10–11.

123. Muhammad Ali Asar, *Adil Shahi daur mein urdu ghazal* (Bangalore: Karnatak Urdu Academy, 2013), 9–14.

124. Purnima Dhavan, *When Sparrows Became Hawks: The Making of the Sikh Warrior Tradition, 1699–1799* (New York: Oxford University Press, 2011), 23–46; Cynthia Talbot, *The Last Hindu Emperor: Prithviraj Chauhan and the Indian Past 1200–2000* (Cambridge: Cambridge University Press, 2015), 29–68; Aparna Kapadia, *In Praise of Kings: Rajputs, Sultans, and Poets in Fifteenth-Century Gujarat* (Cambridge: Cambridge University Press, 2018); Thibaut d'Hubert, *In the Shade of the Golden Palace Ālāol and Middle Bengali Poetics in Arakan* (New York: Oxford University Press, 2018).

125. Shamsur Rahman Faruqi, "A Long History of Urdu Literary Culture, Part I: Naming and Placing a Literary Culture" in *Literary Cultures in History: Reconstructions from South Asia*, ed. Sheldon Pollock (Berkeley: University of California Press, 2003), 819–37.

126. A collaboration between a historian and literary scholar promises to answer some of these questions. See Purnima Dhavan and Heidi Pauwels, "Crafting literary Urdu: Mirza Hatim's Engagement with Vali Dakhani," *Modern Asian Studies* 57, no. 3 (2023): 711–39 as well as their forthcoming work, *Urdu's Origins Revisited: Vali Dakhani and Early Literary Networks in Eighteenth-Century India*.

127. Eaton, *Sufis of Bijapur*, 91–95; Carla Petievich, "The Feminine and Cultural Syncretism," *Annual of Urdu Studies*, 8 (1993): 111; Ali Akbar Hussain, *Scent in the Islamic Garden: A Study of Deccani Urdu Literary Sources* (Karachi: Oxford University Press, 2000), 154.

128. David J. Matthews, "Pem Nem: A 16th Century Dakani Manuscript, A Sixteenth-Century Dakani Manuscript," in *Cairo to Kabul: Afghan and Islamic Studies Presented to Ralph Pinder-Wilson*, ed. Warwick Ball and Leonard Harrow (London: Melisende, 2002), 171.

129. Shamsullah Qadri, *Tārīkh-i zabān- i Urdū: ya'nī Urdū- i Qadīm* (Lucknow: Naval Kishore, 1925); Jamil Jalibi, *Tārīkh- i Adab- i Urdū*, vol. 1 (Delhi: Educational Publishing House, 1977); Mohammed Jamal Shareef, *Dakan main Urdu Shairi Vali se Pehle* (A History of Urdu Poetry before Vali in Deccan), Revised by Dr. Mohd. Ali Asar (Hyderabad: Idara-e-Adabiyat, 2004); Muhiuddin Qadri Zor, *Hindustānī Lisāniyāt* (Hyderabad: Maktabah-yi Ibrahimiya, 1932). Some of this modern historiography of Dakkani has been examined in Kavita Datla, *The Language of Secular Islam: Urdu Nationalism and Colonial India* (Honolulu: University of Hawaii Press, 2013). Future studies could go further by exploring the relationship of this pan-regional vernacular with Persian to examine how its manuscript and literary cultures shaped the evolution of modern Urdu in the eighteenth and nineteenth centuries. Most recently, see Badar Sultana, *Karnātak kī razmīya masnawīyon kā tanqīdī jā'iza* (Bangalore: Karnatak Urdu Academy, 2018) and Oudesh Rani Bawa, *Dakkani zabān-o-adab par dīgar Hindūstānī zabān-o-adab ke asrāt* (Hyderabad: Center for Deccan Studies, 2022).

130. For the argument for "fuzzy" precolonial identities, see Sudipta Kaviraj, *The Imaginary Institution of India: Politics and Ideas* (New York: Columbia University Press, 2010) and Nicholas Dirks, *Castes of Mind: Colonialism and the Making of Modern India* (Princeton, NJ: Princeton University Press, 2001). For "fluid" uses of precolonial identities, see Dirk Kolff, *Naukar, Rajput, and Sepoy: The Ethnohistory of the Military Labour Market of Hindustan, 1450–1850* (Cambridge: Cambridge University Press, 2002), 57–58, 72–73, 169–83, 181–82.

131. David Washbrook, "Progress and Problems: South Asian Economic and Social History c. 1720–1860," *Modern Asian Studies* 22, no. 1 (1988): 57–96 and "Merchants, Markets, and Commerce in Early Modern South India," *Journal of the Economic and Social History of the Orient* 53, nos. 1–2 (2010): 266–89.

2. THE MILITARY BARRACK: IDENTIFYING HOUSEHOLDS, BECOMING MUGHAL

1. The word *chehrah* means countenance or face in Persian. The use of descriptive rolls was not limited to military administration. For instance, in land grant documents in the Batala collection dating from 1527 to 1757 from Panjab, on the front margins and the back, we find multiple *chehreh* alongside signatures and seals recorded on documents generated at the *qāzī's* office. See I.O. Islamic 4720/(28), Batala Collection, British Library, November 8, 1707. A *zamānat nāma* between Shaykh Muhammad and Ghulam Muhammad includes the identifications of those who stood surety (*zāmin*) to the sale of a property. A *siyāha-i-yāddāsht* recorded a *madad ma'āsh* assigned to Shaykh Ni'matullah, son of Shaykh Abdullah recorded a *chehrah* of the grantee. See I.O. Islamic 4720/(29), October 10, 1708.

From the seventy documents in this collection, five include marginal endorsements that have description rolls—I.O. Islamic 4720/(57), I.O. Islamic 4720/(58), I.O. Islamic 4720/(64), Batala Collection, British Library. M. Z. A. Shakeb, *A Descriptive Catalogue of the Batala Collection of Mughal Documents, 1527—1757* (London: India Office Library, 1990), 24–25, 53–54, 59. Also identified with the Arabic word *hilya*, which literally means ornament and refers to the external form or bearing or quality of a person, physical descriptions were recorded at the time of an officer's appointment. See Copy of Memorandum on reinstatement of the *mansab* of Daulat Khan Khokhar, the son of Lashkar Khan, Doc. no. 2. Yusuf H. Khan ed., *Selected Documents of Shah Jahan's Reign* (hereafter *S.D.S.R.*) (Hyderabad: Daftar-i-Diwani, 1950), 4.

2. I thank Brill and in particular Paolo Sartori and James Pickett, editors of a special issue on Islamic Cultures of Documentation, for allowing me to modify a prior contribution, "Making the 'Mughal' Soldier: Ethnicity, Identification, and Documentary Culture in Southern India, c. 1600–1700, *Journal of the Economic and Social History of the Orient*, 62 (2019): 856–924. All rights reserved. Republished by permission of the publisher.

3. James Pickett and Paolo Sartori, "From the Archetypical Archive to Cultures of Documentation," 773–98; James Daybell, *The Material Letter in Early Modern England: Manuscript Letters and the Culture and Practices of Letter-Writing 1512-1635* (Houndmills, Basingstoke: Palgrave Macmillan, 2012); Flood, *Objects of Translation*, 9–12. For the study of materiality in regional socioreligious contexts of early modern South Asia, see Tyler Williams, "If the Whole World Were Paper . . .": A History of Writing in the North Indian Vernacular," *History and Theory* 57, no. 4 (2018): 81–101.

4. For a critique that urges abandoning identity altogether and turns, instead, to the material processes that made identification possible, see Valentin Groebner, *Who Are You? Identification and Surveillance in Early Modern Europe*, (New York: Zone Books, 2007): 2–24.

5. In the case of the Ming-Qing transition, Crossley, Siu, and Sutton ask what mechanisms early modern conquest elites used to foster a theoretical distinction between themselves and the spaces and objects of conquest, see *Empire at the Margins*, 1–26.

6. These terms are often used interchangeably in the following works: Chandra, *Parties and Politics at the Mughal Court 1707-1740*, 17; Joshi and Sherwani, *History of the Medieval Deccan*, vol. 1, 350, 357; S. Inayat Ali Zaidi, "Ordinary Kachawaha Troopers Serving the Mughal Empire: Composition and Structure of the Contingents of the Kachawaha Nobles," *Studies in History* 2: (1980): 57–68 and "Fads and Foibles: Perception of Administrative Traits of the Mughal state," *Indian Historical Review* 29, nos. 1–2, (2002): 96–99; Athar Ali, *The Mughal Nobility under Aurangzeb*; Rafi Ahmad Alavi, *Studies in the History of Medieval Deccan* (Delhi: Idarah-i Adabiyat-i Delli, 1977) and "New Light of Mughal Cavalry," *Proceedings of the Indian History Congress* 31 (1969): 272–87.

7. Ghauri, "Organization of the Army under the Sultanates of the Deccan," 147, 149.

8. On the distinction between institutional mechanisms versus institutions and using regional archival assemblages of Islamic empires, see Konrad Hirschler, "From Archive to Archival Practices: Rethinking the Preservation of Mamluk Administrative Documents," *Journal of the American Oriental Society* 136, no. 1 (January–March 2016): 27; Jurgen Paul, "Archival Practices in the Muslim World Prior to 1500," in *Manuscripts and Archives: Comparative Views on Record-Keeping*, ed. A. Bausi et al. (Berlin: de Gruyter, 2018), 347.

Both Paul and Hirschler make distinctions between five different social sites where documents were generated and preserved. Writing practices on administrative documents that recorded everyday state transactions were at times distinct from but also overlapped with legal documents generated in the office of the *qāzī*.

9. Although far removed from Mughal *ʿarz-o-chehrah*, the current misgivings over the creation of the world's largest biometric scheme—the Unique Identification Authority of India—which requires citizens to acquire an Aadhaar (Foundations) card to avail state-run welfare services, has opened up questions not just about the way users' data can be (mis)used but also about the politics of producing and copying such an identification. In addition to the innumerable complaints about the computers and biometric machines not working, the Aadhaar card's most intriguing criticism is that it has no concept of an "original," for it does not contain a signature or hologram, users are free to print as many copies of an Aadhaar card, as each one can be considered "original." See St Hill, "Privacy, Security and Legality Are Not the Only Problems with Aadhaar: Here Are Four More," *Scroll.in*, March 23, 2017, https://scroll.in/article/832595/privacy-security-and-egality-are-not-the-only-serious-problems-with-aadhaar-here-are-four-more.

10. For two iconic examples, see Kaviraj, *The Imaginary Institution of India* and Dirks, *Castes of Mind*.

11. William Irvine, *The Army of the Indian Moghuls* (Delhi: Eurasia, 1962); Jagadish Narayan Sarkar, *Mughal Polity* (Delhi: Idarah-i Adabiyat-i Delli, 1984); Dirk H. A. Kolff, *Naukar, Rajput, and Sepoy*; Jos Gommans, *Mughal Warfare: Indian Frontiers and High Roads to Empire, 1500–1700* (London: Routledge, 2002); Iqtidar Alam Khan, *Gunpowder and Firearms: Warfare in Medieval India* (New Delhi: Oxford University Press, 2004); Pratyay Nath, *Climate of Conquest: War, Environment, and Empire in Mughal North India* (New Delhi: Oxford University Press, 2019).

12. For the definitions and limits of south-central India or the Deccan region, see P. M. Joshi, "Historical Geography of the Medieval Deccan," in *History of Medieval Deccan*, vol. 1, *1295–1724* (Hyderabad: Government of Andhra Pradesh, 1973), 1–28; Hakim Atishi, *ʿĀdilnāma*, Ms. P. 4300, Telangana State Archaeological Museum, Hyderabad, India, fol. 131, fol. 87.

13. As shown in studies of portraiture and art, Mughal rulers had a keen interest in connecting physiognomy to human character. See Annemarie Schimmel, *The Empire of the Great Mughals: History, Art and Culture* (London: Reaktion Books, 2004), 274; Sanjay Subrahmanyam, "A Roomful of Mirrors: The Artful Embrace of Mughals and Franks, 1550–1700," *Ars Orientalis*, 39 (2010): 39–83.

14. Nur Sobers-Khan, *Slaves without Shackles: Forced Labour and Manumission in the Galata Court Registers, 1560–1572* (Berlin: Klaus Schwarz Verlag, 2014), 106–7, 240–44. See also Pablo E. Pérez-Mallaína, *Spain's Men of the Sea: Daily Life on the Indies Fleets in the Sixteenth Century*, trans. C. R. Phillips (Baltimore: Johns Hopkins University Press, 1998), 49–62; Nancy E. van Deusen, *Global Indios: The Indigenous Struggle for Justice in Sixteenth-Century Spain* (Durham, NC: Duke University Press, 2015), 169–91.

15. The highest ranks among the *khassa mansabdār* in this sample of musters were Doc. Acc. 118-1765, *ʿarz-o-chehrah*, November 28, 1647, ʿAbdullah, son of Burhan ul-mulk, *shirāzī*, 300/100. Doc. Acc. 122-1768, December 6, 1647, Ibrahim, son of Burhan-ul-mulk, *shirāzī*, 200/70. Doc. Acc. 150-418, *ʿarz-o-chehrah*, March 28, 1648, name illegible, son of Bahadur Beg, no identification given, 250/120.

16. M. Athar Ali, *The Apparatus of Empire: Awards of Ranks, Offices and Titles to the Mughal Nobility (1574—1658)* (New Delhi: Oxford University Press, 1985); *The Mughal Nobility under Aurangzeb.*

17. Evyn Kropf and Cathleen. A. Baker, "A Conservative Tradition? Arab Papers of the 12th-17th Centuries from the Islamic Manuscripts Collection at the University of Michigan," *Journal of Islamic Manuscripts* 4 (2013): 4-7. The paper used for Mughal administrative documents was probably locally produced around the areas near the provincial centers in south-central India of Burhanpur, Daulatabad, and Aurangabad, which were also sites of extensive cotton processing and textile production. Even today, textile merchants in the city of Burhanpur are also owners of small paper mills in the region. See B. G. Gokhale, "Burhanpur: Notes on the History of an Indian city in the XVIIth century," *Journal of the Economic and Social History of the Orient* 15, no. 3 (December 1972): 320.

18. Irvine, *The Army of the Indian Moghuls*, 46. Here Irvine is referring to the forces sent in 1739 by the governor of Awadh, Burhan-ul-mulk for the Battle of Karnal with Afsharid ruler, Nadir Shah.

19. Irvine, *The Army of the Indian Moghuls*, 45.

20. Marina Rustow, *The Lost Archive: Traces of a Caliphate in a Cairo Synagogue* (Princeton, NJ: Princeton University Press, 2020), 381-85.

21. Irvine, *The Army of the Indian Moghuls*, 49-50.

22. Iqtidar Alam Khan, "The Matchlock Musket in the Mughal Empire: An instrument of Centralization," *Proceedings of the Indian History Congress* 59 (1998): 350-51.

23. Nand Ram Mukhlis, *Siyāqnāma* (Lucknow: Nawal Kishore, 1879). Like people, animals were further divided into *zāt* or types of different breeds, sometimes associated with regions of origin. Bulls or *nargāo*, for instance, could be *gujarātī, nāgaurī, kehrahdeh*, or *harīnī*. See Mukhlis, *Siyāqnāma*, 151. On this author and similar manuals, see Muzaffar Alam and Sanjay Subrahmanyam, "The Making of a Munshi," *Comparative Studies of South Asia, Africa, and the Middle East* 24, no. 2 (2004): 61-72 and Najaf Haider, "Norms of Professional Excellence and Good Conduct in Accountancy Manuals of the Mughal Empire," *International Review of Social History* 56, no. S19 (2011): 263-74.

24. Mukhlis, *Siyāqnāma*, 147.

25. Ibid., 149.

26. Zaidi, "Fads and Foibles," 91, 98; Alavi, "New Light on Mughal Cavalry": 274; Irvine, *The Army of the Indian Moghuls*, 54-55; J. N. Sarkar, *Mughal Polity*, 340.

27. Doc. 3, *parwancha* or royal order, May 19, 1635, S.D.S.R, 6, 19. Doc. 142, *yāddāsht* or memorandum, Undated, S.D.S.R, 248-49.

28. Doc. 5, November 30, 1635, *parwancha* or royal order, S.D.S.R, 21-22. Doc. 142, undated *yāddāsht* or memorandum, undated, S.D.S.R, 248-49. The latter document cites a *mahzar* (a written collective attestation), which stipulated that an owner was liable to return maintenance money to the state if the horse died. For a recent exploration of the evolution of *mahzar-namas* in Mughal India and the British empire, see Nandini Chatterjee, "*Mahzar-namas* in the Mughal and British Empires: The Uses of an Indo-Islamic Legal Form," *Comparative Studies in Society and History* 58, no. 2 (2016): 379-406.

29. Doc. Acc. VI/40 *dastak*, April 2, 1664, Firoz Tahir, *bakshī* accompanies the army of Namdar Khan to brand the horses of Sayyid Dost Muhammad, son of Sayyid Abdur Rasul, 60 *zāt*. Doc. Acc. VI/34 *Dastak*, April 1, 1664, Docs. Acc. VI/49/59/62/127/129/135/149/152, Mughal Record Room, TSA, Hyderabad, India.

30. Shakeb, *Mughal Archives*, 353. The word *amīn* literary meaning trustee, an imperial officer who checked revenue collections.

31. Doc. Acc. VI/24 *dāgh nāma*, March 28, 1664. Branding certificate of horses of Mir Muhammad Shafi, son of Mir Ali under the supervision of Mir Muhammad Ghazi, *dārogha*, Mir Muhammad Masum, *amīn*, and Dongarmal, *mushrif*. Doc. Acc. VI/155, May 7, 1664, *yāddāsht-i tashīhah-i aspān*. Docs. Acc. VI/2275/2276/2278/2279/2280/2281/2293, December 1, 1663, Mughal Record Room, TSA.

32. Doc. Acc. VI/ 155/156/210/223/224/225/226/227/228, with seal of *mushrif*, Dongarmal, Mughal Record Room, TSA, Hyderabad, India.

33. Doc. Acc. VI/ 1280 *saqtī nāma*, October 15, 1663, death certificate of the horse of Inayat Khan, son of Qutb Khan, *tābinān* of Sayyid Zain ul-abidin Bukhari; died on 26 Safar, 1073. Doc. Acc. VI/1299 *saqtī nāma*, October 21, 1663. Doc. Acc. VI/1261 *saqtī nāma*, October 9, 1663. Doc. Acc. VI/1172 *saqtī nāma*, October 3, 1663.

34. See Doc. Acc. 3076 *fihrist-i mullāzimān-i khalāyaq panāh* or Roll of Imperial Servants. Commentary on the back, written diagonally, records the endorsements of Shah Nawaz Khan and Prince Murad Baksh on different dates.

35. On Ottoman registers, see Guy Burak, "Evidentiary Truth Claims, Imperial Registers, and the Ottoman Archive: Contending Legal Views of Archival and Record-keeping Practices in Ottoman Greater Syria (Seventeenth–Nineteenth Centuries)," *Bulletin of the School of Oriental and African Studies* 79, no. 2 (2016): 233–54.

36. Doc. Acc. 3035, 3076, and 3128, Rolls of Imperial Servants at the military station (*thānajāt*), Burhanpur in Khandesh *sūba* in Payan Ghat. Doc. no. 75, *S.D.S.R.*, 164–65.

37. Doc. Acc. 3076.

38. For two different translations see Shakeb, *Mughal Archives*, 318; Khan, *S.D.S.R.* Doc. no. 23, 63.

39. Doc. Acc. no. 269, '*arz-o-chehreh*, *khassa mansabdār*, Nizam Beg, son of Burj 'Ali, *turkmān*, November 11, 1642.

40. See Doc. 135, *yāddāsht*, undated, *S.D.S.R.*, 242–43.

41. Alavi, *Studies in the history of Medieval Deccan*, 21–23.

42. Shakeb, Doc. Acc. no. 4572, *Mughal Archives*, 321.

43. Ibid.

44. Moosvi, "The Mughal Empire and the Deccan," 374.

45. Flynn, letter 65, 239–40. Opposing directives from Delhi to reduce the pay of *mansabdārs*, Prince Aurangzeb, who served as viceroy of the Deccan twice between 1636 and 1658, expressed dismay that protocol was not being followed: "most of them have still neither brought in their horses for branding, nor mustered their men; so (already) on account of their inability to comply with the (old orders upon) branding and muster, large amounts of arrears have been entered (as outstanding) in the registers of this province against every man."

46. Niccolò Manuzzi, *Storia do Mogor or Mogul India 1653–1708*, trans. William Irvine (London: John Murray, 1907), 1: 449–50.

47. Francis Joseph Steingass, *A Comprehensive Persian-English Dictionary, Including the Arabic Words and Phrases to Be Met with in Persian Literature* (London: Routledge & K. Paul, 1892), 995.

48. See the critique of this debate in the book's introduction, 24–25.

49. Sneath, *The Headless State*, 39–64, 181–204. For an application of this critique to Turani aristocratic orders in early Mughal India, see Anooshahr, "Mughals, Mongols, and Mongrels," 559–77; Gommans, "The Warband in the Making of Eurasian Empires," 316–20, 324–25, 335–36; Gommans, *The Rise of the Indo-Afghan Empire*; Guha, *Beyond Caste*, 73–74.

50. Faruqui, *The Princes of the Mughal Empire*, 146–47; Lisa Balabanlilar, "The Begims of the Mystic Feast: Turco-Mongol Tradition in the Mughal Harem," *Journal of Asian Studies* 69, no. 1 (February 2010): 138–39.

51. For the argument for "fuzzy" precolonial identities, see Kaviraj, *The Imaginary Institution of India* and Dirks, *Castes of Mind*. For "fluid" uses of precolonial identities, see Dirk Kolff, *Naukar, Rajput, and Sepoy*, 57–58, 72–73, 169–83, 181–82.

52. Athar Ali, *The Apparatus of the Mughal Empire*, 104, 122, 131, 134–36, 138–40, 142, 158–63, 171–74, 178–80, 183–84, 186–88, 191–92, 195–98, 203–4, 208–10, 229–31, 234–35, 240–54, 256–58, 262–63, 268–69, 274–77, 282–84, 288–91, 297–300, 319–20. See also Alavi, *Studies in the History of Medieval Deccan*.

53. Athar Ali, *The Apparatus of Empire*, xx–xxi; *The Mughal Nobility under Aurangzeb*, 7–37; Alavi, *Studies in the History of Medieval Deccan*, 20–62.

54. These identification changes in the wake of Mughal expansion are similar to how old and new clan affinities broke down as a result of Mongol rule. Noelle-Karimi has observed this pattern in Khurasan, where commanders also did not share common background with their troops. See Christine Noelle-Karimi, *The Pearl in its Midst: Herat and the Mapping of Khurasan (15th–19th centuries)* (Vienna: Verlag der Österreichischen Akademie der Wissenschaften, 2014): 69–70.

55. Alavi, *Studies in the History of Medieval Deccan*, 21.

56. Ghauri, "Organization of the Bijapur Army," 159–60.

57. Chandra, *Parties and Politics at the Mughal Court*, 16.

58. Yusuf H. Khan, *Selected Documents of Aurangzeb's Reign, 1659–1706* (Hyderabad, Deccan: Central Records Office, Government of Andhra Pradesh, 1958), 64; cf. Athar Ali, *The Mughal Nobility under Aurangzeb*, 26, 28.

59. Doc. Acc. 1086-1373 *arz-o-chehrah, tābinān-i Maloji Bhonsle*, Kayyaji, son of Ranguji, *rājpūt chauhān dakkanī*, April 6, 1647, and Doc. Acc. 1159-1578 *arz-o-chehrah, tābinān-i Maloji Bhonsle*, Temaji, son of Kanhaiyaji, *rājpūt chauhān dakkanī*, June 18, 1647.

60. Guha, *Beyond Caste*, 187–88.

61. Richard M. Eaton, "The Rise and Fall of Military Slavery in the Deccan 1450–1650," in *Slavery and South Asian History*, ed. Indrani Chatterjee and Richard M. Eaton (Bloomington: Indiana University Press, 2006), 115–36.

62. Doc. Acc. 579-804 *arz-o-chehrah, tābinān-i Habash Khan*, Mansur, son of Habash, *rājpūt dakkanī*, May 25, 1646. Doc. Acc. 583-808 *arz-o-chehra-i, tābinān-i Habash Khan*, Daulat, son of Habash, *rājpūt dakkanī*, May 25, 1646.

63. K. C. Malhotra and M. Gadgil, "The Ecological Basis of the Geographical Distribution of the Dhangars: A Pastoral Caste-Cluster of Maharashtra," *South Asian Anthropologist* 2, no. 2 (1981): 49–50.

64. Doc. Acc. 1402-345, name illegible, *rājpūt dakkanī*, July 18, 1643, and Doc. Acc. 1410-2966, Likmuji, son of Maloji, *rājpūt dakkanī*, November 1, 1649.

65. Docs. Acc. 1085-1237 *arz-o-chehrah, tābinān-i Maloji Bhonsle*, dates of branding from 1641 to 1651.

66. Docs. Acc. 2237-2257 'arz-o-chehrah barqandāzān-i-hindustān hazārī ghanshām, ca. 1646–48. The seven non-Rajputs included the following, Doc. Acc. 2240-1092, Hasan, son of Musa, quraishī, September 21, 1646, Doc. Acc. 2288-1146, Alawal, quraishī, October 1, 1646, Doc. Acc. 2297-1155, Sheru, son of Budhan, shaykhzada, Doc. Acc. 2309-1189, Damodar, son of Manik, rājput zunnārdār, October 31, 1646, Doc. Acc. 2323-1367, Mira, son of Jauhar, behlam, March 31, 1647, Doc. Acc. 2349-1823, Chand, son of Feroz, behlam, January 21, 1648, Doc. Acc. 2357-3432, Mahmud, son of Lal, ghorī, January 31, 1648. See also Iqtidar Alam Khan, "The Matchlock Musket in the Mughal Empire," 358n60. Khan cites Doc. 72 in *S.D.S.R*, 160–61 and Irvine, *The Army of the Indian Moghuls*, 168. The same was true for the barqandāzan of the mansabdār Sayyidi Hari Ram (Docs. Acc. 2375–2381) and Hiraman (Docs. Acc. 2358-2365), most of whom were also Baksari Rajputs.

67. Doc. 131, *S.D.S.R.*, 234.

68. Athar Ali, *The Mughal Nobility under Aurangzeb*, 30–31; Alavi, *Studies in the History of Medieval Deccan*, 24–25.

69. Cynthia Talbot, *The Last Hindu Emperor*, 68. Talbot has shown that by the fifteenth century, Chauhan was an amorphous and capacious new social identity with a claim to warrior status.

70. Doc. Acc. 204-450, 'arz-o-chehrah, tābinān-i 'Abdullah, Shaykh Ismail, son of Shaykh 'Abdullah, rajpūt-i kurd, March 8, 1644. Doc. Acc. 2309-1189, 'arz-o-chehrah, barqadāzān-i Hazari Ghansham, Damodar, son of Manik, rājpūt zunnārdār, October 31, 1646. The latter may refer to Bhumihar Rajputs, from eastern Uttar Pradesh and Bihar, who also claim Brahmin descent. My thanks to Purnima Dhavan for suggesting this possibility.

71. Doc. Acc. 981-2027, 'arz-o-chehrah, tābinān-i Kar Talab Khan, Dawood, son of Kalu, rājpūt chauhān, March 14, 1648. Doc. Acc. 983-2029 'arz-o-chehrah, tābinān-i Kar Talab Khan, Chand Muhammad, son of Noor Muhammad, rājpūt chauhān, March 14, 1648. Doc. Acc. 2048-869, 'arz-o-chehrah, tābinān-i Udeji Ram, Osman, son of Ismail, rājpūt chauhān, June 7, 1646. Doc. Acc. 548-559, 'arz-o-chehrah, tābinān-i Darya Gurzani, Yusuf, son of Taj, rājpūt chauhān, November 2, 1644, Doc. Acc. 549-560, 'arz-o-chehrah, tābinān-i Darya Gurzani, Nisar, son of Asad, rājpūt chauhān, November 2, 1644.

72. Doc. Acc. 932-1830, 'arz-o-chehrah, tābinān-i Kar Talab Khan, Qasim, son of Chand, rājpūt, January 23, 1648. Doc. Acc. 915-3192, 'arz-o-chehrah, tābinān-i Jadon Rai, Junaid, son of Shams, rājpūt, January 26, 1650. Doc. Acc. 1506-2611, 'arz-o-chehrah, tābinān-i Qazafi Khan, Dost Muhammad, rājpūt kachwaha, March 13, 1649. Doc. Acc. 930-3173, 'arz-o-chehrah, tābinān-i Jadon Rai, Haibat, son of Bazid, rājpūt, undated. See Doc. Acc. no. 35-669, 'arz-o-chehrah, khassa mansabdār, Malik Ahmad, son of Malik Daulat, son of Malik Zainuddin, of the qaum rājpūt solankī, December 17, 1645. On present-day meanings of caste among South Asian Muslims, see Pervaiz Nazir, "Social Structure, Ideology, and Language: Caste among Muslims," *Economic and Political Weekly* 28, no. 52 (December 1993): 2897–900.

73. The term qaum, according to Lane's *Arabic Lexicon* (ca. 1863), meant "a people or body of persons composing a community, a company or body, part of men without women, or of men and women together." *Lughatnamah Dehkhoda* also notes that qaum refers to men and women together or just a group of men, as well the terms kasān (people) and words connoting relatedness, khweshān or relations. The Persian-Urdu *Lughāt-i Kishorī* (ca. 1904) defines qaum simply as a group of men, or gurūh ādmīyon kā. The term in

musters simply means from the group and was usually indicated along with a chief's name. See Doc. Acc. VI/1218, ʿarz-o-chehrah, Dharamdas, son of Puranshah, from the jamāʿat of Meghraj, bundela-i undcha, October 9, 1663. Doc. Acc. VI/1234, ʿarz-o-chehrah Sawam, son of Ghatam, son of Pratap, from the jamāʿat of Lalman, rājpūt-i baksar, October 9, 1663. Doc. Acc. VI/1245, ʿarz-o-chehrah, Bhiknari, son of Chichak, son of Ghansi, from the jamāʿat of Dharamdas, October 9, 1663.

74. John E. Woods, *The Aqquyunlu: Clan, Confederation, Empire* (Salt Lake City: University of Utah Press, 1999), 16–18; Sanjay Subrahmanyam, "Early Modern Circulation and the Question of ʿPatriotism' between Central Asia and India," in *Writing Travel in Central Asian History*, ed. Nile Green (Bloomington, IN: Indiana University Press, 2014), 43–68; Anooshahr, "Mughals, Mongols, and Mongrels."

75. Doc. Acc. 2193-2258, ʿarz-o-chehrah, tābinān-i Uzbek Khan, illegible, son of Shah ʿAli, sadat bukhārī, July 5, 1648. Doc. Acc. 355-1387, ʿarz-o-chehrah-i khassa mansabdār, Sayyid Jamal, son of Sayyid Mustafa, sadat bukharī, April 7, 1646. Doc. 119-710, ʿarz-o-chehrah, khassa mansabdār, Sayyid Babu, son of Sayyid Khanji, sadat bukhārī, December 6, 1647. Doc. Acc. 874-3070 ʿarz-o-chehrah, tābinān-i ʿIzzat Khan, Lutfullah Beg, son of Mir Badar, arab bukhārī, December 8, 1649. See also T. Barfield, *The Central Asian Arabs of Afghanistan: Pastoral Nomadism in Transition* (Austin: University of Texas Press, 1981), 8–14.

76. A dynast-centered definition of "Mughal" does not account for the word's variable uses and evolution over time and throughout regions. Thus, its use for classifying ahshām or the lowest level of military personnel disturbed the colonial historian, William Irvine, who noted, "*Mughal*: As to these men I can suggest no reason for their appearance in this list of men serving in the infantry, but it is curious to find that they were any Mughals who would deign to serve in this inferior branch of the service" (*The Army of the Indian Moghuls*, 172).

77. Simon Digby, *Sufis and Soldiers in Awrangzeb's Deccan: Malfuzāt-i Naqshbandiyya* (New Delhi: Oxford University Press, 2001), 7–8.

78. Ibid., 135, 177, 270.

79. The term *pathān* used in India to refer to Afghans does not appear at all in this early seventeenth-century muster sample.

80. Doc. Acc. 1435-1446, ʿarz-o-chehrah, tābinān-i Usman Khan Rohilla, April 7, 1646, to May 17, 1648, afghān khalil, afghān. From the two exceptions, one muster has no identification label and the other is of a kāyasth soldier, Doc. 1435-744, ʿarz-o-chehrah, tābinān-i Usman Khan Rohilla, Shankar Das, son of Paras Ram, kāyasth, April 7, 1646.

81. Doc. Acc. 385-504, ʿarz-o-chehrah, tābinān-i Asadullah, June 12, 1646, to November 8, 1649. The range of labels include Afghan, Afghan-i Niyazi, Afghan-i Afridi, Afghan Khalil, Afghan-i Gandhari, Afghan-i Qandhari, Afghan-i Sur, Bhatti, Lodi.

82. Iqbal Husain, "Patterns of Afghan Settlement in India in the 17th Century," *Proceedings of the Indian History Congress* 39, no. 1 (1978): 329–31.

83. In Sayyid Tasadduq Husayn Rizvi's *Lughāt-i Kishorī*, compiled ca. 1907, qabīla is defined as a group from which all people are from the offspring of one father (*woh jamāʿat jis mein sab log ek bāp kī aulād se hon*). The term *tāiʾfa* is defined both as group of men but also as *kisī chīz kā ek tukda*, meaning one part of any object.

84. This purported ancestor Qays was converted to Islam by the Prophet and later fought battles with him in Mecca before returning to what is today the region of Afghanistan. See Nile Green, *Making Space: Sufis and Settlers in Early Modern India* (New Delhi:

Oxford University Press, 2012), 108–9, for an examination of Ni'mat Allah ibn Habib Allah Harawi's *Tārīkh-i khān jahānī wa makhzān-i-afghānī* and its long afterlife in shaping Afghan histories in later centuries. Distinct lineages constitute larger clans (*-khel*), which are further categorized into four broad confederations. See Thomas Barfield, *Afghanistan: A Cultural and Political History* (Princeton, NJ: Princeton University Press, 2010), 24–25.

85. Ibid., 26.

86. Doc. Acc. 1242-2973 '*arz-o-chehra-i tābinān Miyan Dad*, Alwar, son of Sajawal, *afghān-i turkī*, November 1, 1649. Doc. Acc. 54-838, '*arz-o-chehra-i khassa mansabdār*, Jujhar, son of Bahadur, son of Sher, *afghan-i turkī*, June 2, 1646. Doc. 71-1168, '*arz-o-chehra-i khassa mansabdār*, Hatim, son of Rustam, October 18, 1646.

87. Abraham Rosman and Paula G. Rubel, "Nomad-Sedentary Interethnic Relations in Iran and Afghanistan," *International Journal of Middle East Studies* 7, no. 4 (1976): 550; D. Balland, "Bakhtiari of Afghanistan," in *Encyclopedia Iranica* 3 (1988); Richard Tapper, "Who Are the Kuchi? Nomad Self-Identities in Afghanistan," *Journal of the Royal Anthropological Institute* 14, no. 1 (2008): 101.

88. Sumit Guha, "Serving the Barbarian to Preserve the Dharma: The Ideology and Training of a Clerical Elite in Peninsular India c. 1300–1800," *Indian Economic & Social History Review* 47, no. 4 (2010): 509–10. Guha has shown that learning technical skills was limited to members of close-knit communities of low-level scribes, who learnt established documentary conventions and writing strategies through everyday interactions with their peers within institutions.

89. Doc. Acc. VI/1074 *yāddāsht-i tashīha-i aspān*, Mir Muhammad Masum, *darogha* and *amīn*, and Biharidas, *mushrif*, September 24, 1663. Doc. Acc. VI/1076 *yāddāsht-i tashīha*. Dawud Qalich, *bakshī* and *wāqi'a nawīs* of Baglana *sūba*. Doc. Acc. VI/1077 Mir Muhammad Ghazi, *darogha*, Mir Muhammad Amin, *amīn*, Dongarmal, *mushrif*. Doc. Acc. VI/1291 *yāddāsht-i tashīha*, Muhammad Riza, *bakshī* and *darogha*, Keshudas, *amīn*, Shirandas, *mushrif*, October 20, 1663. For names of *wāqi'a nawīs*, see Shakeb, *Mughal Archives*, 58, 64–66, 71–72, 171, 186–188, 197–198, 202, 207, 230–233, 305.

90. We find a sizable number of *kāyasth* soldiers (total of 41 muster rolls) serving in the imperial army, but it is not clear if they fulfilled any scribal function in military administration. Doc. Acc. 206-405, '*arz-o-chehrah, tābinān-i 'Abdullah*, Gobind Das, son of Bhoj Raj, *kāyasth*, July 6, 1645. Doc. Acc. 207-681, '*arz-o-chehrah, tābinān-i 'Abdullah*, Sant Lal, son of Mohan Das, *kāyasth*, December 28, 1647. Doc. Acc. 360-1392 '*arz-o-chehrah, tābinān-i Aman Beg*, Mukand Ram, son of Kapoor Chand, *kāyasth*, April 7, 1646. Doc Acc. 530-2466, '*arz-o-chehrah, tābinān-i Darwesh Beg*, Himmat Singh, son of Roop Sagat Das, *kāyasth*, October 26, 1648. Doc. Acc. 959-1907, '*arz-o-chehrah, tābinān-i Kar Talab Khan*, Rao Paras Ram, son of Ravant Bhim Karan, *kāyasth*, February 8, 1648.

91. Sumit Guha, *Environment and Ethnicity in India 1200—1991* (Cambridge: Cambridge University Press, 1999), 86; Guha, "Serving the Barbarian to Preserve the *Dharma*," 507.

92. For a recent overview of Mughal historiography, see Alam and Subrahmanyam, *Writing the Mughal World: Studies on Culture and Politics*, 1–32.

93. Following Athar Ali, John Richards broke down the Mughal nobility into the following divisions, "*sunnī* Muslim, Turkish-speaking 'Turanis' from Central Asia . . . *sunnī* Muslim, Persian, or Pashto-speaking Afghans, *sunnī* Muslim, Persian-speaking 'Shaikhzādas' or long-domiciled Indian Muslims, and *shi'i* Muslim, Persian-speaking 'Iranis' . . . Hindu,

old Rajasthani-speaking *Rājpūt* nobles . . . and Hindu, Marathi-speaking Maratha chiefs." See John F. Richards, "Norms of Comportment among Mughal Imperial Officers," in *Moral Conduct and Authority: The Place of Adab in South Asian Islam*, ed. B. D. Metcalf (Berkeley: University of California Press, 1984), 257.

94. Nair, "Beyond Exceptionalism," 324–25.

95. See Sherwani, *History of the Qutb Shahi Dynasty*, chaps. 6 and 7; Richards, *Mughal Administration in Golkonda*, 34–51; Verma, *History of Bijapur*, 195–213; Eaton, *Sufis of Bijapur*, 177–201; J. Sarkar, *History of Aurangzeb*, vol. 4, 41–42.

96. Alam and Subrahmanyam, "The Deccan Frontier and Mughal Expansion, ca. 1600," 370–71, 382–83.

97. Iftikhar A. Ghauri, "Central Structure of the Kingdom of Bijapur," *Journal of the Pakistan Historical Society* 18, no. 2 (1970): 88–109 and "Organization of the Army under the Sultanates of the Deccan," 147–71.

98. Fukazawa, *The Medieval Deccan*, 15, 17, 31.

99. Ghauri, "Organization of the Army," 148–150.

100. Faruqui, *The Princes of the Mughal Empire*, 1–23.

101. P. M. Joshi, "The Kingdom of Bijapur" (PhD diss., School of Oriental and African Studies, 1935), 352; Ghauri, "Organization of the Army," 151, 158. Ghauri noted "the famous institution of branding the horses and mustering the soldiers according to their descriptive rolls—a prominent feature of the *mansabdārī* system—does not seem to be a characteristic feature of the Deccan army organization."

102. *Hadīqat*, 111.

103. Ibid., 114–16.

104. M. Ibrahim al-Zubayri, *Tārīkh-i Bījāpūr musamma bi-basātīn al-salātīn* (Hyderabad, ca. 1800s) (hereinafter *Basātīn*): 348–60. Zubayri's *Basātīn* is a much later source, portions of which are copied from earlier chronicles—namely, Zuhur's *Muhammadnāma*, Ms. 26, Bijapur State Archaeological Museum and Abu'l-Qasim al-Husayni's *Guldasta-i gulshan-i rāz dar ta'rīf-i sultān Muhammad 'Ādil Shāh*, Ms. H17 (13), Cambridge University Library, Cambridge, United Kingdom.

105. To my knowledge, no musters have survived from the Deccan sultanates. There is one document, published in Khan's *Selected Documents of Shah Jahan's Reign*, possibly from Golkonda, which provides the salaries and occupations of selected military followers and laborers in the royal army (*khassa khayl*). See a partial translation of this document in Ghauri, "Organization of the Army," 153–57. For Persian transcription, see *S.D.S.R.*, 229–37.

106. *Basātīn*, 356.

107. Atishi, *'Ādilnāma*, fols. 87–88. In one portrait of Bijapur's short-lived alliance with the Mughals to overrun neighboring Ahmadnagar, Atishi recounted how before regional armies set out for battle, Bijapur sultan Muhammad 'Adil Shah instructed his ministers to report back their troop counts to the court.

108. Constantly at odds with regional elites in his court, Sultan Muhammad 'Adil Shah of Bijapur took several other measures to increase direct supervision of forts and military outposts. These changes are also visible in the documentary conventions of seventeenth-century sultanate documents, which began to emulate Mughal documentary salutations and openings. See letters and *farmāns* of Muhammad 'Adil Shah, in Khare's *P.S.I.H.*, vol. 4, 33–34, vol. 2, 1–35.

109. Archivo Histórico de Potosí (AHP) Cajas Reales 203A. My thanks to Kris Lane for sharing materials from Potosí, and for indulging the muster nerd in me.

110. Doc. Acc. no. 35-669, *arz-o-chehrah, khassa mansabdār*, Malik Ahmad, son of Malik Daulat, son of Malik Zainuddin, of the *qaum rājpūt solankī*, December 17, 1645.

111. Kris Lane, *Potosí: The Silver City that Changed the World* (Oakland: University of California, Press, 2019), 92–117.

112. Lane, *Potosí*, 113–15; Bernd Hausberger, "Paisanos, soldados y bandidos: la guerra entre los vicuñas y los vascongados en Potosí (1622–1625)," *Los buenos, los malos y los feos. Poder y Resistencia en América Latina, Publicaciones del Instituto Ibero-Americano e Iberoamericana Vervuert*, Berlín-Madrid 102 (2005): 283–308.

113. Flynn, Letter 65, 239–40. Opposing directives from Delhi to reduce the pay of *mansabdārs*, Prince Aurangzeb, who served as viceroy of the Deccan twice between 1636 and 1658 and later as emperor between 1682 and 1707, expressed dismay that protocol was not being followed: "most of them have still neither brought in their horses for branding, nor mustered their men; so [already] on account of their inability to comply with the [old orders of] branding and muster, large amounts of arrears have been entered [as outstanding] in the registers of this province against every man."

114. See footnote 18 above.

115. Erik-Jan Zürcher, "Introduction: Understanding Changes in Military Recruitment and Employment Worldwide," *Fighting for a Living: A Comparative Study of Military Labour 1500–2000* (Amsterdam: Amsterdam University Press, 2013), 34, 11–42.

116. Mid-twentieth-century archivist-historians began the painstaking work of sorting and cataloging these collections, laying the foundation for Mughal documentary studies. On a pan-India level, major archival reference guides date from the particularly vibrant decades of the 1960s and 1970s, when there was growing national interest in the preservation of premodern collections in Indian languages, especially under the leadership of the Aligarh Muslim University historian, Nurul Hasan, who was union minister for Education and Culture in the Government of India from 1971 to 1977. See Momin Mohiuddin, *Chancellery and Persian Epistolography under the Mughals: From Babar to Shah Jahan (1526–1658)* (Calcutta: Iran Society, 1971); Yusuf H. Khan, *Farmans and Sanads of the Deccan Sultans* (Hyderabad: Government of Andhra Pradesh, 1963); *Selected Documents of Shah Jahan's Reign; Selected Waqai of the Deccan, 1660–1671 A.D.* (Hyderabad: Central Records Office, 1953); *Selected Documents of Aurangzeb's reign: 1659–1706 AD*; M. Z. A. Shakeb, *Mughal Archives: A Descriptive Catalogue of the Documents Pertaining to the Reign of Shah Jahan, 1628–1658*, vol. 1 (Hyderabad: State Archives, Government of Andhra Pradesh, 1977). Originally, Shakeb had planned to publish five volumes of descriptive catalogs for Shah Jahan's period. These included vol. 1 (*Posting and Attendance at Forts and Mughal Checkpoints*), vol. 2 (*Grants and Accounts of Officers*), vol. 4 (*Verification and Branding of Horses*), and lastly, vol. 5 (*Description Rolls of Mughal mansabdārs and tābinān*). Out of the five thousand documents from Shah Jahan's reign, around 2,438 are muster rolls included in the fifth volume's draft catalog. At the time of his departure from Hyderabad in 1980, Shakeb made several indices with accession numbers for the unprocessed documents in volumes 2–4.

117. Scott, *Seeing Like a State*, 2.

3. FROM COURT TO PORT: GOVERNING THE HOUSEHOLD

1. Zuhur, *Muhammadnāma*, fols. 68–73, 88–99, 134–39.
2. Sherwani and Joshi, *History of the Medieval Deccan*, vol. 1, 351–71; Flores, *Unwanted Neighbors*, 186–203.
3. Kruijtzer, *Xenophobia in the Seventeenth-Century India*, 74–105. Partly, the search for origins and a "diaspora" consciousness among premodern South Asian Muslim elites stems from an overreliance on representations in Persian chronicles, the most commonly used sources for writing political history.
4. For a recent overview, see Eaton, *India in the Persianate Age: 1000–1765*; David Gilmartin and Bruce B. Lawrence, eds., *Beyond Turk and Hindu: Rethinking Religious Identities in Islamicate South Asia* (Gainesville: University Press of Florida, 2000).
5. Sarkar, *History of Aurangzib*, vol. 1, 214–25, 246–56.
6. Lennart Bes, "Sultan among Dutchmen? Royal Dress at Court Audiences in South India, as Portrayed in Local Works of Art and Dutch Embassy Reports, Seventeenth-Eighteenth Centuries," *Modern Asian Studies* 50, no. 6 (2016): 1792–1845.
7. Guha, *Beyond Caste*, 19–20; Nazir, "Social Structure, Ideology and Language," 2897–900.
8. Bhavani Raman, *Document Raj: Writing and Scribes in Early Colonial South India* (Chicago: University of Chicago Press, 2012), 29–33; Prachi Deshpande, *Scripts of Power*; Frank Conlon, *A Caste in a Changing World: The Chitrapur Saraswat Brahmans, 1700–1935* (Berkeley: University of California Press, 1977).
9. Sanjay Subrahmanyam and David Shulman, "The Men Who Would Be King? The Politics of Expansion in Early Seventeenth-Century Northern Tamilnadu," *Modern Asian Studies* 24, no. 2 (1990): 225–48; Subrahmanyam, "The 'Pulicat Enterprise,'"17–36.
10. Flores, *Unwanted Neighbors*, 186–203. Kruijtzer, *Xenophobia in Seventeenth-Century India*, 74–105.
11. Flores, *Unwanted Neighbors*, 192–93, 197.
12. VOC 1133, fol. 483.
13. Ibid.
14. VOC 1133, October 20, 1639, Pieter Paets in Vengurla to Governor General Antonio Van Dieman, fols. 517v–518. VOC 1133, fols. 505–6, Pieter Paets in Vengurla to Director General Philip Lucas in Ceylon, fols. 505–7.
15. Flores, *Unwanted Neighbors*, 191–92.
16. Simon Brodbeck, *The Mahabharata Patriline: Gender, Culture, and the Royal Hereditary* (London: Routledge, 2009).
17. Orsini and Sheikh, *After Timur Left*, 1–46.
18. Brajadulal Chattopadhyaya, *Representing the Other? Sanskrit Sources and the Muslims (8th–14th century)* (Delhi: Manohar, 1998); Cynthia Talbot, "Inscribing the Other, Inscribing the Self: Hindu-Muslim Identities in Pre-Colonial India," *Comparative Studies in Society and History* 37, no. 4 (1995): 692–722.
19. Sreenivasan, "Rethinking Kingship and Authority in South Asia," 584–86.
20. Kapadia, *In Praise of Kings*, 44–75, 71.
21. Kruijtzer, *Xenophobia in Seventeenth-Century India*; Fischel, *Local States in the Imperial Lands*.

22. Guha, *History and Collective Memory in South Asia*, 50–82.

23. Philip Wagoner, "The Multiple Worlds of Amin Khan: Crossing Persianate and Indic cultural boundaries in the Qutb Shahi Kingdom," in *Sultans of the South: Arts of India's Deccan Courts, 1323–1687*, ed. Navina Najat Haider and Marika Sardar, 90–101.

24. Zuhur, *Muhammadnāma*, fols. 190–91.

25. My thanks here are extended to Duke University Press for permission to incorporate into this section of the chapter my prior contribution, "Vernacular Conquest: A Persian Patron and His Image in the Seventeenth-Century Deccan," *Comparative Studies of South Asia, Africa and the Middle East* 37, no. 3 (2017): 549–69.

26. Busch citing Pollock, "Hidden in Plain View," 303. Also see Sheldon Pollock, *The Language of Gods in the World of Men: Sanskrit, Culture, and Power in Premodern India* (Oakland: University of California Press, 2009), 511–24.

27. Zuhur, *Muhammadnāma*, fols. 194–209.

28. Purnima Dhavan, *When Sparrows Became Hawks: The Making of the Sikh Warrior Tradition, 1699–1799* (New York: Oxford University Press, 2011), 23–46; Cynthia Talbot, *The Last Hindu Emperor: Prithviraj Chauhan and the Indian Past 1200–2000* (Cambridge: Cambridge University Press, 2015), 29–68: Kapadia, *In Praise of Kings*, 44–75.

29. Subrahmanyam, "Connected Histories: Notes towards a Reconfiguration of Early Modern Eurasia"; Guha, *Beyond Caste*.

30. Jagadish Narayan Sarkar, *The Life of Mir Jumla* (Calcutta: Thacker, Spink, 1951). See reassessments of the life of Mir Jumla and other "portfolio capitalists" in Subrahmanyam, *The Political Economy of Commerce*, 322–336. While the familial was less visible in the aforementioned work, in later collaborations, the question of household, caste, and state-formation was addressed by combining indigenous textual traditions with European-language archives, See Rao, Shulman, and Subrahmanyam, *Symbols of Substance*, 242–304.

31. Jorge Flores, "Marathi Voices, Portuguese Words," *Quaderni storici* (2021): 341–77, where Flores goes beyond the methodological approaches prevalent in postcolonial studies. See Ranajit Guha, "Chandra's Death," in *Subaltern Studies: Writings on South Asian History and Society* (New Delhi: Oxford University Press, 1982). For the broader debate, see Ann Stoler, *Along the Archival Grain: Epistemic Anxieties and Colonial Common Sense* (Princeton, NJ: Princeton University Press, 2009).

32. Fukazawa, *The Medieval Deccan*, 1–41.

33. Ibid., 70–113.

34. Guha, "Serving the Barbarian to Preserve the Dharma," 497–525; Rosalind O'Hanlon, "The Social Worth of Scribes: Brahmins, Kāyasthas and the Social Order in Early Modern India," *Indian Economic & Social History Review* 47, no. 4 (2010): 563–95; Rosalind O'Hanlon and Christopher Minkowski, "What Makes People Who They Are? Pandit Networks and the Problem of Livelihoods in Early Modern Western India," *Indian Economic & Social History Review* 45, no. 3 (2008): 381–416: David Washbrook, "The Maratha Brahmin Model in South India: An Afterword," *Indian Economic & Social History Review* 47, no. 4 (2010): 597–615; Prachi Deshpande, "The Writerly Self: Literacy, Discipline and Codes of Conduct in Early Modern Western India," *Indian Economic & Social History Review* 53, no. 4 (2016): 449–71.

35. Ibid., 40.

36. Subrahmanyam, *Portuguese Empire in Asia*, 184.

37. The early negotiations between Bijapur and the Dutch, as recorded in the embassy of Johan van Twist, are well known, as is the context for the Luso-Dutch rivalry in the Indian Ocean. See P. M. Joshi, "Johan van Twist's mission to Bijapur, 1637," *Journal of Indian History*, nol. 34, 2 (1956), 111–37; C. R. Boxer, "War and Trade in the Indian Ocean and the South China Sea, 16001650," *Mariner's Mirror* 71, no. 4 (1985): 417–35.

38. Om Prakash, "The Dutch Factory at Vengurla," in A. R. Kulkarni, M.A. Nayeem and T.R. de Souza, eds., *Medieval Deccan History. Commemoration volume in honour of Purshottam Mahadeo Joshi* 1, no. 9 (Bombay: Popular Prakashan, 1996), 186; Sachin Pendse, "The Dutch Factory at Vengurla," *International Journal of Maritime History*, 30, no. 4 (2018): 724–32.

39. Prakash, "The Dutch Factory at Vengurla," 187; Collectie Geleynssen de Jonghe, 1.10.30, nos. 196–98, letter of Dominicus Bouwens to the King of Bijapur, October 2, 1640.

40. Ibid. VOC 1133, fol. 517, Pieter Paets in Vengurla to Governor General Antonio van Diemen, October 20, 1639.

41. VOC 1133, fols. 481–83, letter of Pieter Paets to Governor General Antonio Van Dieman, August 15, 1640.

42. Subrahmanyam, *Political Economy of Commerce*, 55. Aside from the region north of Madurai, which supplied saltpeter to most of the Deccan, another area of saltpeter production for the Konkan in the 1640s lay much closer, in Danda Rajapur, north of Goa. During the first half of the seventeenth century, it was controlled by various Indo-African households, including of the Abyssinian Randaula Khan. See VOC 1133, fol. 505v, fol. 517r.

43. Subrahmanyam, "The Pulicat Enterprise," 20–21.

44. Collectie Geleynssen de Jonghe, no. 202, copy and translation of letter of Bijapur king to Dominicus Bouwens, commander of Dutch fleet in Goa, 1641; VOC 1133, fol. 506.

45. VOC 1133, fols. 519–20.

46. VOC 1133, fol. 519v, Pieter Paets to Governor General Antonio van Dieman, October 20, 1639.

47. VOC 1152, fol. 165, letter of the governor of Ponda.

48. Collectie Geleynssen de Jonghe, no. 196, copy and translation of letter of Dominicus Bouwens, commander of Dutch fleet in Goa to Bijapur king, October 2, 1640.

49. Collectie Geleynssen de Jonghe, no. 198.

50. Collectie Geleynssen de Jonghe, no. 196.

51. VOC 1139, fols. 117–18. Sanjay Subrahmanyam, "Holding the World in Balance: The Connected Histories of the Iberian Overseas Empires, 1500–1640," *American Historical Review* 112, no. 5 (2007): 1359–85

52. VOC 1139, fol. 118.

53. My thanks to Sanjay Subrahmanyam for the translations from Portuguese in this chapter and chapter 4. See S. S. Panduronga Pissurlencar, ed., *Assentos do Conselho do Estado*, vol. 2 (hereafter *A.C.E.*) (Bastorá: Tip. Rangel, 1953), 340–41.

54. Ibid., vol. 2, 457–59.

55. M. A. Nayeem, *External Relations of Bijapur Kingdom, (1489–1686 A.D.): A Study in Diplomatic History* (Hyderabad: Bright, 1974), 167.

56. *A.C.E.*, vol. 2, doc. 180, 469.

57. Ibid., vol. 2, doc. 184, 474–78.

58. Ibid., vol. 2, doc. 184, 476–78.

59. The editor of *Assentos de Conselho*, Panduronga Pissurlencar, refers to this Persian *farmān* from Muhammad ʿAdil Shah to Mirza Muhammad Reza at Ponda, dated August 1, 1641, reproduced in Khare ed., *P.S.I.H.*, vol. 4, Poona, 1949, doc. 27.

60. This is a reference to Upper Chaul or Rewadanda, which was the Portuguese section of Chaul. See Sanjay Subrahmanyam, *Explorations in Connected History: Mughals and Franks* (New Delhi: Oxford University Press, 2005), 126.

61. Collectie Geleynssen de Jonghe, Copie van Brieven Boek, Vengurla, ca. 1642–43, fol. 319.

62. Zuhur, *Muhammadnāma*, fols. 145–47; Bhagwat D. Verma, "History in the Muhammad Nama," *Shivaji Nibandhavali Bhag-II*, ed. Narsingh Kelkar (Pune: Government Central Press, 1930), 111.

63. *P.S.I.H.*, vol. 3, no. 37; vol. 5, nos. 56, 68, 54.

64. *A.C.E.*, vol. 2, doc. 180, 469.

65. VOC 1144, fols. 696–697.

66. Ibid., 698.

67. VOC 1152, letter to the governor of Ponda, November 19, 1644.

68. Collectie Geleynssen de Jonghe, November 29, 1644, no. 326.

69. Ibid.

70. VOC 1170, fol. 678v, fol. 681r.

71. VOC 1174, fol. 575.

4. THE ADORNED PALACE: NARRATING CEREMONY AND RELATEDNESS

1. Helen Creese, *Women of the Kakawin World: Marriage and Sexuality in the Indic Courts of Java and Bali* (Armonk, NY: M. E. Sharpe, 2004), 133–47; Jaya Tyagi, *Contestation and Compliance: Retrieving Women's Agency from Puranic Traditions* (New Delhi: Oxford University Press, New Delhi, 2014); Janet Carsten, *Cultures of Relatedness: New Approaches to the Study of Kinship* (Cambridge: Cambridge University Press, 2000), 4–5.

2. Leslie Peirce, *The Imperial Harem: Women and Sovereignty in the Ottoman Empire* (New York: Oxford University Press, 1993); Lal, *Domesticity and Power in the Early Mughal World*.

3. Flatt, *The Courts of the Deccan Sultanates*; Rosalind O'Hanlon, "Manliness and Imperial Service in Mughal North India," *Journal of the Economic and Social History of the Orient* 42, no. 1 (1999): 47–93.

4. Indrani Chatterjee, "A Slave's Quest for Selfhood in Eighteenth-Century Hindustan," *Indian Economic & Social History Review* 37, no. 1 (2000): 53–86: Sunil Kumar, "Service, Status and Military Slavery in the Delhi Sultanate of the Thirteenth and Early Fourteenth Centuries," in Eaton and Chatterjee, eds., *Slavery and South Asian History*, 83–114.

5. Vijaya Ramaswamy, "Households Profane and Divine: Perceptions of Saintly Wives," in Roy, *Looking Within Looking Without*, 234–36.

6. Lal, *Domesticity and Power in the Early Mughal World*, 1–49.

7. D.C. Verma, *History of Bijapur*, 28, 113.

8. Merridee L. Bailey, and Katie Barclay, eds. *Emotion, Ritual and Power in Europe, 1200–1920: Family, State and Church* (Cham: Springer International, 2017).

9. Kaya Şahin, "Staging an Empire: an Ottoman Circumcision Ceremony as Cultural Performance," *American Historical Review* 123, no. 2 (2018): 472.

10. Ibid., 486–90.
11. B.D. Verma, "History in the Muhammad Nama," 73–78; Kruijtzer, *Xenophobia in the Seventeenth-Century India*, 80–81.
12. Duindam, *Dynasties: A Global History*.
13. Monographs on Mughal history are organized either around a single ruler or with chapters that follow each one's reign. See Lisa Balabanlilar, *The Emperor Jahangir: Power and Kingship in Mughal India* (London: Bloomsbury, 2020).; Faruqui, *The Princes of the Mughal Empire*.
14. Marshall Sahlins, *What Kinship Is-and Is Not* (Chicago: University of Chicago Press, 2013), 62–90; Carsten, *Cultures of Relatedness*, 1–36.
15. I. Chatterjee, ed., *Unfamiliar Relations*, 8–14.
16. Ramya Sreenivasan, "Honoring the Family: Narratives and the Politics of Kinship in Pre-colonial Rajasthan," in I. Chatterjee, ed., *Unfamiliar Relations*, 46–72. Within the subcontinent, going beyond dynastic households, studies on Rajput subimperial lineages in western India have presented the richest materials and interpretative breakthroughs on the familial. Sreenivasan examined "historical" narratives of elite Rajput families and their distinct relationship to state-formation, especially in the context of increasing vassalage under the Mughal empire. Her paradigm for the Rajputs holds implications for regional courts across the subcontinent and reading textual traditions that lie beyond imperial purview, attuning us to the different purposes, aspirations, and receptions of a variety of "historical" narratives of kinship.
17. Thus, after comparing manuscript copies of the *Muhammadnāma*, Verma introduced his summary by declaring, "I have been able to take down almost all the historical facts given therein, omitting the poems and the poetic descriptions of the battles, pilgrimages and marriages which do not possess a single idea of any historical importance" (B. D. Verma, "History in the Muhammad Nama," 75–76).
18. Sherwani & Joshi, *History of the Medieval Deccan*, vol. 1, 356–59; Kruijtzer, *Xenophobia in Seventeenth-Century India*; Jorge Flores, *Unwanted Neighbors*, 186–203.
19. *Relação dos Reis Vizinhos* (Account of the neighboring kings, hereafter *Relação*), published by Panduronga Pissurlencar, "A índia em 1629. Relação dos Reis Vizinhos do que ora passão e contão," *Boletim do Instituto Vasco da Gama* 7 (1930): 52–61.
20. Nadine Akkerman ad Birgit Houben, eds., *The Politics of Female Households: Ladies-in-Waiting Across Early Modern Europe* (Leiden: Brill, 2013).
21. Flores, *Unwanted Neighbors*, 186.
22. *Livro das Monções*, no. 13, fols. 447–49v, "Relation of the Neighboring Kings, of What Is Happening Now and Is Related," Historical Archives, Panaji (Goa).
23. Subrahmanyam, *The Portuguese Empire in Asia*, 164–67.
24. Flores, *Unwanted Neighbors*, 186–203. A.C.E., vol. 1, 303–7.
25. *Muhammadnāma*, fol. 17, fol. 27. fols. 121–22.
26. For Mughal narratives of kingly birth, see Lal, *Domesticity and Power in the Early Mughal World*, 176–213.
27. *Muhammadnāma*, fols. 28–29. For the roles of wet nurses in the Mughal context, see Lal, *Domesticity and Power in the Early Mughal World*, 180–90.
28. Zuhur notes that Taj Sultan, Muhammad ʿAdil Shah's mother, died in 1634, shortly before the succession rivalry between Mustafa Khan, Khawas Khan, and Murari Pandit unfolded. See Zuhur, *Muhammadnāma*, fols. 117–22.

29. Ibid., fol. 57.
30. Ibid., fol. 61, fols. 135–38.
31. Ibid., fols. 68–73, 88–98, 134–38.
32. Ibid., fols. 88–91.
33. Zuhur, *Muhammadnāma*, fols. 135–38.
34. Ibid., fol. 69, fol. 89, fol. 135.
35. Sholeh A. Quinn, *Persian Historiography Across Empires: The Ottomans, Safavids, and Mughals* (Cambridge: Cambridge University Press, 2020), 1–19.
36. Kruijtzer, *Xenophobia in Seventeenth-Century India*, 66–69. One common way to read this wedding, in particular, and the 1630s more broadly has been through the lens of multiethnic court factions, particularly as a contest between the Persian Mustafa Khan the Deccanis, Khawas Khan and Murari Pandit.
37. *Hadīqat*, 160–61.
38. Sunil Sharma, "Forging a Canon of Dakhni Literature: Translations and Retellings from Persian," in *Iran and the Deccan: Persianate Art, Culture, and Talent in Circulation, 1400–1700*, ed. Keelan Overton (Bloomington: Indiana University Press, 2020), 408.
39. Khusrau's *Hasht Bihist* (Eight paradises) ca. 1302 was in turn based on Nizami's *Haft Paykar, Seven Beauties*, ca. 1197.
40. Overton, *Iran and the Deccan*, 52.
41. Sayeeda Jafar, ed., Malik Khushnud, *Jannat Singār, 1645* (New Delhi: National Council for the Promotion of the Urdu Language, 1997), 12–13.
42. On the most well-known Indo-African slave-king from the Deccan, Malik Ambar of Ahmednagar, see Eaton, "The Rise and Fall of Military Slavery in the Deccan, 1450–1650," in Chatterjee and Eaton., *Slavery and South Asian History*, 115–35; Omar H. Ali, *Malik Ambar: Power and Slavery across the Indian Ocean* (New York: Oxford University Press, 2016). Precolonial slave narratives often alluded to their multivalent social positions. See Chatterjee, "A Slave's Quest for Selfhood," 53–86.
43. *Hadīqat*, 163.
44. Nusrati, Or. 13533, fols. 10a–10b, fol. 16b.
45. Nusrati, Or. 13533, fols. 16a–16b.
46. My thanks to Keelan Overton for sharing her insights on this manuscript's visual qualities. Writing and its relationship to the phonetics of premodern regional vernaculars such as Dakkani and the social relationships between calligraphers and poets is a subject worth exploring in future projects through the study of manuscripts. See Namrata Kanchan, "A Panegyric from the Deccan's Golden Age," *Asian and African Studies* (blog), February 28, 2023, https://blogs.bl.uk/asian-and-african/2023/02/a-panegyric-from-the-deccans-golden-age.html.
47. *Hadīqat*, 122.
48. Zuhur, *Muhammadnāma*, 134.
49. *Hadīqat*, 133–35.
50. Eaton, "The Rise and Fall of Military Slavery in the Deccan," in Chatterjee and Eaton, *Slavery and South Asian History*, 125–26.
51. *Hadīqat*, 133, 160.
52. Ibid., 134.

53. Zuhur, *Muhammadnāma*, 92.
54. Anooshahr, *Turkestan and the Rise of Eurasian Empires*.
55. Zuhur, *Muhammadnāma*, fols. 94–95.
56. *Hadīqat*, 135, 139.
57. *Hadīqat*, 140–41.
58. VOC 1243 Vengurla 750–52. VOC 1236, 499.
59. Muzaffar Khan is also known as Muzaffar al-din and Khan Muhammad. See Zuhur, *Muhammadnāma*, fol. 131; Zubayri, *Basātīn*, 342. The title "Chanchanna," as observers in the Dutch East India Company noted, would later be given to Bijapuri commander Afzal Khan, known for his attempt to kill the Maratha Bhonsle chief, Shivaji. See VOC 1203 Copie caul aan gouverneur Laurens Pit door Chanchanna, August 10, 1654.
60. Zuhur, *Muhammadnāma*, 136.
61. Ali Akbar Husain, *Scent in the Islamic Garden: A Study of Deccani Urdu Literary Sources*. (Karachi: Oxford University Press, 2000).
62. Dayal, "Vernacular Conquest," 561–62.
63. Hasan Shauqi, *Divān-i Hasan Shauqī: Davīn sadi hijrī mein Urdū shā'irī kī rivayat kā surāgh*, ed. Jamil Jalibi (Karachi: Anjuman-i Taraqqi-yi Urdu Pakistsan, 1971); Shamsur Rahman Faruqi, "A Stranger in the City: The Poetics of Sabk-i Hindi," *Annual of Urdu Studies* 19 (2004): 1–93; Annemarie Schimmel, *A Two-Colored Brocade: The Imagery of Persian Poetry* (Chapel Hill: University of North Carolina Press, 1992), 284, 361.
64. A. A. Seyed-Gohrab, ed., *Metaphor and Imagery in Persian Poetry* (Leiden: Brill, 2012), 4.
65. *Divān-i Hasan Shauqī*, 124–34.
66. A. A. Seyed-Gohrab, "Waxing Eloquent: The Masterful Variations on Candle Metaphors in the Poetry of Ḥāfiẓ and his Predecessors" in *Metaphor and Imagery in Persian Poetry* (Leiden: Brill, 2012), ed. A.A. Seyed-Gohrab, 81–123.
67. *Divān-i Hasan Shauqī*, 122.
68. Irene Bierman, *Writing Signs: The Fatimid Public Texts* (Berkeley: University of California Press, 1998), 114, 48.
69. Steingass, *A Comprehensive Persian-English Dictionary*, 807, 852.
70. *Divān-i Hasan Shauqī*, 124–27.
71. Ibid.
72. Ibid., 127.
73. Thibaut d'Hubert, "Pirates, Poets, and Merchants: Bengali Language and Literature in Seventeenth-Century Mrauk-U," in *Culture and Circulation: Literature in Motion in Early Modern India*, ed. Allison Busch and Thomas de Bruijn (Leiden: Brill, 2014), 51.
74. Sanjay Subrahmanyam, *Courtly Encounters: Translating Courtliness and Violence in Early Modern Eurasia* (Cambridge, MA: Harvard University Press, 2012), 36.
75. *Divān-i Hasan Shauqī*, 131.
76. Ibid., 134–35.
77. Ibid., 127.
78. Eaton, "The Rise and Fall of Military Slavery in the Deccan," 115–35.
79. Navina N. Haider, "Kitāb-i Nauras: Key to Bijapur's Golden Age," in *Sultans of the South: Arts of India's Deccan Courts, 1323–1687*, ed. Navina N. Haider and Marika Sardar (New York: Metropolitan Museum of Art, 2011): 26–43.

5. AT HOME IN THE REGIONAL COURT: CRITIQUING EMPIRE

1. Alam and Subrahmanyam, "The Deccan Frontier and Mughal Expansion, ca. 1600"; M. Z. A. Shakeb, *Relations of Golkonda with Iran*.

2. The first poem in Persian, the *Ādilnāma* of Hakim Atishi (ca. 1637) remains unpublished and available only in manuscript form. Unexamined in both Urdu- and English-language scholarship, a brief survey of Atishi's works can be found in Rahmat Ali Khan, "The Progress of Persian Literature under the Adil Shahi Dynasty of Bijapur, 1489–1686 A.D. (Poetry)" (PhD diss., University of Delhi, 1978); T. N. Devare, *A Short History of Persian Literature at the Bahmani, Adil Shahi, and Qutb Shahi Courts—Deccan* (Pune: S. Devare, 1961), 247–48. The second work in Dakkani, Nusrati's *Ālināma* (ca. 1665), was copied and circulated widely, with many manuscripts dispersed across South Asia and Europe. It has shaped two divergent postcolonial memories of the heavily debated late seventeenth century. In both popular culture and vernacular scholarship in Urdu, Marathi, and Hindi, Nusrati's work has been translated for multiple modern regional publics that contend over the most famous historical figures from this period to allay various nationalist anxieties. See Maulvi Abdul Haq, *Nusrati: The Poet-Laureate of Bijapur—A Critical Study of His Life and Works* (Karachi: Anjuman-i Taraqqi-i Urdu, 1944); Abdul Majeed Siddiqui ed., Nusrati, *Ālināma* (Hyderabad: Salar Jang Dakkani Publications, 1959); Jamil Jalibi, ed., *Divān-i Nusrati* (Lahore: Qausain, 1972); Suresh Dutt Awasthi, *Tarikhe Iskandarī* (Hyderabad: Andhra Pradesh Hindi Academy, 1987); Devisingh Venkatsingh Chauhan, *Dakhani Hinditil Itihas va itar lekh* (Mumbai: Itihas Sansodhak Mandal, 1973); and *Tarikhe Iskandarī* (Pune: Maharashtra Rashtrabhasha Sabha, n.d.). In another world far removed from postcolonial history-writing in Indian vernaculars—namely, English-language historiography—Nusrati's verse remains far less visible and is used only occasionally to affirm Persian chronicle-derived linear political histories. See Jadunath Sarkar, *Shivaji and his Times* (London: Longmans, Green, 1920), 84.

3. In this chapter, I focus on the single manuscript of the *Ādilnāma* currently held at the YSR Reddy State Museum in Hyderabad, India. Atishi's corpus is spread out over three distinct manuscripts. In addition to Ms. P. 4300 of the *Ādilnāma*, Atishi wrote several other masnavī, which survive in two main manuscripts, one in the Salar Jang Museum in Hyderabad and the other in the British Library in London. The *Masnavīyāt-i Atishi* in the Salar Jang Museum contains three texts on distinct themes—*Hidāyatnāma, Muhabbatnāma, Mujmīr-i Anwar* (an imitation of Nizami's *Makhzan al-asrār*). The *Kulliyāt-i Atishi*, in Ethé's catalog, contains an incomplete copy of *Ādilnāma*, missing the poem's beginning chapters. See Hermann Ethé, *Catalogue of Persian Manuscripts in the Library of the India Office*, vol. 1 (Oxford: H. Hart, 1903), 838–39. There are many manuscripts of the *Ālināma* dispersed across museums, private collections, and libraries in South Asia and Europe and one edition. See Nusrati, *Ālināma*, ed. Abdul Majeed Siddiqui (Hyderabad: Salar Jang Dakkani, 1959). It is the earliest contemporary text produced closest to events in the late seventeenth century that were also the subject of later literary texts—for instance, Krishnaji Anant Sabhasad's *Sabhasad Bakhar* (ca. 1695–96) in Marathi and Bhushan's *Sivrajbhusan* (ca. 1673) in Brajbhasha. See Sumit Guha, "Speaking Historically: The Changing Voices of Historical Narration in Western India, 1400–1900," *American Historical Review* 109 (2004): 1099–1100; Allison Busch, *The Poetry of Kings: The Classical Hindi Literature of Mughal India* (New York: Oxford University Press, 2011), 190–93.

4. Rahmat A. Khan, "The Progress of Persian Literature under the Adil Shahi Dynasty of Bijapur (Poetry)" 83–90.

5. Atishi, *Adilnāma*, fol. 82.

6. A. Golchin-Ma'ani, *Kārvān-e Hend: dar ahvāl o āsār-e shā'erān-e 'asr-e Safavi ke be Hendustān rafta-and*, 2 vols., Mashhad: n.p., 1990.

7. Sherwani and Joshi, *History of Medieval Deccan*, vol. 1, 350–59.

8. Nusrati wrote two heroic masnavī—the longest of which is the *Alināma* (ca. 1665) and the shorter of which is *Tārīkh-i sikandarī* (ca. 1672), examined in chapter 6 of this book. Urdu scholars have closely examined Nusrati's literary output while art historians have studied the long afterlife of his work through illustrated manuscripts of his most famous romance written in the masnavī form, *Gulshan-i 'Ishq* (Rose garden of love). For an art historical perspective, see Navina Najat Haidar, "Gulshan-i 'Ishq: Sufi Romance of the Deccan," in *The Visual World of Muslim India: The Art, Culture and Society of the Deccan in the Early Modern Era*, ed. Laura E. Parodi (London: I. B. Tauris, 2014), 295–318. See also Ali A. Husain, *Scent in the Islamic Garden*, 154. For Urdu scholarship on Nusrati, see *Gulshan-i 'Ishq*, ed. Maulvi Abdul Haq (Karachi: Anjuman-i Taraqqi-yi Urdu, 1952); Tayyib Ansari, *Nusrati ki shā'irī* (Hyderabad: Adabi Trust, 1984), 24.

9. Shareef, *Dakan Mein Urdu Sha'iri Vali Se Pehle*, 499–502, 503–5.

10. Peter Gaeffke, "Alexander in Avadhī and Dakkinī Mathnawīs," *Journal of the American Oriental Society* 109, no. 4 (1989): 530–31; Shamsur R. Faruqi, "A Stranger in the City," 24–25; Kevin Schwartz, *Remapping Persian Literary History, 1700–1900* (Edinburgh: Edinburgh University Press, 2020), 14–15; Rajeev Kinra, *Writing Self, Writing Empire: Chandar Bhan Brahman and the Cultural World of the Indo-Persian Secretary* (Oakland, CA: University of California Press, 2015), 201–39.

11. Orsini and Sheikh, *After Timur Left*, 1–46.

12. Kinra, *Writing Self, Writing Empire*; Audrey Truschke, *Culture of Encounters: Sanskrit at the Mughal Court* (New York: Columbia University Press, 2016); Busch, *Poetry of kings*.

13. Audrey Truschke, *The Language of History: Sanskrit Narratives of Indo-Muslim Rule* (New York: Columbia University Press, 2021), 2–10.

14. Purnima Dhavan, *When Sparrows Became Hawks*; Ramya Sreenivasan, "Warrior-Tale at Hinterland Courts in North India, c. 1370–1550" in Orsini and Sheikh, *After Timur Left*, 242–72; Cynthia Talbot, *The Last Hindu Emperor*; Kapadia, *In Praise of Kings*; Thibaut d'Hubert, *In the Shade of the Golden Palace*, 1–20; Kevin L. Schwartz, "The Local Lives of a Transregional Poet: 'Abd al-Qāder Bidel and the Writing of Persianate Literary History," *Journal of Persianate Studies* 9, no. 1 (2016): 83–106; Pankaj Jha, *A Political History of Literature: Vidyapati and the Fifteenth Century* (Oxford: Oxford University Press, 2019).

15. Francesca Orsini, "How to Do Multi-Lingual Literary History: Lessons from Fifteenth- and Sixteenth-Century North India," *Indian Economic and Social History Review* 49, no. 2 (2012): 226–27.

16. Sharma, *Mughal Arcadia*, 12, 28. Sharma argues that multilingualism in the Deccan may be compared to Persian's case in the Ottoman context. Unlike north India, where Urdu flourished much later in the eighteenth century, in the Deccan sultanates, Persian was one among many languages, along with the panregional vernacular (Dakkani) and regional vernaculars (Telugu, Kannada, and Marathi) that competed with each other.

17. Kinra, *Writing Self, Writing Empire*, 2–15; d'Hubert, *In the Shade of the Golden Palace*, 1–20; Mana Kia, "*Adab* as Ethics of Literary Form and Social Conduct: Reading the Gulistan in Late Mughal India" in *No Tapping Around Philology: A Festschrift in Celebration and Honor of Wheeler McIntosh Thackston Jr.'s 70th Birthday*, ed. Alireza Korangy and Daniel J. Sheffield (Wiesbaden: Harrassowitz Verlag, 2014), 281–308.

18. Pasha M. Khan, "Marvellous Histories: Reading the Shāhnāmah in India," *Indian Economic and Social History Review* 49, no. 4 (2012): 527–56; Geert Jan van Gelder, "Some Brave Attempts at Generic Classification in Pre-Modern Arabic Literature," in *Aspects of Genre and Type in Pre-Modern Literary Cultures*, ed. Bert Roest and Herman L. J. Vanstiphout (Leiden: Brill, 1999), 15—32.

19. For the Mughal context, see Appendix B, "The Revolt and Demise of Jujhar Singh Bundela" in Wheeler McIntosh Thackston Jr., "The Poetry of Abu Talib Kalim (d. 1651), Persian Poet-Laureate of Shah Jahan, Mughal Emperor of India" (PhD diss., Harvard University, 1974), 264–79. Given that Kalim spent some time in Bijapur in the early part of his career, we may surmise that he would have known our first poet, Hakim Atishi.

20. Sharma, *Mughal Arcadia*, 130–31.

21. Subah Dayal, "On Heroes and History: Responding to the *Shahnamah* in the Deccan, 1500–1800" in *Iran and the Deccan: Persianate Art, Culture, and Talent in Circulation*, ed. Keelan Overton (Bloomington: Indiana University Press, 2020), 429–38.

22. For a classical study of the "minister-favorite" figure, see John. H. Elliot, *The Count-Duke of Olivares: The Statesman in an Age of Decline* (New Haven, CT: Yale University Press, 1986).

23. Sharma, *Mughal* Arcadia, 30–31.

24. Atishi, *'Ādilnāma*, fols. 38–42, 52–53, 69–70. Between the opening verses in praise of God, the Prophet, and 'Ali to the chapters where heroic narrations of Sultan Muhammad 'Adil Shah begin, Atishi deliberated on a range of existential, poetic, and professional matters, evoking the common tropes of despair, longing for home, and the difficulty of being in a distant land. See Sharma, *Mughal Arcadia*, 23. For a critique of modern scholarship's tendency to dismiss *hikāyāt*, see Kia, "*Adab* as Ethics," 284–85.

25. Sharma, *Mughal Arcadia*, 130.

26. Atishi, *'Ādilnāma*, fols. 35–38; Sharma, *Mughal Arcadia*, 21–22.

27. Atishi, *'Ādilnāma*, fols. 171–73 and fols. 191–93. Atishi discusses Firdawsi in a chapter dispersed between two separate sections of the manuscript, split between narratives of battles between the Mughals and the Deccan sultans.

28. Atishi, *'Ādilnāma*, fols. 30, 171, 176, and 191–93. In these same portions, Atishi also mentions Nizami, Sa'di, and Hafez.

29. Sunil Sharma, *Persian Poetry at the Indian Frontier: Mas'ūd Sa'd Salmān of Lahore* (Delhi: Permanent Black, 2000), 34–36, 43.

30. Steingass, *A Comprehensive Persian-English Dictionary*, 627, where *zangi* is translated as Egyptian/ Ethiopian/black.

31. Atishi, *'Ādilnāma*, fol. 191.

32. Ibid., fols. 71–72, 150, 181. The poet recorded the names of Mustafa Khan's kinsfolk, including his sons and nephews, and commemorated the work in honor of the wedding of his daughter to Sultan Muhammad 'Adil Shah.

33. Ibid., fol. 191.

34. Ibid., fol. 192.
35. Sunil Sharma, "Amir Khusraw and the Genre of Historical Narratives in Verse," *Comparative Studies of South Asia, Africa, and the Middle East* 22, no. 1 (2002): 112–18.
36. Nusrati, *Alināma*, 40.
37. Nurullah Qazi, *Tārīkh-i ʿAlī ʿĀdil Shāhī* (History of ʿAli ʿAdil Shah II), ed. Abu Nasr Khalidi (Hyderabad: Ijaz Press, 1964); Nusrati, *Alināma*, 34.
38. Nusrati, *Alināma*, 38. This is apparent from prefaces of other works from this period. Dakhni poets seemed to have dealt with a crisis of validation from their peers writing in Persian, peers who dominated literary gatherings in Bijapur and Golconda and some of whom undoubtedly looked down on the regional idiom. See Wajhi, *Sab Ras ki Tanqidi Tanvin*, ed. Humaira Jalili (Hyderabad: Aijaz Press, 1983), 182. For a list of Dakhni poets who composed in Persian, see Shareef, *Dakan main Urdu*, 458–69.
39. Nusrati, *Alināma*, 38.
40. Nusrati, *Alināma*, 22, 427.
41. Ibid.
42. Atishi, *Ādilnāma*, fols. 46–51; Nusrati, *Alināma*, 23–29.
43. The poem's first part focuses on Khawas Khan and Murari Pandit, while the manuscript's second half shifts entirely to the prime minister Mustafa Khan and the members of his household, who ousted their competitors in a power struggle during the 1630s. As the narrative progresses, we learn that Mustafa Khan's authority eclipsed that of the reigning sultan Muhammad ʿAdil Shah. At the narrative's outset, Atishi praised both Khawas Khan and Murari (who were executed in the early 1630s, but the actual event is omitted entirely in the poem). The poet casts Murari as a *bandah-yi khās* or a special servant of the Bijapur sultan, and referred to Khawas Khan with the honorific, *khān-i daulat khawās*. Prior to this so-called civil war in the late 1620s, Atishi described Khawas Khan and Mustafa Khan as the indispensable left and right hands of Sultan Muhammad ʿAdil Shah. See *Ādilnāma*, fols. 128, 121, and 158. At no point in his composition does Atishi explicitly mention or name the ethnolinguistic profiles ("Maratha," or "Habshi") of any of these competing household heads. For various narrations of this event in political histories, see Sherwani and Joshi, *History of the Medieval Deccan*, vol 1., 352–57; Kruijtzer, *Xenophobia in Seventeenth-Century India*, 74–104; Jorge Flores, *Unwanted Neighbors*, 186–91.
44. Atishi, *Ādilnāma*, fol. 196.
45. Kia, "*Adab* as Ethics," 282.
46. Atishi, *Ādilnāma*, fol. 192.
47. Ibid., fols. 121, 128, 136–39, 158, 162, and 174. On the patron's duty to take care of the poet, see fols. 46–47, 164, and 171.
48. Ibid., fol. 171.
49. Ibid., fols. 188, 173.
50. Ibid.
51. For Marathi narratives and *bakhar* historiography, see James W. Laine, *Shivaji: Hindu King in Islamic India* (New York: Oxford University Press, 2003), 153–89; Prachi Deshpande, *Creative Pasts Historical Memory and Identity in Western India, 1700–1960* (New York: Columbia University Press, 2007), 26–42.
52. Nusrati, *Alināma*, 43.
53. Nusrati, *Alināma*, 44.

54. Jean-Louis Casaux and Rick Knowlton, *A World of Chess: Its Development and Variations through Centuries and Civilizations* (Jefferson, NC: McFarland, 2017), 359, 11, 15, 17.
55. Kia, "*Adab* as Ethics," 285.
56. Atishi, *Ādilnāma*, fols. 79–100.
57. Ibid., fol. 76.
58. Ibid., fol. 82.
59. Sherwani and Joshi, *History of Medieval Deccan*, 350–59.
60. Atishi, *Ādilnāma*, fol. 97.
61. Ibid., fols. 112–20.
62. Ibid., fols. 108–10.
63. Ibid., fols. 75, 80, 176.
64. Ibid., fol. 105.
65. Ibid., fol. 110.
66. Ibid., fol. 174.
67. There are several such asides where Atishi reprimands himself for digressing from the narrative to imparting advice. See Atishi, *Ādilnāma*, fols. 105, 126, 189.
68. Mehrzad Boroujerdi, ed., *Mirror for the Muslim Prince: Islam and the Theory of Statecraft* (Syracuse, NY: Syracuse University Press, 2013).
69. Kia, "*Adab* as Ethics," 284.
70. Szonyi, *The Art of Being Governed*, 192–215; Tonio Andrade and William Reger, eds., *The Limits of Empire: European Imperial Formations in Early Modern World History*, (London: Routledge, 2012), 137–40; Charles Tilly, "Family History, Social History, and Social Change," *Journal of Family History* 12, no. 1 (1987): 319.
71. See Muzaffar Alam, introduction to *Crisis of Empire in Mughal North India*, 2nd ed. (New Delhi: Oxford University Press, 2013).
72. Stewart Gordon, *The Marathas* (Cambridge: Cambridge University Press, 2016), 70–71.
73. Sarkar, *Shivaji and His Times*, 97–108; Surendranath Sen, *Foreign Biographies of Shivaji* (Calcutta: KP Bagchi, 1977).
74. Gordon, *The Marathas*, 69–76; A. R. Kulkarni, "Maratha Policy towards the 'Adil Shahi Kingdom," *Bulletin of the Deccan College Research Institute* 49 (1990): 221–26; G. T. Kulkarni, "Shivaji-Mughal Relations (1669–80): Gleanings from Some Unpublished Persian Records," *Proceedings of the Indian History Congress* 40 (1979): 336–41; G. T. Kulkarni, "A Note on Mirza Rajah Jai Singh's Purandhar and Bijapur Campaigns—an Unpublished *farmān* of Aurangzeb (1665 A.D.)," *Proceedings of the Indian History Congress* 71 (2010–2011): 274–83; M. N. Pearson, "Shivaji and the Decline of the Mughal Empire," *Journal of Asian Studies* 35, no. 2 (1976): 221–35.
75. Joshi and Sherwani, *History of the Medieval Deccan*, vol. 1, 378–79; Shanti Sadiq Ali, *The African Dispersal in the Deccan: From Medieval to Modern Times* (Hyderabad: Orient Blackswan, 1996), 124. The Siddi Jauhar incident is one among many stock narratives, from theater, television, and film, that pervade nationalist biographies of Shivaji in Marathi and Hindi in contemporary times.
76. Eaton, "The Rise and Fall of Military Slavery in the Deccan, 1450–1650," 115–35.
77. Pashington Obeng, "Service to God, Service to Master/Client: African Indian Military Contribution in Karnataka," *Asian and African Studies* 6 (2007): 271–88; Shanti Sadiq

Ali, *The African Dispersal in the Deccan*; Indrani Chatterjee, "Afro-Asian Capital and Its Dissolution," *Comparative Studies of South Asia, Africa, and the Middle East* 38, no. 2 (2018): 310–29.

78. *P.S.I.H*, vol. 2, *farmān* confirming *in'ām* of Gondaji Pasalkar for helping Salabat Khan/Siddi Jauhar, March 9, 1660, 72–73,. See also *P.S.I.H*, vol. 2, *in'ām* granted to Kedarji Khopade for helping Salabat Khan/Siddi Jauhar on his expedition, 30–31.

79. Nusrati, *'Alināma*, 49.

80. Siddi Jauhar was a slave of 'Abdul Wahhab, the *hākim* of Karnul and a Bijapuri military commander. After 'Abdul Wahab's death, Siddi Jauhar imprisoned his son, Malik Raihan II, and took over Karnul. See Ali, *The African Dispersal in the Deccan*, 124.

81. Nusrati, *'Alināma*, 79–80.

82. Ibid., 82.

83. Ibid., 87–95, 146.

84. Ibid., 46.

85. Cynthia Talbot, "Inscribing the Other, Inscribing the Self: Hindu-Muslim Identities in Pre-Colonial India," *Comparative Studies in Society and History* 37, no. 4 (1995): 705.

86. Ibid.

87. For a chronological narrative in political histories, see Gordon, *The Marathas*, 74, 164; A. R. Kulkarni, "Maratha Policy towards the 'Adil Shahi kingdom," 222; Sarkar, *Shivaji and His Times*, 113–51.

88. Nusrati, *'Alināma*, 187–217.

89. Ibid., 217.

90. Ibid., 218.

91. Political historians have spilled a lot of ink trying to determine whether Shivaji was a Deccani patriot or not. See note 74 above.

92. Nusrati, *'Alināma*, 219. Condemning both Shivaji and Jai Singh, Nusrati concluded this chapter by declaring *farebī donon sakht bad zāt te / yekas yek ke shāgird wa ustād te* (both deceivers with a base character / for they were each other's student and disciple).

93. Echoing Nusrati's viewpoint, but from the opposing side, the later and well-known *Sabhasad bakhar* (ca. 1695–96) in Marathi, for instance, noted that Jai Singh recognized Shivaji as a fellow Rajput.

94. G. S. Sardesai, *New History of the Marathas* (Bombay: Phoenix, 1946), 55.

95. Nusrati, *'Alināma*, 246–47.

96. Nusrati, *'Alināma*, 276–303.

97. For similar enumerations of social groups in Bengali masnavī, see d'Hubert, "Poets, Pirates, and Merchants," 51.

98. Nusrati, *'Alināma*, 183.

99. Ibid., 184–85.

100. Ibid., 249.

101. Qur'an, 105: 1–5.

102. Nusrati, *'Alināma*, 361, 276–77.

103. Lawrence I. Conrad, "Abraha and Muhammad: Some Observations Apropos of Chronology and Literary Topoi in the Early Arabic Historical Tradition," *Bulletin of the*

School of Oriental and African Studies 50, no. 2 (1987): 225–40; Nicola Clarke, *The Muslim Conquest of Iberia: Medieval Arabic Narratives* (London: Routledge, 2012).

104. The Mughal emperor Aurangzeb had a well-known confrontation with the *shaykh al-islām*, who had condemned the Deccan conquest, making the case that it was unjustified to fight fellow Muslim rulers. See Aziz Ahmed, "Dar Al-Islam and the Muslim Kingdoms of Deccan and Gujarat," *Cahiers d'Histoire Mondiale* 7, no. 1 (1962): 787.

105. In future scholarship, it may be worthwhile for literary scholars to examine the ʿ*Alināma* and Nusrati's oeuvre more broadly for its poetics and literary techniques, as has been done by Thibaut d'Hubert for the Middle Bengali poet, Ālāol in Arakan. See d'Hubert, *In the Shade of the Golden Palace*.

106. Guha, *Beyond Caste*, 117–41; Roy, *Looking Within, Looking Without*, 1–15; I. Chatterjee, *Unfamiliar Relations*, 3–45.

107. Muzaffar Alam, "A Muslim state in a non-Muslim Context: The Mughal Case," in *Mirror for the Muslim Prince: Islam and the Theory of Statecraft*, ed. Mehrzad Boroujerdi (Syracuse, NY: Syracuse University Press, 2013), 160–89.

108. Cultural historians have examined Persian-language materials at the highest level of imperial and regional courts—that is, in terms of exchanges between ideologies of dynasts or the frequent traffic of ambassadors and emissaries between capital cities, or as expressions of sociability. For the different kinds of Persian texts used by historians of the Deccan, see Richard Eaton, *Sufis of Bijapur, 1300–1700*; Sherwani, *History of the Qutb Shahi Dynasty*; Kruijtzer, *Xenophobia in Seventeenth-Century India*; Flatt, *The Courts of the Deccan Sultanates*; Fischel, *Local States in an Imperial World*.

109. Sherwani, *History of the Qutb Shahi Dynasty*, 431–600; Eaton, *Sufis of Bijapur*, 177–91.

110. Sinan Antoon, *The Poetics of the Obscene in Premodern Arabic Poetry: Ibn al-Hajjāj and Sukhf* (New York: Palgrave Macmillan, 2014), 64–91.

111. Zuhur, *Muhammadnāma*, fol. 84.

6. FROM BATTLEFIELD TO WEAVING VILLAGE: DISCIPLINING THE COAST

1. J. Sarkar, *History of Aurangzib*, vols 1–2; Nayeem, *External Relations of the Bijapur Kingdom*; Verma, *History of Bijapur*; Sherwani, *History of the Qutb Shahi Dynasty*; Gajanan Bhaskar Mehendale, *Shivaji His Life and Times* (Thane: Param Mitra, 2011).

2. Rosalind O'Hanlon and David Washbrook, "After Orientalism: Culture, Criticism, and Politics in the Third World," *Comparative Studies in Society and History* 34, no. 1, (1992): 141–67.

3. John F. Richards, *Mughal Administration in Golconda* (Oxford: Clarendon Press, 1975).

4. Nayeem, *External Relations of the Bijapur Kingdom*, 118–44; Verma, *History of Bijapur*, 113–48; Sherwani, *History of the Qutb Shahi Dynasty*, 431–62; Bahadur and Srinivasachari, *A History of Gingee and its Rulers*, 152–88.

5. The story of European-Asian encounters or "cross-cultural interactions" in settings such as diplomatic missions, embassies, and court protocol, so often reconstructed through the VOC's records, has been well narrated recently for the Mughals and post-Vijayanagara nayaka kingdoms of southern India. See Markus Vink, *Encounters on the Opposite*

Coast: the Dutch East India Company and the Nayaka state of Madurai in the seventeenth century (Leiden: Brill, 2015); Lennart Bes, *The Heirs of Vijayanagara* (Leiden: Brill, 2022); Guido van Meersbergen, *Ethnography and Encounter: The Dutch and English in Seventeenth-Century South Asia* (Leiden: Brill, 2022).

6. There are varieties of this scholarship broadly split between the earlier (Portuguese, Dutch, Danish) and later colonial European materials (French and English). See Sinappah Arasaratnam, *Merchants, Companies and Commerce on the Coromandel Coast, 1650–1740* (Delhi: Oxford University Press, 1986); Subrahmanyam, *The Political Economy of Commerce*. And, for the later period, see Raman, *Document Raj*; for a more recent account, see Robert Travers, *Empires of Complaint: Mughal Law and the Making of British India, 1765–1793* (Cambridge: Cambridge University Press, 2022).

7. For the northern Coromandel, in the port cities north of Madras that fell under the Golkonda sultanate, the historiography is comparatively thicker. See Sinnappah Arasaratnam, "Coromandel Revisited: Problems and Issues in Indian Maritime History," *Indian Economic & Social History Review* 26, no. 1 (1989): 101–10. See also the following works by J. J. Brennig: "The Textile Trade of Seventeenth Century Northern Coromandel: A Study of a Pre-Modern Asian export industry" (PhD diss., the University of Wisconsin, Madison, 1975); "Textile Producers and Production in Late Seventeenth Century Coromandel," *Indian Economic & Social History Review* 23, no. 4 (1986): 333–55; "Chief Merchants and the European Enclaves of Seventeenth-Century Coromandel," *Modern Asian Studies* 11, no. 3 (1977): 321–40.

8. Deccan chroniclers commented on this famous episode with considerable admiration for Khan Jahan Lodi. See Ahmad, *Hadīqat*, 106–7.

9. For an overview, see Gordon, *The Marathas 1600–1818*. For more detailed studies, see Wink, *Land and Sovereignty in India*; Prachi Deshpande, *Creative Pasts*, 43–68; Sumit Guha, "An Indian Penal Regime: Maharashtra in the Eighteenth Century," *Past & Present* 147, no. 1 (1995): 102.

10. Jadunath Sarkar, *House of Shivaji* (Calcutta: M. C. Sarkar & Sons, 1955); Kruijtzer, *Xenophobia in Seventeenth Century India*, 265–284.

11. John D. Fryer, *New Account of East India and Persia 1672–1681* (London: Hakluyt Society, 1909), 43–45, 53–55; Kruijtzer, *Xenophobia in Seventeenth Century India* and "Madanna, Akkanna and the Brahmin Revolution: A Study of Mentality, Group Behaviour and Personality in Seventeenth-Century India," *Journal of the Economic and Social History of the Orient* 45, no. 2 (2002): 260–61. For the earliest arguments against such essentialisms, see A. R. Kulkarni, "Maratha Policy Towards the Adil Shahi Kingdom," *Bulletin of the Deccan College Research Institute* 49 (1990): 221–26.

12. Irina Efremova, "Delimiting the Ghar in Socio-Cultural Space," 41–57.

13. Gilmartin and Lawrence, *Beyond Turk and Hindu*, 1–20.

14. Deshpande, *Creative Pasts*, 42–65.

15. David E. Ludden, *Peasant History in South India* (Princeton, NJ: Princeton University Press, 1985); David Washbrook, "Progress and Problems: South Asian Economic and Social History c. 1720–1860," *Modern Asian Studies* 22, no. 1 (1988): 57–96; David Washbrook, "Merchants, Markets, and Commerce in Early Modern South India," *Journal of the Economic and Social History of the Orient* 53, nos. 1–2 (2010): 266–89.

16. Sanjay Subrahmanyam, "Noble Harvest from the Sea: Managing the Pearl Fishery of Mannar, 1500–1925," in *Institutions and Economic Change in South Asia*, ed. Burton Stein

and Sanjay Subrahmanyam (Delhi: Oxford University Press, 1996), 134–72; Markus Vink, *Encounters on the Opposite Coast*, xx–xxviii.

17. François Martin, *India in the 17th Century, (Social, Economic, and Political): Memoirs of Francois Martin 1670-1694*, ed. and trans. Lotika Varadarajan (New Delhi: Manohar, 1981), vol. 2, part 1, 823–25.

18. Vijaya Ramaswamy, *Textiles and Weavers in South India*, 2nd ed. (Delhi: Oxford University Press, 2006), 63–116; Vink, *Encounters on the Opposite Coast*, 218.

19. Chris Bayly and Sanjay Subrahmanyam, "Portfolio Capitalists and the Political Economy of Early Modern India," *Indian Economic & Social History Review* 25, no. 4 (1988): 401–24.

20. Ibid., 419.

21. Various Afghan shipowners on the Coromandel coast begin appearing in the incoming correspondence of the VOC toward the end of the seventeenth century, participating in freight trade across the Bay of Bengal, with operations in Tenasserim and Mergui. Subah Dayal, "From Golkonda to Siam: Secret Letters, Envelopes, and Diplomatic Crisis in the Mughal port-city," (presentation, Muzaffar Alam and The New Mughal Historiography Conference, Yale University, April 26–27, 2024).

22. See Ramaswamy, *Textiles and Weavers in South India*, 58–59, 107–12, for the disputes between the so-called *idangai* (left-hand) and *valangai* (right-hand) castes.

23. As noted by Varadarajan in the introduction to her translation (Martin, *India in the 17th Century*, xvi). For further exploration of Afghan lineages in eighteenth-century south India, see Hannah Archambault, "Geographies of Influence: Two Afghan Military Households in 17th and 18th Century South India" (PhD diss., University of California, Berkeley, 2018).

24. Martin, *India in the 17th century*, vol. 1, part 1, 5, 120. In late 1670, when Martin was first invited by Lodi to trade in his territories, he remarked very briefly that he had learned from an Armenian about the production of good quality cloth and the abundance of weaving centers in the countryside around Senji.

25. Muzaffar Alam and Sanjay Subrahmanyam, "Letters from a Sinking Sultan," in *Writing the Mughal World: Studies on Culture and Politics*. In addition, see the authors' other collaborations on documentary genres in Arabic and Persian across the Indian Ocean world, including "Letters from Kannur, 1500–1550: A Little Explored Aspect of Kerala History," in *Clio and Her Descendants: Essays for Kesavan Veluthat*, ed. Manu Devadevan (Delhi: Primus Books, 2018), 99–131.

26. For the late eighteenth century and the nineteenth century, the question of merchants and weavers under the English East India Company has a rich historiography. See Prasannan Parthasarathi, *The Transition to a Colonial Economy: Weavers, Merchants and Kings in South India*, 1720–1800 (Cambridge: Cambridge University Press, 2001); Prasannan Parthasarathi, "The State of Indian Social History," *Journal of Social History* 37, no. 1 (2003): 47–54; Karuna Dietrich Wielenga, "Repertoires of Resistance: The Handloom Weavers of South India, c. 1800–1960," *International Review of Social History* 61, no. 3 (2016): 423–58, and *Weaving Histories: the Transformation of the Handloom Industry in South India, 1800–1960* (Delhi: Oxford University Press, 2020). For merchant groups, see Kanakalatha Mukund, *The Trading World of the Tamil Merchant: Evolution of Merchant Capitalism in the Coromandel* (Hyderabad: Orient Blackswan, 1999).

27. Danna Agmon, *A Colonial Affair: Commerce, Conversion, and Scandal in French India* (Ithaca, NY: Cornell University Press, 2017); Anna Winterbottom, *Hybrid Knowledge in the Early East India Company World* (Cham: Springer, 2016); Guido van Meersbergen, *Ethnography and Encounter: The Dutch and English in Seventeenth-Century South Asia* (Leiden: Brill, 2022).

28. Agmon, *A Colonial Affair*, 1–18.

29. Zoltán Biedermann, "Three Ways of Locating the Global: Microhistorical Challenges in the Study of Early Transcontinental Diplomacy," *Past & Present* 242, no. 14 (2019): 110–41; I. Chatterjee, "Connected Histories and the Dream of Decolonial History."

30. J.N. Sarkar, *The Life of Mir Jumla*, 62–80; J. Sarkar, *History of Aurangzib*, vol. 1.

31. Wink, *Land and Sovereignty in India*, 157–250.

32. Chief merchant Joan Tack, from Delhi, to Governor Laurens Pit in Coromandel, VOC 1215 1656 fols. 1007–9. A decade later, it was noted that ʿAli II himself had sent away his mother, VOC 1255 1667 fol. 934, Governor Anthonij Paviljoen to Heeren XVII.

33. The figure of Khadija Sultana occupies a fraught position in both the earliest and the most recent political histories of the Deccan sultanates. The tendency to vilify Bari Sahiba and her "regency," as outside dynastic time and succession, remains consistent among male chroniclers and modern historians in the past and the present. See John D. Fryer, *New Account of East India and Persia. Being Nine Years' Travels, 1672–1681*, vol. 2, 53–55; Bernier, *Travels in the Mogul Empire*, 196–98. A more measured appraisal may be found in the work of the only female historian to write about her in the twentieth century. See Zeenat Sajida, ʿ*Ali ʿĀdil Shah Sānī* (Hyderabad: Silsila-yi Matbuʾāt hyderābād ūrdū akādemī, 1962). See also Verma, *History of Bijapur*, 195; B. G. Paranjape, *English Records on Shivaji* (Pune: Shiva Charitra Karyalaya, 1931), 32–33; Mehendale, *Shivaji His Life and Times*, 161; Gijs Kruijtzer, "Bari Sahiba bint Muhammad Qutb Shah," in *Christian-Muslim Relations. a Bibliographical History*, vol. 11, *Asia, East Africa and the Americas (1600–1700)* (Boston: Brill, 2016), 231–37.

34. *English Records on Shivaji*, 3; Bernier, *Travels in the Mogul Empire*, 197.

35. Nurullah Qazi, *Tārīkh-i ʿAli ʿĀdil Shāhī* (Telangana State Archives, Ms. 308), 18–23.

36. *English Records on Shivaji*, 1–3; VOC 1236 1661 fols. 479–96, 481r, Pieter van Santvliet in Vengurla to Batavia.

37. VOC 1232 1661 fols. 59–60.

38. VOC 1236 1661 fols. 479–98, Pieter van Santvliet in Vengurla to Batavia on April 28. VOC 1236 1661 fols. 923–24, Governor Laurens Pit in Coromandel to Batavia September 9, VOC 1243 1661 fols. 735–52, fols. 721–813. Pieter van Santvliet in Vengurla to Batavia, January 10.

39. VOC 1236 1661 fols. 479–98, Pieter van Santvliet in Vengurla to Batavia on April 28, *English Records on Shivaji*, 1–21.

40. Ibid., fol. 498.

41. VOC 1236 1661, fols. 194–95, fols. 183–202, Pieter van Santvliet in Vengurla to Batavia, January 10.

42. VOC 1256 1666, fol. 679v, Governor Anthonij Paviljoen in Fort Geldria to Governor General Joan Maetsuycker and Council of the Indies in Batavia February 8. VOC 1236 1661 fol. 497. VOC 1232 1661, fols. 59r–61.

43. VOC 1236 1661 fols. 498–99, Pieter van Santvliet in Vengurla to Batavia on April 28; letters from Vengurla to Batavia. The rumors mentioned by the Dutch resident intersect with the Jedhe chronology, which mentions the murder of Bahlol Khan (*shrāvan mansī bahlol khān mārela*) but does not specify that it was one of ʿAbdul Karim's brothers. See D. V. Apte and S. M. Divekar, eds., *Shivajicharitra Pradip* (Pune: Bharata Itihasa Sanshodhaka Mandala, 1925), 19.

44. VOC 1245 1664 fols. 467r, translation of a letter of the king of Bijapur to Governor Speelman November 5.

45. Ibid.

46. B. Muddachari, "Maratha Court in the Karnatak," *Proceedings of the Indian History Congress* 28 (1966): 177–79.

47. VOC 1261 1667, fols. 840–43, Leendeert Leendertsz in Vengurla to Heeren XVII November 28.

48. VOC 1232 1661, fols. 76–77, VOC 1234 1662, fols. 95–99, VOC 1238 1663, fols. 197–98. Martin, *India in the 17th Century*, vol. 1, part 2, 471.

49. VOC 1238 1663, fols. 197–98.

50. VOC 1234 1661 fols. A 95–99. VOC 1236 1661, fol. 605, Laurens Pit in Fort Geldria to Governor General Joan Maetsuycker in Batavia, 4 August 1661.

51. Future studies could examine the participation of the Mughal agents in the slave trade between the southern Coromandel to northern Sri Lanka in the late seventeenth and early eighteenth centuries. For northern India, Irfan Habib has argued that Mughal *faujdārs* regularly enslaved peasants who could not meet revenue demands or used robbery as an excuse to raid villages and take slaves, *Agrarian System of Mughal India*, 370–71. I thank Sumit Guha for this reference.

52. VOC 1232 1661, fols. 73—74.

53. VOC 1231 1660, fols. 795–96, Laurens Pits in Fort Geldria to Governor General Joan Maetsuycker in Batavia, 11 October 1659. VOC 1232 1661, fol. 382–83, From Laurens Pit in Fort Geldria to Heeren XVII, 9 August 1660. For the VOC's role in the slave trade after abolition and entrenching the role of dominant Vellalar caste in late eighteenth century Jaffna, see Nira Wickramasinghe and Alicia Schrikker, "The Ambivalence of Freedom: Slaves in Jaffna, Sri Lanka, in the Eighteenth and Nineteenth Centuries," *Journal of Asian Studies* 78, no. 3 (2019): 497–519. For a broad overview of oscillations in the VOC's slave trade in the Coromandel, see Tapan Raychaudhuri, *Jan Company in Coromandel* (Leiden: Brill, 1962), 156–59. A mention of the slave trade from Coromandel to Sri Lanka was made by Arasaratnam (*Merchants, Companies, and Commerce on the Coromandel Coast*, 104–5), which was substantially revised by Markus Vink in "'The World's Oldest Trade'": Dutch Slavery and Slave Trade in the Indian Ocean in the Seventeenth Century, *Journal of World History* 14, no. 2 (June 2003): 142. See also Vink, *Encounters on the Opposite coast*, 290.

54. VOC 1203 1655 587v, Caul issued by Commander Khan Muhammad of Bijapur for Laurens Pit, Captain of the Dutch in Pulicat 10 August 1654. VOC 1203 1655, 588v Caul of the King of Bijapur 12 August 1654.

55. Martin, *India in the 17th Century*, vol. 1, part 2, 686–87.

56. Subrahmanyam, "The 'Pulicat Enterprise.'"

57. Maulvi Abdul Haq, *Nusratī: malik-us shuʿarā'-ye Bījāpūr ke hālāt aur kalām par tabsirah* (New Delhi: Anjuman Taraqqī-yi Urdū, Hind, 1940); Devisingh Venkatsingh

NOTES   239

Chauhan, ed., *Tarikhe iskandarī, umarānī kā yudhha, Mulla nusratikṛta* (Pune: Maharashtra Rashtrabhasha Sabha, 1969); Jamil Jalibi, ed., *Divān-i Nusratī* (Lahore: Qausain, 1972); Suresh Dutt Awasthi, ed., *Tarikhe iskandarī* (Hyderabad: Andhra Pradesh Hindi Academy, 1987). *Tārīkh-i sikandarī* has been utilized in Marathi-language biographies of Shivaji. See Gajanan Bhaskar Mehendale, *Shri Raja Shivchatrapati*, (Pune: Diamond, 1999). Mehendale translated his biography of Shivaji from Marathi to English; there he draws on Devi Singh Chauhan's Devanagari edition of the text. Mehendale, *Shivaji His Life and Times*, 653–54, 459–60.

58. Before independence, Maulvi Abdul Haq's printed 1940 edition was well-known and accessible to Indian historians and literary scholars. But variations in the ability to read Dakkani in different scripts shaped how the *Tārīkh-i sikandarī* was edited by different individuals in the twentieth century. The very first complete transcription of the single manuscript in Maulvi Abdul Haq's library in Karachi was done by renowned Urdu scholar Sakhawat Mirza, which formed the basis for Jamil Jalibi's 1972 *Divān-i Nusratī*, one section of which included the *Tārīkh-i sikandarī*. I am indebted to Abdus Sattar Dalvi, Retired Professor, Department of Urdu, University of Mumbai, for sharing a copy of the original manuscript, Sakhawat Mirza's transcription, and the letters they exchanged about the text in the 1970s. Suresh Dutt Awasthi, a Hindi scholar who is well-versed in the Perso-Arabic script, based his 1987 edition in Devanagari script on Jalibi's 1972 Urdu edition. In contrast, as was well known in Urdu and Marathi circuits in Bombay at the time, Devi Singh Chauhan, who could not read Perso-Arabic script, used to sit down with a *maulvi*, who would explain each verse to him from Abdul Haq's partial Urdu edition, which he then quoted and glossed with an interpretation in his 1969 Devanagari edition.

59. Orsini, "How to Do Multi-Lingual Literary History?" 232.

60. In his edition, Awasthi even contested Nusrati's origins as a Muslim poet. See Suresh Dutt Awasthi's introduction to *Tarikhe iskandarī*.

61. Renowned Maratha historian and editor of Persian documents, and former director of Bharata Itihasa Sanshodhaka Mandala, G. H. Khare, wrote the preface for Devi Singh Chauhan's 1969 edition, published from the Maharashtra Rashtriyabhasa Sabha, Pune. While, as a professional historian, Khare still questioned the text's historicity, he nevertheless congratulated Chauhan on unearthing a source of and by a Muslim poet that could be used to contest the claims of historians who relied exclusively on Persian chronicles. See Khare's foreword to Devisingh Chauhan edition, *Tarikhe iskandarī*, 3–4.

62. Guha, *History and Collective Memory in South Asia*, 3–8.

63. Here, along with the *Tārīkh-i sikandarī* and *Shivrajbhusan* from the 1670s, we may also include Shivaji's Sanskrit-Persian dictionary of bureaucratic terms, *Rajvyahārkosh* (ca. 1678). See A. D. Marathe, ed., *Chhatrapatīñchyā Preraṇene Jhālelā Rājkosh* (Pune: Diamond, 2008).

64. J. Sarkar, *History of Aurangzib*, vol. 4, 112–16: Mehendale, *Shivaji His Life and Times*, 161–97.

65. Mehendale, *Shivaji His Life and Times*, 180.

66. Martin, *India in the 17th Century*, vol. 1, part 2, 510–12, 516, 529–34, 539–49, 554–56.

67. Ibid., 595–96.

68. Ibid.

69. Ibid., 560–62, 572–78, 580–86.

70. Ibid., 506–9; D.C. Verma, *History of Bijapur*, 203–5.
71. Ibid., 583.
72. Ibid., 621.
73. J. Sarkar, *Shivaji and His Times*, 228–342. The text's historicity is contested in Mehendale, *Shivaji His Life and Times*, 459–60.
74. VOC 1236 1661 fols. 498–99, Pieter van Santvliet in Vengurla to Batavia on April 28 Letters from Vengurla to Batavia.
75. Ali Anooshahr, *The Ghazi Sultans and the Frontiers of Islam* (London: Routledge, 2009), 14.
76. Umrani is a small village, located around sixty kilometers northwest of Bijapur, in the Miraj-Kolhapur district that lies at the intersections of the modern-day states of Maharashtra and Karnataka.
77. Nusrati, *Tārīkh-i sikandarī*, 17.
78. Sunil Sharma, "The City of Beauties in Indo-Persian Poetic Landscape," *Comparative Studies of South Asia, Africa and the Middle East* 24, no. 2 (2004): 73, 77.
79. Nusrati, *Tārīkh-i sikandarī*, 19.
80. Ibid., 17.
81. Ibid., 21.
82. Ibid., 18.
83. D.C. Verma, *History of Bijapur*, 203–5.
84. Nusrati, *Tārīkh-i sikandarī*, 20.
85. Ibid., 25.
86. Ibid., 34.
87. Ibid., 21.
88. Ibid., 21–22.
89. Ibid., 27, 31.
90. Vikas Rathee, "Narratives of the 1658 War of Succession for the Mughal Throne, 1658–1707" (PhD diss., University of Arizona, 2015).
91. Nusrati, *Tārīkh-i sikandarī*, 31.
92. Supriya Gandhi, *The Emperor Who Never Was* (Cambridge, MA: Harvard University Press, 2020), 224–27.
93. Nusrati, *Tārīkh-i sikandarī*, 31–32.
94. Gandhi, *Emperor Who Never Was*, 224–27.
95. Nusrati, *'Alināma*, 246–47.
96. Rao, Shulman, and Subrahmanyam, *Symbols of Substance*, 242–304; Markus Vink, *Encounters on the Opposite Coast*; Bes, *The Heirs of Vijayanagara*.
97. The problem of deindustrialization is one of the first foundational lessons taught in the standard curriculum of modern Indian history.
98. Ian C. Wendt, "Four Centuries of Decline? Understanding the Changing Structure of the South Indian Textile Industry" in *How India Clothed the World*, ed. Giorgio Riello and Tirthankar Roy (Leiden: Brill, 2009), 193–216.
99. Ibid.
100. Prasannan Parthasarthi, *The Transition to a Colonial Economy: Weavers, Merchants and Kings in South India, 1720–1800* (Cambridge: Cambridge University Press, 2001), 15–17, 121–48.

101. For the west coast of India in the late eighteenth century, Lakshmi Subramanian's *Indigenous Capital and Imperial Expansion: Bombay, Surat, and the West Coast* (New York: Oxford University Press, 1996) was among the first works to reconstruct the complex triangular social relations between regional upper-caste Hindu banking and mercantile castes, urban Muslim artisans, and the English East India Company, forcefully making the case for an "Anglo-bania order" that fueled and sustained imperial expansion. In an iconic debate in *Modern Asian Studies*, Subramanian's reply to Torri made clear the stakes for not shying away from examining intersectarian and intercaste conflicts during early colonial rule. See Lakshmi Subramanian, "The Eighteenth-Century Social Order in Surat: A Reply and an Excursus on the Riots of 1788 and 1795," *Modern Asian Studies* 25, no. 2 (1991): 321–65; Michelguglielmo Torri, "Surat During the Second Half of the Eighteenth Century: What Kind of Social Order?: A Rejoinder to Lakshmi Subramanian," *Modern Asian Studies* 21, no. 4 (1987): 679–710.

102. Vijaya Ramaswamy, *Textiles and Weavers in Medieval India*.

103. Ibid., 83–85, 142.

104. Vijaya Ramaswamy, "The Genesis and Historical Role of the Master Weavers in South Indian Textile Production," *Journal of the Economic and Social History of the Orient* (1985): 294–325.

105. Subrahmanyam, *Political Economy of Commerce in Southern India*, 307–14; Brennig, "Chief Merchants and the European Enclaves."

106. Martin, *India in the 17th Century*, Vol. 1, Part 1, 120.

107. Daniel Havart, *Op- en Ondergang van Cormandel . . . ook Op- en ondergang der Koningen, die zedert weynige jaren, in Golconda, de hoofd-stad van Cormandel geregeerd hebben* (three parts in one volume) (Amsterdam: Jan Claesz ten Hoorn, 1693), 15; Subrahmanyam, *Political Economy of Commerce in Southern India*, 206; Varadarajan, introduction to *India in the 17th Century*, xxii.

108. Subrahmanyam, "Niches and Networks: Staying On, 1665–1700," in *The Portuguese Empire in Asia*, 191–226. In the second half of the seventeenth century, the Indo-Portuguese, operating under Bijapur's protection or under the English, continued to serve in various capacities in Porto Novo and St. Thomé, and had small-scale commercial operations in Sumatra and Siam. See VOC 1256 1667, fol. 660, Antonio Paviljoen in Pulicat to Heeren XVII, November 15, 1666.

109. Subrahmanyam, "Noble Harvest from the Sea"; Subrahmanyam, Rao, Shulman, *Symbols of Substance*, 242–304; Markus Vink, *Encounters on the Opposite Coast*, 18; Subrahmanyam, *The Portuguese Empire in Asia*, 99. The Paravas were a low-status community of the Pearl Fishery Coast, who were converted by the Portuguese ecclesiastical mission in the 1530s. Preexisting economic rivalries existed between the Christian Paravas and the Muslim Maraikayyars, who controlled pearl fishery and revenue farms granted by nayaka rulers.

110. Takya Shu'ayb 'Alim, *Arabic, Arwi, Persian in Sarandib and Tamil Nadu: A Study of the Contributions of Sri Lanka and Tamil Nadu to Arabic, Arwi, Persian, and Urdu languages, literature, and education* (Chennai: Imāmul Arūs Trust, 1993), 1–24.

111. Havart, *Op- en Ondergang van Cormandel*, 16.

112. VOC 1302, 401–2, 408.

113. Martin, *India in the 17th Century*, vol. 1, part 2, 525, 587.

114. Ibid., 621.

115. For a study based on French sources, see Glenn Ames, *Colbert, Mercantilism, and the French Quest for Asian Trade* (DeKalb: Northern Illinois University Press 1996); VOC 1291 1673, fol. 56, French director Baron to De la Haye in Masulipatnam. VOC 1304 1674, fols. 246–47, De la Haye to Governor Anthonio Paviljoen, September 22, 1674. VOC 1302 1674, fols. 452–56, articles of peace over the city of St. Thomé between Anthonio Paviljoen and the Council of the Indies with the French general De la Haye, September 6, 1674.

116. Martin's first volume covers the sieges of St. Thomé, recounting French negotiations with Lodi and the Dutch. See Martin, *India in the 17th Century*, vol. 1, part 1, 118–84, 369–443; Subrahmanyam, *The Portuguese Empire in Asia*, 211–14.

117. For Martin Pit's career, see Havart, *Op- and Ondergang van Cormandel*, part 3, 51. Martin, *India in the 17th Century*, vol. 1, part 1, 311–13, 328–29, 323–24. Martin's account also reports on numerous visits to Lodi's camp and on Dutch attempts to oust the French from Pondicherry but does not include the letters to and from Lodi. VOC 1302 1674, fols. 401–8, report of chief merchant Martin Pit and Secretary Nicolas Ruijser to Anthonio Paviljoen on their visit to Sher Khan Lodi, March 30, 1674.

118. VOC 1302 1674, fols. 410–11, translated Telugu letter of Sher Khan Lodi to Governor Anthonio Paviljoen, March 25, 1674.

119. VOC 1302 1674, fol. 412, translated Telugu letter of Sher Khan Lodi to Governor Paviljoen, 1 June 1674. Martin, *India in the 17th Century Vol. I, Part I*, 389.

120. VOC 1302 1674, fols. 413–41, translated Telugu letter of Sher Khan Lodi in Valikondapuram to Governor Paviljoen, June 30, 1674.

121. Ibid., fols. 402–17.

122. VOC 1302, fols. 404–5, Sher Khan Lodi's qaul translated from Tamil to Anthonio Paviljoen, governor and director of the Coromandel Coast.

123. Ibid.

124. Translations of indigenous documentary genres appear a dime a dozen in the VOC archives, with distinct document types distributed across different regions. While the qaul form was prevalent on the Coromandel, Konkan, and Kanara coasts and the Deccan more broadly, it is largely absent in the case of Mughal domains, Surat and Bengal, where the *hasb ul-hukm* (order), issued directly by the Mughal ruler, was used. For just a few examples of such orders from Bengal, see 1692 VOC 1518, 679–80, 1692 VOC 7968 73–74, 1699 VOC 1624 Bengalen 1, 57–61; for Surat, see 1698 VOC 1611 394–95, VOC 1611, 1701 VOC 1649 Surat 385–86. The usage of the qaul form was common across different polities in southern India, irrespective of their religious and linguistic affiliation. For the nayaka kingdoms, see Markus Vink, *Encounters on the Opposite Coast*, 17–20, 314–16, 323–27, 353–58; Lennart Bes, *The Heirs of Vijayanagara*, 328, 332.

125. Prachi Deshpande, "The Marathi *kaulnāmā*: Property, Sovereignty and Documentation in a Persianate Form," *Journal of the Economic and Social History of the Orient* 64 (2021): 583–614.

126. Nawab Aziz Jung Vila, *Jami' ul-'atiyāt*, ed. Ziauddin Shakeb and Hasanuddin Ahmed (Hyderabad: Vila Academy, 1974), 157–59; Nawab Aziz Jung (d. 1924) was a Nawayati Muslim born in Nellore (present-day Andhra Pradesh), who worked in the Nizam's judicial department for over two decades. He collected and collated Mughal manuals on *siyāq* account-keeping and grant typologies, using them to teach staff in the newly formed archive offices of the Hyderabad state in the early twentieth century.

127. Ibid. See also Nader Nasiri-Moghaddam, "Persian Documents In the National Archives (Torre Do Tombo) of Portugal and Their Importance for the History of the Persian Gulf in the 16th–17th Centuries," *International Journal of the Society of Iranian Archaeologists* 2, no. 3 (Winter–Spring, 2016): 59.

128. *Jami' ul-'atiyāt*, 159.

129. Ibid.

130. Deshpande, "The Marathi *kaulnāmā*," 591–92.

131. Khare, P. S. I. H., vol. 2, letters from the Khopade family of Ambade (Bhor-Pune), 32–33. One among many published qauls, this one dated from June 17, 1665, from the eighth regnal year of the Mughal king Aurangzeb (d. 1707), and was addressed to hereditary office holders from the Khopade family of Ambade (near Pune) in western India.

132. Ibid.

133. Yusuf H. Khan, *Diplomatic Correspondence Between Mir Nizam Ali Khan and the English East India Company* (Hyderabad: Central Records Office, 1958); Deshpande, "The Marathi *kaulnāmā*," 607.

134. Deshpande, "The Marathi *kaulnāmā*," 598.

135. For instance, in many Persian qaul from the Nizam's period, we find instances of commercial taxes levied on the sale of textiles by the Marwari communities in Hyderabad state.

136. Many individuals and groups were contacted to make sure Lodi's qaul would be adhered to, including Lodi's arch-rival, the Indo-African Nasir Muhammad, in Senji, the havaldārs of Porto Novo and those of other districts south up to Point Calimere, the English agent William Langhorne in Madras, and various officials of the Danish East India Company in Tranquebar, and most importantly, the merchants of Porto Novo.

137. VOC 1302., fol. 410r.

138. Ibid.

139. VOC 1302, fol. 403r.

140. VOC 1236 1661, fols. 498–99.

141. Rao, Shulman, and Subrahmanyam, *Symbols of Substance*, 242–304; Vink, *Encounters on the Opposite Coast*, 323–30, 494–505.

142. I thank Sanjay Subrahmanyam for deciphering these names and titles. The collective included names like Hasan Maraikkayar, Aramugam Nalla Tambi Chetti, Kutti Ambala (Criambole) Chetti, Badi' (Batia) Maraikkayar, Sayyid Maraikkayar, Brahma (Pramma) Reddi, Mudaliyan Chetti, Nayiniappa Mudaliyar, Periya Nayina (Nia) Pillai Maraikkayar, Qadir Miyan (Cartamia) Pillai Maraikkayar, Kaliyatta (Caliata) Pillai.

143. Rao, Shulman, and Subrahmanyam, *Symbols of Substance*, 264–67; David Shulman and Sanjay Subrahmanyam, "Prince of Poets and Ports: Cītakkāti, the Maraikkāyars and Ramnad, ca. 1690–1710," in *Islam and Indian Regions*, ed. Anna Libera Dallapiccola and Stephanie Zingel-Avé Lallement, vol. 1 (Stuttgart: Steiner, 1993), 497–535.

144. VOC 1302 1675, fol. 408. The complete biographies of Sunni Muslim Maraikayyars, proficient in Arabic and Tamil, and how they combined their scribal skills with mercantile interests are difficult to reconstruct in this part of the seventeenth century. They may have certainly been precursors to controversial figures in the early nineteenth century such as Casi Chettiar, who used his scribal position in the treasury department in the Coimbatore collector's office to further entrench his private trade interests, which Bhavani Raman has evocatively reconstructed. See Raman, *Document Raj*, 43–50.

145. Cynthia Talbot, "A Revised View of 'Traditional' India: Caste, Status, and Social Mobility in Medieval Andhra," *South Asia: Journal of South Asian Studies* 15, no. 1 (1992): 17–52.

146. Ibid., 33–35, 46–48.

147. VOC 1302 1675, fols. 416–17. Anthonio Paviljoen to the merchants of Porto Novo, May 18, 1674.

148. Ibid.

149. VOC 1302 1675, fol. 407.

150. Ramaswamy, *Textiles and Weavers in South India*, 14–15. The other major *jāti* or subcaste were the *sales or salingas*, divided further into more divisions and hierarchies—for instance, between the silk weavers, who ranked themselves higher than cotton weavers.

151. *Annual Report of South-Indian Epigraphy*, 1943–45, 287.

152. A range of groups fell in and out of this system of social organization, marked by conflict as well as by an underlying unity. See Ramaswamy, *Textiles and Weavers in South India*, 107–12, 160–66; Niels Brimnes, *Constructing the Colonial Encounter: Right- and: Left-Hand Castes in Early Colonial South India* (London: Routledge, 2019).

153. For the Bijapuri Indo-African Khan Muhammad's relations with the VOC, particularly with regard to the control of the import trade of tin, see VOC 1203 1654, fol. 583, Khan-i Khanan from Governor Laurens Pit, September 6, 1654. VOC 1203 1654, fols. 584–85, translated letter of Khan-i Khanan to Governor Laurens Pit, September 6, 1654. VOC 1203 1654 fols. 586–87 Copy of Khan-i Khanan's caul issued to Laurens Pit. VOC 1203 1654 fols. 589–90, Khan-i Khanan to Laurens Pit, August 18, 1654.

154. VOC 1269 1670, fols. 105–7.

155. Ibid., fols. 105–6.

156. VOC 1270 1669, fol. 413r, letters from governor to Heeren XVII, November 2, 1669. VOC 1274 1670, fols. 569–70, fols. 550–613, letters from the governor to Batavia, February 13, June 24, July 5, August 6, September 29, and October 6, 1670. In the southern Coromandel, merchants and weavers specialized in painted cotton cloth, meant to be exported to markets within Asia. See J. J. Brennig, "The Textile Trade of Seventeenth Century Northern Coromandel," 23, 243, 254.

157. VOC 1269 1670, fol. 105v.

158. Cherian, *Merchants of Virtue*, 1–8, 69–76.

159. Kothiyal, *Nomadic Narratives*, 27–49, 90–110.

160. One of the earliest studies to engage with the question of precolonial inequality on the eve of colonialism was Dharma Kumar, *Land and Caste in South India: Agricultural Labour in the Madras Presidency during the Nineteenth Century* (Cambridge: Cambridge University Press, 1965).

161. For the early colonial period, see chapter 3 of Raman, *Document Raj*, 81–105.

7. POSTSCRIPT: FORGETTING HOUSEHOLDS, MAKING DYNASTIES

1. Munshi Muhammad ʿAzimuddin ibn Muhammad Faizuddin Dalvi, *Tārīkh-i Dilīr-jangī* (Jāmiʿ ul-akhbār: 1262 Hijri/1847 CE) (hereafter *Tārīkh-i Dilīr-jangī*), 4–5.

2. On the household anthology under the Safavids, see Kathryn Babayan, *The City as Anthology*, 63–107.

3. Muzaffar Alam and Sanjay Subrahmanyam, "Witnesses and Agents of Empire: Eighteenth-Century Historiography and the World of the Mughal Munshi," *Journal of the Economic and Social History of the Orient* 53, nos. 1–2 (2009): 393–423; C. Skinner, "Transitional

Malay Literature: Part 1—Ahmad Rijaluddin and Munshi Abdullah," *Bijdragen tot de Taal-, Land- en Volkenkunde* 134 (1978): 467–70.

4. Khera, *The Place of Many Moods*, 117–43: Kapadia, *In Praise of Kings*, 129–57; Asif, *Loss of Hindustan*, 181–219; Talbot, *The Last Hindu Emperor*, 183–218.

5. Asif, *Loss of Hindustan*, 205.

6. Indrani Chatterjee, *Gender, Slavery and Law in Colonial India* (New Delhi: Oxford University Press, 1999); Durba Ghosh, *Sex and the Family in Colonial India: The Making of Empire* (Cambridge: Cambridge University Press, 2006).

7. Sumit Guha, "The Family Feud as Political Resource in Eighteenth-Century India," in I. Chatterjee, *Unfamiliar Relations*, 77.

8. Krishnaji Nageshrao Chitnis, *The Nawabs of Savanur* (Delhi: Atlantic, 2000), 9, 52.

9. Justin Jones, *Shi'a Islam in Colonial India: Religion, Community and Sectarianism* (Cambridge: Cambridge University Press, 2011); Asiya Alam, "Polygyny, Family and Sharafat: Discourses amongst North Indian Muslims, circa 1870–1918," *Modern Asian Studies* 45, no. 3 (2011): 631–68 and *Women, Islam and Familial Intimacy in Colonial South Asia* (Leiden: Brill, 2021).

10. 'Azimuddin, *Tārīkh-i Dilīr-jangī*, 224.

11. Ibid., 225.

12. Ibid., 239.

13. Ibid., 257.

14. Ibid., 233.

15. Ibid., 256–63.

16. Ibid., 49–51.

17. Ibid., 20–23, 49–51, 145, 225.

18. These include texts such as Mir Hussein Ali Khan Kirmani, *The History of the Reign of Tipu Sultan: Being a Continuation of the Neshani Hyduri*, trans. W. Miles (London: Oriental Translation Fund), 1844.

19. *Tārīkh-i Dilīr-jangī*, 61–62.

20. *Annual Report of the Mysore Archaeological Department*, 1944, 172, 181.

21. *Tārīkh-i Dilīr-jangī*, 66. Here, 'Azimuddin was drawing on Kirmani's *The History of the Reign of Tipu Sultan*.

22. For instance in James Grant Duff, *History of the Mahrattas*, vol 3. (Calcutta: R. Cambray, 1918) and more recently in Chitnis, *The Nawabs of Savanur*.

23. *Tārīkh-i Dilīr-jangī*, 73; *Bombay Gazetteer*, 667.

24. *Tārīkh-i Dilīr-jangī*, 78.

25. This is a rare moment in the *Tārīkh-i Dilīr-jangī* when the author emphasizes the Afghanness of Savanur, when emphasizing a comparison against the Sunni Muslim rulers of Mysore, when in most of the account, there appears to be little to no discussions of a sense of ethnic solidarity.

26. The trope of Afghan solidarity went back several centuries, occurring in well-known late Mughal texts, such as Bhimsen's *Tārīkh-i Dilkusha* and his account of the Deccan conquest as well as in earlier texts from the Deccan sultanates from the early seventeenth century. See *Hadīqat*, 106–7.

27. These types of genealogical accounts were common in Afghan histories, as Nile Green has shown in the foundational text, *Tārīkh-i Afghanha*. See his chapter "Tribe, Diaspora, and Sainthood in Indo-Afghan History," in *Making Space: Sufis and Settlers in Early Modern India* (Delhi: Oxford University Press, 2012), 65–115.

28. *Tārīkh-i Dilīr-jangī*, 15–16.
29. Ibid., 86.
30. Keelan Overton and Kristine Rose-Beers, "Indo-Persian Histories from the Object Out: The St. Andrews Qur'an Manuscript between Timurid, Safavid, Mughal and Deccani Worlds," in Overton, *Iran and the Deccan*, 257–336.
31. Guha, *Beyond Caste*; Subrahmanyam, "Connected Histories"; Chatterjee, "Connected Histories and the Dream of Decolonial history."
32. Asif, *The Loss of Hindustan*.
33. Pankaj Jha, Nitin Sinha, Nitin Varma, eds., *Servants' Pasts: Sixteenth to Eighteenth Century, South Asia, Vol. 1* (Hyderabad: Orient Blackswan, 2019). Rosalind O'Hanlon and David Washbrook, "After Orientalism: Culture, Criticism, and Politics in the Third World," *Comparative Studies in Society and History* 34, no. 1 (1992): 141–67.
34. F. Hasan, *Paper, Performance, and the State*, 121–31.
35. Faruqui, *The Princes of the Mughal Empire*; Azfar A. Moin, *The Millennial Sovereign: Sacred Kingship and Sainthood in Islam* (New York: Columbia University Press, 2014); Truschke, *Culture of Encounters*; Kinra, *Writing Self, Writing Empire*.
36. Not at all unique to the case of Islam in South Asia, this dilemma is part of a larger pattern of how the discourse on Islam is framed and received in the West. See Mahmood Mamdani, *Good Muslim, Bad Muslim: America, the Cold War, and the Roots of Terror* (New York: Pantheon Books, 2004).
37. Manu Pillai, *Rebel Sultans: The Deccan from the Khilji to Shivaji* (New Delhi: Juggernaut Books, 2020), 6–7.
38. For a critique of origins, see Manan Ahmed Asif, *A Book of Conquest* (Cambridge, MA: Harvard University Press, 2016).
39. Kaicker, *The King and The People*; Chatterjee, *Negotiating Mughal Law*; Cherian, *Merchants of Virtue*; F. Hasan, *Paper, Performance, and the State*.
40. Sumit Guha, *Beyond Caste*, 19; Nazir, "Social Structure, Ideology and Language," 2897–900; Kancha Ilaiah Shephard, "Why Didn't India's Muslim Rulers and Thinkers Confront the Inequities of the Caste System?" *The Wire*, January 8, 2023, https://thewire.in/caste/why-didnt-indias-muslim-rulers-and-thinkers-confront-the-inequities-of-the-caste-system.
41. M. Athar Ali, *The Mughal Nobility under Aurangzeb*, 14–15. Future studies promise to illustrate how well caste fit into Hanafi jurisprudence, helping forge a pansubcontinental, highly centralized Mughal legal order. See Naveen Kanalu Ramamurthy, "Mirrors and Masks of Sovereignty: Imperial Governance in the Mughal World of Legal Normativism, c. 1650s–1720s," (PhD diss., University of California, Los Angeles, 2021).
42. For a recent study that examines contentious debates among Smarta-Saiva Brahmins and the works of the seventeenth-century poet Nilakantha Dikshita from southern Tamil Nadu, see Elaine M. Fisher, *Hindu Pluralism: Religion and the Public Sphere in Early Modern South India* (Oakland, CA: University of California Press, 2017). For a study that accounts for heterogeneity and disagreement among Muslim elites in the early Delhi Sultanate, see Sunil Kumar, *The Emergence of the Delhi Sultanate, 1192—1286* (New Ranikhet: Permanent Black, 2007) and "The Ignored Elites: Turks, Mongols and a Persian Secretarial Class in the Early Delhi Sultanate" *Modern Asian Studies* 43, 1 (2009): 45–77.

ACKNOWLEDGMENTS

Over the past decade, the generosity of an eclectic set of scholars, teachers, friends, interlocuters, and institutions helped make this book possible. First books take much too long to come to light, and along the way we lose some of our most cherished mentors. I must begin by thanking two teachers who taught me the virtues of circulating between multiple disciplines and worlds: M. Z. A. Shakeb (d. 2021), historian-archivist and maker of the Mughal Record Room in the Telangana State Archives, and Rahmat Ali Khan (d. 2022), Keeper of Manuscripts at the Salar Jung Museum Library in Hyderabad, India. Both were part of a tireless first generation of postindependence scholars, from different regions of Hindustan who devoted their lives to listening to the precolonial past and doing everything possible to preserve its material remains in our present. They taught me that the children who do not inherit a private library or come from an illustrious family lineage can also learn to decipher documents and help in reimagining the archives of times past.

This book is the result of studying under these unconventional teachers, along with the more traditional set of resources afforded by graduate schools, language programs, research fellowships, and so forth. I thank the Library of Congress in Washington, DC, where this book was completed with the support of a Kluge Fellowship during the academic year 2021–22. In particular, I thank Michael Stratmoen and Travis Hensley of the John W. Kluge Center, and Jonathan Loar and Charlotte Giles of the Asia Division, for accommodating my many requests as a harried new mom. I take full responsibility for the inevitable inadequacies and errors of this work and credit all its strengths to this long list of teachers and loved ones who made it come to fruition.

The kernel of this book began at the Department of History at the University of California, Los Angeles, where conversations with Sanjay Subrahmanyam, along with his irreverence and sense of humor, helped me get through many ups and downs during and long after graduate school. At UCLA, I also thank Nile Green, Roy Bin Wong, Margaret Jacob, Michael Cooperson, Geoffrey Robinson, Caroline Ford, Muriel McClendon, and my first

Dutch teacher, Cisca Brier. In Los Angeles, I also thank Julia Maher and Karen Leonard for offering comfortable homestays in between trips to Hyderabad. I thank my undergraduate teachers Sumit Guha and Indrani Chatterjee for the earliest lessons about all things household and for their enthusiastic support for the idea of reversing the flow that led me to pursue an advanced degree at Jawaharlal Nehru University in New Delhi, where Radhika Singha, Neeladri Bhattacharya, Lakshmi Subramanian, and the late Rajat Datta first introduced me to the addictive smell of an archive. I am most grateful to Muzaffar Alam, who helped me find my teachers. He first directed me to Sanjay, an advisor amenable to working with a strange combination of languages, and then to Shakeb Sahib, who enabled my turning away from the glamorous side of the Mughals to the gritty, mundane realities of an empire trying to govern the unruly peninsula.

I thank the friends who helped me navigate the learning curve that comes after graduate school, Garry Bertholf, M. Ty, Macabe Keliher, and Joel Blecher. In 2016, Garry and M. Ty kept me sane during nine months of taco deprivation in South Carolina, where we entertained ourselves by going to Dave and Buster's. I thank fellow *khatmal* destroyer, Joel, for his boundless kindness ever since our fateful journey to the Deccan in 2011. At Emory, Scott Kugle, Harshita Mruthinti Kamath, and Roxani Margariti helped restore my senses on weekend trips to Atlanta. In New Orleans, I thank colleagues at Tulane University where I taught for two years, particularly Kris Lane, whose door was always open to nerd out on all things early modern. And the Young Turks of Hébert Hall—Karissa Haugeberg, Felipe Fernandes Cruz, Sara Madandar, M. Kathryn Edwards, Yiğit Akin, and Zulal Fazlıoğlu Akın. In Tulane's Sociology Department, a big thanks go to Mariana Craciun and Camilo Arturo Leslie, the drill sergeants who taught us how to sleep train our infant daughter so that I could get back to writing this book.

At New York University, I am surrounded by colleagues who supported me through many professional and personal transitions. Thank you to Dipti Khera, David Ludden, Guy Burak, and Barry Flood for help with figuring out NYU's complex topography and Ulrich Baer and the Center for Humanities for a Book Subvention Grant. Dipti has wiped off many kinds of tears while continuing to engage with my work in critical ways. Her comments, along with the meticulous feedback of Purnima Dhavan in my manuscript workshop, transformed the book's content and organization. Guy remains a consistent interlocutor always ready to share another rant over dosas. Many thanks to Jyoti Gulati Balachandran, a patient reader and merciless editor, who taught me how to write the difficult genres of proposals and introductions. Without my book development editor, Petra Shenk, I would have probably never written this book. Thank you to Kim Greenwell for a final edit of the introduction.

At Gallatin, my mentors Ritty Lukose and Ali Mirsepassi, pushed me at the right moments to stop deliberating and just get it done. A big thanks to Sinan Antoon, Gianpaolo Baiocchi, Paula Chakravartty, Kwami Coleman, Mehmet Darakçıoğlu, Anne DeWitt, Hallie Franks, Rosalind Fredericks, Andrea Gadberry, Shatima Jones, Marie Cruz Soto, David Spielman, and Duncan Yoon. I want to especially thank the two deans who have supported my work, Susanne Wofford and Victoria Rosner, Faculty of Arts and Science Vice Dean Susan Antón, as well as associate deans Millery Polyné and Alejandro Velasco for their generous and unwavering support of junior faculty, including an award from the Gallatin Publications Subvention Fund. I thank Associate Dean of Finance Linda Wheeler Reiss, as well as our amazing staff, including Marissa Mattes, Gisela Humphreys, Ivy Marie Garcia, and Anna Brown, all of whom have made Gallatin an academic home.

I thank the entire staff at the University of California Press, especially my editor, Eric Schimdt, who enthusiastically supported the project through the steps of publication, along with his editorial assistant, Jyoti Arvey, and copy editor, Gabriel Bartlett. I thank the anonymous reviewers who offered incisive comments on a late draft of the manuscript, as well as Ali Anooshahr, Rajeev Kinra, Sunil Sharma, Prachi Deshpande, Eric Lewis Beverley, Manan Ahmed, Jorge Flores, Usman Hamid, and Pasha M. Khan who read individual chapters. Thank you to Keelan Overton and Jake Benson for sharing sources and for their erudite estimates in deciphering illegible words.

In India, the list of individuals, institutions, and many households that helped make this book possible is long. The late scholar-administrator Vasant Kumar Bawa and renowned Urdu scholar, Oudesh Rani Bawa, hosted me for many years and taught me about Hyderabad's history, culture, and bureaucracy, helping make this city a second ghar. In Bijapur, Dr. Abdul Ghani Imaratwale of Anjuman Degree College and Sujit Nayan and Smita Kumar of the Archaeological Survey of India, who shared materials, and Ameen Hollur for coordinating the logistics of trips. Qamarunissa Qadri, the granddaughter of Shamsullah Qadri (d. 1953), and the wife of my late teacher, Rahmat Ali Khan, who welcomed me to their home and library. Farhat Ahmed and the entire family of Shakeb Sahib dispersed over Hyderabad, London, and the Gulf. Retired professor from the Department of Urdu, Osmania University, Mohammed Ali Asar who, despite his illness, has been generous with his time and ideas on Dakkani. At what is now the Telangana State Archives, Director Zarina Parveen and Assistant Directors Ramakrishna and T. Purandhar. Downstairs in the Mughal Record room, Abdul Moeed, Senior Research Assistant, and Mohammad Abdul Raqeeb, Assistant Director. At Idara-i Adabiyat Urdu, Hyderabad, the descendants of M. Q. Zor, especially Rafiuddin Qadri Zor, and Tasneem Zor of Fairfax, VA, and librarian Amir Shah, who made available secondary sources. At the Government Oriental Manuscripts Library and Research Institute, Hyderabad, Rafat Rizwana and Tanveer Madam. At the YSR Reddy State Museum, Hyderabad, manuscript clerk, Vasanthi Madam, and Director Suguna Sharma. At Abu'l Kalam Azad Oriental Research Institute in Hyderabad, Ahmed Ali Khan for making available many out-of-print works. At Osmania University library, the staff of the dissertations and Urdu periodicals sections.

Among the current generation of scholars of premodern Dakkani, I have cherished my friendship with Dr. Badar Sultana of Maulana Azad National Urdu University, the author of two indispensable monographs on narrative poems in Dakkani who continues to edit and process the rarest premodern manuscripts in this language. Badar and I owe much to an earlier generation of women who led the way in working across literary and nonliterary archives—Zeenat Sajida, Najma Siddiqua, Zaib Hyder, S. Basheerunissa Begam, Sayeeda Jafar, and Humairah Jalili, all of whom are no longer with us. In Mumbai, Abdus Sattar Dalvi and the late Nurus Sayeed Akhter, both of the University of Mumbai, who generously shared copies of materials from the Anjuman Taraqqi-i Urdu in Karachi, Pakistan. Gautam Pemmaraju for sharing his knowledge of the contemporary performance traditions of Dakkani poetry and satire. In Indore, Mukesh Dube and Shraddha Goswami for their hospitality and for arranging a road trip to Burhanpur. In Burhanpur, the Archaeological Survey of India staff, Toofan Singh, and local historian, Major Gupta, for sharing tales of his frontier city. I thank you all.

In the Netherlands, many thanks go to the staff of Nationaal Archief, especially Frank Devanand Kanhai. In Leiden, Carolien Stolte, Lennart Bes, and Norifumi Daito shared their meticulous knowledge of VOC materials. Kees Stal, of the Municipal Archives in Den

Haag, first introduced me to the dizzying handwriting of archival documents. My Dutch teachers, Ingrid Marek and An Vanderhelst, held my hand through the toughest VOC materials. At the British Library in London, the staff of the Asia and Africa Studies Reading Room. Conversations with the late David Matthews and Christopher Shackle, the earliest scholars to closely examine Indian vernaculars like Dakkani and Panjabi, helped me recognize the limits of my own engagement with such materials. Thank you to Fasih ul-Islam for always advising me to do the right thing at the right time.

A set of friends and family, within and beyond academia and across continents have sustained me through the years: Naveen Kanalu, the radioactive proton that has no off button, with whom I share a love for all the contradictions of the pre-modern past. Adventures with Rohit, Mahboubeh, and Suranjan—whether watching a *kabaddi* match in Barkas or trying the rickety rides at *numaish* or the endless pursuit of gluttony—helped make the best memories of Bombay and Hyderabad. Thank you to Suzanne Schulz and Ali Sengul and Trudy Rebert and Sid Jha, who helped us feel at home when we first moved back east in 2019. My dear friend, an archaeologist of early medieval South Asia, Kanika Kalra, stayed with me through many crazy events and created all the maps for this book shortly after delivering her second child. A special thanks to my *nani*, N. P. Kaura, the original matriarch who presided over a lineage of formidable women, including my mother, Devika Dayal. I miss you, Mama. Thank you (and Pop and Bhai) for doing everything possible to support my bizarre fantasy to be a historian, this one is for you. The Patros, Peterson, and Kotnour families in La Crosse, Wisconsin, in particular, my mother-in-law Cynthia Patros, who stepped in during many summer and winter breaks to take care of our daughter. Several cross-country moves, floods, broken femurs, grief, and all the rest, we survived it all, Tyson and Selma! You two are my whole world and I cannot thank you enough.

Subah Dayal
New York City, 2024

BIBLIOGRAPHY

MANUSCRIPTS

Atishi, Hakim. Ms. '*Ādilnāma*. Ms. P. 4300. YSR Reddy State Museum. Hyderabad, Telangana, India. ca. 1637.
Documents under Shah Jahan (ca. 1628–58). Acc. nos. 1–541 to 2838–3152. Mughal Record Room. State Archives, Telangana, Hyderabad.
al-Husayni, Abu'l Qasim. *Guldasta-i gulshan-i rāz dar ta'rīf-i sultartān Muhammad 'Ādil Shāh*. Ms. H17 (13). Cambridge University Library. n.d.
Muqim, Mirza, *Fathnāma-i Ikkerī*. Ms. No. 1/225, Qadim 2/40 Jadid, Anjuman Taraqqi-i Urdu, Karachi, Pakistan.
Nusrati. *Tarjī'-band (poem with return-tie) on the Occasion of Khadija Sultana and Muhammad 'Adil Shah's Wedding*. Ms. Or. 13533. British Library, n.d.
Qazi, Nurullah. *Tārīkh-i 'Ali 'Adil Shāhī*. Ms 308. Telangana State Archives, Hyderabad, n.d.
Zuhuri, Zuhur ibn. *Muhammadnāma*. Ms. 26. Bijapur State Archaeological Museum, Karnataka, ca. 1648.

Nationaal Archief (National Archives), The Hague

Collectie Geleynssen de Jonghe: 1.10.30, nos. 196, 198, 202.
Overgekomen Brieven and Papieren (OBP):
Coromandel VOC 1203, 1215, 1231, 1232, 1234, 1236, 1238, 1243, 1245, 1255, 1256, 1261, 1291, 1269, 1270, 1274, 1302, 1304.
Vengurla VOC 1130, 1133, 1139, 1144, 1152, 1170, 1174, 1243, 1236.

Editions and Translations

Ahmad, Nizamuddin. *Hadīqat al-salātīn (A History of the Reign of ʿAbdullah Qutb Shah of Golkonda [1662–1672 A.D.])*. Edited by Syed Ali Asghar Bilgirami. Hyderabad: Islamic Publications Society, 1961.

Annual Report on South-Indian Epigraphy for the Year 1943–1945. Calcutta: GOI Central Publication Branch.

Bernier, François. *Travels in the Mogul Empire AD 1656–1668*. London: W. Pickering, 1826.

Dalvi, Munshi Muhammad ʿAzimuddin ibn Muhammad Faizuddin. *Tārīkh-i Dilīr-Jangī*. Jamiʿal-akhbār, 1262 Hijri/1846 CE.

al-Fazl, Abuʾl. *The History of Akbar*. Edited by W. M. Thackston. Vol. 8. Murty Classical Library of India. Cambridge, MA: Harvard University Press, 2022.

Fryer, John D. *A New Account of East India and Persia: 1672–1681*. London: Hakluyt Society, 1909.

Havart, Daniel. *Op- en Ondergang van Cormandel . . . ook Op- en ondergang der Koningen, die zedert weynige jaren, in Golconda, de hoofd-stad van Cormandel geregeerd hebben* (three parts in one volume). Amsterdam: Jan Claesz ten Hoorn, 1693.

Khan, Yusuf H. *Diplomatic Correspondence between Mir Nizam Ali Khan and the East India Company, 1780–1798*. Hyderabad: Central Records Office, 1958.

———. *Selected Documents of Aurangzeb's Reign, 1659–1706*. Hyderabad, Deccan: Central Records Office, Government of Andhra Pradesh, 1958.

———. *Selected Documents of Shah Jahan's Reign*. Hyderabad: Daftar-i-Diwani, 1950.

———. *Selected Waqai of the Deccan: (1660–1671 A.D.)*. Hyderabad: Central Records Office, 1953.

Khare, Ganesh Hari, ed. *Aitihāsik Fārsī sāhitya / Persian Sources of Indian History*. Vols. 1–3. Pune: Bharata Itihasa Sanshodhaka Mandala, 1934.

Khushnud, Malik. *Jannat Singār, 1645*. Edited by Sayeeda Jafar. New Delhi: National Council for Promotion of Urdu Language, 1997.

Manuzzi, Niccolò. *Storia do Mogor or Mogul India 1653–1708*. Vol. 2. Translated by William Irvine. London: John Murray. 1907.

Martin, François. *India in the 17th Century, (Social, Economic, and Political): Memoirs of Francois Martin 1670–1694*. Translated and annotated by Lotika Varadarajan. New Delhi: Manohar, 1981.

Mukhlis, Nand Ram. *Siyāqnāma*. Lucknow: Nawal Kishore, 1879.

Nusrati. *ʿAlināma*. Edited by Abdul Majeed Siddiqui. Hyderabad: Salar Jang Dakkani Publications, 1959.

———. *Tarikhe Iskandari*. Edited by Devisingh Venkatsingh Chauhan. Pune: Maharashtra Rashtrabhasha Sabha, n.d.

———. *Tārīkh-i Sikandarī*. Edited by Jamil Jalibi. Lahore: Qausain, 1972.

———. *Tarikhe Iskandari*. Edited by Suresh Dutt Awasthi. Hyderabad: Andhra Pradesh Hindi Academy, 1987.

Pissurlencar, Panduronga S. S., ed. "A índia Em 1629. Relação Dos Reis Vizinhos Do Que Ora Passão e Contão (Account of the Neighbouring Kings.) *Boletim do Instituto Vasco da Gama* 7 (1930): 52–61.

———. *Assentos do Conselho do Estado*. 5 Vols. Bastorá, Goa: Tip. Rangel, 1953–57.

Qazi, Nurullah. *Tārīkh-i ʿAlī ʿĀdil Shāhī*. Edited by Abu Nasr Khalidi. Hyderabad: Ijaz Press, 1964.

Sharif, Ja'far. *Qanoon-e-Islam: or the Customs of the Mussulmans of India*. Translated by G. A. Herklots. London: Parbury, Allen, 1832.
Shauqi, Hasan. *Divān-i Hasan Shauqī: Dasvīn sadi hijrī mein Urdū shā'irī kī rivāyāt kā surāgh*. Edited by Jamil Jalibi. Karachi: Anjuman-i Taraqqi-yi Urdu Pakistan, 1971.
al-Zubayri, M. Ibrahim. *Tārīkh-i Bījāpūr musamma bi-basātīn al-salātīn*. Hyderabad, 1800s.

SECONDARY SOURCES

'Alim, Tayka Shu'ayb. *Arabic, Arwi and Persian in Sarandib and Tamil Nadu: A Study of the Contributions of Sri Lanka and Tamil Nadu to Arabic, Arwi, Persian and Urdu Languages, Literature, and Education*. Chennai: Imāmul Arūs Trust, 1993.
Adams, Julia. *The Familial State: Ruling Families and Merchant Capitalism in Early Modern Europe*. Ithaca, NY: Cornell University Press, 2005.
Agmon, Danna. *A Colonial Affair: Commerce, Conversion, and Scandal in French India*. Ithaca, NY: Cornell University Press, 2017.
Ahmed, Aziz. "Dar Al-Islam and the Muslim Kingdoms of Deccan and Gujarat." *Cahiers d'Histoire Mondiale* 7, no. 1 (1962): 787.
Akhter, Nurus Syed. "Fathnāmah-yi Ikkerī az Mirza Muqīm par Tahqīqī Nazr." *Seh Mahi Urdu*, 2 (1988): 108–37.
Akkerman, Nadine, and Birgit Houben. *The Politics of Female Households: Ladies-in-Waiting across Early Modern Europe*. Leiden: Brill, 2013.
Alam, Asiya. "Polygyny, Family and Sharafat: Discourses amongst North Indian Muslims, circa 1870–1918." *Modern Asian Studies* 45, no. 3 (2010): 631–68. https://doi.org/10.1017/s0026749x10000168.
———. *Women, Islam and Familial Intimacy in Colonial South Asia*. Leiden: Brill, 2021.
Alam, Muzaffar. *The Crisis of Empire in Mughal North India: Awadh and Punjab, 1707–48*. 2nd ed. New Delhi: Oxford University Press, 2013.
———. "A Muslim State in a non-Muslim Context: The Mughal Case." In *Mirror for the Muslim Prince: Islam and the Theory of Statecraft*, edited by Mehrzad Boroujerdi, 160–89. Syracuse: Syracuse University Press, 2013.
———. "The Zamindars and Mughal Power in the Deccan, 1685–1712." *Indian Economic and Social History Review* 11, no. 1 (1974): 74–91. https://doi.org/10.1177/001946467401100103.
Alam, Muzaffar, and Sanjay Subrahmanyam. "The Deccan Frontier and Mughal Expansion, Ca. 1600: Contemporary Perspectives." *Journal of the Economic and Social History of the Orient* 47, no. 3 (2004): 357–89. https://doi.org/10.1163/1568520041974666.
———. "Letters from Kannur, 1500–1550: A Little Explored Aspect of Kerala History." In *Clio and Her Descendants: Essays for Kesavan Veluthat*, edited by Manu Devadevan, 99–131. Delhi: Primus Books, 2018.
———. "Witnesses and Agents of Empire: Eighteenth-Century Historiography and the World of the Mughal Munshī." *Journal of the Economic and Social History of the Orient* 53, nos. 1–2 (2009): 393–423. https://doi.org/10.1163/002249910x12573963244647.
———. *Writing the Mughal World: Studies on Culture and Politics*. New York: Columbia University Press, 2012.
Alavi, Rafi Ahmad. "New Light of Mughal Cavalry." *Proceedings of the Indian History Congress* 31 (1969): 272–87.
———. *Studies in the History of Medieval Deccan*. Delhi: Idarah-i Adabiyat-i Delli, 1977.

Ali, Daud. *Courtly Culture and Political Life in Early Medieval India.* Cambridge: Cambridge University Press, 2011.

Ali, M. Athar. *The Apparatus of Empire: Awards of Ranks, Offices and Titles to the Mughal Nobility (1574–1658).* New Delhi: Oxford University Press, 1985.

———. *The Mughal Nobility under Aurangzeb.* New Delhi: Oxford University Press, 2001.

Ali, Omar H. *Malik Ambar: Power and Slavery across the Indian Ocean.* New York: Oxford University Press, 2016.

Ali, Shanti Sadiq. *The African Dispersal in the Deccan: From Medieval to Modern Times.* Delhi: Orient Blackswan, 1996.

Amanat, Abbas, ed. *The Persianate World: Rethinking a Shared Sphere.* Leiden: Brill, 2018.

Ames, Glenn J. *Colbert, Mercantilism, and the French Quest for Asian Trade.* DeKalb: Northern Illinois University Press, 1996.

Andrade, Tonio. "A Chinese Farmer, Two African Boys, and a Warlord: Toward a Global Microhistory." *Journal of World History* (2010): 573–91.

Anooshahr, Ali. *The Ghazi Sultans and the Frontiers of Islam.* London: Routledge, 2009.

———. "Mughals, Mongols, and Mongrels: The Challenge of Aristocracy and the Rise of the Mughal State in the Tarikh-i Rashidi." *Journal of Early Modern History* 18, no. 6 (2014): 559–77. https://doi.org/10.1163/15700658-12342420.

———. *Turkestan and the Rise of Eurasian Empires: A Study of Politics and Invented Traditions.* New York: Oxford University Press, 2020.

Ansari, Tayyib. *Nusrati ki shāʿirī.* Hyderabad: Adabi Trust, 1984.

Antoon, Sinan. *Poetics of the Obscene in Premodern Arabic Poetry: Ibn Al-Hajjaj and Sukhf.* New York: Palgrave Macmillan, 2014.

Apte, D. V., and S. M. Divekar, eds. *Shivajicharitra Pradip.* Pune: Bharata Itihasa Sanshodhaka Mandala, 1925.

Arasaratnam, Sinnappah. "Coromandel Revisited: Problems and Issues in Indian Maritime History." *Indian Economic and Social History Review* 26, no. 1 (1989): 101–10. https://doi.org/10.1177/001946468902600105.

———. *Merchants, Companies and Commerce on the Coromandel Coast, 1650–1740.* Delhi: Oxford University Press, 1986.

Archambault, Hannah. "Geographies of Influence: Two Afghan Military Households in 17th and 18th Century South India." PhD diss., University of California, Berkeley, 2018.

Asar, Muhammad Ali. *ʿĀdil Shahī daur mein urdu ghazal.* Bangalore: Karnatak Urdu Academy, 2013.

Asher, Catherine, and Cynthia Talbot. *India Before Europe.* 2nd ed. Cambridge: Cambridge University Press, 2022.

Sebouh Aslanian, Joyce E. Chaplin, Ann McGrath, and Kristin Mann. "AHR Conversation How Size Matters: The Question of Scale in History." *American Historical Review* 118, no. 5 (2013): 1431–72.

Asif, Manan Ahmed. *A Book of Conquest: The Chachnama and Muslim Origins in South Asia.* Cambridge, MA: Harvard University Press, 2016.

———. *The Loss of Hindustan: The Invention of India.* Cambridge, MA: Harvard University Press, 2020.

Babayan, Kathryn. *The City as Anthology: Eroticism and Urbanity in Early Modern Isfahan.* Stanford, CA: Stanford University Press, 2021.

Bailey, Merridee L., and Katie Barclay, eds. *Emotion, Ritual and Power in Europe, 1200–1920: Family, State and Church*. Cham: Springer International, 2017.
Balabanlilar, Lisa. The Begims of the Mystic Feast: Turco-Mongol Tradition in the Mughal Harem." *Journal of Asian Studies* 69, no. 1 (February 2010): 138–39.
———. *The Emperor Jahangir: Power and Kingship in Mughal India*. London: Bloomsbury, 2020.
Balachandran, Jyoti Gulati. *Narrative Pasts: The Making of a Muslim Community in Gujarat, Ca. 1400–1650*. New Delhi: Oxford University Press, 2020.
Balland, D. "Bakhtiari of Afghanistan." In *Encyclopedia Iranica*, last updated December 15, 1988. https://iranicaonline.org/articles/baktiaris-of-afghanistan.
Barfield, Thomas. *Afghanistan: A Cultural and Political History*. Princeton, NJ: Princeton University Press, 2010.
Barry, Ellen. "Families feud over Delhi Estates." *New York Times*, September 9, 2014. https://www.nytimes.com/2014/09/10/world/asia/families-feud-over-delhi-estates.html.
Bawa, Oudesh Rani. *Dakkani Zabān-o-adab par dīgar Hindūstānī Zabān-o-adab ke asrāt*. Hyderabad: Center for Deccan Studies, 2022.
Bentley, Jerry H. "Sea and Ocean Basins as Frameworks of Historical Analysis." *Geographical Review* 89, no. 2 (1999): 215–24.Berkel, Maaike van, and Jeroen Duindam, eds. *Prince, Pen, and Sword: Eurasian Perspectives*. Leiden: Brill, 2018.
Bes, Lennart. "Sultan among Dutchmen? Royal Dress at Court Audiences in South India, as Portrayed in Local Works of Art and Dutch Embassy Reports, Seventeenth–Eighteenth Centuries." *Modern Asian Studies* 50, no. 6 (2016): 1792–1845. https://doi.org/10.1017/S0026749X15000232.
———. *The Heirs of Vijayanagara*. Leiden: Leiden University Press, 2022.
Biedermann, Zoltán. "Three Ways of Locating the Global: Microhistorical Challenges in the Study of Early Transcontinental Diplomacy." *Past and Present* 242, no. Supplement_14 (2019): 110–41. https://doi.org/10.1093/pastj/gtz040.
Bierman, Irene. *Writing Signs: The Fatimid Public Texts*. Oakland: University of California Press, 1998.
Blake, Stephen P. "Returning the Household to the Patrimonial-Bureaucratic Empire: Gender, Succession, and Ritual in the Mughal, Safavid and Ottoman Empires." In *Tributary Empires in Global History*, edited by Peter Fibiger Bang and C. A. Bayly, 214–26. London: Palgrave Macmillan, 2011.
Boxer, C. R. "War and Trade in the Indian Ocean and the South China Sea, 1600–1650." *Mariner's Mirror* 71, no. 4 (1985): 417–35. https://doi.org/10.1080/00253359.1985.10656052.
Brennig, Joseph J. "Chief Merchants and the European Enclaves of Seventeenth-Century Coromandel." *Modern Asian Studies* 11, no. 3 (1977): 321–40. https://doi.org/10.1017/S0026749X00014177.
———. "Textile Producers and Production in Late Seventeenth Century Coromandel." *Indian Economic and Social History Review* 23, no. 4 (1986): 333–55. https://doi.org/10.1177/001946468602300401.
———. "The Textile Trade of Seventeenth Century Northern Coromandel: A Study of a Pre-Modern Asian Export Industry." PhD diss., University of Wisconsin, Madison, 1975.
Brimnes, Niels. *Constructing the Colonial Encounter: Right and Left Hand Castes in Early Colonial South India*. London/New York: Routledge, 2019.

Brodbeck, Simon. *The Mahabharata Patriline: Gender, Culture, and the Royal Hereditary.* London: Routledge, 2009.
Bruijn, Thomas de, and Allison Busch, eds. *Culture and Circulation: Literature in Motion in Early Modern India.* Leiden: Brill, 2014.
Busch, Allison. "Hidden in Plain View: Brajbhasha Poets at the Mughal Court." *Modern Asian Studies* 44, no. 2 (2010): 267–309. https://doi.org/10.1017/s0026749x09990205.
———. *Poetry of Kings: The Classical Hindi Literature of Mughal India.* New York: Oxford University Press, 2011.
Burak, Guy. "Evidentiary Truth Claims, Imperial Registers, and the Ottoman Archive: Contending Legal Views of Archival and Record-keeping Practices in Ottoman Greater Syria (Seventeenth-Nineteenth centuries)." *Bulletin of the School of Oriental and African studies* 79/2 (2016): 233–54.
Casey, James. *Family and Community in Early Modern Spain: The Citizens of Granada, 1570–1739.* Cambridge: Cambridge University Press, 2007.
Carsten, Janet. *Cultures of Relatedness: New Approaches to the Study of Kinship.* Cambridge: Cambridge University Press, 2000.
Casaux, Jean-Louis, and Rick Knowlton. *A World of Chess: Its Development and Variations through Centuries and Civilizations.* Jefferson, NC: McFarland, 2017.
Chandra, Satish. "The Deccan Policy of the Mughals—A Reappraisal." *Indian Historical Review* 4, no. 2 (1978).
———. *Parties and Politics at the Mughal Court: 1707–1740.* New Delhi: Oxford University Press, 1959.
———. "Some Considerations on the Religious Policy of Aurangzeb during the Later Part of His Reign." *Proceedings of the Indian History Congress* 47, no. 1 (1986): 369–81.
Chatterjee, Indrani. "Afro-Asian Capital and Its Dissolution." *Comparative Studies of South Asia, Africa and the Middle East* 38, no. 2 (2018): 310–29. https://doi.org/10.1215/1089201x-6982073.
———. "Connected Histories and the Dream of Decolonial History." *South Asia: Journal of South Asian Studies* 41, no. 1 (2018): 69–86. https://doi.org/10.1080/00856401.2018.1414768.
———. *Forgotten Friends: Monks, marriages, and memories of Northeast India.* New Delhi: Oxford University Press, 2013.
———. *Gender, Slavery and Law in Colonial India.* New Delhi: Oxford University Press, 1999.
———. "A Slave's Quest for Selfhood in Eighteenth-Century Hindustan." *Indian Economic and Social History Review* 37, no. 1 (2000): 53–86. https://doi.org/10.1177/001946460003700103.
———. *Unfamiliar Relations: Family and History in South Asia.* New Brunswick, NJ: Rutgers University Press, 2004.
Chatterjee, Indrani, and Richard M. Eaton, eds. *Slavery and South Asian History.* Bloomington: Indiana University Press, 2006.
Chatterjee, Indrani, and Sumit Guha. "Slave-Queen, Waif-Prince: Slavery and Social Capital in Eighteenth-Century India." *Indian Economic and Social History Review* 36, no. 2 (1999): 165–86. https://doi.org/10.1177/001946469903600202.
Chatterjee, Nandini. "Mahzar-namas in the Mughal and British Empires: The Uses of an Indo-Islamic Legal Form." *Comparative Studies in Society and History* 58/2 (2016): 379–406.

———. *Negotiating Mughal Law: A Family of Landlords across Three Indian Empires*. Cambridge: Cambridge University Press, 2022.
Chattopadhyaya, Brajadulal. *Representing the Other?: Sanskrit Sources and the Muslims: Eighth to Fourteenth Century*. Delhi: Manohar, 1998.
Chauhan, Devisingh Venkatsingh. *Dakhani Hinditil Itihas Va Itar Lekh*. Mumbai: Itihas Sansodhak Mandal, 1973.
Cherian, Divya. *Merchants of Virtue: Hindus, Muslims, and Untouchables in Eighteenth-Century South Asia*. Oakland: University of California Press, 2022.
Chitnis, Krishnaji N. *The Nawabs of Savanur*. New Delhi: Atlantic Publications and Distributors, 2000.
Clarke, Nicola. *The Muslim Conquest of Iberia: Medieval Arabic Narratives*. London: Routledge, 2012.
Cohn, Bernard S. "The Initial British Impact on India: A Case Study of the Benares Region." *Journal of Asian Studies* 19, no. 4 (1960): 418–31. https://doi.org/10.2307/2943581.
Conlon, Frank. *A Caste in a Changing World: The Chitrapur Saraswat Brahmans, 1700–1935*. Oakland: The University of California Press, 1977.
Conrad, Lawrence I. "Abraha and Muhammad: Some Observations apropos of Chronology and Literary *Topoi* in the Early Arabic Historical Tradition." *Bulletin of the School of Oriental and African Studies* 50, no. 2 (1987): 225–40. https://doi.org/10.1017/s0041977x00049016.
Creese, Helen. "Balinese Babad as Historical Sources; a Reinterpretation of the Fall of Gèlgèl." *Bijdragen tot de taal-, land- en volkenkunde / Journal of the Humanities and Social Sciences of Southeast Asia* 147, no. 2 (1991): 236–60. https://doi.org/10.1163/22134379-90003188.
———. "Judicial Processes and Legal Authority in Pre-Colonial Bali." *Bijdragen tot de taal-, land- en volkenkunde / Journal of the Humanities and Social Sciences of Southeast Asia* 165, no. 4 (2009): 515–50. https://doi.org/10.1163/22134379-90003631.
———. *Women of the Kakawin World: Marriage and Sexuality in the Indic Courts of Java and Bali*. Armonk, NY: M. E. Sharpe, 2004.
Crossley, Pamela K., Helen F. Siu, and Donald S. Sutton, eds. *Empire at the Margins: Culture, Ethnicity, and Frontier in Early Modern China*. Oakland: University of California Press, 2007.
Dallapiccola, Anna L., and Stephanie Zingel-Avé Lallemant, eds. *Islam and Indian Regions*. Vol. 1. Stuttgart: Steiner, 1993.
Datta, Pradip Kumar. *Rabindranath Tagore's the Home and the World: A Critical Companion*. London: Anthem Press, 2005.
Dayal, Subah. "From Golkonda to Siam: Secret Letters, Envelopes, and Diplomatic Crisis in the Mughal port-city." Presentation at Conference for Muzaffar Alam and The New Mughal Historiography, Yale University, New Haven, CT, April 26–27, 2024.
———. "Making the 'Mughal' Soldier: Ethnicity, Identification, and Documentary Culture in Southern India, Ca. 1600–1700." *Journal of the Economic and Social History of the Orient*, 62 (2019): 856–924.
———. "Vernacular Conquest: A Persian Patron and His Image in the Seventeenth-Century Deccan." *Comparative Studies of South Asia, Africa and the Middle East* 37, no.3 (2017): 549–69.
Daybell, James. *Material Letter in Early Modern England: Manuscript Letters and the Culture and Practices of Letter-Writing 1512–1635*. London: Palgrave Macmillan, 2012.

Datla, Kavita. *The Language of Secular Islam: Urdu Nationalism and Colonial India.* Honolulu: University of Hawaii Press, 2013.

Deshpande, Prachi. *Creative Pasts: Historical Memory and Identity in Western India, 1700–1960.* Ranikhet: Permanent Black, 2007.

———. "The Marathi *kaulnāmā*: Property, Sovereignty and Documentation in a Persianate Form." *Journal of the Economic and Social History of the Orient* 64, nos. 5–6 (2021): 583–614. https://doi.org/10.1163/15685209-12341547.

———. *Scripts of Power: Writing, Language Practices, and Cultural History in Western India.* Ranikhet: Permanent Black, 2022.

———. "The Writerly Self: Literacy, Discipline and Codes of Conduct in Early Modern Western India." *Indian Economic and Social History Review* 53, no. 4 (2016): 449–71. https://doi.org/10.1177/0019464616662137.

Devare, T. N. *A Short History of Persian Literature at the Bahmani, Adil Shahi, and Qutb Shahi Courts.* Pune: S. Devare, 1961.

Devadevan, Manu V. *The "Early Medieval" Origins of India.* Cambridge: Cambridge University Press, 2020.

Dhavan, Purnima. *When Sparrows Became Hawks: The Making of the Sikh Warrior Tradition, 1699–1799.* New York: Oxford University Press, 2011.

Dhavan, Purnima, and Heidi Pauwels. "Crafting Literary Urdu: Mirza Hatim's Engagement with Vali Dakhani." *Modern Asian Studies* 57, no. 3 (2023): 711–39.

———. *Urdu's Origins Revisited: Vali Dakhani and Early Literary Networks in Eighteenth-Century India* (Monograph forthcoming).

Digby, Simon. "Before Timur Came: Provincialization of the Delhi Sultanate through the Fourteenth Century." *Journal of the Economic and Social History of the Orient* 47, no. 3 (2004): 298–356. https://doi.org/10.1163/1568520041974657.

———. *Sufis and Soldiers in Awrangzeb's Deccan: Malfūzāt-i Naqshbandiyya.* New Delhi: Oxford University Press, 2001.

Dirks, Nicholas B. *Castes of Mind: Colonialism and the Making of Modern India.* Princeton, NJ: Princeton University Press, 2001.

Duindam, Jeroen. *Dynasties: A Global History of Power, 1300–1800.* Cambridge: Cambridge University Press, 2016.

Eaton, Richard M. *India in the Persianate Age: 1000–1765.* Oakland: University of California Press, 2019.

———. "The Rise and Fall of Military Slavery in the Deccan, 1450–1650." In *Slavery and South Asian History*, edited by Indrani Chatterjee and Richard M. Eaton, 115–36. Bloomington: Indiana University Press, 2006.

———. *A Social History of the Deccan, 1300–1761: Eight Indian Lives.* Cambridge: Cambridge University Press, 2005.

———. *Sufis of Bijapur 1300–1700: Social Roles of Sufis in Medieval India.* Princeton, NJ: Princeton University Press, 1978.

Eaton, Richard M., and Phillip B. Wagoner. *Power, Memory, Architecture: Contested Sites on India's Deccan Plateau, 1300–1600.* New Delhi: Oxford University Press, 2013.

Elliot, John H. *The Count-Duke of Olivares: The Statesman in an Age of Decline.* New Haven, CT: Yale University Press, 1986.

Ethé, Hermann. *Catalogue of Persian Manuscripts in The Library Of The India Office.* Vol. 1. Oxford: H. Hart, 1903.

Fallon, S. W. *Hindustani-English Dictionary of Idioms and* Proverbs. Banaras: Medical Hall Press, 1886.
Faruqi, Shamsur R. "A Stranger in the City: The Poetics of Sabk-i Hindi." *Annual of Urdu Studies* 19 (2004): 1–93
Faruqui, Munis D. *The Princes of the Mughal Empire, 1504–1719*. Cambridge: Cambridge University Press, 2015.
Fischel, Roy S. *Local States in an Imperial World: Identity, Society and Politics in the Early Modern Deccan*. Edinburgh: Edinburgh University Press, 2020.
Fisher, Elaine M. *Hindu Pluralism: Religion and the Public Sphere in Early Modern South India*. Oakland: University of California Press, 2017.
Flatt, Emma J. *The Courts of the Deccan Sultanates: Living Well in the Persian Cosmopolis*. Cambridge: Cambridge University Press, 2020.
Flood, Finbarr Barry. *Objects of Translation: Material Culture and Medieval "Hindu-Muslim" Encounter*. Princeton, NJ: Princeton University press, 2009.
Flores, Jorge. *Unwanted Neighbors: the Mughals, the Portuguese, and Their Frontier Zones*. New Delhi: Oxford University Press, 2018.
———. "Marathi Voices, Portuguese Words." *Quaderni storici* 167 / a. LVI, n. 2, Bologna, Il Mulino (August 2021): 341–77.
Flynn, Vincent John Adams. "An English Translation of the Adab-i-Alamgiri: The Period before the War of Succession Being the Letters of Prince Muhammad Aurangzib Bahadur to Muhammad Shihabu'ddin Shah Jahan Sahib-i-Qiran-i-Sani Emperor of Hindustan." Dissertation, Australian National University, 1974.
Fukazawa, Hiroshi. *The Medieval Deccan: Peasants, Social Systems and States, Sixteenth to Eighteenth Centuries*. New Delhi: Oxford University Press, 1991.
Gaeffke, Peter. "Alexander in Avadhī and Dakkinī Mathnawīs." *Journal of the American Oriental Society* 109, no. 4 (1989): 527–32.
Gandhi, Supriya. *The Emperor Who Never Was*. Cambridge, MA: Harvard University Press, 2020.
Gelder, Geert Jan van. "Some Brave Attempts at Generic Classification in Pre-Modern Arabic Literature." In *Aspects of Genre and Type in Pre-Modern Literary Cultures*, edited by Bert Roest and Herman LJ Vanstiphout, 15–31. Leiden: Brill, 1999.
Ghauri, Iftikhar A. "Central Structure of the Kingdom of Bijapur." *Journal of the Pakistan Historical Society* 18, no. 2 (1970): 88–109.
———. "Organization of the Army under the Sultanates of the Deccan." *Journal of the Pakistan Historical Society* 14, no. 3 (1966).
Ghobrial, John Paul. "Moving Stories and What They Tell Us: Early Modern Mobility between Microhistory and Global History," and "Introduction: Seeing the World Like a Microhistorian." Supplement, *Past & Present* 242, no. 14 (2019): 1–22, 243–80.
Ghosh, Durba. *Sex and the Family in Colonial India: The Making of Empire*. Cambridge: Cambridge University Press, 2006.
Gilmartin, David, and Bruce B. Lawrence. *Beyond Turk and Hindu: Rethinking Religious Identities in Islamicate South Asia*. Gainesville: University Press of Florida, 2000.
Gluškova Irina, and Rajendra Vora. *Home, Family and Kinship in Maharashtra*. New Delhi: Oxford University Press, 1999.
Gokhale, B. G. "Burhanpur: Notes on the History of an Indian City in the XVIIth Century." *Journal of the Economic and Social History of the Orient* 15, no. 3 (1972). https://doi.org/10.2307/3596070.

Golchin-Maʿani, A. *Kārvān-e Hend: Dar ahvāl o āsār-e shāʿerān-e ʿasr-e Safavi ke be Hendustān Rafta-And*. 2 vols. Mashhad, n.p., 1990.
Gommans, Jos. *Mughal Warfare: Indian Frontiers and Highroads to Empire 1500–1700*. London: Routledge, 2002.
———. *The Rise of the Indo-Afghan Empire, Ca. 1710–1780*. Leiden: Brill, 1995.
———. "The Warband in the Making of Eurasian Empires." In *Prince, Pen, and Sword: Eurasian Perspectives*, edited by Jeroen Duindam and M. van Berkel, 297–383. Leiden: Brill, 2018.
Gordon, Stewart. *The Marathas: 1600–1818*. Cambridge: Cambridge University Press, 2016.
Green, Nile. *Making Space Sufis and Settlers in Early Modern India*. New Delhi: Oxford University Press, 2012.
———. *The Persianate World: The Frontiers of a Eurasian Lingua Franca*. Oakland: University of California Press, 2019.
———. *Writing Travel in Central Asian History*. Bloomington: Indiana University Press, 2014.
Groebner, Valentin. *Who Are You?: Identification, Deception, and Surveillance in Early Modern Europe*. New York: Zone Books, 2007.
Guha, Ranajit. "Chandra's Death." In *Subaltern Studies: Writings on South Asian History and Society*. New Delhi: Oxford University Press, 1982.
Guha, Sumit. "Bad Language and Good Language: Lexical Awareness in the Cultural Politics of Peninsular India, 1300–1800." In *Forms of Knowledge in Early Modern Asia: Explorations in the Intellectual History of India and Tibet*, edited by Sheldon Pollock, 49–68. Durham, NC: Duke University Press, 2011.
———. *Beyond Caste: Identity and Power in South Asia, Past and Present*. Ranikhet: Permanent Black, 2016.
———. *Ecologies of Empire in South Asia 1400–1900*. Seattle: University of Washington Press, 2023.
———. "Empires, Languages, and Scripts in the Perso-Indian World." *Comparative Studies in Society and History* Published online (2024): 1–27.
———. *Environment and Ethnicity in India, 1200–1991*. Cambridge: Cambridge University Press, 1999.
———. "The Family Feud as Political Resource in Eighteenth-Century India." In *Unfamiliar Relations: Family and History in South Asia*, edited by Indrani Chatterjee, 73–94. New Brunswick, NJ: Rutgers University Press, 2004.
———. *History and Collective Memory in South Asia, 1200–2000*. University of Washington Press, 2019.
———. "An Indian Penal Regime: Maharashtra in the Eighteenth Century." *Past and Present* 147, no. 1 (1995): 101–26. https://doi.org/10.1093/past/147.1.101.
———. "Patronage and State-making in early modern empires in India and Britain." In *Patronage as Politics in South Asia*, edited by Anastasia Piliavsky, 104–22. Cambridge: Cambridge University Press, 2014.
———. "Rethinking the Economy of Mughal India: Lateral Perspectives." *Journal of the Economic and Social History of the Orient* 58, no. 4 (2015): 532–75.
———. "Serving the Barbarian to Preserve the Dharma: The Ideology and Training of a Clerical Elite in Peninsular India ca. 1300–1800." *Indian Economic & Social History Review* 47, no. 4 (2010): 497–525.

———. "Speaking Historically: The Changing Voices of Historical Narration in Western India, 1400–1900." *American Historical Review* 109 (2004): 1099–1100. https://doi.org/10.1086/ahr/109.4.1084.

Habib, Irfan. *The Agrarian System of Mughal India: 1556–1707*. New Delhi: Oxford University Press, 2004.

Haider, Najaf. "Norms of Professional Excellence and Good Conduct in Accountancy Manuals of the Mughal Empire." *International Review of Social History* 56, no. S19 (2011): 263–74.

Haider, Navina N. "Gulshan-i 'Ishq: Sufi Romance of the Deccan." In *The Visual World of Muslim India: The Art, Culture and Society of the Deccan in the Early Modern Era*, edited by Laura E. Parodi, 295–318. London: I. B. Tauris, 2014.

———. "Kitāb-i Nauras: Key to Bijapur's Golden Age." In *Sultans of the South: Arts of India's Deccan Courts, 1323–1687*, edited by Navina N. Haider and Marika Sardar, 26–43. New York: Metropolitan Museum of Art, 2011.

Hamid, Usman, and Pasha M. Khan. "Introduction: Moving across the Persian Cosmopolis." *Comparative Studies of South Asia, Africa and the Middle East* 37, no. 3 (2017): 491–93.

Haq, Maulvi Abdul. *Nusrati: The Poet-Laureate of Bijapur: A Critical Study of His Life and Works*. New Delhi: Anjuman-e-Taraqqi-e-Urdu, 1944.

Hasan, Farhat. *Paper, Performance, and the State: Social Change and Political Culture in Mughal India*. Cambridge: Cambridge University Press, 2022.

———. *State and Locality in Mughal India: Power Relations in Western India, Ca. 1572–1730*. Cambridge: Cambridge University Press, 2004.

Hathaway, Jane. *The Arab Lands under Ottoman Rule, 1516–1800*. 2nd ed. London: Routledge, 2020.

———. *The Politics of Households in Ottoman Egypt: The Rise of the Qazdağlis*. Cambridge: Cambridge University Press, 2002.

Hausberger, Bernd. "Paisanos, soldados y bandidos: la guerra entre los vicuñas y los vascongados en Potosí (1622–1625)." *Los buenos, los malos y los feos. Poder y Resistencia en América Latina, Publicaciones del Instituto Ibero-Americano e Iberoamericana Vervuert*. Berlín-Madrid 102 (2005): 283–308.

Hill, St. "Privacy, Security and Legality Are Not the Only Problems with Aadhaar: Here Are Four More." Scroll.in. March 23, 2017. https://scroll.in/article/832595/privacy-security-and-egality-are-not-the-only-serious-problems-with-aadhaar-here-are-four-more.

Hirschler, Konrad. "From Archive to Archival Practices: Rethinking the Preservation of Mamluk Administrative Documents." *Journal of the American Oriental Society* 136, no. 1 (2016). https://doi.org/10.7817/jameroriesoci.136.1.1.

Hodgson, Marshall. *The Venture of Islam*. Vol. 3, *The Gunpower Empires and Modern Times*. Chicago: University of Chicago Press, 1974.

d'Hubert, Thibaut. *In the Shade of the Golden Palace Ālāol and Middle Bengali Poetics in Arakan*. New York: Oxford University Press, 2018.

———. "Pirates, Poets, and Merchants: Bengali Language and Literature in Seventeenth-Century Mrauk-U." In *Culture and Circulation: Literature in Motion in Early Modern India*, edited by Allison Busch and Thomas de Bruijn, 47–74. Leiden: Brill, 2014.

Husain, Ali Akbar. *Scent in the Islamic Garden: A Study of Deccani Urdu Literary Sources*. Karachi: Oxford University Press, 2000.

Husain, Iqbal. "Patterns of Afghan Settlement in India in the 17th Century." *Proceedings of the Indian History Congress* 39, no. 1 (1978): 329–31.
Hussain, Zakir. "Aurangzeb's First Viceroyalty of the Deccan." *Proceedings of the Indian History Congress* 70 (2009): 310–17.
Irvine, William. *The Army of the Indian Moghuls*. Delhi: Eurasia, 1962.
Jalibi, Jamil. *Tārīkh-i Adab- i Urdu*. Vol. 1. Delhi: Educational Publishing House, 1977.
Jha, Pankaj. *A Political History of Literature: Vidyapati and the Fifteenth Century*. Oxford: Oxford University Press, 2019.
Pankaj Jha, Nitin Sinha, Nitin Varma, eds. *Servants' Pasts: Sixteenth to Eighteenth Century, South Asia*. Vol. 1. Hyderabad: Orient Blackswan, 2019.
Jones, Justin. *Shi'a Islam in Colonial India: Religion, Community and Sectarianism*. Cambridge: Cambridge University Press, 2011.
Joshi, P. M. "Johan van Twist's Mission to Bijapur, 1637." *Journal of Indian History* 34, no. 2 (1956): 111–37.
———. "The Kingdom of Bijapur." PhD diss., School of Oriental and African Studies, London, 1935.
Kadam, V. S. "Forced Labour in Mahārāṣṭra in the Seventeenth and Eighteenth Centuries: A Study in Its Nature and Change." *Journal of the Economic and Social History of the Orient* 1 (1991): 55–87.
Kaicker, Abhishek. *The King and the People: Sovereignty and Popular Politics in Mughal Delhi*. New York: Oxford University Press, 2020.
Kallander, Amy Aisen. *Women, Gender, and the Palace Households in Ottoman Tunisia*. Austin: University of Texas Press, 2013.
Kanchan, Namrata. "A Panegyric from the Deccan's Golden Age." *Asian and African Studies* (blog). February 28, 2023. https://blogs.bl.uk/asian-and-african/2023/02/a-panegyric-from-the-deccans-golden-age.html.
Kapadia, Aparna. *In Praise of Kings: Rajputs, Sultans and Poets in Fifteenth-Century Gujarat*. Cambridge: Cambridge University Press, 2018.
Kaviraj, Sudipta. *The Imaginary Institution of India: Politics and Ideas*. New York: Columbia University Press, 2010.
Keliher, Macabe. "The Problem of Imperial Relatives in Early Modern Empires and the Making of Qing China." *American Historical Review* 122, no. 4 (2017): 1001–37. https://doi.org/10.1093/ahr/122.4.1001.
Kelkar, Narsingh, ed. *Shivaji Nibandhavali Bhag-II*. Pune: Government Central Press, 1930.
Khan, Iqtidar Alam. *Gunpowder and Firearms: Warfare in Medieval India*. New Delhi: Oxford University Press, 2004.
———. "The Matchlock Musket in the Mughal Empire: An instrument of Centralization." *Proceedings of the Indian History Congress* 59 (1998): 341–59.
Khan, Pasha M. "Marvellous Histories: Reading the Shāhnāmah in India." *Indian Economic and Social History Review* 49, no. 4 (2012): 527–56. https://doi.org/10.1177/0019464612463807.
Khan, Rahmat Ali. "The Progress of Persian Literature under the 'Adil Shahi Dynasty of Bijapur, 1489–1686 A.D. (Poetry)." PhD diss., University of Delhi, 1978.
Khera, Dipti. "Arrivals at Distant Lands: Artful Letters and Entangled Mobilities in the Indian Ocean Littoral." In *The Nomadic Object: The Challenge of World for Early Modern Religious*, edited by Christine Göttler and Mia M. Mochizuki, 571–605. Leiden: Brill, 2018.

———. *The Place of Many Moods: Udaipur's Painted Lands and India's Eighteenth Century*. Princeton, NJ: Princeton University Press, 2020.

Kia, Mana. "Adab as Ethics of Literary Form and Social Conduct: Reading the Gulistan in Late Mughal India." In *No Tapping Around Philology: A Festschrift in Celebration and Honor of Wheeler McIntosh Thackston Jr.'s 70th Birthday*, edited by Alireza Korangy and Daniel Sheffield, 281–308. Wiesbaden: Harrassowitz Verlag, 2014.

———. *Persianate Selves: Memories of Place and Origin before Nationalism*. Stanford: Stanford University Press, 2020.

Kinra, Rajeev. *Writing Self, Writing Empire: Chandar Bhan Brahman and the Cultural World of the Indo-Persian State Secretary*. Oakland: University Of California Press, 2015.

Kolff, Dirk H. A. *Naukar, Rajput, and Sepoy: The Ethnohistory of the Military Labour Market in Hindustan, 1450–1850*. Cambridge: Cambridge University Press, 1990.

Kothiyal, Tanuja. *Nomadic Narratives: A History of Mobility and Identity in the Great Indian Desert*. Cambridge: Cambridge University Press, 2016.

Kropf, Evyn, and Cathleen A. Baker. "A Conservative Tradition? Arab Papers of the 12th–17th Centuries from the Islamic Manuscripts Collection at the University of Michigan." *Journal of Islamic Manuscripts* 4, no. 1 (2013): 1–48. https://doi.org/10.1163/1878464-13040101.

Kumar, Dharma. *Land and Caste in South India: Agricultural Labour in the Madras Presidency during the Nineteenth Century*. Cambridge: Cambridge University Press, 1965.

Kruijtzer, Gijs. "Bari Sahiba bint Muhammad Qutb Shah." In *Christian-Muslim Relations: A Bibliographical History*, edited by David Thomas and John Chesworth, 231–37. Vol. 11, *Asia, East Africa and the Americas (1600–1700)*. Leiden: Brill, 2017.

———. "Madanna, Akkanna and the Brahmin Revolution: A Study of Mentality, Group Behaviour and Personality in Seventeenth-Century India." *Journal of the Economic and Social History of the Orient* 45, no. 2 (2002): 231–67. https://doi.org/10.1163/15685 2002760247122.

———. *Xenophobia in Seventeenth-Century India*. Leiden: Leiden University Press, 2009.

Kulkarni, A. R. "The Deshmukh *watan* with Special Reference to Indapur." *Indian Historical Review* 3 (1976): 289–300.

———. "The Jedhe Gharane (The House of the Jedhes)." In *Home, Family and Kinship in Maharashtra*, edited by Irina Gluškova and Rajendra Vora, 173–84. New Delhi: Oxford University Press, 1999.

———. "Maratha Policy Towards the Adil Shahi Kingdom." *Bulletin of the Deccan College Research Institute* 49 (1990): 221–26.

———. *The Marathas*. Pune: Diamond, 2008.

Kulkarni, G. T. "A Note on Mirza Rajah Jai Singh's Purandhar and Bijapur Campaigns— an Unpublished Farmān of Aurangzeb (1665 A.D.)." *Proceedings of the Indian History Congress* 71 (2010).

———. "Shivaji-Mughal Relations (1669–80): Gleanings from Some Unpublished Persian Records." *Proceedings of the Indian History Congress* 40 (1979): 336–41.

Kumar, Sunil. *The Emergence of the Delhi Sultanate, 1192–1286*. Ranikhet: Permanent Black, 2007.

———. "The Ignored Elites: Turks, Mongols and a Persian Secretarial Class in the Early Delhi Sultanate." *Modern Asian Studies* 43, no. 1 (2009): 45–77. https://doi.org/10.1017 /s0026749x07003319.

———. "Service, Status and Military Slavery in the Delhi Sultanate of the Thirteenth and Early Fourteenth Centuries." In *Slavery and South Asian History*, edited by Indrani Chatterjee and Richard M. Eaton, 83–114. Bloomington: Indiana University Press, 2006.

Laine, James W. *Shivaji: Hindu King in Islamic India*. New York: Oxford University Press, 2003.

Lal, Ruby. *Domesticity and Power in the Early Mughal World*. Cambridge: Cambridge University Press, 2005.

Lane, Kris E. *Potosí: The Silver City That Changed the World*. Oakland: University of California Press, 2019.

Lewis, Bernard. "Watan." *Journal of Contemporary History* 26, no. 3 (1991): 523–33. https://doi.org/10.1177/002200949102600309.

Ludden, David E. *Peasant History in South India*. Princeton, NJ: Princeton University Press, 1985.

Majumdar, Rochona. *Marriage and Modernity: Family Values in Colonial Bengal*. Durham, NC: Duke University Press, 2009.

Malhotra, K. C., and M. Gadgil. "The Ecological Basis of the Geographical Distribution of the Dhangars: a Pastoral Caste-Cluster of Maharashtra." *South Asian Anthropologist* 2, no. 2 (1981).

Mamdani, Mahmood. *Good Muslim, Bad Muslim: America, the Cold War, and the Roots of Terror*. New York: Pantheon Books, 2004.

Markovits, Claude, Jacques Pouchepadass, and Sanjay Subrahmanyam, eds. *Society and Circulation: Mobile People and Itinerant Cultures in South Asia, 1750–1950*. New York: Anthem Press, 2006.

Matthews, David. "Pem Nem: A Sixteenth-Century Dakani Manuscript." In *Cairo to Kabul: Afghan and Islamic Studies Presented to Ralph Pinder-Wilson*, edited by Warwick Ball and Leonard Harrow, 170–75. London: Melisende, 2002.

Meersbergen, Guido van. *Ethnography and Encounter: The Dutch and English in Seventeenth-Century South Asia*. Leiden: Brill, 2021.

Mehendale, Gajanan Bhaskar. *Shivaji His Life and Times*. India: Param Mitra, 2011.

Menon, Dilip. "Houses by the Sea: State-Formation Experiments in Malabar, 1760–1800." *Economic and Political Weekly* 34, no. 29 (July 17, 1999): 1995–2003.

Mohiuddin, Momin. *Chancellery and Persian Epistolography under the Mughals: From Babar to Shah Jahan (1526–1658)*. Calcutta: Iran Society, 1971.

Moin, A. Azfar. *The Millennial Sovereign: Sacred Kingship and Sainthood in Islam*. New York: Columbia University Press, 2014.

Moosvi, Shireen. "The Mughal Empire and the Deccan: Economic Factors and Consequences." *Proceedings of the Indian History Congress* 43, no. 1 (1982): 365–82.

Muddachari, B. "Maratha Court in the Karnatak." *Proceedings of the Indian History Congress* 28, (1966): 177–79.

Mukund, Kanakalatha. *The Trading World of the Tamil Merchant: Evolution of Merchant Capitalism in the Coromandel*. Hyderabad: Orient Blackswan, 1999.

Nath, Pratyay. *Climate of Conquest: War, Environment, and Empire in Mughal North India*. New Delhi: Oxford University Press, 2019.

Nair, Janaki. "Beyond Exceptionalism: South India and the Modern Historical Imagination." *Indian Economic and Social History Review* 43, no. 3 (2006): 323–47.

Nasiri-Moghaddam, Nader. "Persian Documents in the National Archives (Torre Do Tombo) of Portugal and Their Importance for the History of Persian Gulf In the 16th–17th Centuries." *International Journal of the Society of Iranian Archaeologists*, Winter-Spring, 2, no. 3 (2016): 54–88.

Nayeem, M. A. *External Relations of the Bijapur Kingdom, (1489–1686 A.D.): A Study in Diplomatic History*. Hyderabad: Bright, 1974.

Nazir, Pervaiz. "Social Structure, Ideology and Language: Caste among Muslims." *Economic and Political Weekly* 28, no. 52 (1993): 2897–900.

Noelle-Karimi, Christine. *The Pearl in Its Midst: Herat and the Mapping of Khurasan, 15th–19th Centuries*. Vienna: Verlag der Österreichischen Akademie der Wissenschaften, 2014.

Obeng, Pashington. "Service to God, Service to Master/Client: African Indian Military Contribution in Karnataka." *Asian and African Studies* 6 (2007): 271–88.

O'Hanlon, Rosalind. "Manliness and Imperial Service in Mughal North India." *Journal of the Economic and Social History of the Orient* 42, no. 1 (1999): 47–93. https://doi.org/10.1163/1568520991445597.

———. "The Social Worth of Scribes: Brahmins, Kāyasthas and the Social Order in Early Modern India." *Indian Economic and Social History Review* 47, no. 4 (2010): 563–95. https://doi.org/10.1177/001946461004700406.

O'Hanlon, Rosalind, and Christopher Minkowski. "What Makes People Who They Are? Pandit Networks and the Problem of Livelihoods in Early Modern Western India." *Indian Economic and Social History Review* 45, no. 3 (2008): 381–416. https://doi.org/10.1177/001946460804500303.

O'Hanlon, Rosalind, and David Washbrook. "After Orientalism: Culture, Criticism, and Politics in the Third World." *Comparative Studies in Society and History* 34, no. 1 (1992): 141–67. https://doi.org/10.1017/S0010417500017461.

Orsini, Francesca. "How to Do Multi-Lingual Literary History: Lessons from Fifteenth- and Sixteenth-Century North India." *Indian Economic and Social History Review*, 49, 2 (2012): 225–46.

Orsini, Francesca, and Samira Sheikh. *After Timur Left: Culture and Circulation in Fifteenth-Century North India*. New Delhi: Oxford University Press, 2014.

Overton, Keelan H., ed. *Iran and the Deccan: Persianate Art, Culture, and Talent in Circulation*. Bloomington: Indiana University Press, 2020.

Overton, Keelan H., and Kristine Rose-Beers. "Indo-Persian Histories from the Object Out: The St. Andrews Qur'an Manuscript between Timurid, Safavid, Mughal and Deccani Worlds." In *Iran and the Deccan: Persianate Art, Culture, and Talent in Circulation*, edited by Keelan H. Overton, 257–336. Bloomington: Indiana University Press, 2020.

Paranjape, B. G. *English Records on Shivaji: (1659–1682)*. Poona: Shiva Charitra Karyalaya, 1931.

Parker, Geoffrey. "Crisis and Catastrophe: The Global Crisis of the Seventeenth Century Reconsidered." *American Historical Review* 113, no. 4 (2008): 1053–79. https://doi.org/10.1086/ahr.113.4.1053.

Parthasarathi, Prasannan. "The State of Indian Social History." *Journal of Social History* 37, no. 1 (2003): 47–54. https://doi.org/10.1353/jsh.2003.0152.

———. *The Transition to a Colonial Economy: Weavers, Merchants and Kings in South India, 1720–1800*. Cambridge: Cambridge University Press, 2001.

Paul, Jurgen. "Archival Practices in the Muslim World Prior to 1500." In *Manuscripts and Archives: Comparative Views on Record-Keeping*, edited by Alessandro Bausi, Christian Brockmann, Michael Friedrich and Sabine Kienitz, 339–60. Berlin: Walter de Gruyter, 2018.
Pearson, Michael N. "Shivaji and the Decline of the Mughal Empire." *Journal of Asian Studies* 35, no. 2 (1976): 221–35.
Perlin, Frank. "The Pre-Colonial Indian State in History and Epistemology: A Reconstruction of Societal Formation in the Western Deccan from the Fifteenth to the early Nineteenth century." In *The Study of the State*, edited by Henri J. Claessen and Peter Skalnik, 275–302. Berlin: De Gruyter Mouton, 2011.
——. "State Formation Reconsidered: Part Two." *Modern Asian Studies* 19, no. 3 (April 1984): 415–80.
Peirce, Leslie P. *The Imperial Harem: Women and Sovereignty in the Ottoman Empire*. New York: Oxford University Press, 1993.
Pendse, Sachin. "The Dutch Factory at Vengurla." *International Journal of Maritime History* 30, no. 4 (2018): 724–32. https://doi.org/10.1177/0843871417746104.
Perdue, Peter. *China Marches West: The Qing Conquest of Central Asia*. Cambridge, MA: Belknap Press, 2010.
Pérez-Mallaína, Pablo E. *Spain's Men of the Sea: Daily Life on the Indies Fleets in the Sixteenth Century*. Baltimore: Johns Hopkins University Press, 1998.
Pernau, Margrit, and Helge Jordheim, eds. *Civilizing Emotions: Concepts in Nineteenth-Century Asia and Europe*. Oxford: Oxford University Press, 2015.
Petievich, Carla. "The Feminine and Cultural Syncretism." *Annual of Urdu Studies* 8 (1993): 110–21.
Pfeiffer, Helen. *Empire of Salons: Conquest and Community in Early Modern Ottoman Lands*. Princeton, NJ: Princeton University Press, 2022.
Pickett, James, and Paolo Sartori. "From the Archetypical Archive to Cultures of Documentation." *Journal of the Economic and Social History of the Orient* 62, nos. 5–6 (2019): 773–98. https://doi.org/10.1163/15685209-12341493.
Pillai, Manu S. *Rebel Sultans: The Deccan from Khilji to Shivaji*. New Delhi: Juggernaut, 2020.
Plamper, Jan. "The History of Emotions: An Interview with William Reddy, Barbara Rosenwein, and Peter Stearns." *History and Theory* 49, no. 2 (2010): 237–65. https://doi.org/10.1111/j.1468-2303.2010.00541.x.
Platts, John T. *A Dictionary of Urdu, Classical Hindi, and English*. London: W. H. Allen, 1884.
Pollock, Sheldon. *The Language of the Gods in the World of Men: Sanskrit, Culture, and Power in Premodern India*. Oakland: University of California Press, 2009.
——. *Literary Cultures in History: Reconstructions from South Asia*. Berkeley: University of California Press, 2007.
Prakash, Om. "The Dutch Factory at Vengurla in the Seventeenth Century." In *Medieval Deccan History: Commemoration volume in honour of Purshottam Mahadeo Joshi*, edited by A. R. Kulkarni, M. A. Nayeem and T. R. de Souza, 185–190. Bombay: Popular Prakashan, 1996.
Putnam, Lara. "The Transnational and the Text-Searchable: Digitized Sources and the Shadows they Cast." *American Historical Review* 121, no. 2 (2016): 377–402.

Qadri, Shamsullah. *Tārīkh- i zabān- i Urdū: ya 'nī Urdū- i Qadīm*. Lucknow: Nawal Kishore, 1925.
Quinn, Sholeh A. *Persian Historiography across Empires: the Ottomans, Safavids, and Mughals*. Cambridge: Cambridge University Press, 2020.
Ramachandran, Ayesha. *The Worldmakers: Global Imagining in Early Modern Europe*. Chicago: University of Chicago Press, 2015.
Ramamurthy, Naveen Kanalu. "Mirrors and Masks of Sovereignty: Imperial Governance in the Mughal World of Legal Normativism, Ca. 1650s–1720s." PhD diss., University of California, Los Angeles, 2021.
Raychaudhuri, Tapan. *Jan Company in Coromandel 1605–1690*. Leiden: Brill, 1962.
Raman, Bhavani. *Document Raj: Writing and Scribes in Early Colonial South India*. Chicago: University of Chicago Press, 2012.
Ramaswamy, Vijaya. "The Genesis and Historical Role of the Master Weavers in South Indian Textile Production." *Journal of the Economic and Social History of the Orient* 28, no. 3 (1985): 294. https://doi.org/10.2307/3631842.
———. *Textiles and Weavers in South India*. 2nd ed. Delhi: Oxford University Press, 2006.
———. "Households Profane and Divine: Perceptions of Saintly Wives." In *Looking within, Looking without: Exploring Households in the Subcontinent through Time: Essays in Memory of Nandita Prasad Sahai*, edited by Kumkum Roy, 233–52. New Delhi: Primus Books, 2015.
Rana, R. P. *Rebels to Rulers: The Rise of Jat Power in Medieval India, Ca.1665–1735*. New Delhi: Manohar, 2006.
Rao, Velcheru Narayana, David Shulman, and Sanjay Subrahmanyam. *Symbols of Substance: Court and State in Nayaka Period Nadu*. New Delhi: Oxford University Press, 1998.
Rathee Vikas. "Narratives of the 1658 War of Succession for the Mughal Throne, 1658–1707" PhD diss., University of Arizona, 2015.
Reger, William, and Tonio Andrade, eds. *The Limits of Empire: European Imperial Formations in Early Modern World History*. London: Routledge, 2012.
Reid, Anthony. "The Seventeenth-Century Crisis in Southeast Asia." *Modern Asian Studies* 24, no. 4 (1990): 639–59. https://doi.org/10.1017/s0026749x00010520.
Richards, John F. "The Imperial Crisis in the Deccan." *Journal of Asian Studies* 35, no. 02 (1976): 237–56. https://doi.org/10.1017/s0021911800080700.
———. *Mughal Administration in Golconda*. Oxford: Clarendon Press, 1975.
———. "Norms of Comportment among Mughal Imperial Officers." In *Moral Conduct and Authority: The Place of Adab in South Asian Islam*, edited by Barbara D. Metcalf, 255–89. Berkeley: University of California Press, 1984.
Riello, Giorgio, and Tirthankar Roy, eds. *How India Clothed the World*. Leiden: Brill, 2009.
Rizwi, Sayyid Tasadduq Husayn Rizvi. *Lughāt-i Kishorī*. Lucknow: Naval Kishore, 1907.
Rosenwein, Barbara H. *Anger's Past: The Social Uses of an Emotion in the Middle Ages*. Ithaca: Cornell University Press, 1998.
———. "Worrying about Emotions in History." *American Historical Review* 107, no. 3 (2002): 821–45. https://doi.org/10.1086/ahr/107.3.821.
Rosman, Abraham, and Paula G. Rubel. "Nomad-Sedentary Interethnic Relations in Iran and Afghanistan." *International Journal of Middle East Studies* 7, no. 4 (1976): 545–70. https://doi.org/10.1017/s0020743800024697.

Roy, Kumkum, ed. *Looking Within, Looking Without: Exploring Households in the Subcontinent through Time; Essays in Memory of Nandita Prasad Sahai*. Delhi: Primus Books, 2015.

Rustow, Marina. *The Lost Archive: Traces of a Caliphate in a Cairo Synagogue*. Princeton, NJ: Princeton University Press, 2020.

Safley, Thomas M. *Family Firms and Merchant Capitalism in Early Modern Europe: The Business, Bankruptcy and Resilience of the Höchstetters of Augsburg*. New York: Routledge, 2019.

Sahai, Nandita Prasad. *Politics of Patronage and Protest: The State, Society, and Artisans in Early Modern Rajasthan*. New Delhi: Oxford University Press, 2006.

Şahin, Kaya. "Staging an Empire: an Ottoman Circumcision Ceremony as Cultural Performance." *American Historical Review* 123, no. 2 (2018): 463–92.

Sahlins, Marshall. *What Kinship Is and Is Not*. Chicago: University Of Chicago Press, 2013.

Sajida, Zeenat. *'Ali 'Ādil Shah Sani*. Hyderabad: Silsila-yi Matbu'at Hyderabad Urdu Akademi, 1962.

Sardar, Marika, and Navina Haider, eds. *Sultans of Deccan India: 1500–1700; Opulence and Fantasy*. New York: Metropolitan Museum of Art, 2015.

Sardesai, G. S. *New History of the Marathas*. Bombay: Phoenix, 1946.

Sarkar, Jadunath. *History of Aurangzib*. Vol. 4. Calcutta: M. C. Sarkar & Sons, 1919.

———. *House of Shivaji*. Calcutta: M. C. Sarkar & Sons, 1955.

———. *Shivaji and His Times*. London: Longmans, Green, 1920.

Sarkar, Jagadish Narayan. *The Life of Mir Jumla: The General of Aurangzeb*. Calcutta: Thacker, Spink, 1951.

———. *Mughal Polity*. Delhi: Idarah-i Adabiyat-i Dilli, 1984.

Sartori, Paolo. "Seeing Like a Khanate: On Archives, Cultures of Documentation, and Nineteenth-Century Khvārazm." *Journal of Persianate Studies* 9, no. 2 (2016): 228–57.

Schimmel, Annemarie. *The Empire of the Great Mughals: History, Art and Culture*. London: Reaktion Books, 2004.

———. *A Two-Colored Brocade: The Imagery of Persian Poetry*. Chapel Hill: University of North Carolina Press, 1992.

Schwartz, Kevin L. "The Local Lives of a Transregional Poet: 'Abd Al-Qāder Bidel and the Writing of Persianate Literary History." *Journal of Persianate Studies* 9, no. 1 (2016): 83–106.

———. *Remapping Persian Literary History, 1700–1900*. Edinburgh: Edinburgh University Press, 2020.

Scott, James C. *The Art of Not Being Governed: An Anarchist History of Upland Southeast Asia*. New Haven, CT: Yale University Press, 2009.

———. *Seeing Like a State: How Certain Schemes to Improve the Human Condition Have Failed*. New Haven, CT: Yale University Press, 1998.

Sen, Surendranath. *Foreign Biographies of Shivaji*. Calcutta: K. P. Bagchi, 1977.

Seyed-Gohrab, A. A. "Waxing Eloquent: the Masterful Variations on Candle Metaphors in the Poetry of Ḥāfiẓ and His Predecessors." In *Metaphor and Imagery in Persian Poetry*, edited by A. A. Seyed-Gohrab, 81–123. Leiden: Brill, 2012.

Shakeb, M. Z. A. "The Black Sheep Tribe from Lake Van to Golkonda." *Itihas: Journal of the State Archives Andhra Pradesh* 3, no. 2 (1975): 60–65.

———. *A Descriptive Catalogue of the Batala Collection of Mughal Documents: 1527–1757 AD*. London: India Office Library and Records, 1990.

———. *Mughal Archives: A Descriptive Catalogue of the Documents Pertaining to the Reign of Shah Jahan, 1628–1658*. Hyderabad: State Archives, Government of Andhra Pradesh, 1977.

———. *Relations of Golkonda with Iran: Diplomacy, Ideas, and Commerce, 1518–1687*. New Delhi: Primus Books, 2017.

Shareef, Mohammad Jamal. *Dakan Mein Urdu Sha'iri Vali Se Pehle (Urdu Poetry in the Deccan before Vali)*. Hyderabad: Idara- i- Adabiyat Urdu, 2004.

Sharma, Sunil. "Amir Khusraw and the Genre of Historical Narratives in Verse." *Comparative Studies of South Asia, Africa, and the Middle East*, 22, 1 (2002): 112–18.

———. "Forging a Canon of Dakhni Literature: Translations and Retellings from Persian." In *Iran and the Deccan: Persianate Art, Culture, and Talent in Circulation, 1400–1700*, edited by Keelan H. Overton, 401–20. Bloomington: Indiana University Press, 2020.

———. *Mughal Arcadia: Persian Literature in an Indian Court*. Cambridge, MA: Harvard University Press, 2017.

———. *Persian Poetry at the Indian Frontier: Mas'ūd Sa'd Salmān of Lahore*. New Delhi: Permanent Black, 2000.

Sheikh, Samira. "Aurangzeb as Seen from Gujarat: Shi'i and Millenarian Challenges to Mughal Sovereignty." *Journal of the Royal Asiatic Society* 28, no. 3 (2018): 557–81. https://doi.org/10.1017/s1356186318000135.

Shephard, Kancha Ilaiah. "Why Didn't India's Muslim Rulers and Thinkers Confront the Inequities of the Caste System?" *The Wire*, January 8, 2023. https://thewire.in/caste/why-didnt-indias-muslim-rulers-and-thinkers-confront-the-inequities-of-the-caste-system.

Sherwani, H. K. *The Bahmanis of the Deccan*. New Delhi: Munshiram Manoharlal, 1985.

———. *History of the Qutb Shahi Dynasty*. Delhi: Munshiram Manoharlal, 1974.

Sherwani, H. K., and P. M. Joshi. *History of Medieval Deccan*, vols. 1 and 2. Hyderabad: Government of Andhra Pradesh, 1973.

Siddiqua, Najma. *Persian Language and Literature in Golkonda*. New Delhi: Adam, 2011.

Skinner, Cyril. "Transitional Malay Literature: Part 1—Ahmad Rijaluddin and Munshi Abdullah." *Bijdragen tot de Taal-, Land- en Volkenkunde* 134, no. 4 (1978): 466–87.

Skocpol, Theda, Peter B. Evans, and Dietrich Rueschemeyer. *Bringing the State Back In*. Cambridge: Cambridge University Press, 1985.

Sneath, David. *The Headless State: Aristocratic Orders, Kinship Society & Misrepresentations of Nomadic Inner Asia*. New York: Columbia University Press, 2007.

Sobers-Khan, Nur. *Slaves without Shackles: Forced Labour and Manumission in the Galata Court Registers, 1560–1572*. Berlin: Klaus Schwarz Verlag, 2014.

Sreenivas, Mytheli. *Wives, Widows, and Concubines: The Conjugal Family Ideal in Colonial India*. Bloomington: Indiana University Press, 2008.

Sreenivasan, Ramya. "Honoring the Family: Narratives and the Politics of Kinship in Pre-Colonial Rajasthan." In *Unfamiliar Relations: Family and History in South Asia*, edited by Indrani Chatterjee, 46–72. Ranikhet: Permanent Black, 2004.

———. "Rethinking Kingship and Authority in South Asia: Amber (Rajasthan), Ca. 1560–1615." *Journal of the Economic and Social History of the Orient* 57, no. 4 (2014): 549–86. https://doi.org/10.1163/15685209-12341358.

Srinivasachari, C.S., and Rao Bahadur. *The History of Gingee*. Madras: Annamalai University, 1943.
Stein, Burton. "State Formation and Economy Reconsidered." *Modern Asian Studies* 19, no. 3 (1985): 387–413.
Stein, Burton, and Sanjay Subrahmanyam. *Institutions and Economic Change in South Asia*. New Delhi: Oxford University Press, 1996.
Steingass, Francis Joseph. *A Comprehensive Persian-English Dictionary, Including the Arabic Words and Phrases to Be Met with in Persian Literature*. London: Routledge & K. Paul, 1892.
Stern, Philip J. *The Company-State: Corporate Sovereignty and the Early Modern Foundations of the British Empire in India*. New York: Oxford University Press, 2011.
Stoler, Ann Laura. *Along the Archival Grain: Epistemic Anxieties and Colonial Common Sense*. Princeton, NJ: Princeton University Press, 2009.
Subrahmanyam, Sanjay. "A Roomful of Mirrors: The Artful Embrace of Mughals and Franks, 1550–1700." *Ars Orientalis*, 39 (2010): 39–83.
———. "Aspects of State Formation in South India and Southeast Asia, 1500–1650." *Indian Economic and Social History Review* 23, no. 4 (1986): 357–77.
———. "Connected Histories: Notes towards a Reconfiguration of Early Modern Eurasia." *Modern Asian Studies* 31, no. 3 (1997): 735–62. https://doi.org/10.1017/s0026749x00017133.
———. *Courtly Encounters: Translating Courtliness and Violence in Early Modern Eurasia*. Cambridge, MA: Harvard University Press, 2012.
———. "Early Modern Circulation and the Question of 'Patriotism' between Central Asia and India." In *Writing Travel in Central Asian History*, edited by Nile Green, 43–68. Bloomington: Indiana University Press, 2014.
———. *Empires between Islam and Christianity, 1500–1800*. Albany: State University of New York Press, 2018.
———. *Explorations in Connected Histories: From the Tagus to the Ganges*. New Delhi: Oxford University Press, 2005.
———. *Explorations in Connected Histories: Mughals and Franks*. New Delhi: Oxford University Press, 2005.
———. "Hybrid Affairs: Cultural Histories of the East India Companies." *Indian Economic and Social History Review* 55, no. 3 (2018): 419–38.
———. "Noble Harvest from the Sea: Managing the Pearl Fishery of Mannar, 1500–1925." In *Institutions and Economic Change in South Asia*, edited by Burton Stein and Sanjay Subrahmanyam, 134–72. Delhi: Oxford University Press, 1996.
———. *The Political Economy of Commerce: Southern India, 1500–1650*. Cambridge: Cambridge University Press, 1990.
———. *The Portuguese Empire in Asia, 1500–1700: A Political and Economic History*. Chichester: John Wiley and Sons, 2012.
———. "The 'Pulicat Enterprise': Luso-Dutch Conflict in South-Eastern India, 1610–1640." *South Asia: Journal of South Asian Studies* 9, no. 2 (1986): 17–36. https://doi.org/10.1080/00856408608723084.
———. "Writing History 'Backwards': Southeast Asian History (and the Annales) at the Crossroads." *Studies in History* 10, no. 1 (1994): 131–45. https://doi.org/10.1177/0019464618778408.

Subrahmanyam, Sanjay, and C. A. Bayly. "Portfolio Capitalists and the Political Economy of Early Modern India." *Indian Economic and Social History Review* 25, no. 4 (1988): 401–24. https://doi.org/10.1177/001946468802500402.

Subrahmanyam, Sanjay, and David Shulman. "The Men Who Would Be King? The Politics of Expansion in Early Seventeenth-Century Northern Tamilnadu." *Modern Asian Studies* 24, no. 2 (1990): 225–48. https://doi.org/10.1017/s0026749x00010301.

Subramanian, Lakshmi. "The Eighteenth-Century Social Order in Surat: A Reply and an Excursus on the Riots of 1788 and 1795." *Modern Asian Studies* 25, no. 2 (1991): 321–65. https://doi.org/10.1017/s0026749x00010702.

———. *Indigenous Capital and Imperial Expansion: Bombay, Surat, and the West Coast*. New York: Oxford University Press, 1996.

Subtelny, Maria Eva. "Centralizing Reform and Its Opponents in the Late Timurid Period." *Iranian Studies* 21, nos. 1–2 (1988): 123–51. https://doi.org/10.1080/00210868808701712.

Sultana, Badar. *Karnātak kī razmīya masnawīyon kā tanqīdī jā'iza*. Bangalore: Karnatak Urdu Academy, 2018.

Swaminathan, K. D. *The Nayakas of Ikkeri*. Madras: P. Varadachary, 1957.

Szonyi, Michael. *The Art of Being Governed: Everyday Politics in Late Imperial China*. Princeton, NJ: Princeton University Press, 2017.

Talbot, Cynthia. "Anger and Atonement in Mughal India: An Alternative Account of Akbar's 1578 Hunt." *Modern Asian Studies* 55, no. 5 (2021): 1413–60. https://doi.org/10.1017/s0026749x21000172.

———. "Inscribing the Other, Inscribing the Self: Hindu-Muslim Identities in Pre-Colonial India." *Comparative Studies in Society and History* 37, no. 4 (1995): 692–722. https://doi.org/10.1017/s0010417500019927.

———. *The Last Hindu Emperor: Prithviraj Chauhan and the Indian Past, 1200–2000*. Cambridge: Cambridge University Press, 2015.

———. *Precolonial India in Practice: Society, Region, and Identity in Medieval Andhra*. New Delhi: Oxford University Press, 2001.

———. "A Revised View of 'Traditional' India: Caste, Status, and Social Mobility in Medieval Andhra." *South Asia: Journal of South Asian Studies* 15, no. 1 (1992): 17–52. https://doi.org/10.1080/00856409208723159.

Tapper, Richard. "Who Are the Kuchi? Nomad Self-Identities in Afghanistan." *Journal of the Royal Anthropological Institute* 14, no. 1 (2008): 97–116. https://doi.org/10.1111/j.1467-9655.2007.00480.x.

Thackston Jr., Wheeler M. "The Poetry of Abu Talib Kalim, Persian Poet-Laureate of Shah Jahan, Mughal Emperor of India." PhD diss., Harvard University, 1974.

Tilly, Charles. "Family History, Social History, and Social Change." *Journal of Family History* 12, nos. 1–3 (1987): 319–30. https://doi.org/10.1177/036319908701200118.

Torri, Michelguglielmo. "Surat during the Second Half of the Eighteenth Century: What Kind of Social Order?" *Modern Asian Studies* 21, no. 4 (1987): 679–710. https://doi.org/10.1017/s0026749x00009288.

Travers, Robert. *Empires of Complaints: Mughal Law and the Making of British India, 1765–1793*. Cambridge: Cambridge University Press, 2022.

Trivellato, Francesca. "Is There a Future for Italian Microhistory in the Age of Global History?" *California Italian Studies* 2, no. 1 (2011).

Truschke, Audrey. *Culture of Encounters: Sanskrit at the Mughal Court*. New York: Columbia University Press, 2016.

———. *The Language of History: Sanskrit Narratives of Indo-Muslim rule*. New York: Columbia University Press, 2021.

Tyagi, Jaya. *Contestation and Compliance: Retrieving Women's Agency from Puranic Traditions*. New Delhi: Oxford University Press, 2014.

———. *Engendering the Early Household: Brahmanical Precepts in the Early Grhyasutras, Middle of the First Millenium B.C.E.* Delhi: Orient Longman, 2008.

Vatuk, Sylvia. "Shurreef, Herklots, Crooke, and Qanoon-E-Islam: Constructing an Ethnography of 'the Moosulmans of India.'" *South Asia Research* 19, no. 1 (1999): 5–28. https://doi.org/10.1177/026272809901900102.

Verma, Bhagwat D. "History in the Muhammad Nama." In *Shivaji Nibandhavali Bhag-II*, edited by Narsingh Kelkar, 73–134. Pune: Government Central Press, 1930.

Verma, D. C. *History of Bijapur*. Delhi: Kumar Brothers, 1974.

Vila, Nawab Aziz Jung. *Jami ʿal-ʿAtiyāt*, edited by M. Z. A. Shakeb and Hasanuddin Ahmed. Hyderabad: Vila Academy, 1974.

Vink, Markus. *Encounters on the Opposite Coast: The Dutch East India Company: The Dutch East India Company and the Nayaka State of Madurai in the Seventeenth Century*. Leiden: Brill, 2015.

———. "'The World's Oldest Trade': Dutch Slavery and Slave Trade in the Indian Ocean in the Seventeenth Century." *Journal of World History* 14, no. 2 (June 2003): 131–77.

Wagoner, Philip. "The Multiple Worlds of Amin Khan: Crossing Persianate and Indic Cultural Boundaries in the Qutb Shahi Kingdom." In *Sultans of the South: Arts of India's Deccan Courts, 1323–1687*, edited by Navina N. Haider and Marika Sardar, 90–101. New York: Metropolitan Museum of Art, 2011.

Washbrook, David A. "Merchants, Markets, and Commerce in Early Modern South India." *Journal of the Economic and Social History of the Orient* 53, nos. 1–2 (2009): 266–89. https://doi.org/10.1163/002249910X12573963244485.

———. "Progress and Problems: South Asian Economic and Social History ca. 1720–1860." *Modern Asian Studies* 22, no. 1 (1988): 57–96. https://doi.org/10.1017/s0026749x00009410.

———. "South India 1770–1840: the Colonial Transition." *Modern Asian Studies* 38, no. 3 (2004): 479–516.

Wickramasinghe, Nira, and Alicia Schrikker. "The Ambivalence of Freedom: Slaves in Jaffna, Sri Lanka, in the Eighteenth and Nineteenth Centuries." *Journal of Asian Studies* 78, no. 3 (2019): 497–519. https://doi.org/10.1017/s0021911819000159.

Wielenga, Karuna Dietrich. "Repertoires of Resistance: The Handloom Weavers of South India, ca. 1800–1960." *International Review of Social History* 61, no. 3 (2016): 423–58. https://doi.org/10.1017/s0020859016000535.

———. *Weaving Histories: The Transformation of the Handloom Industry in South India, 1800–1960*. Oxford: Oxford University Press, 2020.

Wigen, Kären. "Mapping Early Modernity: Geographical Meditations on a Comparative Concept." *Early Modern Japan* 5, no. 2 (1995): 1–13.

Williams, Tyler. "If the Whole World Were Paper . . .': A History of Writing in the North Indian Vernacular." *History and Theory* 57, no. 4 (2018): 81–101.

Wink André. *Land and Sovereignty: Agrarian Society and Politics under the Eighteenth-Century Maratha svarjya*. Cambridge: Cambridge University Press, 1986.

Winterbottom, Anna. *Hybrid Knowledge in the Early East India Company World*. Cham: Springer, 2016.
Woods, John E. *The Aqquyunlu: Clan, Confederation, Empire*. Salt Lake City: University of Utah Press, 1999.
Zaidi, S. Inayat Ali. "Fads and Foibles: Perception of Administrative Traits of the Mughal State." *Indian Historical Review* 29, nos. 1-2 (2002): 87–114. https://doi.org/10.1177/037698360202900206.
———. "Ordinary Kachawaha Troopers Serving the Mughal Empire: Composition and Structure of the Contingents of the Kachawaha Nobles." *Studies in History* 2 (1980): 57–68.
Zor, Muhiuddin Qadri. *Hindustānī Lisāniyat*, Hyderabad: Maktabah-yi Ibrahimiya, 1932.
Zürcher, Erik Jan. *Fighting for a Living: A Comparative Study of Military Labour 1500-2000*. Amsterdam: Amsterdam University Press, 2013.

INDEX

Abraha, 138–39
'Abdul Hakim Khan, 186, 188, 189–90
'Abdul Karim Bahlol Khan, 146, 148, 149, 152–54, 158–60, 162–66, 176
'Abdul Khair Khan, 189
'Abdul Rauf Khan, 192. See also Miyanas
Abu'l-Faraj Muhammad ibn 'Ubayd Allah al-Lajlaj, 126
Abu'l-Fazl, 11; *Akbarnāma*, 96
Abyssinian, 49, 92, 99, 105, 124, 138, 223n42. See also *habshī*; Indo-Africans
accession, 92–97
Aceh, 79, 144, 176
adab (rules of etiquette and conduct), 22, 125, 129, 141
'Ādilnāma, 30, 115*fig.*, 116, 120–25, 129, 140. See also Atishi, Hakim
'Adil Shah, Muhammad (sultan), 56–57, 61, 65–67, 68, 78, 79, 80–84, 90, 92–93, 96, 97, 99, 128, 151, 231n43; weddings of, 88*fig.*, 97–112, 114
'Adil Shah, Sikandar (sultan), 161. See also *Tārīkh-i sikandarī*
'Adil Shah II, 'Ali (sultan), 115, 116, 122, 126, 131–32, 135, 151–54, 158, 159
'Adil Shah II, Ibrahim (sultan), 79, 92, 93, 96, 100, 112, 121
'Adil shahs of Bijapur, 12, 15, 27, 138; alliance with Mughals, 135. See also Bijapur
Afghans, 7, 10, 16, 19, 48, 51–52, 70, 71, 81, 115, 124, 126, 134, 142–43, 147, 148*map*, 163, 165, 191, 217n79, 218n93; military recruitment in northern and southern armies, 51–53. See also Miyanas
Afzal Khan, 131, 153
Asad Khan, 64*fig.*, 66
aghore. See *aghor panthis*
aghor panthis (mendicant order), 71. See also *avadhūt*
agnatic descent, 47–48, 51–53, 58, 66, 187
Ahmad Maymandi, 121
Ahmadnagar, 12, 14–15, 27, 55–56, 93–94, 116, 127, 128, 203n61, 219n107
Akbar (Mughal emperor), 1, 41–42, 67–68
akhlāq, 125, 129
Ali, M. Athar, 197
Aliya Rama Raya, 109. See also Ramraj
alliance(s): across sect and caste, 18; critiques of the theory of, 16, 104; role of marriages in, 87–92. See also *under* 'Adil shahs; Bijapur; Deccan Sultanates; Mughal Empire
Andhra, 3, 13, 30, 134, 174
Andries, Pieter, 66
Arabian Sea, 13, 61, 78, 151
Arabic, 168, 174, 193
archives: literary and non-literary, 25–27, 140; Mughal, 3–4, 220n116; true copy, 40
Ardestani, Mir Jumla Muhammad Sayyid, 85, 151, 168, 176
Ariyalur, 159, 169
'arzdāsht, 17

275

276 INDEX

'arz-o-chehreh. See muster roll
Asaf, 110–11
Asar, Mohammad Ali, 26
Asif, Manan Ahmed, 181
Asirgarh, 1–3, 180
Astarabadi, Fuzuni, 64*fig.*, 68
Astarabadi, Mir Mu'min, 99
Atishi, Hakim, 30, 36–37, 64*fig.*, 115–30, 136, 142, 145, 228n2, 230nn24,27, 231n43
Atlantic Ocean, 58
Aurangzeb (Mughal emperor), 19, 22, 131, 138, 151, 164–65, 191, 192, 204n76, 214n45, 220n113, 234n104, 243n131
avadhūt, 71
Awadhi, 13
Awasthi, Suresh Dutt, 157, 239n58
'Azimuddin, Muhammad, 31, 181–94; *Tārīkh-i Dilīr-jangī*, 181–94, 245n25

Babayan, Kathryn, 22
Babur (Mughal emperor), 11
bāghī, 132
Bahlol Khan. See also Miyanas
Bahmanis, 12, 55
Baksar, 50, 216n66
Bankapur, 65–66, 69–70, 153–54, 166
banquet, 101, 106, 111
Bardes, 154
Barid shahs of Bidar, 12
Bari Sahiba. See Khadija Sultana
Barlas, 51, 52
barracks, 28, 32–60
Basātīn us-Salātīn, 149
Basavappa Nayaka II, 188
bastard, 93–94, 121, 152
Battle of Samugarh, 164–65
Battle of Talikota, 110
Battle of Umrani, 160
bazm, 107, 108–9
Bednur, 62, 65, 70
Belgaum, 65–66, 80, 85
believer, 71, 133, 135, 163
belonging, 4–5, 7–10, 11, 15–16, 25–29, 36, 47, 60, 62, 63, 67, 76, 88, 100, 117–19, 127, 140, 145, 158, 160–61, 163, 165, 178
Bengal, 77, 144, 155; Bay of, 148, 154, 166, 168, 176, 180
betel nut, 72, 112. See also *pān*
betrayal, 126, 131, 137, 141, 143, 163
Bhatkal, 78
Bheemunipatnam, 13
Bhonsle (family), 18, 30, 49–50, 135, 146, 151, 154–56; in verse, 156–66. See also Marathas

Bhor, 17
Bhushan, 158, 228; *Shivrajbhusan*, 158, 239n63
Bidar, 12, 116
Bidnur, 187–88
Bijapur, 12–14, 30, 49, 55–57, 61, 65, 67, 78, 131, 145–47, 152, 158–59, 161, 170, 178, 180, 204n77, 219nn107,108; alliance with Mughals, 128; civil war in, 124; court politics of, 93; literary portraits of, 92; Mughal incursions into, 192; sovereignty of, 173–74; weddings in, 90, 97–107. See also 'Adil shahs
bilingualism, 72, 122–23
Bombay, 182, 185, 186
borders, 3, 33, 54, 72–74, 85, 101–2, 117–18, 192. See also frontier(s); *sarhad*; threshold
Bouwens, Dominicus, 79
Brahmins, 50, 149; Konkani, 76; Maratha, 53, 55, 105, 124; Shenvi, 64, 65; Smart-Saiva, 246n42
Brajbhasha, 158, 165
branding, 42–44, 56–57, 102, 214n45
broker, 167–68
Bundeli, 142
bureaucracy, 47, 60, 63, 171; maritime, 75–77; military, 57
bureaucrats, 76, 84; new, 77
Burhanpur, 3–4, 33*fig.*, 39, 42, 58–59, 65, 102, 249, 259
Burma, 77, 170

Cape Comorin. See Kanyakumari
caste, 9, 20, 76, 166, 167, 174, 197; heads of, 176; left-hand, 175; right-hand, 175; upper, 177, 241n101; weaving sub-castes, 149, 175–77
Catholic church, 169
centralization, 55. See also Mughal Empire: attempts at centralization
ceremony, 87–143, 189
Ceylon, 168
Chandragiri, 168
Chatterjee, Indrani, 200n9,12
Chatterjee, Nandini, 24
Chauhan, 46, 48, 49, 50, 219n69
Chauhan, Devi Singh, 239nn58,61
Chaul, 82–83, 94
chehrah, 39–40, 210n1
chehrah āqāsī. See *chehrah nawīs*
chehrah nawīs, 37, 44–53
Chennabasavappa Nayaka, 188
Chennai, 147, 148, 154, 166, 168, 176
Cherian, Divya, 22, 177
chess, 124–27
chetti, 174, 176, 243n142
Chinanna Chetti, 168

INDEX 277

chirurgijn, 66
Chitradurg, 187, 189
circulation, 3, 5–10, 11, 15–16, 18–20, 26–29, 97–98, 194, 197; book and manuscript, 192–93; labor, 166–67, 175–77; Perso-Arabic literary, 6
circumcision, 91
citizen, 8, 212n9
cleanliness, 75, 189, 190–91
Coimbatore, 169, 243n144
collective memory, 157
colonialism, 4, 5, 146, 166–67, 178, 194
colorism, 132
commensality: caste and, 187, 189, 191; rituals of, 91, 111. *See also* dining
consumption, 29, 87, 102, 104, 110–11
coreligionists: political critiques of, 12–13, 114, 145, 187, 189
Coromandel, 159, 235n7, 238n53; coast, 7, 14, 30, 77–78, 106, 142–43, 145–47, 148*map*, 150, 166–68, 170–71, 174, 175, 177, 236n21; plains near, 61
Count-Duke of Olivares, 94
counternarratives, 140, 141
court, 6, 20–25, 29, 43, 69, 90, 142, 178; Deccan, 55, 114–43
Courteen Association, 85
Cuddalore, 148, 149, 156, 159, 166, 178

Dabhol, 78, 83, 116
Dakkani (language), 25–27, 29, 41, 67–75, 226n46; poets, 231n38; prestige of, 122; verse, 156–66; writing in, 89–91, 99, 106–12, 116–17, 122, 125, 140, 142, 156. *See also under* literati
dakkanī (social identification): southerner, 48–49, 56
dāmād, 67, 80, 89
Damghani, ʿAli ibn Naqi al-Husayni al-, 88*fig*., 100
Danda Rajapur, 83, 85, 94, 152, 223n42
Danes, 170
Danish East India Company, 173, 243n136
Dara Shikoh, 164–65
dārogha, 42, 44–45
Darvish (prince), 95
Daulatabad, 39, 42, 43–44, 65, 102, 180, 213n17
Daulat Khan. *See* Khawas Khan
Dávila, Pedro Juan, 58
Deccan, 1–3, 31, 85, 140, 142, 147, 183; as *ghar*, 9, 11–15; language in, 62; Mughal sites in, 35*map*; political organization in, 9, 126, 165
Deccani (political category), 48–49, 53, 127, 158; armies, 138

Deccan Sultanates, 11–15, 11*map*, 16, 23, 48–50, 90, 168; alliances, 127; decline of, 151; inter-marriages in, 102; resilience of the, 45; soldiering in, 55
deed of submission, 12, 116, 124. *See also inqiyādnāma*
deindustrialization, 166, 240n97
Delhi, 3, 4, 7, 10, 15, 39, 128, 134, 136, 162, 163, 190, 195
desai, 17, 18, 55, 76, 84, 131, 154
description: physical, 36–41, 58
deshkulkarni, 76
deshmukh, 84, 172
deshpande, 76, 172
Deshpande, Prachi, 171, 172
Devanampattinam, 24, 168
devangulu, 149. *See also* caste: weaving sub-castes
Dharwar, 185
diaspora, 221n3
difference, 27, 63, 67–68, 70, 131, 136, 156, 158, 165; ethno-linguistic, 95; sectarian, 134–35, 141, 142
Digby, Simon, 51
Dilir Jang Bahadur, Nawab Dilir Khan, 180–94
Dimgal, 68
dining, 183, 187, 190–91. *See also* commensality
disloyalty, 132–33, 137, 143
documents, 34, 36–46, 211n8, 213n17; materiality of, 24, 57–60
donkey, 186–87
dowry, 99, 100, 101, 105, 108, 110
Duke of Lerma, 94
Dutch, 14, 25, 61, 79, 90, 151, 152–53, 170–71, 173–77, 223n37
Dutch (language), 76, 81
Dutch East India Company, 14, 24, 27, 65–66, 77, 78–80, 83, 84, 145–46, 149, 153–58, 168, 170, 172–76, 205n85, 234n5, 236n21, 242n124; documents, 24, 145, 146; dynasty, 21, 31, 141, 165, 182–83, 205n86; negotiations with Goa, 79, 81, 84

East India Company, 6, 179; archive, 150, 193–94. *See also* Danish East India Company; Dutch East India Company; English East India Company; French East India Company
Eaton, Richard, 23
economy, 6, 145, 147; Indian Ocean littoral, 6, 27, 30, 31, 143, 145, 147, 149, 151, 154, 167, 168; political, 159
eighteenth century, 10, 14, 22, 24, 26, 27, 36, 39, 77, 87, 130, 145, 161

Ekoji Bhonsle, 159, 135–36, 159, 166, 169.
  See also Bhonsle (family)
Elizabeth I (Queen of England), 14
Ellichpur, 43–44
émigré, 12, 16, 19, 28, 30, 36, 62–63, 65, 67, 70, 75, 77; Central Asian, 95, 120; household, 84, 107
empires: definition of, 4–5, 15, 136; Islamic, 6, 7–11, 21
English, 151
English (language), 181
English East India Company, 1, 14, 27, 31, 62, 77, 149, 166–67, 172, 180–82, 184, 185–86, 236n26, 241n101
Estado da Índia, 6, 29
ethnicity, 10, 46–54
ethnography, 68, 70, 72, 73; colonial, 25
European languages, 6, 63, 76, 80, 145, 194
Europeans, 14, 20, 29, 66, 79, 99, 133, 135, 170, 176

faith, 133–34, 135, 138
family, 9, 16–18, 21, 22, 29, 46, 62, 65, 76, 79–81, 84–85, 192, 225n16; in history-writing, 31, 91, 180, 181, 182, 184–89
fareb, 128, 136–37, 223n92
farmān, 18, 39, 43, 72, 82, 224n59
"far south," 3
Faruqi dynasty of Khandesh, 1
father, 32; name of, 8, 36, 41
fathnāma. *See* poetry, martial
feasting, 108, 109, 113. *See also* commensality; dining
fihrist, 39, 42–43
Firdawsi, 119, 120–23, 142, 220n27; *Shāhnāma*, 121–22
Firishta, Muhammad Qasim, 12; *Gulshan-i Ibrāhīmī*, 12
Flatt, Emma, 23
Flores, Jorge, 14, 65, 76
foreigner, 25, 62, 146, 158, 159
Franks, 110, 133, 135
French, 173, 175
French East India Company, 149, 168, 169–71
frontier(s), 3, 4–5, 14, 62, 166. *See also* borders; *sarhad*; threshold
Fukazawa, Hiroshi, 76, 77, 84

Gabbur, 3
Gandikota, 3, 151
gāon, 158
gender, 22, 29, 87, 93–95, 107, 188–89
Gesudaraz, Banda Nawaz Khwaja, 116
ghanīm, 163

Ghansham, 50
ghar, 3, 4, 7–11, 15, 16, 18–19, 24–25, 29–30, 60, 75, 92, 108–9, 119, 123, 131–32, 134, 139, 146–47, 158, 161–62, 182, 184, 187, 195, 201n19; creating, 63, 85; destruction of, 161; and literary patronage, 118; loyalty to, 141; meaning of, 36, 113, 114, 127, 136, 193; as metaphor, 100; naming of, 32, 36, 195; as political category, 19, 114, 118; politics of, 140; shared, 147, 163; as social identification, 32. *See also* dynasty; home; house; household; kin; space
Ghats: Eastern, 13, 147; Western, 13, 17, 61, 147
Ghawasi (poet), 100
ghaza, 159
ghazal (lyric), 26, 27
gifting, 87, 109–10
Goa, 14, 65, 77–79, 84–85, 94. *See also* Portuguese Empire
Golkonda, 12, 13, 15, 27, 49, 85, 93, 97–101, 103–5, 131, 138, 147, 151, 152, 168, 169, 173, 176; weddings in, 90. *See also* Qutb Shah, ʿAbdullah (sultan); Qutb Shah, Muhammad Quli (sultan)
Gondaji Pasalkar, 131–32
Gopikabai, 188
Great Mughal, 66, 114
Green, Nile, 25
Grhyasutras, 8
griha. *See ghar*
Guha, Sumit, 141, 204nn68,78, 205n80, 238n51
Gujarat, 14, 58, 68, 181
Gujri, 117
Gulbarga, 36–37
Gulf of Mannar, 148*map*, 155, 205n85
Gutti, 85, 151

Habash Khan, 49
habshī, 48–49, 70, 115, 119, 124, 142. *See also* Abyssinian; Indo-Africans
Hafiz, 119
Haider ʿAli, 183, 189–90
halālkhor, 17. *See also namak halālī*
Haq, Maulvi Abdul, 228n2, 239n58
harām-zādagī, 17
Harderwijk, 78
Harrison, William, 185
Hasan, Farhat, 24
havaldār, 17, 55, 63, 66, 67, 79–82, 84, 85, 144, 170, 243n136
Haveri, 31
de la Haye (Admiral), 169
hierarchy, 47, 67, 95, 125

Hijaz, 139
hikāyāt, 120, 129
Hind, 136, 138, 162,
Hindawi (language), 13, 41
Hindi (language), 3, 122, 123, 157, 196, 228n2, 232n75; Khari Boli, 27
Hindus, 22, 62, 70–72, 169; bureaucratic elite, 63, 77; merchant, 148, 174
Hindustan, 11, 15, 85, 137, 142; Mughal, 16, 49, 51, 54, 162, 183
historiography, 7; of Deccan sultanates, 10, 23; of Indian subcontinent, 19–20, 24–25
home, 3, 4, 7 10. See also *ghar*; house; household
honor, 131–32
hookah, 190
Hormuz, 77, 95, 116
horse, 32, 35–38, 41, 58, 83, 105, 214n45; death certificate of, 42, 214nn28,33
hospitality, 87, 97; politics of, 111–13, 169, 189–91
house, 183–90. See also dynasty; *ghar*; home; household
household, 5–6, 9, 10, 15–21, 28, 75–76, 113, 117, 132, 141, 167–68, 181–83, 187; agrarian, 201n27; aristocratic-military, 56–57; autonomy of, 77, 90; dynastic, 86; elite, 24, 205n85; émigré, 63; governing the, 61–86; itinerant, 60; making of, 89; patrimonial head, 63, 120, 125, 134, 144; Persian, 204n71; politics, 124–27; power, 78–86, 125, 182, 197; Sufi, 27. See also dynasty; *ghar*; home
Humayun (Mughal emperor), 192
Husayni Habz Khan, 105
Husayni, Sayyid ʿAbd al-Rahman, 97
Hyderabad, 29, 56, 105, 106, 176, 180, 183; siege of, 151. See also Golkonda

Iberian Union, 79
Ibrahim Rauza, 100
idangai, 175
identification, 46–54, 195
identity, 10, 28, 31, 36–46, 47, 195, 206n93; language and, 26, 117; Mughal obsession with, 37, 60; neither fuzzy nor fluid, 28, 47, 210n130, 215n51; political, 141; premodern, 34, 36, 54–55; social, 47; as social practice, 5, 20, 25
Ikhlas Khan, 159–60
Ikkeri, 12, 62, 65–72, 80, 84. See also Mirza Muqim: *Fathnāma-yi Ikkeri*
ʿImad Shahs of Berar, 12
India: definitions of, 3–4 141, 157; peninsular, 1, 2*maps*1, 2, 7, 9, 15, 61, 102, 141, 191, 195

Indianness, 25, 197
Indian Ocean, 11–15, 30, 58, 75, 77, 95, 138, 143, 144; early modern, 150; intersections with the Persianate, 6–7, 150
Indo-Africans, 16, 18, 19, 30, 49, 74*map*, 83, 99, 124, 126, 131–34, 136, 142, 148*map*, 151, 155, 158–59, 178, 226n42, 243n136. See also Abyssinians; *habshī*
Indo-Islamic, 13, 22, 76, 77
Indo-Portuguese, 168, 142n108
influence, 5, 62
inqiyādnāma, 12. See also deed of submission
institutions: in north and south, 54–57, 60, 77, 102, 194, 197
insults: for intimate rivals, 68, 69, 71, 72, 75, 132–33, 160; for sultans, 120–21; for the Mughals, 128, 138–39
Iranian Olivares. See Mustafa Khan
Iranians, 46, 51, 62, 74*map*, 107, 134, 142
Irvine, William, 39, 217n76
Islam, 246n36; caste in, 39, 63–64, 246n40; Shiʿi, 12, 28, 98, 116; in South Asia, 8, 197; Sufi, 13, 27, 47; Sunni, 12, 191

Jafar, Sayeeda, 99
Jaffna, 144, 155
jāgīr, 56, 132
jahez. See dowry
Jai Singh, Mirza Raja, 127, 130, 131, 134, 135, 233nn92,93
jāti, 9, 20, 24, 49, 63, 84
Jedhe (family), 16, 204n70, 238n43. See also Khopades (family)
Johor, 79

Kachawaha, 50
Khadija Sultana, 64*fig.*, 88*fig.*; court politics, 151–54, 159, 173, 237n33; marriage proposal, 101–6; poetic circuit of, 97–101
Kaicker, Abhishek, 24
kaikkolar, 149, 174. See also caste: weaving sub-castes
Kanara, 74*map*, 153; coast, 84, 180, 194
Kannada (language), 29, 41, 171
Kans, 66
Kanyakumari, 147
Kapadia, Aparna, 68
Karim Saheb, 189
Karnatak, the, 12, 31, 67, 69, 75, 77, 85, 106, 154–55, 170, 174, 176, 177, 178, 192; lowlands, 3, 144, 149, 155
Karnul, 18, 132, 233n80

Kar Talab Khan, 50
Kaveri River, 148, 148*map*; delta, 12, 13, 174
kāyasth (scribes), 45–46, 53–54; as soldiers, 218n90. *See also* scribes
Kedarji Khopade, 17–19
Keladi, 188
Khan Jahan Lodi, 146, 203n61, 235n8
Khan Jahan Pathan, 203n61
Khan Muhammad, 155, 159, 244n153
khāna, 8–9, 16. See also *ghar*; house; household
khānazād, 9, 48, 83, 105
Khan Baba. *See* Mustafa Khan
khāndān, 9, 183, 186, 191
Khandesh, 20, 37, 155
Khandoji Khopade, 17–18, 204n76
Khare, G. H., 239n61
Khawas Khan, 92, 94-96, 98, 124, 125, 158–60, 231n43
khāssa mansabdār, 38, 39, 40
Khopade (family), 17–19, 24, 204nn70,76, 243n131. *See also* Jedhe (family)
Khushnud, Malik (poet), 92, 99–100; *Jannat Singār*, 99
Khusrau, Amir, 99, 122; *Hasht Bihisht*, 99
khutba, 127
Kia, Mana, 125
kin, 8, 56, 69, 75–77, 86, 127, 162–63, 185–86; extended, 93. See also *ghar*
kinship, 21, 29, 89, 91, 96, 113, 128, 164, 188, 206n93; narratives, 90. *See also* relatedness
Kirmani, Mir Husain ʿAli Khan, 188, 192; *Nishān-i Haidari*, 188, 192
Kitāb-i Nauras, 112
Koddaikarai. *See* Point Calimere
Konkan, 13, 14, 20, 29, 74*map*, 76, 80, 81, 83; coast, 84, 93, 180
kothī, 7. See also *ghar*
Kothiyal, Tanuja, 22
Krishna River, 13, 15, 29, 37, 57, 128, 129, 131, 148*map*
kula, 8
Kulkarni, A. R., 16, 201n19

Lal, Ruby, 200n12
Lar, 61, 116
lashkar nawīs. See *chehra nawīs*
lineage, 16, 52, 55, 70, 90, 132, 142–43, 145, 158, 162. See also *nasl*
Lingayats, 55
literati, 116–18, 120, 136, 142; Dakkani, 130; Persianate, 89, 113–15, 120, 122–23, 127, 129, 140–41; premodern, 140, 142

loyalty, 7, 34, 56, 104, 114, 124, 141, 163, 187; political, 48, 119, 132–35, 141, 143
Luso-Dutch conflict, 65, 77, 203n56, 223n37

Madhya Pradesh, 28
Madras. *See* Chennai
Madurai, 154, 166, 168, 174
Maetsuycker, Joan, 152
Mahabharata, 66
Maharashtra, 3, 13, 17, 28, 29, 154, 180, 201n19, 240n76
Mahmud of Ghazna (sultan), 120–21, 123
Mahmud Khan, 170
majmūʿa, 181, 182
Malacca, 144, 170, 176
Malay Peninsula, 77
Malfuzāt-i Naqshbandiyya, 51
Malik Ahmad, 33*fig.*, 58
Malik Jahan, 93, 95
Maloji Bhonsle, 49
Malwa, 23, 39
māmā, 66, 188
mansabdārs, 47, 49–50, 51–52, 55, 146, 220n113
Man Singh, Raja, 67–68
Manuzzi, Niccolò, 45
Maraikkayars, 168, 174, 241n109, 243n144; Shafiʿi, 148, 175. *See also* Muslims
Marathas, 10, 16, 19, 24, 30, 49, 53, 70, 74*map*, 77, 124, 131, 134, 142, 148*map*, 151, 172, 183, 201n19
Marathi (language), 41, 142, 165, 232n75
marriage, 66, 88, 101–2, 189-191; dynastic, 102–3; proposal for, 89, 92, 101–6
Martin, Francois, 169, 172; *India in the Seventeenth Century*, 149
Marwar, 177–78, 243n135
masnavī, 26, 99, 114, 118, 129, 139, 147, 157
Masulipatnam, 168
Maval, 17
Melaka, 77, 78, 79
memorandum, 43–44
merchants, 167, 169, 174, 236n26, 243n144; Indo-Portuguese, 168; Porto Novo, 175–77
military, 32–60
Ming state, 21, 211n5
Miraj, 154
Mir Jumla. *See* Ardestani, Mir Jumla Muhammad Sayyid
Mirza Muqim, 64*fig.*, 67, 68–75, 107; *Fathnāma-yi Ikkeri*, 62–63, 65, 67–69, 75
Mirza, Sakhawat, 239n58
Miyanas (family), 30, 31, 145, 147, 149, 151, 153–56, 158–60, 168, 170, 175–76, 178, 185–86, 191;

partnership with the French, 173; in verse, 156–66. *See also* Afghans; ʿAbdul Karim Bahlol Khan
Mocha, 99, 152, 173
Mormugão, 79
Muazzam Khan (prince), 192
Mughal, 48, 54, 127, 136–37, 140, 217n76; social identifications, 51-52
Mughal-Deccan Wars, 12, 144–45, 155, 166
Mughal Empire, 1, 2*map*1, 4, 9, 11–16, 20–25, 89–91, 94, 131, 134, 159, 182, 194–97; alliance with Bijapur, 128, 134, 223n37, 242nn124,126; archives of, 59; army of, 32–60, 66, 80, 137, 138; attempts at centralization, 13, 15, 24, 28, 36, 45, 55; bureaucratic practices, 171; critiques of, 114, 120, 136–39, 144; definition of, 35; frontier of, 4–5, 17–18, 21, 26, 30, 32, 88, 102, 142, 181, 192; institutions of, 28; as Muslim rulers, 138; negotiations with Mustafa Khan, 125; occupation by, 101–2; presence in southern India, 55; service to, 15–16, 29; state-formation in, 47, 208n114. *See also* suzerainty; Timurids
Muhammad Amin. *See* Mustafa Khan
Muhammad Rafiʿ, 43–44
Muhammad Reza, 64*fig.*, 66–67, 79, 82–84
Muhammad Sharif, 43
Mukhlis, Nand Ram, 40–41; *Siyāqnāma*, 40
mulk, 9, 147, 158, 161, 162
multilingualism, 62, 67–75, 117, 229n16
Munawwar Khan, 185
Muslims, 62–63, 72, 76, 102; Indic, 77, 189; merchants, 79; rulers, 146; Tamil, 148. *See also* Islam
muster roll, 32–35, 33*fig.*, 36–47, 48, 49, 51–54, 59–60, 212n9; in the Deccan Sultanates, 219n105
Mustafa Khan, 61–86, 64*fig.*, 92, 93–94, 95, 96, 97, 106–7, 120–21, 124, 125, 230n32, 231n43; arrest of, 81; household of, 65–68
Muzaffar Khan, 106–12, 227n59
mutabannā, 152
Mysore, 190–91, 245n25

Nad ʿAli Sabzwari, Khwaja, 43
Nagapattinam, 148, 149, 151, 155, 158, 168, 170, 173, 174, 176, 180
Nair, Janaki, 54, 199n3
namak halālī, 163. *See also halālkhor*
namak harāmī, 133, 163
naming, 46–54
Nana Saheb Balaji Rao, Peshwa, 187–98

Narmada River, 1, 3, 15
Narsoji Dhangar, 49
Nasir Muhammad, 156, 159–60, 170, 243n136
nasīhat, 127–28, 129
nasl, 133, 162. *See also* lineage
nationalism, 24, 156–57, 194, 228n2
naukarī: service under a master, 9–10, 15–16, 28–29, 34, 57, 60, 162–63
Nawaz Begam, 189
nayaka, 135, 154, 166, 168, 169, 171, 174, 186–89
Neknam Khan, 176
Nizami, 119, 120
Nizams of Hyderabad, 171–72, 183, 187, 189
Nizam Shah, Burhan (sultan), 94
Nizam shahs of Ahmadnagar, 12, 27, 55–56, 116, 128
Nizamuddin Ahmad (chronicler), 98, 99, 100, 101–6; *Hadīqat al-Salātīn*, 29, 101–2
north, the, 3–4, 22, 54, 208n113
Nurullah Qazi (chronicler), 122; *Tārīkh-i ʿAlī ʿĀdil Shāhī*, 122
Nusrati, 19, 30, 92, 100–101, 107, 114–18, 122–27, 129–39, 142, 145–47, 156, 157, 158, 161, 164, 178, 229n8, 233nn92,93; *ʿAlīnāma*, 30, 107, 114–15, 122–27, 131, 140; *Gulshan-i ʿIshq*, 100; *Tārīkh-i sikandarī*, 30, 146, 156–66, 184, 238n57, 239n58

occupation(s), 9, 18, 28, 29, 32, 40, 42, 43, 46, 47–50, 60; non-combatants in the Mughal army, 50; roles in bureaucracy, 62, 63, 77, 84
orientalism, 91, 93, 194
Orissa, 155
Orsini, Francesca, 117
Other, 67, 131, 146, 158, 162. *See also* self
otherness, 70, 132, 135, 160, 196
Ottoman Empire, 6, 21, 23, 43, 91

Paets, Pieter, 66, 78
Pakhtun, 52–53
Palar River, 148
Palk Strait, 148, 148*map*, 155
pān, 111
pand, 127–28, 138
Pandit, Murari, 56, 105, 124, 125, 231n43
Panhala (fort), 18, 131–32, 153, 204n77
Panjabi, 27, 136–37, 250
paper: of documents, 38–40, 41, 42–44
Paravas, 168, 241n109
pathān, 163, 217n79
patrimonial, 19, 21, 73, 114, 118, 204n78
Paviljoen, Anthonio, 170–71, 173

INDEX

Pearl Fishery Coast, 147, 148, 242n109
Pennar River, 3
Persian (language), 6, 13, 16, 23–27, 29, 33, 41, 58, 67–75, 76, 80, 81, 94–95, 99, 109, 114, 123, 149, 160, 171, 181, 193, 210nn1,129, 234n108; ethical literature in, 125, 141; poetry in, 119, 127, 140, 161; prose chronicles, 12, 15, 23, 25, 89, 90–91, 95, 97–98, 107, 113, 118, 140, 141, 144, 182, 183
Persianate, 6, 7, 20, 21, 24, 25, 62, 65, 66, 70, 81, 90, 95, 96, 107, 110, 112, 117–18, 119–29, 142, 147, 149–50, 167, 177, 183–84. *See also under* literati
Persian Gulf, 3, 78, 95, 116
Perso-Arabic, 9; literary circuits, 6; forms, 26–27, 107–8, 181–82, 239n58; script, 13, 27, 157, 239n58
Persographia, 25
Peshwas, 183, 186–89
phenotype, 13
Pit, Martin, 169, 171, 173, 174, 242n117
poet, 70, 71, 87, 89–90, 98–99, 123, 140, 147; as political commentator, 124–27
poetry, 97–101, 108, 113–14; complaining in, 119–24; forms of, 26, 27, 141; homage to masters of, 119–24; martial, 127, 140, 142; meter in, 109; plagiarism in, 120; politics in, 118; question of originality in, 123
Point Calimere, 148, 166, 168, 174, 243n136
polyvocality, 26, 62, 75, 85, 88, 98, 107–8
Ponda, 64*fig.*, 66, 67, 74*map*, 79–80, 84, 85, 93
Pondicherry, 3, 148, 149, 168–71, 173, 242n117
portfolio capitalists, 149–50, 167
Portmans, Martin, 85
Porto Novo, 148, 149, 154, 168, 170, 173, 174, 175, 176, 177, 241n108, 243n136
portraiture, 37, 59, 76, 89, 195, 212n13; literary, 67, 69, 90, 92, 102, 104, 125, 138, 158–59
Portuguese (language), 25, 65, 76, 81, 82, 93, 95, 96
Portuguese Empire, 14, 61, 65–66, 77, 78–83, 90, 95, 168; alliance with Paravas, 168, 241n109; faith of, 133. *See also* Goa
Potosí, 58–59
power, 21–22, 89, 91; elasticity of, 91; elite, 63; imperial, 114, 128; kingly, 89; stratification of, 55
Pratap Rao, 160
proverbs, 7; on *ghar*, 186–87
Pulicat, 78, 168, 176
Pune, 17, 131, 154, 159, 180, 185, 188
Purandar, 134

qabā'il, 18
qaul, 79, 80, 170–77, 242n124, 243nn131,135,136; agrarian vs. maritime, 172

qaum, 9, 40, 46, 51, 58, 191, 216n73
Qutb Shah, 'Abdullah (sultan), 56, 64*fig.*, 85, 98–101, 103–6, 173. *See also* Golkonda
Qutb Shah, Muhammad Quli (sultan), 112. *See also* Golkonda
Qutb shahs. *See* Golkonda

Raichur, 7, 194
Rajasthan, 22, 52, 178, 181, 218n93, 225n16
rājpūt (social identification), 33*fig.*, 46, 68, 48–51, 58; Solanki, 48, 50–51
Raman, Bhavani, 243n144
Ramanathapuram, 110. *See also* Ramnad
Ramaswamy, Vijaya, 167
Ramnad, 148, 168, 169, 174, 205n85, 243n143. *See also* Ramanathapuram
Ramraj, 110. *See also* Aliya Rama Raya
Randaula Khan, 82, 83–84, 223n42
Ranmal of Idar, 68
Rao, Narayana Velcheru, 23
Rashid Khan Ansari, 52
razm, 107, 108–9, 161. *See also* war
recruitment, 15, 41, 48, 59; in Deccan Sultanates, 47–52, 54–55, 57; descriptions in manuals and chronicles, 41–42, 55–56; pan-subcontinent military, 28, 46, 55, 102
relatedness, 87–113; literary representations of, 87–88; politics of, 134; rituals of, 104–6, 111. *See also* kinship
Revington, Henry, 152
Rewadanda (Upper Chaul), 82, 224n60
Reza Quli Beg. *See* Khan, Neknam
Rohida (fort), 17, 18
Rohilla, 137, 206n03
Ruijser, Nicolas, 169, 171, 173–75, 242n117
Rustami, Kamal Khan (poet), 99; *Khāvarnāma*, 99
Rustam Zamān, 82, 83, 152. *See also* Randaula Khan

sabk-i hindī, 116–17
Sabzwari, Khwaja Nad 'Ali, 43
Sa'di, 119, 120
Safavid Empire, 22, 23, 78, 91, 95
Şahin, Kaya, 91
Sahyadri Mountains. *See* Ghats, Western
Salabat Khan, *See* Siddi Jauhar
sale, 149. *See also* caste: weaving sub-castes
saltpeter, 78, 83, 155, 223n42
Sankaraji Banaji, 17
Sanskrit, 8, 13, 23, 68, 109, 113, 117, 157, 239n63
sarhad, 15. *See also* borders; frontier(s); threshold
Sarkar, Jadunath, 22

INDEX 283

Savanur, 31, 180, 182–93, 245n25
sayyid, 51, 53, 81
Scott, James, 4; *Seeing Like a State*, 4
scribe, 32–33, 37, 42–46, 48, 52–53, 60, 63, 76, 171, 174, 181, 185, 243n144
seals, 40, 42
secondary centers, 13–14, 23
self, 67, 87, 158. See also Other
Senji, 145, 154, 168, 170, 171, 176, 236n21, 243n136
setti. See *chetti*
Setupatis, 174, 175
Shah Jahan (Mughal emperor), 65, 102, 128
Shah Saheb (Xa Saibo), 64*fig.*, 66, 80
shahr-āshob, 161
Shaivite, 13, 28–29, 62, 71
sharāfat, 184, 190
Shah Abu'l Hasan, 64*fig.*, 66, 103
Shahaji Bhonsle, 135, 152, 154
Shahu Bhonsle, 77
Shah Nawaz Khan, 43
Shaista Khan, 130, 131
Sharma, Sunil, 161, 229n16
shatter zones, 20–21, 23
Shauqi, Hasan (poet), 92, 107–12; *Fathnāma-yi Nizām Shah*, 110; *Mezbanīnāma*, 97, 107–12, 113
Shaykh Muhyi-ud-Din, 94
Shaykh Rahim, 103
Shivaji Bhonsle, 19, 131–35, 127, 138, 142, 149, 152–54, 157, 158–60, 162–64, 169, 232n75, 233nn92,93. See also Bhonsle (family)
Shulman, David, 23
Siddi Jauhar, 127, 131–34, 152–53, 156, 159, 232n75, 233n80
Sivappa Nayak, 62, 69, 70–72, 75
slave, 92, 99, 131–32, 154; trade, 238nn51,53
soldiers, 45–46; identifications for, 46–54
south, the, 3, 22, 54, 48–49
southerner. See *dakkanī* (social identification)
sovereignty, 13, 15–20, 76, 124
space, 4–8; terms for, 158, 161–62. See also *ghar*
Speelman, Cornelis, 154
Sreenivasan, Ramya, 67–68
stadthouder van Decan, 65. See also Mustafa Khan
state, 6, 8, 20–25, 142; early modern, 33; formation, 151; imperial, 5; modern, 4, 28; precolonial, 4, 19
stratification, 94, 96; labor, 150, 167
St. Thomé, 148, 149, 169–71, 174–75, 241n108
Subrahmanyam, Sanjay, 23, 201nn17,18, 205n85, 223n53
Subramanian, Lakshmi, 241n101
sulahnāma, 187–88

Sultan Begam, 189
Surat, 14, 80, 130–31, 138, 241n101
suzerainty, 97; Company, 180; Mughal, 9, 55, 56, 65, 77, 88, 90, 97, 103, 107, 112, 118, 124, 127, 134, 136, 139, 141, 144, 145, 151, 176, 178

Tagore, Rabindranath, 7; *Ghare Baire*, 7
Taj Sultan, 93, 95–96
Taj Jahan Begam, 64*fig.*, 97
Talbot, Cynthia, 134, 174
Tamil (language), 148, 149, 167, 168, 171, 174, 176
Tamil Nadu, 3, 13–14, 30, 144, 147, 246n42
Tanjavur, 12, 135, 154, 155, 159, 166
tankhwāh, 36, 50
Tapti River, 1
tārīkh, 25, 113, 181, 182
tarjī'-band, 88*fig.*, 100–101
tatsama, 109, 157
tax, 84, 128, 167, 172
Teganapatnam, 25, 144, 149, 151, 154, 168–70, 173, 174, 176, 178
Telangana, 20, 29, 37, 93, 102, 155
Telugu, 3, 13, 27, 41, 68, 148–49, 167–68, 171, 174–77, 179, 205n85
threshold, 15. See also borders; frontier(s); *sarhad*
Timurids, 11–13. See also Mughal Empire
tin, 78, 170, 190, 244n153
Tipu Sultan, 172, 183, 187, 189
titles, 69, 127, 132; status, 174, 243n142
tolls, 78, 144, 156
trade, 63, 78–79, 84, 155–56, 172; freight, 166; guns, 83; textile, 14, 155, 166, 167–68, 175–77
Tranquebar, 170, 243n136
translation, 97; in administrative documents, 146, 170–72, 242n124; in literature, 99
translator, 72, 171, 174
Transoxiana, 137
travelogues: European, 140, 144
Turanis, 28, 46, 51–52
Turko-Mongol, 12, 21, 194
Turktaz Khan Bahadur, 51
Tyagi, Jaya, 8

Umrani, 148*map*, 240n76
unbelonging, 8
Urdu, 26, 117, 157, 161, 171, 185, 192
Usman Khan Rohilla, 52
Utroli, 17

valangai, 175
valido, 65, 93–94
Valikondapuram, 166, 168, 171, 173–76

Vengurla, 65–66, 77–86, 151–54, 158
Venkatapa Nayak, 153
Verenigde Oostindische Compagnie (VOC).
    See Dutch East India Company
Vijayanagara Empire, 13, 110, 166–67, 234n5
Viramma of Bidnur, 188–89
Vithoji Kantiya, 56

Wagoner, Phillip, 23
war, 32–36, 145, 149, 155, 161, 164.
    See also *razm*
war front, 7, 28, 33, 195; coastal, 150–56, 166; in Karnatak, 18, 66–67, 82; in upper Deccan, 16, 45, 55, 59–60, 172
wārisdār, 17
War of Succession, 130, 137, 151–52, 164
watan, 9, 147, 158, 161
watandār, 16–18

watan jāgīr, 9
weavers, 166–77, 236n26; weaving castes, 149, 155, 175–79
wedding, 88*fig.*, 89, 99–101, 107–12, 189–91, 226n36
Wigen, Kären, 20

Xa Saibo. *See* Shah Saheb

Yacama, 205n85
Yusufzai, 52

zakāt, 83
zamīndār, 23, 207n103
zāt, 38, 40, 43, 58, 59, 213n23
Zubayri, Ibrahim, 149, 193
Zuhuri, Zuhur ibn (chronicler), 64*fig.*, 68, 95–96, 101–7, 225n28; *Muhammadnāma*, 96, 101, 219n104, 225n17

Founded in 1893,
UNIVERSITY OF CALIFORNIA PRESS
publishes bold, progressive books and journals
on topics in the arts, humanities, social sciences,
and natural sciences—with a focus on social
justice issues—that inspire thought and action
among readers worldwide.

The UC PRESS FOUNDATION
raises funds to uphold the press's vital role
as an independent, nonprofit publisher, and
receives philanthropic support from a wide
range of individuals and institutions—and from
committed readers like you. To learn more, visit
ucpress.edu/supportus.